The Fleet Air Arm: An Illustrated History

Alan Key

Written by Alan Key

British Library Cataloguing in Publication Data
A catalogue record for this book is available from the British Library

ISBN: 978 1 902236 10 0

Published by:
SCOVAL Publishing Ltd
PO BOX 36
Ponteland
Newcastle-upon-Tyne
NE20 9WE
Tel: (01661) 820 838
Fax: (01661) 822 911

Printed by:
Kyodo Printing Co (S'Pore) Pte Ltd

Designed and typeset in 11 on 13pt Quorum by S Henderson for SCOVAL Publishing Ltd

Edited by S Henderson & C Hymers

CONTENTS

Acknowledgements

This book could not have been written without the help of many and if I have omitted your name, it is merely an oversight on my part. My thanks go out to my family who have encouraged me in the project and to the following who have given me information and photographs:

Len Allen, Chris Bailes, Fred Ballam, John Bishop, Mike Caws, Ed Cole, Graham Cooper, Dennis Day, Scott Henderson, George Inglis, Brian Johnson, Chris Knight, Norman Laughlan, John McPhilp, Ken Pagan, David Reader, Robbie Robinson, Brian Russell, Dave Saxton, Jock Scott, John Shears, Tony Turpin, Dick Ward, British Aerospace, Westlands Helicopters, Bond Helicopters, Boeing Aerospace, Lockheed Martin, the MoD, the Gosport Aviation Society, Submarine Museum and HMS Sultan Museum.

The biggest thanks go to Mr FAA - Ray Sturtivant, who has given me many photographs and much of the information required to complete the book.

Foreword

This book is a history book written to tell the world of the development and actions of the Royal Navy's flying branch, beginning with the use of balloons to the current proposed aircraft and ships of tomorrow. During its history, it has been instrumental in developing a good number of aviation warfare techniques, weapons and systems - strategic bombing, torpedo and depth charge weapons, aerial photography, pathfinder and anti-submarine warfare methods to name just a few.

It has been instrumental in developing naval aviation practices, equipments and techniques used worldwide, having taken the lead in carrier and small ships' flight operations. It has developed the most fundamental pre-requisites of the modern aircraft carrier; angled deck, catapults, arrester wires and the ski-ramp, plus helicopter operations in the ASW role, SAR, amphibious assault role and as an integral weapon for frigates and destroyers.

It has had some turbulent times and some truly magnificent times. It has produced some brilliant and brave aviators and some equally brilliant engineers. Its future is, I believe, uncertain with the policy of Joint Forces, a system that has not worked too well in other countries, neither did it work in Britain between the two World Wars. However I am an optimist and can see it remaining as the most valuable arm of the Royal Navy, the most professional Navy in the world.

You will not find any aircraft serial numbers or pilots' anecdotes, nor in-depth histories of squadrons or ships between these covers (they can be found in other books), only the facts about the FAA's work. The book is written as a tribute to the service and all who have made it what it is today - the finest military force in the world.

Balloons Kites and Wires

The Beginning of Naval Aviation

The first idea for the use of lighter than air devices in the Royal Navy (RN) was a suggestion by Rear Admiral C H Knowles. He suggested the use of a balloon launching ship to watch over the French preparations for the invasion of Britain in 1803. This was ignored, although three years later kites were used from HMS *Pallas* to drop leaflets over France.

Kites were next used at the turn of the century, during March 1903, when trials were conducted at Whale Island in Portsmouth harbour. After many failures, the idea was further developed with kites capable of holding a man aloft being produced. During August 1908 these were used for 'observation trials', with the man kite being towed behind ships. Although it proved the feasibility, no evidence is available to show the concept was seriously used.

In 1907 the Wright brothers offered the British Admiralty the patents to their Wright Flyer. This was spurned by the Admiralty with a written reply indicating that the opinion of the Lords of the Admiralty was that they would not be of any practical use. How wrong they were to be proved over the next 90 years.

Fortunately this was not to be the final say in the matter of Naval Aviation. The following year, Captain R H S Bacon was in France to observe the world's 1st International Air Races at Rheims on behalf of the Admiralty. In view of the advances Germany was making in constructing Zeppelins, he submitted his findings on 21st July to Admiral Sir John Fisher (1st Sea Lord) which included the following proposals:-

i) A Naval Air Assistant be added to the staff of the Admiralty.

ii) The War Office allow the Superintendent of Ballooning be consulted by the Admiralty.

iii) That Vickers Sons & Maxim build a rigid airship for the Royal Navy.

These recommendations were accepted by Fisher, the Board of the Admiralty and subsequently the Commission of Imperial Defence, and £35,000 was allotted for the 1909-1910 Naval Estimates for a rigid airship. Captain Murray Sueter was appointed to the Naval Staff as Inspecting Captain of Aircraft, with Commander Oliver Schwann as his Assistant and Chief Artificer-Engineer A Sharpe as the overseer for the building of the airship.

Shorts S27

Furthering the heavier than air possibilities, two Lieutenants at Fort Blockhouse, Gosport experimented with the launching of a powered aircraft from a ramp. The site used was a piece of land between two forts used by the Royal Garrison Artillery, which was eventually to become Grange airfield, Gosport, one of the country's first five airfields.

THE MAYFLY

A contract was signed with Vickers on 7th May 1909 for the construction of No. 1 Rigid Naval Airship to be named 'The Mayfly', an airship of 640,000 cubic feet with a length of 540ft. It was designed for aerial scouting with an endurance of 24 hours at 40 knots at an altitude of 1500ft. The Mayfly was handed over to the Navy two years later in May 1911, but unfortunately the airship was to break its back whilst being manoeuvred out of its hangar, without ever having flown.

On 24th September, as the craft was being moved out of the hangar, a gust of wind caught the nose swinging it round and the fuselage was levered against the hangar breaking its back; this after it had carried out successful mooring trials withstanding winds of 40 knots.

THE FIRST NAVAL AVIATORS

When volunteers were sought for pilot training in 1911, more than two hundred officers volunteered, and four officers were chosen to learn to fly at the Royal Aero Club (R.A.C.) flying school at Eastchurch.

Shorts Pusher

Shorts S27 on board HMS Hibernia

These four Lieutenants - R Gregory, A M Longmore, C R Samson and G Wildman-Lushington were to learn to fly in Shorts S27s with Mr George Cockburn as their instructor. Lieutenant E L Gerrard from the Royal Marines Light Infantry replaced Lt. Wildman-Lushington who became ill prior to the course, although he did join later following his recovery.

These Officers were to receive instruction on the handling of the aircraft and a complete technical course on aircraft engineering - the first time a course of this nature had been established (it is now standard practice known as 'ground school'). The technical course was designed and taught by Mr Horace Shorts from Shorts Brothers Engineering, the aircraft's manufacturers.

It is difficult to speculate as to whether this training would have gone ahead if there had not been an offer from Mr Francis Maclean to use his aircraft, as well as the instruction from George Cockburn and Horace Shorts free of charge!

The course began on 2nd March and was completed within two months with all four initial students receiving their 'wings' within six weeks. Lt. Samson persuaded the Admiralty that aviation would become an important factor in the military and that more personnel should receive this training. December 1911 saw the Admiralty purchase some aircraft and rent ten acres of the airfield at Eastchurch from the R.A.C. With a nucleus of twelve naval ratings, the Naval Flying School was established as the first British military flying school, at the first (of many) Naval Air Stations. This continued to operate as a Naval Flying Training School after the formation of the Central Flying School at Upavon in June 1912. The school was the venue for Winston Churchill to learn to fly when in the office of The First Lord of the Admiralty in 1912.

The maintenance of the aircraft for this new Air Department of the Royal Navy was to be the work for naval artificers. Volunteers were recruited mostly from engine room artificers (engineers who had completed an apprenticeship) and were taught the rudiments of aircraft design and servicing by Shorts.

Shorts S27 Folder (First aircraft designed for stowage aboard ship)

THE RN's PRIVATE PILOTS

The Officers who attended the Naval Flying School were not the only aviators in the service. Lt. G C Colmore RN was the Royal Navy's first aviator when he received Aviator's Certificate No. 5 on 21st June 1910 at his own expense. Commander Oliver Schwann also paid for his own flying lessons after purchasing his own Avro Type D aeroplane. During November 1911, he began trials in Cavendish Docks at Barrow-in-Furness with the aircraft to which he had fitted floats, thus becoming the first aviator to take off and land from water in an aircraft. He then went on to learn to fly (April 1912).

As other naval officers became pilots, more experimental flying was carried out. Lt. Longmore and Sub. Lt. Sippe assisted Oliver Schwann in the 'seaplane' flying, the trial flights being funded by fellow naval officers as the Admiralty did not supply a budget for them. Support was given by the Shorts brothers who developed the Longmore designed seaplanes for the trials.

The major navies of the world were developing and building submarines to equip their Fleets. These weapons had not (yet) been used as a major instrument in these navies' arsenals, but Lt. H Williamson, a submariner who had received flying training, wrote a paper advocating the bombing of submarines by aircraft. His thesis was to drop 50lb bombs specially designed to burst 20ft below the surface to inflict major damage to the submarine. The weapon that was to be developed for the role became known as the depth charge.

This group of Naval Aviators were to set out the requirements of the role of naval aircraft operations for the RN. The aircraft and their aircrew would have the following duties:-

i) Identify enemy vessels in port for the blockading naval squadron.

ii) Identify enemy ships at sea, 'over the horizon' from the Fleet.

iii) Fly above the Fleet to identify enemy submarines.

iv) Detect minefields.

v) Direct naval gunfire.

vi) Aerial bombing of enemy harbours and installations.

EARLY PROGRESS IN NAVAL AVIATION

Shorts Brothers Engineering had now become Shorts Brothers Aircraft Company (the world's first aircraft construction company) and many of the aircraft used by the Naval Wing, and later the Royal Naval Air Service (RNAS), were from their design office. Their first design, the Type S41, was delivered as early as 1912, taking part in the Fleet Review at Weymouth in May of that year.

The year 1912 saw some remarkable records being achieved by these Naval pilots. On 10th January, Commander Charles Rumney Samson carried out the first take-off from a British Warship when he took off in his Shorts S27 from the cruiser HMS *Africa* at anchor in Sheerness. The ship had been rigged with staging over the front gun turret and bows as a flight deck. This feat had already been achieved by Eugene Ely, an American who had taken off from the USS *Birmingham* fourteen months earlier.

Samson's exercise was a practice for the real event which was staged on 2nd May at the Royal Fleet Review in Weymouth Bay in front of King George V, when he flew off HMS *Hibernia*, at anchor in the Bay, which was fitted with a 45ft platform over the front turret. In the Bay a week later, whilst the ship was steaming at 10.5 knots, Samson took off in his Shorts S27 thus achieving the world's first take-off from a ship underway. The aircraft had been fitted with airbags as floatation support in case the aircraft failed to reach sustained flight - the first time such devices had been fitted to an aircraft. Fortunately they were not needed.

Other trials were carried out in 1912 to establish procedures for the duties of Naval aviation laid down previously; wireless and telegraphy exercises for transmitting messages and position findings, anti-submarine spotting, aerial photography, more seaplane research and long distance flights. Cdr. Samson successfully dropped a 100lb bomb from a Shorts Biplane whilst Lt. Wilfred Parke carried out the first known recovery from a spin in an Avro biplane on 25th August.

By the end of the year, there were 22 Naval pilots equipped with sixteen aeroplanes. The Admiralty awarded a contract to Vickers to design and build a prototype fighting aeroplane, and the first 'mobile' air stations using portable Bessoneau hangars were developed.

THE ROYAL FLYING CORPS

In November 1911, the Committee of Imperial Defence received a memorandum from the Prime Minister, Mr. H Asquith, requesting that they consider the future of military aviation and the means of establishing an efficient military air service. They were asked to co-ordinate a study of aviation in the navy and army, and to advise whether steps should be taken to form a corps of military aviators.

Airship Gamma

A study was carried out involving naval and army aviators, aircraft designers and naval intelligence personnel. Their findings, which were presented to the Committee on 27th February 1912, recommended:-

i) The formation of a Flying Corps, a single service with Naval and Military wings.

ii) The setting up of a central flying school administered by the War Office.

iii) The formation of the Air Committee.

iv) The establishing of flying grounds.

v) A combined pool of naval and army pilots available for flying with either service.

These recommendations were accepted and passed to the Government. The Parliamentary White Paper of 11th April was accepted and the Royal Flying Corps (RFC) was constituted on 13th April by Royal Warrant. One month later, on 13th May 1912, the RFC came into being consisting of separate Naval and Military Wings with a Central Flying School at Upavon. A series of naval air stations were approved, with the Isle of Grain being the first to be commissioned (December 1912) followed by four more of these 'Coastal Stations' - Calshot, Cromarty, Felixstowe and Yarmouth, with the first airship station established at Kings North.

The Admiralty continued its own training at Eastchurch whilst opposing the recommendation of a pool of pilots, feeling that all pilots in the Naval Wing should be naval officers. The Admiralty set up the Air Department (AD) with Captain Murray Sueter as its Director and Captain G W Vivian in command of naval flying, both ashore and afloat.

Shorts S38

HMS Ark Royal

THE ART OF DROPPING BOMBS

One of the recommended duties of naval aircraft was that of bombing enemy targets. Trials had been carried out with dummy bombs dropped from the cockpit, whilst Shorts had designed a device to hold a 100lb bomb beneath its pusher biplane, with the bomb being released by the pilot operating a mechanism. Cdr. Samson carried out the first trials and discovered that the release of the bomb had little effect on the aircraft, however the inaccuracy of the fall of the weapon to the target needed improvement. With the assistance of Lt. R C Hall, a naval gunnery officer, Samson designed a bombsight which improved the accuracy to an acceptable level, and this was to become the world's first aircraft bombsight.

Further bombing trials were carried out to discover the altitudes at which bombs could be released safely. A destroyer fitted with a cable extended behind it was used in these trials, and explosive charges attached to the cable were fired as an aircraft was flying above them. The results found that it would be safe to drop 100lb bombs from a height of 350ft without incurring any danger to the aircraft. A Maurice Farman Longhorn was modified as a floatplane, with the forward elevator removed, and successfully proved the ability of aircraft to absorb the shock waves produced when bombs were dropped.

Under the guidance of Samson and with the full backing of Winston Churchill, the AD was to develop the art of bombing strategic targets. It was seen as a way of attacking an enemy at its supply sources, thus preventing the manufacture of weapons for use against the British Forces. The War Office opposed this idea of 'Strategic Bombing', as aircraft would be needed to assist the front line fighting.

Undeterred, the AD continued with its idea but Sueter realised the available aircraft would not be able to penetrate any potential enemy's factories. What was needed was a long range bomber aircraft, so he commissioned Handley Page to develop such an aircraft which he coined as "A Bloody Paralyser". Thus the world's first Bomber aircraft was conceived as a requirement of the Air Department of the RN.

THE FIRST AVIATION SHIPS

Four Abercrombie 14" gun monitors were converted in 1913 to carry two Sopwith Type 807 Folder floatplanes each. The aircraft were operated from the ship's stern using a crane to raise and lower the aircraft onto the sea, and they were the first aircraft to be built with the innovative invention of folding wings. This feature, still used today for carrier-borne and land based aircraft, was the idea of Winston Churchill as a means of reducing the stowage area required for aircraft aboard ships.

HMS *Hermes*, a converted cruiser, became the Naval Wing's first aircraft carrier when it recommissioned on 7th May 1913 as a seaplane carrier under the command of Captain Vivian. She was fitted with a two-track launch platform in the forecastle and a canvas shelter on the quarterdeck as a hangar. During the first naval exercises involving aircraft, the Naval Manoeuvres in July, the ship embarked a Shorts Folder Seaplane and a Caudron GIII Amphibian.

Hermes carried out trials launching aircraft from its Shorts flying deck, and the Caudron seaplane fitted with wheels was successfully launched before the trials ended. The aftermath of these exercises resulted with £81,000 in the 1914-15 Naval Estimates being allotted for the world's first purpose built 'aircraft carrier' - HMS *Ark Royal*, a name now synonymous in the Fleet Air Arm.

The ship was laid down as a merchantman in the Blyth Shipbuilding yard, but it was considered to be at a stage of building where it could be redesigned as a seaplane carrier. The redesign included an internal hangar, aircraft support facilities - workshops, aircraft stores areas, aviation fuel and oils storage areas and aviation ordnance magazines, all features still incorporated in aviation ships today.

AIRSHIPS

With the build-up of the German Forces, the Admiralty ordered two rigid and six non-rigid airships to be constructed for the Naval Wing. Even though the Army was already using four airships at this time, these were handed over to the Naval Wing and the Navy was responsible for all airship operations during W.W.I.

The Admiralty purchased the non-rigid airship, the Astra Torres, from France. This was the only British airship to carry armament - a single Hotchkiss machine gun, and was the fastest airship in the world. The

Astra Torres

Naval Airship No. 3 began trials at Farnborough in June 1913, being accepted during July. Parseval Airship No. 4, a semi-rigid airship which had been built in Germany, had already been accepted after its trials, and Vickers were to build three more under licence for use as training airships.

TORPEDOES DELIVERED BY AIR

As Lt. Williamson's depth charge ideas were under development, Murray Sueter and other flying officers were looking at the torpedo as an airborne weapon against submarines. The torpedo had been designed by Mr Robert Whitehead 40 years earlier and Lt. Hyde-Thomas, recently qualified in torpedo warfare, suggested to Commodore Sueter the possibility of the weapon being used with aircraft. This was accepted and Hyde-Thomas joined the Air Service as an adviser.

The Sopwith Aeroplane Company was contracted to build two seaplane aircraft for the research; one was for preliminary work, not intended to reach flight, only taxiing on the water. The aircraft, a Sopwith Canton-Unne, was designed to fly with a 14" torpedo, and it successfully took off from the Solent at the end of 1913 although the pilot was not allowed to drop the weapon.

The development work was carried out under the auspices of the Aircraft Torpedo Development Unit (ATDU) located at the Woolwich Arsenal. The unit moved to the airfield at Grange in Gosport in July 1914 (for a stay of 44 years), ideally located to use the Solent as the exercise area.

The development of aircraft and torpedo compatibility was to eventually result in the first torpedo dropping on 27th July 1914. Gordon Bell, the Shorts' test pilot, carried out the first dropping of a torpedo from an aircraft when he dropped a 14" Whitehead torpedo from his Shorts 184 Seaplane. The following day, Squadron Commander Longmore carried out the same exercise. Although these torpedo droppings were only in their infantile stages, development of this form of aerial warfare was expedited when war broke out six days later, culminating in the first sinking of a ship by this method thirteen months later.

THE ROYAL NAVAL AIR SERVICE

An important date in the Fleet Air Arm's (FAA) history is 1st July 1914, the date that the RFC Naval Wing was granted independence to become the Royal Naval Air Service (RNAS) still under the command of Murray Sueter, giving the RN control of all its aviation facilities, bases, aircraft and pilots.

Sopwith Gun Bus

New ranks were established, with Wing Captain and Wing Commander taking over from Captain and Commander respectively. Lt. Commander became Squadron Commander, Lieutenants became either Flight Commander or Flight Lieutenant depending on seniority and experience, and Sub-Lieutenants assumed the title of Flight Sub-Lieutenant. The pilots wore a gilt eagle badge on their left sleeve above their gilt rank rings.

The fledgling air arm continued to carry out development trials, with Engineering Lt. C Hall RN successfully firing a 1.5lb gun from the nose of a Sopwith Gun Bus. Eng. Lt. Briggs raised the world altitude record to 14,920ft in a Bleriot monoplane in April 1914, and night flying was developed with Cdr. Travers flying over the Spithead Fleet Review at night in his Sopwith Bat Boat.

The Fleet Review, held on 18th-22nd July 1914, was to see the first display of formation flying when the RNAS flew above the assembled Fleet in 'V' formation, followed by seventeen seaplanes, whilst four airships flew higher still trailing White Ensigns, the flag of the RN. This was the largest display of military aircraft seen over the skies of Britain. The military and naval aviation review at Hendon (28th September 1912) had been the first gathering of air assets but at that time neither air arm had large compliments.

Following a nationwide tour, the aircraft of the RNAS were ordered to assemble at Eastchurch on 27th July. Two days later, the Cabinet informed the Admiralty that RFC would be required to support the Army if it were to be sent abroad, as a confrontation was extremely likely. If this was the case, the air defence of Britain would be the responsibility of the RNAS. This event had been foreseen and the RNAS had been practicing air fighting in the skies over Chatham in Kent, with two aircraft attacking the naval dockyard whilst six defended. These exercises, possibly the first such exercises carried out above the British skies, gave the pilots of the RNAS invaluable training for actions soon to be flown with much zeal.

Shorts S184

ABOVE: Avro 504

LEFT: Felixstowe F2S

BOTTOM: HMS *Campania*

The War to End All Wars

For two years a war had been fought in the Balkans with the aim of elimination of the Turkish Ottoman rule in the area, with hostilities ending on 10th August 1913. The area was still unstable and the Austria-Hungary alliance had desires on taking some of the area for themselves. This alliance was supported by the German and Italian Governments (the Central Powers), but the opposition to any further confrontation in the area was from the alliance of Great Britain, France and Russia (the Allied Powers).

The heir to the Austria-Hungarian throne, Archduke Franz Ferdinand, and his wife were assassinated at Sarajevo on 28th June 1915 by Serbian terrorists. War was declared on Serbia one month later and the Russians began mobilisation on its borders. Germany declared war on the Russians on 1st August, invaded Belgium and Luxembourg, and then declared war on France two days later. Britain declared war on Germany on the 4th August, thus 'the war to end all wars' had begun.

THE GREAT WAR BEGINS - 1914

Britain entered the war against Germany on 4th August at 23.00hrs. When the war began, the RNAS was given the task of defending British air space due to most squadrons of the RFC departing across the channel with the British Expeditionary Force (BEF). The RNAS 'front line' aircraft had assembled at Eastchurch having 39 'land' aircraft, 52 seaplanes, 7 airships, 128 officers and 700 ratings. The BEF began departure across the English Channel almost immediately, and the first air action of the war involved the German built Naval Airship No. 4 escorting the convoys of troops on the first full day.

The Eastchurch wing, under the command of Wing Cdr. Samson comprising of ten aeroplanes (two BEs, two Bleriots, one Bristol, one Farman, one Shorts and two Sopwiths) and the Astra Torres, was the first naval wing to join the fighting across the water, arriving at Ostend race course on 27th August before moving on to St. Pol near Dunkirk. The unit commandeered many vehicles which Samson had protected with heavy armour (the armoured car was born) and even designed their own 'Seabrook' armoured car built on an American Standard Truck Co. chassis, the outcome being fifteen squadrons of armoured vehicles belonging to the RN Armoured Car Division.

Shorts 74

Now with the identification of No. 1 Wing RNAS, their task was to patrol an area within 100 miles of Dunkirk. The Wing was reinforced with the arrival of the aircraft from Hendon and Eastchurch to form the Dunkirk Wing with redefined objectives; those of coastal patrol/anti-submarine patrol and opposition to the German Zeppelin force.

The Wing provided the aviation world with many "first's" during these early days of the war. On 22nd September, four aircraft were despatched to attack the Zeppelin sheds at Dusseldorf in Germany, but only one aircraft reached the target due to mist in the Rhine valley. The pilot, Flt. Lt. C Collet dropped his 20lb bombs on the sheds which unfortunately failed to explode, however the mission gave Collet the place in history as the first British aviator to carry out an aerial bombing raid.

The attack was repeated sixteen days later when Flt. Lt. R Marix successfully attacked the sheds in his Sopwith Tabloid and destroyed Zeppelin Z9 before it had even made its maiden flight. This was the first ever successful bombing raid, and the RNAS was laying down the foundations of strategic bombing as conceived earlier.

Wg. Cdr. Samson became the first pilot to carry out a night bombing mission when he attacked the German gun batteries at Ostend (21st December 1914) flying a Maurice Farman. Aerial bombing was proving to be a forte of the RNAS with

Balloon Ship "Artil"

Nieuport 12

successful attacks on Zeppelin sheds and other targets including the railway station at Cologne. These successes resulted in the most daring aviation raid to date.

THE FREDRICHSHAFEN RAID

Four Avro 504s were dispatched by sea and rail to the French aerodrome of Belfort on the Swiss German border where they were reassembled for a raid on the Zeppelin factory at Fredrichshafen on Lake Constance 250 miles behind enemy lines. The four pilots who volunteered for the raid were Sqdn. Cdr. Featherstone Briggs, Flt. Cdr. Babington, Flt. Lt. Sippe and Flt. Sub. Lt. Cannon.

Three of the aircraft took off for the mission on 21st November but the other aircraft, flown by Cannon, became unserviceable prior to take-off. After avoiding Swiss territory, the three aircraft reached the target and dropped eleven 20lb bombs successfully damaging workshops, a Zeppelin under construction and the gas plant which was totally destroyed. The Germans built heavy defences around the factory against further attacks - which never materialised.

After the mission the 1st Sea Lord, Lord Fisher, was compelled to dispatch the RNAS's first signal of congratulations: "This fine feat of endurance, courage and skill reflects great credit on all who took part in the raid and through them on the Air Service to which they belong."

MILITARY AVIATION STRUCTURE AS WE KNOW IT

1914 saw the birth of the structure of military aviation which is still in existence worldwide today, based around the formation and operation of squadrons. At Gosport, No. 1 Sqdn. RNAS was formed under the command of Sqdn. Cdr. Longmore - with four Bristol Tractor TB8s, whilst Sqdn. Cdr. Gerrard formed No. 2 Sqdn. at Eastchurch. Both these squadrons were formed on 17th October, then Samson's Wing became No. 3 Sqdn. on 26th February 1915 prior to its departure from Dover to the Aegean. This format would change temporarily to wing status before returning to squadron units similar to the present day.

THE AIRCRAFT CARRIERS

The Admiralty realised the need for faster aviation ships to allow spotting for the battle fleet. HMS *Ark Royal*, still four months from commissioning, would not be able to keep up with the Fleet, which only left HMS *Hermes* fast enough but not a true conversion to aircraft carrier. The RN requisitioned three cross-channel packets from the South Eastern and Chatham Railway Company (HMS *Empress*, HMS *Engadine* and HMS *Riviera*), two Isle of Man Steam Packet Company boats (HMS *Ben-My-Chree* and HMS *Vindex*) and the Cunard liner HMS *Campania* - all ships which could be quickly converted into aircraft carriers.

After carrying out the operating trials, HMS *Hermes* was returned to operations as a cruiser but was soon reconfigured to operate aircraft when the hostilities began. She was the world's first aircraft carrier ever to become operational but unfortunately her life as an aircraft carrier was not going to last very long. The ship was involved with delivering personnel and equipment to Dunkirk for the proposed naval air station on 30th October. Whilst returning across the Channel the following day to collect another load she was sunk by a U-Boat attack, thus becoming the first aircraft carrier casualty. Ironically the reason for this new base was for anti-submarine patrols.

All was not lost however, as the three smaller packets had been converted and were in commission, and HMS *Ark Royal* was launched on 5th September and commissioned on 10th December. The ship had a 130ft forward flush deck and an after hangar for the stowage of its ten seaplanes. The three larger conversions were due for delivery early in the new year.

FIRST AIRCRAFT CARRIER OPERATION

Christmas Day 1914 saw the first true naval air attack take place when aircraft from three seaplane carriers (HMS *Empress*, HMS *Engadine* and HMS *Riviera*) were briefed to attack the Zeppelin sheds at Cuxhaven. Each ship supplied three Shorts aircraft for the raid; Empress - Shorts 74s led by Flt. Cdr. Oliver; Engadine - Shorts Folders led by Flt. Cdr. Ross, and Riviera - Shorts 135s led by Flt. Cdr. Hewlett.

Only seven seaplanes were able to get airborne but, on reaching the area, hampered by thick fog, heavy anti-aircraft fire and engine problems, they failed to find the target so bombed Wilhemshaven instead. Whilst the attack was in progress the assembled Fleet was itself attacked by enemy aircraft and a Zeppelin.

Only three of the aircraft arrived back at the carriers. Of the others, one landed near

Moraine Saulner Parasol

to a Dutch merchant ship whilst the other three alighted at a rendezvous point at Norderney Gat where the pilots were taken aboard HM *Submarine E11*. The three aircraft were sunk by the action of another supporting submarine.

U-BOATS MENACE

The Germans were busy building two classes of submarines, coastal 'UB' and a larger 'UC' class, in alarming numbers which were beginning to achieve results against British shipping and warships. On 4th February 1915, the German Admiralty declared all-out war against British shipping and neutral shipping found inside British territorial waters.

The RNAS were now tasked with aerial assaults on known U-boat pens in Belgium, beginning a week later when thirteen aircraft reached their targets. However they were only armed with 20lb bombs which did no damage, and later attacks with 100lb bombs also had little affect. This was noted by Lord Fisher who sought alternative defences against this menace.

Lord Fisher decided one answer would be using airships to patrol the Dover Straits and Irish Narrows. Sueter was tasked with supplying these airships - now ! Within three weeks the first such airship was operational; this was the modification of an old Willows airship with a BE2C aircraft fuselage attached below it. It was to be the 'prototype' of 36 Submarine Scout (SS) airships, with an endurance of eight hours at 40 knots. These airships would spot submarines then direct a surface ship to attack the enemy.

To support these airships, five airship stations were constructed; Capel near Folkestone, Polegate near Eastbourne and Marquise in France for patrolling the Channel, Anglesey and Luce Bay for the Irish Sea.

BALLOONS BECOME AN ASSET

A balloon depot and training base was also established for use against the submarines. The balloons were to embark on converted tramp steamers and trawlers, having a crew for observation who would report on any submarines which were on the surface recharging their batteries. HMS *Manica* was the first tramper to be converted fitted with a sloping fore deck, a balloon winch and a wireless house for the crew to report to. Facilities were also fitted to some of the seaplane carriers for balloon operations, and HMS *Engadine* was to successfully tow a balloon at 22kts whilst at 3000ft altitude.

The effort produced limited success but it was normal for the submarine to spot the balloon and escape the ensuing destroyers. It did however keep the submarine below water reducing their capacity to recharge their batteries. HMS *Patriot* successfully sank the U69 after being directed to the target by a crew from a balloon. The balloons were to be redeployed for naval gunfire spotting duties, operating in the Dardanelles and off the Belgian coast.

Naval Airship

DARDANELLES - THE TURKS JOIN IN

The Turks joined forces with the Central Powers on 29th October, leaving the Russians now cut off from the Allied Powers. The Turks denied access through the Dardanelles, the passage from the Aegean Sea to the Sea of Marmara and then the Black Sea. This situation was untenable and had to be resolved, and the only way was to open the route from the Aegean to the Black Sea.

HMS *Ark Royal*, with eight aircraft aboard, arrived at Tenedos on 17th February 1915 in support of the operations against the Turkish forces and the forthcoming attack on Gelibolu (Gallipoli), a strategic area at the entrance to the Sea of Marmara. Within two hours of arriving, her aircraft began flights over the area and Flt. Lt. C Butler completed the world's first recorded photo-reconnaissance flights, taking over 700 photographs of the Turkish positions.

These photographs were used to interpret strikes in support of the British and Commonwealth troops and, on the 19th, Ark Royal's aircraft, under the command of Samson now a Wing Cdr., began bombarding the Turkish fortresses, shipping and the airfield at Canakkale (Chanak) where an aircraft was destroyed in the hangar.

Sopwith 1½ Strutter

Sopwith Pup

During March 1915, No. 3 Sqdn. RNAS moved to help in the unsuccessful campaign. During missions in this theatre, Samson dropped the first 500lb bomb to be used in the war (the heaviest bomb at that time to be flown underneath an aircraft) on a Turkish Army barracks building, totally destroying it. Another innovation of Samson was aerial incendiary bombs, a 20 gallon drum of petrol fitted with an explosive charge. He dropped these over Turkish lines but the petrol scattered over a large area failing to produce a blaze of fire.

The landings began at Cape Helles on 25th April with the RNAS supporting the ground forces with close air support, bombing of the Turkish forces and in spotting for the Fleet bombardment. Later, in these early operations, the eyes in the skies were able to report on troop positions and activities.

Flt. Cdr. Marix spotted such a build-up of Turkish forces on 17th May at Ak Bashi Uiman where a large camp had been established near the port. He loaded his Breguet Biplane with bombs and, crewed by Wing Cdr. Samson, attacked the camp. The report of this build-up of the enemy enabled the British Army to prepare for a possible attack. This occurred the following night but the enemy was defeated suffering so many losses that a temporary ceasefire was asked for to allow them to bury their dead.

AERIAL LAUNCHED TORPEDO STRIKES

When HMS *Ben-My-Chree* launched Flt. Cdr. C H K Edmonds RN in his Shorts 184 fitted with a 14" torpedo on 12th August, during the second assault phase, his mission was to attack enemy shipping in the Sea of Marmara. He returned to the ship after successfully sinking an enemy supply ship, thus becoming the first pilot to sink a ship by an air launched torpedo.

Only five days later there were two more successful sinking of ships by aircraft and torpedo. The first was again by Edmonds, but the second of the day was an unconventional launch of the weapon, albeit still successful, when Flt. Lt. G B Dacre sank a Turkish tug after releasing his torpedo whilst taxiing on the water due to engine problems.

After this second assault on Gallipoli failed, it was seen as an impossible operation with no ground being made as the Turkish forces defended their territory with tenacity. The Allied Force withdrew after the loss of 500,000 lives from both sides. The fight for the Dardanelles was over after eight months of fighting.

THE SUEZ CANAL

The Turkish military leaders had been planning to take the Suez Canal, an important strategic target, but during the initial Turkish advance on the canal, they were observed by allied aircraft. When eventually out of the range of these aircraft, seaplanes of the RNAS were called upon to seek out the enemy and report their positions.

Two seaplane tenders were despatched, HMS *Anne* and HMS *Raven II*, and both captured German boats equipped with Nieuport aircraft. The enemy were spotted on 18th January 1915, and their position and strengths were reported to the British Forces waiting for them. The aircraft were busy with their spotting duties and some clandestine operations for three weeks, reporting daily on their progress.

When the Turks attacked the British positions on 3rd February, they were driven back by the troops and the naval supporting gunfire on the enemy positions. The Nieuports were used as bombers during the assault and the Turkish troops failed in their mission, withdrawing the following day. The RNAS continued their observation flights until the Turks were out of range but, without these seaplanes, the results may have been different.

ZEPPELIN RAIDS - THE RNAS's FIRST VC

February was a busy month for the RNAS. The Germans began nightly bombing attacks on coastal ports using Zeppelin airships, eventually reaching London, and the Government called on the Admiralty to increase their efforts against these attacks. Early attempts at reducing the activities of these monsters were to attack their radio station at Norddeich, but using aircraft from the seaplane carriers, including the recently commissioned HMS *Ben-My-Chree*, proved costly and ineffective.

On 17th May, Flt. Cdr. Bigsworth severely

HMS Engadine

crippled LZ39 when four bombs from his Avro 504B hit the Zeppelin but failed to explode. The following month (7th June), the first aerial success against the airships resulted in Flt. Sub-Lt. R Warneford receiving the RNAS's first VC of the war after dropping six bombs onto the Zeppelin.

He was flying the aircraft at 7000ft at about 2.25am when he dropped the bombs which then exploded causing his aircraft to lift and invert out of control. It then nose dived to the ground before he was able to regain control. The action had also fractured a fuel pipe near to the tank so insufficient fuel was being fed to the fuel pump forcing him to land, effect a repair and take off again. He had considered setting the aircraft on fire but as he had landed unobserved, he repaired the aircraft. Whilst returning to his unit, he became lost in the fog so again he landed (at Cape Griz Nez) where he refuelled before eventually returning to Furnes at 10.30am, 9hrs 30mins after leaving the airfield.

Unfortunately ten days later (17th June), Rex Warneford VC was killed when his Henri Farman broke up in the air sending him and his American passenger Henry Needham, a reporter, to their deaths. Warneford had received his VC on 11th June and on the day of his untimely demise he had been decorated with the French Legion d'Honneur. The accident had occurred on his return flight to No. 1 Naval Squadron.

THE KONIGSBERG

The RNAS was active in Africa with the mission to destroy the German cruiser Konigsberg hiding in the Rufiji River in Tanganyika to effect repairs after being damaged by the light cruiser HMS *Pegasus*, which she subsequently sank.

Mr H Cutler, a civilian who was flying two Curtiss flying boats on pleasure flights in Durban, South Africa, was given a temporary commission in the RNAS. He was despatched to the RN base at Niororo Island eighteen miles north east of the delta, to search for the Konigsberg, with support from HMS *Chatham*.

During his first mission on 19th November 1914, he was forced to land on an inhabited island due to a heavy storm. His second mission, on 22nd, was successful when he located the ship twelve miles up the river. He then carried out a third mission which resulted in him being taken prisoner on 10th December after an emergency landing on the river due to engine failure. His aircraft was rescued by a motor boat and armed tug which dashed up the river and towed the aircraft back to the base.

Shorts 166 Seaplane

More RNAS aircraft were to play a part in the mission to destroy the ship but unfortunately the first two aircraft, Sopwith 807 seaplanes under the command of Flt. Lt. J Cull which arrived from Bombay on 21st February 1915, disintegrated due to the climate. These were replaced with three Shorts Folders, used for observing the Konigsberg, one was damaged during the first mission on 25th April and another was destroyed on 5th May.

May saw the arrival of four land planes; two Henri Farman F27s and two Caudron GIIIs which were able to operate from the newly constructed 'airfield' at Mafia complete with a hangar. These aircraft practised the art of naval gunfire spotting, observation flights and, on 2nd July, a bombing strike, whilst awaiting the true strike on the ship by two monitors.

March 1915 saw the despatch of two shallow draught river monitors; HMS *Severn* and HMS *Mersey* with 6" guns, arriving at the base under tow on 3rd June. After preparing the ships, a brief period of practice was carried out to combine the operation of the boats with the aircraft. The first operation on 6th July produced hits for both sides but more practice in spotting fall of shots was needed by the aircrew.

After further exercises, the aircrew had improved their skills sufficiently to carry out another attack, with a Caudron flown by Flt. Lt. Cull with Sub-Lt. H Arnold as observer accurately spotting the fall of shot from HMS *Severn*. The Konigsberg was finally destroyed on the 11th July. These missions were the first time aircraft had been involved in naval engagements and Cull received the Distinguished Service Order (D.S.O.) and Arnold the Distinguished Service Cross (D.S.C.).

FLT. LT. R BELL DAVIES VC

The second VC was awarded to Flt. Lt. R Bell Davies RN for his daring rescue of Flt. Lt. Smylie after both pilots had been attacking Ferejik railway junction in an action against Bulgarian troops on 15th November 1915. Smylie had been shot down and landed in a dried up watercourse and, after setting fire to his aircraft which was still armed with a bomb, he hid in a hollow.

SSZ Airship

RNAS Airships, "The Delta" in the foreground

Bell Davies, seeing the smoke from the burning aircraft, flew down to look for his comrade who waved to him. Davies landed his Nieuport Scout to pick up Smylie, who attached himself to the aircraft's struts, and they took off just before the alerted Bulgarian troops arrived at the scene. For this act of unselfish bravery, his VC was awarded on 1st January 1916.

THE AIR DEPARTMENT BECOMES OFFICIAL

Since the outbreak of war, the RNAS had been steadily growing in both size and manpower, however there was no cohesion between the air stations at home and the aircraft carrying out duties in the different theatres and with the Fleet.

A radical change was required which would properly co-ordinate the training to meet the tasks, acquire the correct type of aircraft for the roles, ensure that older aircraft were replaced with modern types and to encourage the development of aircraft carriers and naval aviation. There was also a need to instil the correct amount of discipline into the aviators, who were acting very much as individuals rather than members of a team, even though they were gaining results.

An important date in the RNAS history was 1st August 1915 when the RNAS was reorganised. The Air Department became a fully integrated department of the RN, with Rear Admiral Vaughan-Lee as the Director of Air Services and Commodore Sueter given the position Superintendent of Aircraft Construction. This department would develop the resources of the RNAS into a better, more disciplined, and therefore more effective force.

The only aircrew in the RNAS were pilots, the rear gunner or observer being enlisted men. This changed in 1916 with the forming of the Observer Officer Branch which were men trained in the art of aerial surveillance, spotting, photography and communication with land forces and ships. These new observers would wear smaller 'folded' wings on their sleeves - as they still do to this day.

DEVELOPMENT OF AIRCRAFT CARRIERS

After commissioning during September 1915, the seaplane carrier HMS *Vindex* was used as a trials ship for the launching of aircraft from the deck of a ship, in continuation of the earlier experiments in both the UK and USA. They resulted in Flt. Sub-Lt. H F Towler launching from her deck in a Bristol Scout C in November whilst the ship was steaming into wind at 12 knots, the first time an aircraft with wheels had achieved this feat from a ship specifically designed to operate aircraft.

Earlier feasibility trials had been held on board HMS *Campania*, the ex-Cunard liner which joined the Fleet in April under the command of Cdr. Schwann. The ship was fitted with a 120ft forward flying-off deck, but it was not tested until 6th August when a Sopwith Schneider Seaplane, adapted with wheels, took off from the deck for the beginning of a range of trials in the North Sea.

The trials were held over a six month period but resulted in only seven actual days of flying. The seaplanes were able to fly on only three of these days due to varying reasons but mainly the sea conditions and weather. Cdr. Schwann's report pointed out the problems with operating seaplanes and that the flying-off deck was only suitable for small light planes - alright for attacking airships but not for scouting duties.

He felt that there were two solutions for operating the aircraft in support of the Fleet; that the seaplanes were made larger, therefore more capable of operating in the harsh sea conditions, and that the flying-off deck be extended to allow larger aircraft the ability to launch from it. Both these solutions would require extensive alterations to the ship. The result was that the ship was refitted with a longer deck, returning to the Fleet in November.

AVIATION DEVELOPMENTS

Following time spent on board HMS *Ark Royal* at the Dardanelles, Flt. Cdr. H Williamson (of depth charge fame) had designed a ship capable of operating aircraft safely. Williamson, although a submariner, had gained his pilot's licence and had transferred to the RNAS. His design incorporated a superstructure on the starboard side of the ship and arrestor wires for stopping the aircraft, but unfortunately this proposal was rejected in September 1915 (although not forgotten).

As in any war time, developments and trials are prevalent by all sides involved, and weapons were being developed to supersede those already in service at a greater pace than had ever been, especially in the new weapon - aircraft. In terms of British aviation and especially Naval aviation, 1916 was probably the year that saw the most innovative trials and aircraft development ever achieved in a single year - many that were to have a lasting effect on military aviation in the future.

EVENTS NOT PURSUED (AT THIS TIME)

Trials were held on 21st February to see if airships could carry an aircraft and then launch it whilst airborne. This British trial involved an airship playing mother to a BE2C, and the aircraft was to be released at 4000ft. Unfortunately the aircraft was released before the crew were ready and it fell from the airship and turned onto its back, resulting in the pilot falling to his death. The aircraft crashed killing the other occupant, putting an end to this idea within the RNAS.

After the war, No. 212 Sqdn. RAF reactivated the trials using a Sopwith Camel attached to the airship R23. The first successful launch was carried out by Lt. Keys on the 6th November 1918 but there were no further developments on completion of the trials. The concept was however perfected by the Americans who eventually built three airships fitted with 'parasite fighters'; USS Los Angeles, Akron and Macon with their Sparrowhawk fighters.

A similar idea using two aircraft was also tried when Cdr. Porte flew a Porte Baby

Sopwith Pup

flying boat as mother to a Bristol Scout on its upper wing. This aircraft was successfully flown after being released by the pilot, Flt. Lt. M J Day. Although a success, it was not an experiment that was repeated.

April saw trials for submarines carrying aircraft when two Sopwith Schneiders were taken aboard HM *Submarine E22*. They were attached aft of the conning tower and the submarine flooded its aft tanks to submerge the rear of the boat to launch the aircraft down the specially built ramp. Three attempts were made to launch the aircraft but these were not a success and the idea was shelved until after the war.

Successful trials were carried out for arrestor aircraft when landing. The first type of arrestor gear, designed by Williamson at the Isle of Grain, involved flexible steel wires stretched fore and aft across a deck bringing the aircraft to a safe stop in 60ft. Across the Medway at Port Victoria aircraft repair yard, Flt. Lt. Wright was carrying out another set of trials based on an American idea of using ropes with a weight at the end. An Avro Biplane fitted with a rigid hook was successfully arrested safely by this method, and a combination of both these systems was eventually to produce a single system incorporated into future ships at a later date.

SOPWITH AIRCRAFT

Sopwith developed the $1^{1/2}$ strutter as the first British aircraft with a synchronised forward firing fixed gun which enabled the pilot to use the aircraft as a true fighter - the first British two-seat fighter bomber aircraft in service. It was to be the first two-seater to take off from a British warship two years later. There were also some single seat variants which carried a load of twelve bombs within the fuselage.

Experimental flights had been flown earlier in the year to prove the feasibility of night flying and these proved to be successful, resulting in the RNAS flying operations against the enemy. During a night mission on 2nd August, a No. 5 Wing Sopwith $1^{1/2}$ Strutter was the first to act as 'pathfinders' when its crew fired Very lights to assist its Squadron's Caudron GIV bombers.

The RNAS formed the world's first strategic bomber unit on 27th July, the honour going to No. 3 Wing also equipped with $1^{1/2}$ Strutters based at Luxeuil, bombing many enemy industrial targets, dockyards and arsenals. Sir Douglas Haig, however, objected to this unit on the grounds that this sort of action was only of a minor importance and the defence of the ground forces was more paramount. The operations ceased after less than nine months on 15th April 1917 - how different to future conflicts!

Another Sopwith design joined the RNAS this year with the arrival of the Scout, better known as the Sopwith Pup. These aircraft were superior fighter aircraft which could fly higher than any other fighter aircraft used by either side.

MONUMENTAL IDEAS STILL IN USE

The world's first in-flight refuelling operations were carried out during May 1916, when 60 gallons of fuel was transferred from HMS *Carysfort* to the airship C1. Further trials in September had the cruiser HMS *Canterbury* towing the airship at 26 knots, and the crew were changed whilst it was at 12 knots. This proved the concept of sustaining prolonged flights without the necessity of landing, now an everyday event in the world's air forces' operations.

A development of the Sopwith Pup was by the shipbuilder Beardsmore who redesigned the aircraft with folding wings and undercarriage for stowage aboard the aircraft carriers. Beardsmore had moved into aircraft manufacture and had been awarded a contract to build Pups for the

Sopwith Schneider onboard the E22. (RN Submarine Photograph Archive)

Sopwith Triplane

RNAS. This redesigned aircraft, the Beardsmore WBIII, was the first aircraft designed for use aboard ships. The redesign, however, reduced the 'Pups' performance and handling characteristics and only a few were modified, some having the retractable undercarriage whilst others had a jettisonable type.

These Sopwith designs and the WBIII were used to develop floatation devices to allow salvage of the aircraft or at least the recovery of the pilot. The designs and trials were conducted at the Isle of Grain to keep the aircraft on an even keel until the rescue ship could arrive alongside the aircraft. During one trial a Pup was to remain afloat for six hours.

The floats were fitted either in the rear fuselage, lower forward fuselage or alongside the cockpit and were supplied with air from the engine. Although not embodied in production aircraft, they would eventually be fitted to helicopters 40 years later.

THE WESTERN FRONT AND JUTLAND

Following the Battle of the Somme, the RFC needed reinforcements on the front and, to meet this demand, the RNAS formed No. 8 (Naval) Squadron on 16th October with flights from Nos. 1, 4 and 5 Wings. Initially using Sopwith Pups, 1½ Strutters and Nieuports, before standardising with Pups, the unit was formed specifically as a support unit for the Army on the Western front.

It claimed 27 aircraft either destroyed or forced down during its three short months on the front, operating from Vert Galand under the command of Sqdn. Cdr. G Bromet. The unit was replaced on 7th February by No. 3 Naval Sqdn. also with Pups, who were later succeeded by No. 9 Naval Sqdn. on 15th June after claiming over 80 victories.

During operations against Zeppelin sheds at the end of March 1916 by the Harwich squadron and the Battle-Cruiser squadron, the German High Seas Fleet put to sea to attack the British ships. Due to the prevailing conditions, however, they returned to the sanctuary of their harbour although the British Grand Fleet had been alerted of the impending confrontation and had sailed to intercept the Germans.

On 3rd May 1916, another attack on the Zeppelin sheds at Trondern was planned using HMS *Engadine* and HMS *Vindex* with the hope that the German Fleet would again put to sea to oppose the British, but the Germans remained in port.

At the end of the month, increased radio traffic alerted the British that the German Fleet could be putting to sea and, on 30th May, the Cruiser squadron with HMS *Engadine* and the Grand Fleet with HMS *Campania* were ordered to sail. However the signal to sail was not received by Campania so the Grand Fleet sailed without her.

HMS *Engadine* launched Flt. Lt. Rutland and Asst. Paymaster Trewin to look for the German Fleet. They found the Fleet and relayed its position to Engadine, but unfortunately the information was not passed to Admiral Beatty due to a breakdown in the ships W/T equipment and the failing weather. The RNAS only played a small part in this the last great Grand Fleet action in any war, but it was however the first successful aerial reconnaissance mission during a naval battle.

THE BALKANS AND MIDDLE EAST

The RNAS attacked Constantinople (now Istanbul) on 15th April, dropping sixteen small incendiary bombs. Two aircraft flew from the RNAS at Imbros Island 180 miles from the city, one aircraft returning safely whilst the other landed in the Gulf of Xeros. Six months later, another long distance flight from the air station was undertaken by a flight of five aircraft to Bucharest 310 miles away, but one aircraft got lost and landed at Ismail 400 miles away in Russia.

A combined operation by the RNAS and RFC Military Wing was carried out over a fifteen day period from 15th-29th April to assist the Army's 6th Division who were besieged at Kit El Amera. They needed re-supplying or they would capitulate so aircraft were modified with a crude beam and release mechanism operated from the cockpit and the beams were then loaded with stores and supplies. The aircraft then flew over the Division and released their load to the British troops thus ensuring their existence. This was the first time stores had been delivered by this method.

The world's first carrier force, The East Indies and Egypt Seaplane Squadron of HMSs *Ben-My-Chree*, *Empress*, *Anne* and *Raven II*, saw action against the Turks in Palestine, Sinai and the Yemen. The two latter ships, ex-German ships now RN vessels, had been operated by the French until the arrival of the French Carrier FNS *Campinas*, after which they were operated by RN crews. The squadron, the only specifically organised naval force during W.W.I, formed at Port Said during January 1916. The squadron was initially operating in the role of spotting for naval bombardments, reconnaissance flights and the bombing of enemy installations, ships, encampments and troops around the Aegean, Eastern Mediterranean and North Africa. HMS *Ben-My-Chree* was also involved in supporting the Arab irregular forces of T E Lawrence in the defeat of the Turks and their surrender of the Red Sea port of Jidda.

Successful attacks were made against the railway between Bulgaria and Turkey resulting in the destruction of the railway bridges across the Nester River. On 15th October, three Farmans attacked the Buk Bridge taking out its centre span followed two weeks later when the Shimshirli Bridge had its two-centre spans destroyed. However the Turkish army would also have a degree of success with the sinking of the Ben-My-Chree on 9th January 1917, when she was bombarded from the shore battery off the island of Castelorizo and became the second carrier loss of the war.

ZEPPELINS AND U-BOAT SUPERIORITY

The giant Zeppelin airships were increasing their attacks across the North Sea, but unfortunately attacks on these airships were infrequent due to their ability to rise, by venting their ballast tanks, to a higher altitude at a faster rate than was possible by the pursuing aircraft of the time. The first interception of an airship from a seaplane carrier occurred when a Bristol Scout aircraft from HMS *Vindex* unsuccessfully attacked Zeppelin L17 on 2nd August. The aircraft fired some 'Rankin Darts' (a canister of 24 darts released in groups of three at a time, developed by Lt. F Rankin, Engineer) at the airship but it escaped. Unfortunately the Scout suffered engine failure and was lost.

One of the few successful attacks was achieved with a combined strike by three BE2Cs in November. Zeppelin L21 was returning home after attacking Barnsley and Wakefield when the three aircraft, flown by Flt. Lt. E Cadbury, Sub-Lt. E Pulling and Sub-Lt. G Fane, attacked the airship with both bombs and their Lewis guns, sending the vessel to the sea in a mass of flames.

Anti-submarine warfare saw an increase by the end of the year and into 1917. The first Coastal class non-rigid airship entered service at Pembroke airship station in June, and the station itself was commissioned in January to be followed by five more by August. These 'C' class airships were capable of eleven hours duration at 45 knots and 27 were delivered.

The RNAS also began taking delivery of the Sea Scout Zero (SSZ) class airships, and a total of 66 of these improved SS class were received.

Sopwith Camel

De Havilland DH4

The submarine attacks by the enemy were, in the main, crippling the British and Allied merchant fleet and, in the first four months of 1917, over two million tons were sunk accounting for nearly 1200 vessels. Under the guidance of Lt. J Porte, the RNAS had been developing flying-boat operations for the anti-submarine role. Porte, one of the RNAS's early aviators, moved to the USA to assist Glenn Curtiss on the development of the flying boat after being medically discharged with Tuberculosis, but he rejoined the RNAS at the outbreak of the war and became an important player in the war against the U-boat.

Early flying boats were not very successful as they were under-powered and unsafe, but improved boats eventually entered service, mainly the Felixstowe and Large America. Although Porte was unhappy with the range of these aircraft, large areas of the North Sea had to be covered which was not possible with the present aircraft in service, so he devised an ingenious plan of using destroyers to tow the aircraft on lighters into the operating areas, thus increasing their operating range.

A systematic patrol pattern of search was devised known as the Spider's Web, an octagonal pattern enabling 4000 sq. miles of sea to be searched by the flying boat patrols. The first time this system was operated, beginning on 13th April 1917 and lasting three weeks in an area close to the North Hinder Light Vessel, eight submarines were sighted and three were bombed. The system, albeit refined, is still the basis of sea searches carried out throughout the world to this day.

The Large America was a very successful aircraft responsible for some good early victories. On 14th May 1917, Sub-Lt. Leckie and his crew shot down the first Zeppelin (L22) by a flying boat, and Flt. Sub-Lt. C Morrish sank the first submarine by an aircraft when he destroyed U36 in the North Sea six days later (20th May). These results were achieved after less than three weeks of operations of this type.

HMS Argus

Leckie was the pilot of an H12 flying boat which was involved in the rescue of the crew of a DH4 shot down on 5th September. They picked up the two crew but were unable to take off with the extra weight. After attempting to taxi back to Yarmouth, short of fuel in heavy seas and with a shell hole in the aircraft hull, the engines eventually stopped and the aircraft was dependant on the elements. After four days they were themselves rescued 100 miles from Yarmouth by HMS *Halcyon* who took the aircraft in tow. It was repaired and soon back in operation. This is the first known rescue of aircrew from the sea by another aircraft.

Many methods were used to locate submarines, the most imaginative being the hydrophone - a microphone lowered down into the water to listen for the engine noise from the submarine. The SS airships, as well as seaplanes alighted on the water, were to carry out trials on this 1917 development. Again, this system was to come into its own with the use of helicopters as sub hunters 40 years later.

THE FIRST REAL AIRCRAFT CARRIER

It was realised that seaplane carriers were not very effective in front line naval battles because of the time taken to launch and recover the aircraft and the reliance on the aircraft's ability to take off. After consulting with Captain Oliver Schwann from HMS *Campania*, Admiral Jellicoe forwarded a proposal to the Admiralty that an aircraft carrier with a flight deck be designed and built, allowing aircraft to take off from the carrier in support of naval operations, rather than having to take off from the sea.

The Lords Commissioners considered designs submitted by Beardsmore & Co., shipbuilder and from Lt. R Holmes RNVR who had been serving on the seaplane carrier HMS *Riviera*. They decided to build a special aviation ship and a keel laid down in June 1914 for a cargo liner, the Conte Rosso belonging to the Italian Lloyd Sabaudo Line, was acquired. The building of the ship had ceased at the outbreak of war so it remained as a frame work. It was deemed more prudent to modify the remainder of the ship and complete it as a clear flush deck ship rather than build a new ship from the keel up. The ship was launched in December 1917 as HMS *Argus*, the world's first purpose designed aircraft carrier.

THE GRAND FLEET AIRCRAFT COMMITTEE

The Zeppelin problem was still paramount with their attacks on the mainland and the RNAS was being rebuffed for their lack of results against these attacks. The Commander-in-Chief, Admiral Beatty, set up a Grand Fleet Aircraft Committee to solve the problem. The main problems were the slow speed of the converted packet ships and their usable available space was limited, thus limiting the size and amount of aircraft carried. Another problem was the time lost launching and recovering the seaplanes by the carriers.

Fairey IIID

The Committee forwarded its report, which had two main suggestions, to Admiral Beatty on 5th February 1917. The first suggestion was that the light cruiser HMS *Furious*, nearing completion, be remodelled as a ship capable of operating aeroplanes as well as seaplanes. The other suggestion was an idea which involved the use of aeroplanes from capital ships.

In March, HMS *Furious* was ordered to be redesigned with a forward flight deck and hangar replacing the forward gun turret. It joined the Fleet on 4th July with a compliment of five Sopwith Pups and three Shorts 184 seaplanes. During the ship's sea trials, Sqd. Cdr. E Dunning carried out the first deck landing on board a ship underway (2nd August), whilst the ship was making way at 25 knots in Scapa Flow.

Dunning was to bring the aircraft over the deck to allow a deck crew to grab hold of the toggles specifically attached to the aircraft and hold the aircraft whilst he shut down the engine. This feat was achieved to the great satisfaction of all involved and further landings were made. Five days later, however, Dunning stalled the engine of his aircraft as he approached the deck, the Pup fell over the side of the ship and Dunning was drowned.

The Grand Fleet Aircraft Committee recommended that HMS *Furious* be modified by the removal of the aft 18" gun replacing it with another hangar and a landing deck. These modifications were carried out at the end of 1917, and Furious rejoined the Fleet at Rosyth on 15th March 1918 with 1½ Strutters replacing the Shorts 184s.

The trials by Cdr. Dunning also produced a safety device for stopping the aircraft falling off the front of the ship, a large rope hawser safety barrier. It was first fitted to HMS *Argus* during its build and to HMS *Furious* during its refit, and is still current in today's aircraft carriers, although not for what it was initially conceived for.

GUN TURRET LAUNCHES

During 1917, flights from ships' gun turrets were reactivated using Sopwith Pups, with Sqd. Cdr. F Rutland launching from the forward turret of the light cruiser HMS *Yarmouth* on the 28th June. These trials culminated with Flt. Sub-Lt. B Smart taking off from Yarmouth to attack and successfully destroy Zeppelin LZ66 (L23) on 21st August. In this successful attack, Smart climbed to 7000ft before attacking and destroying the airship, the first from an aircraft launched from a gun turret.

Rutland further improved operations from capital ships when he had a 'runway' built on the forward 'B' gun turret of HMS *Repulse* in such a way that the turret could be swung into the relative wind, thus allowing the ship to remain on its course whilst launching the aircraft. On 1st October, he flew off the runway in a Pup whilst the ship was steaming at 24 knots, and the turret was swung into wind producing over 30 knots of head wind. Ten days later he carried out a launch from the after 'Y' turret.

These operations resulted in eleven battleships, eleven battle-cruisers and fifteen cruisers being fitted with ramps on their gun turrets and equipped with their own Sopwith Pup. The aircraft had to ditch into the sea on flotation bags and be hoisted onboard the ship if no land was nearby.

The Commander in Chief, Admiral Sir David Beatty, was still not completely happy with this development as the ships were still required to stop and pick up the pilot after the mission and the aircraft itself was likely to be lost, a wastage which needed to be alleviated. Also, as the Pup was only a single seater, it was not very effective in the role of Fleet spotter. The first two-seater aircraft, a Sopwith 1½ Strutter, was successfully launched from HMS *Australia's* mid-ship turret fitted with a longer platform on 4th April 1918.

After the varied 'success' of these aviation trials throughout the Fleet, Beatty saw the huge potential of aircraft in the Fleet and wrote to the Admiralty on 7th October, suggesting that eight suitable ships be requisitioned which were capable of 16-20

Shorts 184 Seaplane

De Havilland DH9

knots fitted with flight decks fore and aft.

TRIPLANES AND CAMELS IN THE WESTERN FRONT

Sopwith continued to develop and produce outstanding aircraft, and February 1917 saw the introduction of their Triplane (nicknamed the Tripehound) entering service with No. 1 and No. 8 Naval Squadrons. No. 10 Naval Squadron was next to receive the aircraft, and 'B' Flight was manned by Canadians under the leadership of Flt. Lt. R Collishaw.

The five aircraft of 'Black' Flight were all personalised with names to suit this high scoring unit. All the names began with the suffix 'Black'- Death, Maria, Prince, Roger and Sheep. In action between May and July, Collishaw (who was to finish the war as the top scoring Naval pilot having 60 victories) destroyed sixteen aircraft in only 27 days, whilst the Flight accounted for 87 aircraft.

These aircraft were built as a faster climbing derivative of the Pup, but only 152 were built, 139 of which were delivered to the RNAS. They were soon replaced by the Camel in November, arguably the most successful British fighter of the war with 386 victories. This is attributed to its twin Vickers front firing machine guns, the first British fighter so fitted. There were two versions of the Camel, the F.1 which was used by both the RFC and RNAS, and the Naval 2F1 which had steel tubular centre-section struts and a fuselage which was in two parts to allow for easier shipboard stowage. The aircraft replaced the Pup onboard the capital ships.

LORD CURZON'S ILL-FATED REPORT

1916 had ended with a damning report from the Air Board, set up in May to promote closer co-operation between the RNAS and RFC, to formulate an Air Service policy and review the organisation of the two air arms. Lord Curzon's report to the War Committee, submitted in October, condemned the RNAS as a gung-ho brigade formed under the guidance of Winston Churchill. Its findings indicated that it would be better to combine the RNAS and RFC to encourage the correct tactics, material procurement and development.

His report inferred that the poor results achieved by the RNAS were mainly due to the lack of authority imposed on the aviators and the fact that the service was run by seamen, not airmen. He recommended one body to control aviation assets, materials and personnel which would produce positive results. Thus the seeds for the future Royal Air Force were sown.

Following the Curzon report, no immediate action was taken by the Government but this changed drastically after German Gotha bombers and Zeppelins reached London to drop their weapons relatively unopposed. The Government was forced to look at the problem and investigate British military aviation and its resources and operations.

Lt. Gen. Sir David Henderson was commissioned to look into the problems of the two air services with the aim of resolving the unsettled imbalance between them. His memo of 19th July 1917 came out in favour of a unified Force; a department with a full staff responsibility for war in the air, whilst supporting the requirements of the Navy and Army during operations in progress at the time; and a unified system of training where, upon specialisation of pilots and mechanics, they were earmarked for service with either Force as necessary.

General Jan Smuts, a South African who was neutral to both the RNAS and RFC, was appointed to assist the Prime Minister, Mr Lloyd George, to investigate the roles of the air services to see if a workable solution could be produced. Their report, issued on 17th August, was in favour of a single air arm.

This amalgamation was founded after professional advice was sought from the principal senior officers in their respective 'fields'. They were to advocate that both the services should keep their own autonomy. The downfall, however, was to be the constant bickering over the design, material supplies and requirements of the aircraft needed to defend Britain and its services.

So it was on 8th November 1917 that the Air Force Bill had its reading in the House of Commons, becoming law on 1st April (All Fools Day!!) 1918, when the functions of the RFC and RNAS would be performed by one air unit - the Royal Air Force. The rank structure of those transferring would be as in the Army; the RFC squadrons would retain their numbers whilst the RNAS squadrons would adopt numbers in the 200 series i.e. No. 1 Sqdn. RNAS became No. 201 Sqdn. RAF.

THE FIRST AIRCRAFT SIMULATOR

Wing Capt. Schwann, who was still in command of HMS *Campania*, designed and

HMS Argus

proposed the first simulator in August 1917. The design comprised of a twin-seater tractor fuselage mounted on a revolving platform to give a horizontal circular motion. To enable the rudder to be effective in turning the aircraft, a small engine was required and the cockpit was to be fitted with controls, instrumentation and W/T equipment.

THE OFFENSIVE

A major task was given to No. 2 Wing in March 1918, that of photographing the harbours of Ostend and Dunkirk for the impending blockades of their channels and canals. Many flights were carried out in the Unit's DH4s taking hundreds of photographs, with the aircraft flying through intense enemy defensive fire at heights of 50ft. The results were such that scale models of both ports were able to be produced for use in the planning of the operation.

The first bombing missions were carried out by Handley Page heavy bombers of No. 214 Sqdn. RAF (No. 14 Sqdn. RNAS) on 11th April. Following the naval operation to secure the blockade, the DH4s were again required to carry out a photographic reconnaissance mission on 23rd, but the results showed that the blockade at Ostend had not been successful and a second mission was necessary. This was achieved on 9th May when again the HP O/100 bombers were in support, dropping six of the new 550lb bombs for the first time.

RETURN OF HMS FURIOUS

HMS *Furious* was refitted with a 300ft landing-on deck after the removal of its aft gun turret, main mast and some of the superstructure before rejoining the Fleet in March 1918. Trials on the landing deck were carried out by Sopwith Pups which were modified by the removal of their wheels and the fitting of skids which were to catch the wires rigged fore and aft on the deck.

Only three of the thirteen landings were successful, the others resulted in either the aircraft going over the edge of the deck or crashing into the barrier rigged on the deck for the purpose of stopping the aircraft before it struck the superstructure. The trials were stopped because the eddy currents caused by the superstructure and funnel exhaust gases were the primary causes of the failure of the landings so the use of the deck for landing ceased.

Those who were 'lucky' enough to be stopped by this barrier became the first naval aviators to be saved by the device which later was to be an incorporated design feature of Fleet aircraft carriers.

Handley Page 0/100 heavy bomber

THE ROYAL AIR FORCE

All Fools Day was the day which was the beginning of a new era in British military aviation with the forming of the Royal Air Force (RAF). Although this was good for the country after the Great War, it would soon be detrimental to both the Royal Navy and British Army during the inter war years.

On the morning of 1st April the strength of the RNAS was 2949 aircraft, 103 airships and 126 air stations manned and operated by some 67,000 officers and men. These men were given the choice of transferring to the new service or remaining with the Navy. Those who transferred were given ranks equivalent to that held in the RNAS with an eventual change of uniform to light blue.

Unfortunately for the future of naval aviation, the majority transferred but of those who stayed, one of the most notable was Cdr. Richard Bell Davies RN VC. The Air Staff consisted of two senior naval officers, Rear Admiral Mark Kerr as Deputy Chief and Commodore Godfrey Pain as Master General of Personnel. The Squadrons of the RNAS immediately took up new identification, with the Wings numbered from No. 61 and the Squadrons from No. 200.

THE FALL OF THE 'RED BARON'

Captain Roy Brown (previously Flt. Cdr.) was credited with the successful shooting down of Baron Manfred Von Richtofen (The Red Baron) with a single shot to the chest. This is however contested by three Australian soldiers, Sgt. Popkin, Gunner Evans and Gunner Buie, who believe that one of them fired the fateful shot on that April day (21st). Unfortunately the post-mortem was only able to discover that the Baron had been hit by a single small calibre shot to the chest and it is mostly accepted that Roy Brown is the most probable victor.

THE USE OF TOWED LIGHTERS

During May 1918, Samson decided to utilise the lighters developed by Porte for use by fighter aircraft, with grooves fitted fore and aft to guide the aircraft skids which were to replace wheels. Piloting a Sopwith Camel, he attempted a launch whilst being towed at 32 knots by the destroyer HMS *Truculent*. The aircraft travelled a few feet down the grooves before it fell off the lighter which then travelled over the top of the aircraft.

Samson survived the accident and undeterred proceeded to redesign the lighter by reconstructing it so the angle of the deck

HMS Furious

Fairey IIIC

would be parallel to the sea when the aircraft (reverted back to wheels) would make its take-off run. The first successful take-off was carried out by Lt. S D Culley, and the lighters became operational within the Fleet, being towed behind the capital ships.

A force of ships patrolling in the Heligoland Bight during August included HMS *Redoubt* towing a lighter with a Camel on board - flown by Culley. The aircraft was launched on the morning of 11th August to attack Zeppelin L53 which was shadowing the Fleet. Culley climbed in pursuit of the Zeppelin, taking an hour to reach it, but the Camel was at its maximum ceiling and Culley had no response from the controls.

He pulled back the controls and let go with a burst of gunfire until he ran out of ammunition. The aircraft fell away from the airship and Culley reloaded his Vickers synchronised guns for a second attack which resulted in the airship being set alight and crashing to the sea. As Culley descended, he could not find the ships and, running low on fuel, was preparing to land near some Dutch trawlers. However he then sighted the squadron and as he approached them, he looped and rolled the Camel in a Victory salute. This was not only the first successful mission carried out by a barge launched fighter, but also the last Zeppelin to be destroyed in the war. For his actions, Culley was recommended for a V.C. but received a D.S.O. instead.

The success of the attack induced the Squadron Commander Vice Admiral Tyrewhitt to signal his ships - "*Attention is drawn to Hymn 224 Verse 72 in the naval prayer book. This reads 'Oh happy band of pilgrims, look upwards to the skies, where such a little affliction, shall win so great a prize'.*"

THE FINAL "FIRST'S" OF THE WAR

The 18th of June saw the first air warfare action to be launched from an aircraft carrier. Sopwith Camels attacked four enemy floatplanes over the Skagerraks; one being destroyed, the other three driven off. The aircraft had been launched from the forward deck of HMS *Furious*.

On 19th July, the first and only carrier launched land attack of the war took place when six aircraft, again from HMS *Furious*, carried out the final air/sea operations successfully bombing the Zeppelin sheds at Tondern destroying L54 and L60 at the base. This operation was proof that airborne attacks, launched from ships to attack land targets, were a reality not just a dream.

The world's first aircraft carrier with a completely unobstructed flat deck, HMS *Argus,* joined the Fleet during September with the ship receiving her first aircraft, a 1½ strutter flown by Bell Davies VC. The ship was laid down in 1914 as an Italian merchantman before being redesigned as a seaplane carrier in 1916, then redesigned once more in 1917 with an unobstructed deck. These changes in design, for the better operation of aircraft, meant commissioning of the ship was delayed. The ship had four hangar sections separated by fireproof curtains, two aircraft lifts, weapons stores and aircraft workshops to support the embarked aircraft.

In 1915, after operating off HMS *Ark Royal,* Cdr. H A Williamson submitted ideas for constructing the superstructure on the starboard side of a ship, thus leaving the deck clear. This suggestion was possible due to the British driving on the left, but it is recorded that the starboard side was the natural position as the gyroscopic effect of an aircraft's rotary engine forced the nose up when turning the aircraft to the left (the opposite turning to the right).

A dummy structure, which became known as the island, was erected on the deck of HMS *Argus* for trials in October 1918 which proved the theory. The design was incorporated in the build of HMS *Eagle* launched in June of 1918 and commissioned in 1924. This is now standard on all aircraft carriers built since W.W.I.

Sopwith Cuckoo

FINAL OPERATIONS

During August the 'old Sea Salts', now in the RAF, were still achieving 'RNAS' victories. Sqdn. Cdr. (now Major) E Cadbury attacked the last two airships to venture into British airspace. Zeppelins L65 and L70 were crossing the Norfolk coast on the 5th when he attacked them in his Camel, successfully destroying the latter but L65 escaped as his guns jammed. On board the L70 was Peter Strasser, the driving influence on airship warfare in the German Naval Airship Division.

Eight days later, 50 RNAS Camels led by Lt. W Grey attacked the enemy's main airfield at Varssenaere escorted by a squadron of DH4s. Their arrival at the target was planned for early morning which was achieved, arriving over the airfield as the enemy aircraft were being prepared for their first sorties of the day. The attack by the Camels totally destroyed the airfield and all the aircraft returned home safely.

Although the war was at last drawing to an end, convoys were still plying the sea lanes escorted by the airships. On 16th September, the last sinking of a German submarine of the war occurred when UB103 was successfully attacked by one of the Sea Scout Zero airships. These, and the other airships built to protect the convoys, had carried out sterling work since their arrival into service. Through their operations, many ships and countless lives were saved from the torpedoes of the German U-boats.

The last operation of the war was carried out on the final night of the conflict, when No. 214 Sqdn. RAF bombed the railway station and yard at Louvain with their Handley Page O/100 heavy bombers. The following morning, 11th November, the armistice was signed at 11am.

At the Armistice, the RNAS (even though it was now part of the fledgling RAF) had more than 2650 aeroplanes and seaplanes, 103 airships and 150 flying boats, which was the world's largest naval air strength. There were more than 100 of the aircraft operating from capital ships, 22 cruisers had flying-off platforms equipped with one aircraft, whilst all battleships and battle cruisers were equipped with a two-seat aircraft operating from their forward platform and a single-seat fighter from their aft platform. The Royal Navy had more ships operating these aircraft than all the world's navies combined.

HMS Argus

HMS VINDICTIVE

Laid down as the cruiser HMS *Cavendish*, HMS *Vindictive* was redesigned as an aircraft carrier with two hangars, a forward flying-off deck and an after-landing deck, and she was to accommodate two fighter aircraft and six spotter aircraft. Commissioned on 1st October 1918, Vindictive joined the Grand Fleet Flying Squadron on the 18th but she was to see no operational service before the Armistice six weeks later.

The after-landing deck was only to see one aircraft landing carried out upon it when, on 1st November, a landing was made by W W Wakefield in a Sopwith Pup. This was also synonymous as the aircraft was the Fleet's sole remaining operational Sopwith Pup from about 290 which had served in the RNAS since the type's first flight in early 1916.

The ship was initially used for trials including the first trials with the unsuccessful Grain Griffin. This was a two-seat Fleet spotter reconnaissance aircraft conceived at the RNAS experimental depot on the Isle of Grain. The aircraft was to see action in the Baltic during the British assistance to the White Russians.

A final act, carried out on 21st November, was the flight of the 'naval aircraft' - seaplanes, flying boats, airships and aircraft, flying above the Grand Fleet escorting the defeated German High Seas Fleet to Scapa Flow, a victory that could not have been achieved without them.

Fairey Flycatcher

TOP: Nieuport Nightjar

LEFT: Parnell Panther

BOTTOM: Parnell Panther

The Next Battle - One for Survival

Fairey Flycatcher

POST W.W.I - THE DECLINE OF NAVAL AVIATION

With the end of hostilities there was a rapid reduction in the British Forces and many aircraft orders were cancelled. The strength of the RAF was reduced to 25 squadrons including one Spotter-reconnaissance squadron, 1/2 a Torpedo Squadron and single flights of fighter, seaplane and flying boat aircraft in support of the Fleet.

The amalgamation of the RNAS and RFC did not eliminate the inter-forces rivalry. The new RAF hierarch who originated from the two previous Forces seemed to forget their roots (mainly due to the influence of Lord Trenchard and his insistence on The Unity of the Air Policy), and began to ignore the requirements of their past service masters. Much to the chagrin of the RN and British Army, all efforts in British military aviation were to the detriment of them. As far as aircraft delivered to operate on behalf of the Fleet was concerned, they were mostly only derivatives of RAF types, not specific 'naval' aircraft.

The emphasis from the Great War, which was indicating the importance of aircraft as a major part of the RN, began to wane from the cessation of the hostilities, getting progressively worse as more ex-naval aviators were to 'retire' to civilian street.

On 4th December 1918, there was a meeting between the Director of the Air Department and the Admiralty on the future of the RN and its aviation requirements. This resulted in the decision to keep six operational aircraft/seaplane carriers - HMSs *Argus, Furious, Nairana, Pegasus, Vindex* and *Vindictive*, and to receive the two under construction - HMSs *Eagle* and *Hermes*. HMS *Ark Royal* would be retained for aviation trials.

Capital ships would retain a flight on board with the added agreement that future capital ships would include aircraft as a standard compliment (light cruisers one aircraft and larger ships two aircraft). The RAF would embark aircraft flights as required to fulfil the tasking of the Admiralty under the command of the ship's Captain.

Following this meeting, the Navy assumed that there would be squadrons under their direct responsibility but the 1919 Defence White Paper did not give this directive. It did, however, mention that a small part of the RAF would be trained for operations aboard ships. This was the first real indication the RN would have to battle with the Air Ministry if it was to have any control on naval aviation matters. This attitude and the ignorance to the Fleet's needs were to continue for nearly twenty years, with the RN fighting its corner producing results during these years and eventually winning control in 1937.

NAVAL AIRCRAFT JOIN THE RAF

Sopwith designed the Cuckoo, the first landplane able to carry a torpedo (prior to this only seaplanes had been capable of carrying this weapon). Second to this was the rudimentary fact that it was designed to operate from ships. The aircraft entered service with the naval element of the RAF on 7th October 1918 with No. 185 Sqdn. at East Fortune, embarking on board HMS *Argus* twelve days later. Unfortunately they

HMS Glorious

were too late to take part in the war but went on to serve for another five years.

Sopwith designed the aircraft after consultation with Sueter two years earlier. The first prototype flew in June 1917 but it took many months of development work to produce the ultimate torpedo carrier. The torpedo casing froze in flight which meant it did not perform as desired when released, but this problem was cured by heating the casing with hot air from the aircraft's engine.

With the introduction of this torpedo aircraft, a training school was established at Grange airfield (now RAF Gosport), working alongside the ATDU. The school would train all torpedo aircraft pilots until the outbreak of the Second World War, with the airfield having a carrier deck marked out for this training. Also located at Gosport was the catapult training establishment where all pilots for catapult flights had to successfully complete a day of catapult launches.

Another great aircraft to have its maiden flight in June of 1918 was the Fairey IIIA. The type originated from the F128/FN10 seaplane and was further developed into a range of aircraft. The Fairey IIIC was possibly the world's first multi-role aircraft used for both scouting and bombing duties. The improved IIID arrived in 1924 and was operated from all launch scenarios; from land, aircraft carriers, capital ships and the sea. During October 1925, Wing Cdr. Burlington carried out the first catapult launch of a standard seaplane from a warship at sea in an IIID. The final model was the IIIF of which the FAA received more than 350 during its service career from 1928 until 1940.

Fairey IIID

Parnell developed the Panther, a two-seat reconnaissance aircraft designed for carrier deck operations, fitted with hooks on its axles to catch the longitudinal wires when recovering on board. The aircraft had a novel feature, that of a folding fuselage to allow reduced stowage space when on board ship. The aircraft first flew in 1917 and entered service in 1919, serving in four flights until 1926, seeing service on board both Argus and Hermes.

SUPPORT FOR THE 'WHITE RUSSIANS'

After the Armistice was signed, the British Government formed an allegiance with the 'White Russians' in their struggle against the Bolsheviks. The allegiance was to include France and the USA who hoped they would be able to assist the White Russians to overcome the forces led by Leon Trotsky.

The first naval aviation exploits involved two Russian merchant ships which had been commandeered in the Caspian Sea and which operated with No. 266 Sqdn. from the port of Petrovsk. The Orlionoch was put to use carrying two Shorts seaplanes during late 1918, followed by the Alader Yousanoff in January 1919. The aircraft were operational on both reconnaissance and bombing missions, and the ships were handed over to the White Russians when the British Forces withdrew from the area during August.

The seaplane carriers, HMS *Empress* and HMS *Riviera,* delivered the DH9s of No. 221 Sqdn. RAF to Batumi, the Black Sea port on the Russian Turkish border, arriving on 5th January 1919. The ships were then returned to the UK prior to them being decommissioned and returned to their previous owners.

HMS Eagle

The last day of the year saw a new RAF Squadron form for anti-shipping operations in the Caspian Sea. The squadron, No. 186, was formed using volunteer crews from No. 185 Sqdn. whilst aboard HMS *Argus* and was to be equipped with DH9s. The requirements of the squadron were, however, cancelled but its aircraft were still needed so they were transferred to No. 221 Sqdn. and taken to the theatre aboard HMS *Ark Royal.*

May to September 1919 saw five RN carriers in action with the B.E.F. against the Bolsheviks, at Archangel'sk in the White Sea and the Baltic. A seaplane base was established on the beach at Troitsa on the river Dvina for the aircraft of the Archangels River Seaplane Squadron which had been transported to the area aboard HMS *Pegasus.* Fairey IIICs from Pegasus were to bomb four Bolshevik naval vessels on 8th June and, during July, HMS *Argus* delivered more IIICs to Pegasus in its first operational mission since commissioning in September 1918.

HMS *Nairana* operated five Campania seaplanes whilst operating with the B.E.F. which was her last operation before being sold. These aircraft were the first to be designed specifically to operate from ships, their name being taken from HMS *Campania* for which they were originally intended to operate from (the Beardsmore WBIIIs were conversions of the Sopwith Pup).

July saw HMS *Vindictive* sail to join the British Forces in the Baltic with twelve aircraft aboard (Camels, $1^{1/2}$ Strutters, Type 184s and Grain Griffins), but unfortunately she was embarrassingly grounded at Reval for eight days. The operation to bomb Kronstad on 30th July involved all twelve aircraft and, to accommodate all the aircraft on the deck together and increase the aircraft's take-off run, she had to have the take-off deck extended by 118ft.

HMS *Furious* joined Vindictive for a few weeks operating Camels, returning to Portsmouth during November and joining the reserve Fleet on the 21st. When the operations in the Baltic were completed on 22nd December, HMS *Vindictive* returned to Portsmouth to be paid off and join Furious in reserve.

During December 1919, HMS *Ark Royal* was operating as an aircraft transporter during the minor skirmish in British Somali-land. Twelve DH9 aircraft and personnel of the RAF 'Z' Force were transported to support the 'Camel Corps' for operations against Mohammed Ben Abdullah's native insurgents. She was to carry out a similar role exactly twelve months later transporting Fairey IIIDs of No. 267 Sqdn. to Kilja Bay in the Dardanelles for use by the British Forces patrolling the neutral line.

THE ROYAL NAVY's FINAL AIRSHIP OPERATION

The last airship operated by the Royal Navy before final handing over to the RAF was the R34. This machine flew the first transatlantic crossing when it took off from East Fortune airfield on 2nd July 1919 arriving in Long Island, New York on the 6th after completing the 3130 mile journey after 108hrs 12mins flying time. Three days later it began its return flight, landing on the 13th after 75hrs 3mins, thus making the first ever two-way crossing of the Atlantic.

THE NAVY's AVIATION ASSETS

Aircraft operated by the RAF in support of the Fleet were incorporated in the RAF

HMS Eagle at high speed

Fairey Flycatcher

system, being units numbered in the '200' series. No. 186 Squadron RAF, the torpedo development unit, was reformed as No. 210 Squadron at Gosport on 1st February 1920 as the Naval Torpedo Training Unit equipped with Sopwith Cuckoos. Also based in the Solent area was the School of Naval Co-operation, the seaplane training unit located jointly at Calshot and Lee-on-the-Solent operating Shorts 184 seaplanes and Fairey IIIDs.

HMS Furious

The Fleet was to have another two squadrons at its disposal from 1920. No. 203 Sqdn., a Fleet fighter squadron equipped with Sopwith Camels, was reformed at RAF Leuchars in Scotland on 1st March. This unit was the original RNAS Eastchurch Squadron from 1914. No. 205 Sqdn. was reformed with Parnell Panthers on 15th April, also at Leuchars, as the Fleet reconnaissance squadron. This squadron could trace its past back to No. 5 Naval Wing.

Of the seventeen squadrons of the RNAS to be 'accepted' into the RAF on 1st April 1918 (Nos. 201-217 Sqdns), these were the only three remaining as 'naval' squadrons. The remainder had disbanded; No. 209 Sqdn. - Camels and No. 211 Sqdn. - DH9s 24th Jan 1919; No. 215 Sqdn. - HP O/400 18th Oct 1919; No. 217 Sqdn. - DH4s 19th Oct 1919; No. 208 Sqdn. - Snipes 7th Nov 1919; No. 201 Sqdn. - Snipes, No. 204 Sqdn. and No. 213 Sqdn. - Camels on 31st Dec 1919; No. 207 Sqdn. - HP O/400 20th Jan 1920; No. 202 Sqdn. - DH9s on 22nd Jan 1920; No. 214 Sqdn. - HP O/400 1st Feb 1920 and No. 212 Sqdn. - Camels 9th Feb 1920. Although No. 206 Sqdn. (renumbered No. 47 Sqdn.) and No. 216 Sqdn. remained as RAF squadrons, they had no ties with the RN.

THE NAVAL AIR SECTION

The Admiralty initiated a Naval Air Section (NAS) in 1920, under the command of Admiral Chatfield (later as First Sea Lord, to be instrumental in regaining control from the RAF), who appointed Bell Davies VC RN as the only member of this section. The role of the NAS was to oversee the Fleet's aviation requirements to ensure full support was achieved from the RAF. The minimum requirements for the support of aviation missions within the Fleet were determined as four aircraft carriers in service with 45 spotter aircraft, 22 reconnaissance aircraft and twelve torpedo spotter aircraft.

A major problem was from the RAF personnel who had not previously been in the naval side of aviation. They were not keen to serve in detachments to the Fleet and they did not like to be separated from their families (as is the norm for naval people). The RAF service was cosy in comparison to the Army and Navy thus they did not like the living facilities on board ships i.e. giving up their warm beds for hammocks and, above all, service with the Fleet came with a small reduction in pay. Most of the RAF types appointed to units operating with the Fleet wanted their period of service to pass quickly so they could return to the comforts of their service. This resulted in reduced enthusiasm during naval exercises involving the aircraft carriers which showed a distinct lack of professionalism and skill.

THE RN AIRCREW OBSERVERS

From the very early flying within the RNAS

there were specially trained spotters flying in naval aircraft. With the end of hostilities, many returned to civilian life, while those that remained transferred to the RAF as navigators with a completely different role. This resulted in the loss of expertise in the role of the 'eyes' flying in Fleet spotter aircraft. Thus the level of operational competence within the Fleet's aviation fraternity was reduced even further.

Westland Walrus

To rectify some of these deficiencies, the Observer Officer branch was formed in 1921 ensuring that only specialist navy observers would fly as 'backseaters' in aircraft operating with the Fleet. These aviators were able to begin to reinstate some of the professionalism and skill back into aviation at sea. This was also a major step in the direction of the autonomy of RN aviation, although it was still going to take another eighteen years before complete control was secured.

The 21st October 1921 saw the 'birth' of another Fleet squadron when No. 3 Sqdn. was reformed at Leuchars from part of No. 205 Sqdn. The role of the squadron was designated as the Naval Co-operation Unit initially equipped with DH9A aircraft until the arrival of its Westland Walrus aircraft in January 1922. Although the Walrus was a three-seat deck landing development of the DH9A, it is recognised as the first post W.W.I British naval aircraft. The additional crew member (the DH9A had only two crew) was an observer who had a prone position cockpit.

THE CHANAK CRISIS

The British Forces were required to show their strength during 1922, when Turkish troops crossed the neutral line in a bid to regain control of land held by the British since the Armistice. Two of the old seaplane carriers were once again operating in the Dardanelles during this disturbance. HMS *Pegasus* was operating her Fairey IIICs whilst HMS *Ark Royal* was used as an aircraft transport and depot ship in support of HMS *Argus*, transporting twelve Bristol F2B Fighters to the ship.

No. 203 Sqdn. with its six Nieuport (Gloster) Nightjars was transferred to Kilja Bay from Leuchars during September aboard Argus, arriving on the 27th. This new fighter aircraft served in the theatre for nearly three months before being returned to Leuchars at the end of December, once again aboard Argus. The ship was eventually to receive her own flight of Nightjars when No. 401 flight formed on 1st April 1923.

HMS ARGUS PROVES HER DESIGN

HMS *Argus* had a busy 1922, being employed on many of the trials to improve safety and operating procedures on aircraft carriers as she was the only full flush deck aircraft carrier until the arrival of the new HMS *Hermes* due the following year. She did take part in some naval exercises but she proved to be too slow in general so was mainly involved in proving the design concept for future aircraft carriers.

An idea proposed by the Royal Aircraft Establishment (RAE) at Farnborough was the use of remote control drones for naval gunfire. These trials with the RAE 1921 Target were carried out from her deck in August but proved unsuccessful, however later trials were to succeed and the ship became the operating deck for DH Queen Bee drones.

THE FLEET GETS ITS 'OWN' UNITS

A change in the numbering of the squadrons of the RAF which were directly associated with operating with the RN were once again to be renumbered. With effect from 1st April 1923, all these units were to be redesignated as flights with numbers in the '400' series as follows:- 401-419 Fleet Fighters, 420-439 Fleet Spotters, 440-459 Fleet Reconnaissance and 460 upwards as Fleet Torpedo Units.

The flights had two main operating bases; RAF Leuchars in Scotland and RAF Gosport in the Solent. The flights were allocated to their specific aircraft carrier for operations, disembarking to either of the bases when the ship was in their base port. Seaplane training was carried out at the bases of Calshot and Lee-on-the-Solent.

At this time, combined with the allocating and renumbering of Fleet aircraft units, colour codes were painted on the aircraft to indicate which aircraft carrier the unit was operating from (with the new ships, as they entered service):- HMS *Argus* - green rectangle, HMS *Ark Royal* (1938) - blue/red/blue band, HMS *Courageous* (1928) - light blue diagonal band, HMS *Eagle* (1924) - black rectangle, HMS *Furious* - red diagonal band, HMS *Glorious* (1930) - yellow diagonal band with white edges and HMS *Hermes* - white diamonds, post 1933 a green band.

Blackburn Blackburn

Fairey IIIF

ARRESTOR WIRE DEVELOPMENTS

As mentioned earlier, the initial methods of arresting aircraft landing on carrier decks was with longitudinal (fore and aft) wires, which were supposed to guide the aircraft to a safe stop. This system was further developed by combining the wires with a series of ramps. The idea was conceived by accident after an aircraft landed on the deck of HMS *Argus* whilst the lift was partially lowered, resulting in a rapid deceleration of the aircraft.

A variation of this method was installed aboard HMS *Eagle* with the wires mounted on hinged flaps which acted as a braking device being knocked down by the aircraft as it ran along the deck, thus slowing it down. These were still not a guaranteed safe landing aid and eventually, beginning in 1924, all arrestor wires were removed from carrier decks as the ships went into dock for maintenance/refit, the aircraft making free landings for the next nine years.

FAIREY FLYCATCHER

The delivery of a new fighter to No. 402 Flight heralded an era of twelve years when the Fairey Flycatcher would reign as the Fleet's most versatile fighter. This small compact aircraft served on board all the RN carriers of the period as normal 'wheeled' aircraft and from capital ships, operating as an amphibian (not very successfully) or as a normal seaplane. Most aircraft designed for operating from carriers normally incorporated folding wings, but this was not the case with this aircraft, instead the fuselage could be dismantled for stowage on board.

The prototype aircraft was carrying out operating trials aboard Argus during February 1923 most specifically to test the new arrestor gear, two steel jaws on the aircraft's undercarriage, and the aircraft's revolutionary (in naval aircraft terms) hydraulic wheel brakes. Until the final removal of the fore and aft wires from British aircraft carriers, Flycatchers were fitted with the steel jaws but not the braking system, which had proved so satisfactory that the brakes reduced the aircraft's stopping distance to 150ft.

The aircraft was also fitted with the patent 'Fairey camber change mechanism' which altered the trailing edge profile of the mainplane for landing and take-off. The edge was fitted with adjustable flaps which increased the camber reducing the aircraft's stalling speed, a feature still fitted to aircraft.

NEW CARRIERS

The world's first official ship designed as an aircraft carrier, HMS *Hermes*, was commissioned during July 1923. The ship, with a 580ft unobstructed flight deck, the 'island' on the starboard side and a 400ft hangar below, was to be the accepted design for aircraft carriers the world over. A feature built on the ship which came from the previous seaplane carriers was the 'ship's crane'. Located behind the island, this was to feature on all the future RN carriers, although not always located behind the island.

Work began on the conversion of the two light cruisers, HMS *Courageous* and HMS *Glorious* (sister ships to HMS *Furious*) to fast (30kt) aircraft carriers in 1923. These two ships would be completed

HMS Hermes at Wei-Hai-Wei

incorporating all the latest designs for operating aircraft and have a forward flying-off deck direct from the hangar (as was being initiated in the refit of HMS *Furious*).

HMS *Eagle* was commissioned on 26th February 1924 at Portsmouth where she had been for two years fitting out. She was originally laid down as the battleship Almirante Cochrane for the Chilean Navy over ten years earlier in 1913, but January 1918 saw the Admiralty decide to complete it as a strike carrier although work on the ship progressed slowly.

SUBMARINES AS AIRCRAFT CARRIERS

The idea of operating aircraft from submarines (shelved after the E22 trials of 1916) was reactivated when Captain M Horton RN - Captain First Submarine Sqdn. proposed the operation of aircraft from submarines by refitting the Monitor ('M') Class of submarines with a hangar and catapult track forward of the conning tower.

This proposal was eventually accepted by the Admiralty after being passed to them by C-in-C Atlantic Fleet in July 1923. The Head of the Air Section, however, felt that it was no use pursuing the idea unless a suitable aircraft could be designed and procured. The Air Ministry therefore raised aircraft specification 16/24 for a stainless steel seaplane with folding wings, with a width no greater than 8ft when folded and a height less than 11ft, capable of operating from a submarine.

Parnell designed an aircraft to meet the proposal and were awarded a contract to build two prototypes to be called the Peto after Lt. Cdr. Francis Peto RN who was the Commanding Officer of the M2, the submarine that was chosen for the refit. The submarine went into its £60,000 refit at Chatham in September 1925.

THE BIRTH OF THE FLEET AIR ARM

After the Admiralty won the argument for Naval Observers in 1921, the first of many committees was set up to investigate the requirements of naval aviation. The Balfour Committee sat during late 1923 and issued their findings in 1924. The report by Lord Salisbury agreed to the Admiralty's request that all aircraft observers and up to 70% of all pilots operating aircraft in the Fleet be Royal Navy or Royal Marine officers.

The discipline and administration procedures for cross-operating were formulated by the RN. Naval officers seconded to the RAF were to be given

Blackburn Dart

Fairey Flycatcher over Grand Harbou Malta

Submarine M2/Parnell Peto

Hawker Osprey

equivalent RAF Officer rank but carry out naval type duties only, whilst initial pilot training would be given at the RAF's Central Flying Schools prior to the specialised naval flying training.

Aviation units designated for operations with the Fleet were to be known as The Fleet Air Arm (FAA) of the RAF from 1st April 1924, and none of these units were to be withdrawn without consultation with the Admiralty or Government consent. The Air Ministry would be responsible for the aircraft ordered by the Admiralty and would pay for the aircraft required for the Fleet. So the FLEET AIR ARM was officially 'born'.

Three months later, the Spithead Fleet Review on 26th July was to have its first aircraft carrier in amongst the 200 assembled Fleet. Although it was not the first time aircraft had taken part in a review, it was the first time aircraft of the FAA had been flown over an assembled Fleet. Even though they were officially RAF aircraft!

PEGASUS RETIRES - FURIOUS RETURNS

HMS *Pegasus* had joined the Royal Navy in August 1918 as the last seaplane/ aeroplane carrier and was the only one retained after hostilities ended. Besides operating with the Grand Fleet during the war, she also saw service against the Bolsheviks and at Chanak against the Turks.

The ship, redesignated as an aircraft tender after having its launching platform removed during 1923, was tasked with the role of supporting a Far Eastern Photographic Expedition for twelve months from March. She sailed for Singapore on 21st March with six Fairey IIIDs specially modified for the exercise, returning to Plymouth on 31st March 1925. This was to be her last operation actively operating aircraft, and she was placed in reserve on 5th July.

Now fitted with a complete flush deck, HMS *Furious* completed its full carrier refit in 1925. It had a unique feature, that of a 60ft flying-off deck which was served by the upper hangar, allowing aircraft to get airborne directly from it. This feature was also incorporated into its sister ships, Courageous and Glorious, and was normally used for the launching of Fairey Flycatchers, the ship's fighter flight (known as the 'slip flight').

CATAPULT TRIALS

The Isle of Grain had been an instrumental part of the developments in naval aviation. Trials had been held for both arrestor wires and catapult launching of aircraft during the war but had been cancelled as 'more pressing' work was needed. During the period 1917-1919, a specialised ship was commissioned for carrying out catapult trials. The ship, HMS *Slinger*, initially used Shorts Type 184 seaplanes until the arrival of the sole Fairey F127 catapult float plane. This aircraft was stressed for the trials which proved successful but no further developments were made.

The catapult trials were eventually restarted at the RAE Farnborough, but the trials began not in the launching of pilots, but with sheep in the aircraft's cockpit. Complete with pilots' goggles, sheep were used to determine the effects on the body from the 'G' forces before using the real thing! These first catapults were high pressure air driven propulsive rams (no 'pun' intended).

The destroyer HMS *Stronghold* was fitted with a basic counter weight catapult during 1924 which was used to launch a radio controlled flying bomb developed by RAE Farnborough. The small light aircraft, misleadingly called Royal Aircraft Factory Aerial Targets, were launched from the ship's bows during the trials in 1925, possibly the first exercises with this type of weapon.

No further trials were held until a new lease of life was given to HMS *Vindictive* in 1925, with the installation of a 'Carey' aircraft catapult above her hangar. She conducted trials using Fairey IIID and Flycatcher float planes and, on 30th October, she launched a IIID flown by Wing Cdr. Burlington for the first catapult launch of a standard British naval seaplane.

Other trials with compressed air and cordite charges resulted in capital ships being fitted with catapults as standard, HMS *Frobisher* receiving the first air operated model in 1927. The final type of catapult was a hydro-pneumatic version which shot a reusable towing bridle along a slot in the deck.

THE FIRST CARRIER TASK FORCE

During September 1926, the first RN carrier task force was deployed to the South China Seas in support of the British Merchant ships and the Shanghai Defence Force against Chinese Nationalist rebels. Merchant ships were regularly pirated and attacked by rebel Chinese forces near Shanghai. The task force consisted of HMSs *Argus*, *Hermes* and *Vindictive* and,

Blackburn Dart

once on station, the ships' Fairey IIIDs and Flycatchers were operating from the Shanghai Kiangnan racecourse and the Whangpoo River.

Hermes and Argus assisted the Shanghai Defence Force against the Chinese rebel forces, led by General Chaing Kai-Shek, for over twelve months until Hermes returned home in September 1927 followed by Argus in November. Vindictive mostly operated from the northern anchorage at Wei-hai-Wei on anti-piracy duties and was to remain on station until March 1928.

The task force also operated from Hong Kong utilising a landing strip from a piece of land at Kai Tak. The first aircraft to operate from the strip were the air group aboard Hermes; Flycatchers of 403 Flt. and Fairey IIIDs of 440 Flt. The strip was soon to be developed into a permanent air base for aircraft from the aircraft carriers.

NEW ARRIVALS AND NEW TRIALS

April 1928 saw HM *Submarine 'M2'* begin trials operating the Parnall Peto seaplane. Its crew of six officers and 49 ratings included two pilots, Lt. C Byas and Lt. C Keighly-Peach, and three aircraft ratings. The submarine was fitted with a 'sealable' aircraft hangar which was entered from the pressure hull prior to the submarine surfacing, a 'Carey' compressed air catapult and a derrick above the hangar to recover the aircraft back to the catapult, the track acting as a guide for hangar stowage. Once inside the hangar a large door was raised to effect the seal.

To launch the aircraft, ten men were required to get the aircraft out of the hangar and spread. The routine would be that the pilot would warm up the engine prior to the door being opened, once surfaced the door was lowered and track inserts fitted to join the inner and outer rails, the aircraft was then pushed forward onto the catapult track where the wings were spread. The submarine would turn into wind and increase its speed up to 15 knots where the pilot would open the throttle and the aircraft would be launched.

HMS *Courageous* commissioned in May 1928, having previously been a light cruiser which was proposed for conversion (along with its sister ship HMS *Glorious* - recommissioned March 1930) after the Washington Naval Treaty which limited the size of aircraft carriers to 22,000 tons. The ship was to operate three new squadrons; No. 407 Fleet Fighter Flt. with Flycatchers; No. 445 Fleet Reconnaissance Flt. with Fairey IIIFs and No. 463 Fleet Torpedo Flt. with Darts, which had all commissioned on

Hawker Nimrod

1st September 1927. The aircraft embarked for work in the summer of 1928 when the ship was with the Home Fleet, and it was to see its first operational missions twelve months later.

During August 1929, the Palestinians were attacking Jewish villages in Palestine which, at that time, was a British Protectorate. HMS *Courageous* was dispatched from Malta on 26th August arriving at Jaffa two days later where she disembarked her aircraft to Gaza. The aircraft carried out attacks on Arab villages and deterrent flights against the Arab agitators for four weeks before returning to the ship when the disturbances ceased. The ship transported an Army battalion to the area - was this the forerunner of the commando carrier of the 1960's?

CATAPULT FLIGHTS

The School of Naval Co-operation at Lee-on-the-Solent became the parenting home of the capital ships' catapult flights in 1930:

No. 447 Flight (IIIF and Flycatcher) -1st Cruiser Sqdn. (Mediterranean Fleet),

No. 444 Flight (IIIF and Flycatcher) -1st Battle Sqdn. (Capital Ships/Home Fleet),

Battle Cruiser Sqdn. (Cap. Ships/Med. Fleet),

No. 407 Flight (Flycatcher) - 2nd Cruiser Sqdn. (Home Fleet),

No. 443 Flights (IIIF and Flycatcher) - 2nd Cruiser Sqdn. (Home Fleet),

No. 444 Flight (IIIF and Flycatcher) - 2nd Battle Sqdn. (Cap. Ships/Home Fleet),

No. 445 Flight (Flycatchers) - 3rd Cruiser Sqdn. (Med. Fleet),

No. 406 Flight (Flycatcher) - 4th Cruiser Sqdn. (East Indies),

Nos. 403 and 405 Flights (Flycatcher) - 5th Cruiser Sqdn. (China Station),

No. 443 Flight (IIIF) - 6th Cruiser Sqdn. (South Africa),

No. 443 Flight (IIIF) - 8th Cruiser Sqdn. (West Indies and America).

M2/Parnell Peto

Avro Bison II

Most of the flights were parenting three detachments (Nos. 403, 406, 407 and 445), No. 443 Flt. had five detachments in two squadrons whilst No. 444 Flt. had four detachments also in two squadrons. The largest flight was No. 447 Flt. which was responsible for seven flights in the Mediterranean. Most of the Fairey IIIFs and Flycatchers were replaced with the Hawker Osprey Fighter Reconnaissance aircraft (developed from the RAF's Hart day bomber) from 1932 and Supermarine Walrus from 1933.

CONTINUATION OF CARRIER TRIALS

During July 1926, night operating trials were held on HMS *Furious* by No. 462 Flight operating Blackburn Darts. On the 1st, Flt. Lt. Boyce successfully carried out the first night landing on board the ship. This landing, followed by more trials over the next few years, resulted in the procedures for operating aircraft at night being laid down and perfected.

Another set of trials in 1930, which would one day be used in anger, was the perfecting of making a smoke screen using aircraft. A Fairey IIIF was used for the exercise. The system was to be used over the Normandy beaches by Swordfish aircraft fourteen years later.

After spending many years as a transportation and depot ship, the old HMS *Ark Royal* was given a new lease of life in 1930 as the catapult trials ship. She continued in the role of catapult trials and training ship until the outbreak of W.W.II, although by the time war was declared she had been renamed HMS *Pegasus* (in 1935, the original seaplane carrier by that name was broken up in 1931).

Throughout the early 1930s, with aircraft becoming faster, heavier and more widely operated within the RN, developments in safety requirements on board the ships had become paramount, not only to safeguard the deck personnel but also the ships and aircraft.

Safety trials were carried out in 1930 aboard Eagle and Furious to check the suitability of the deck safety nets and palisades, using redundant DH9A aircraft which were deliberately crashed into the palisades. Arrestor wires, based on the American designed system of transverse wires controlled by electric winches, were to be refitted to aircraft carriers from 1931 onwards as programmed refits were carried out. Barriers would also be fitted to prevent the aircraft striking other aircraft already on the deck.

The following year saw first landing trials of an aircraft fitted with a spring loaded deck hook attached to a tubular 'A' frame carried out aboard HMS *Courageous*, now fitted with its transverse wires across the deck. The system was installed on a Fairey IIIF and was designed to lower below the fuselage of the aircraft upon selection by the pilot but remain flush to the fuselage during flight.

This design of deck hook was used on many aircraft types and is still the basis of hooks on today's aircraft. Hawker's Nimrod fighter and Osprey fighter-reconnaissance aircraft were the first two aircraft to enter service to be fitted with an arrestor hook as standard. The hook/wires combination was seen as a success, however the electrical winches were replaced with hydraulic ones in 1933 - which is also the basis of today's modern arrestor gear systems.

THE LOSS OF HMSUBMARINE M2

Disaster struck the Submarine service and Fleet Air Arm on 26th January 1932 with the loss of the M2 with its crew of 60. For nearly four years the submarine had successfully carried out trials and operations with the Parnell Peto, to an extent that it had been able to launch the aircraft in twelve minutes from the submarine being at periscope level (recovery taking ten minutes).

More trials were being carried out off Portland Bill during the morning when the submarine was lost at a depth of 17 fathoms (102ft). It is not clear what went wrong, but divers found that both the hangar door and access hatch were open allowing water into the hull of the boat. This put an end to any further development of submersible aircraft carriers in the Royal Navy (the Japanese and German Navy employed aviation elements on submarines during W.W.II).

SQUADRON REDESIGNATION

Now that the RAF Flights for naval operations were increasing both in number and aircraft compliment, they were to be redesignated as proper squadrons with numbers in the 700 and 800 series which are still in use to this day. If the flight had more than nine aircraft it became its own squadron, if it had less it would merge with another to become a squadron, whilst catapult flights were to retain their Flight status for the time being.

Blackburn Ripon II

The system was organised such that catapult flights were eventually numbered 700-749, training and support squadrons 750-799, fighters were numbered 800-809 and 870-899, torpedo bombers 810-819, and spotter reconnaissance 820-859. The initial redesignation was of the front line units which became effective from 1st April 1933 with the commissioning of the squadrons on the 3rd as follows:-

No. 800 Sqdn. - from 402 and 404 Flights (Nimrods and Ospreys)

No. 801 Sqdn. - from 401 Flight (Flycatcher and Nimrods)

No. 802 Sqdn. - from 408 and 409 Flights (Nimrods and Ospreys)

No. 803 Sqdn. - from 409 Flight (Ospreys)

No. 810 Sqdn. - from 463 and 464 Flights (Darts)

No. 811 Sqdn. - from 465 and 466 Flights (Ripons)

No. 812 Sqdn. - from 461 and 462 Flights (Ripons)

No. 820 Sqdn. - from 445 and 450 Flights (IIIFs)

No. 821 Sqdn. - from 445 and 446 Flights (IIIFs)

No. 822 Sqdn. - from 442 and 449 Flights (IIIFs)

No. 823 Sqdn. - from 441 and 448 Flights (IIIFs)

No. 824 Sqdn. - from 440 and 460 Flights (IIIFs)

Each carrier was allocated its own squadrons; HMS *Courageous* - Nos. 800, 810, 820 and 821 Sqdns; HMS *Eagle* - Nos. 803 and 824 Sqdns; HMS *Furious* - Nos. 801, 811 and 822 Sqdns; HMS *Glorious* - Nos. 802, 812 and 823 Sqdns, whilst HMS *Hermes* was undergoing a refit and would take on the squadrons from the next ship to refit - Eagle - a system which still operates today.

THE FIRST TSR II

A landmark in British Naval Aircraft, an aircraft that was to surpass the history of all previous and future naval aircraft types, (although probably matched by the Supermarine Walrus and much later the McDonnell Douglas FG MkI Phantom II), was the Fairey TSR I - (Torpedo Strike Reconnaissance) which flew for the first time on 21st March 1933. After this aircraft

Fairey Swordfish

Hawker Nimrod

Fairey Seal

Blackburn Baffin

crashed in September, the second aircraft, the TSR II, was to take to the air on 17th April 1934 with a redesigned tail assembly. The aircraft was subsequently named the Swordfish (colloquially the Stringbag).

The aircraft entered service on 19th February 1936 as the MkI. The MkII, with stronger lower mainplane to allow the aircraft to carry rocket launchers, followed in 1943, as did the radar equipped ASV MkIII. A total of 2,393 aircraft were built (including the two prototype TSRI and TSRII) of which 1,699 were actually 'Blackfish', that is they were built under licence by Blackburns.

The aircraft served on every aircraft carrier operated by the RN until it was finally retired on 28th June 1945 upon disembarking from HMS *Empire Mackay* - the last operational biplane flight of an aircraft in British military service. As will be seen later, it operated in every theatre of the war with great distinction and with some truly remarkable victories.

STILL MORE 'OLD' NEW AIRCRAFT TYPES

From 1933, older aircraft were being replaced with more 'modern' equipment. Fairey IIIFs were replaced with the Fairey Seal spotter-reconnaissance aircraft which was the naval variant of the RAF's Fairey Gordon. Improvements included the hydraulic braking system trialed on the Flycatcher a decade earlier. It was the first Fairey aircraft fitted with the triangular steel arrestor hook beneath the rear fuselage which was to become a prominent feature of many subsequent Fairey types. It was accepted into service by Nos. 820 and 821 Sqdns., both squadrons being allocated to HMS *Courageous*.

During 1934, the Blackburn Dart and Ripon aircraft were being withdrawn as Blackburn Baffins were introduced. Once again the newer aircraft was a development of the aircraft it was replacing, in this case the Ripon (the prototype Baffin was originally named the Ripon V). It entered service with No. 812 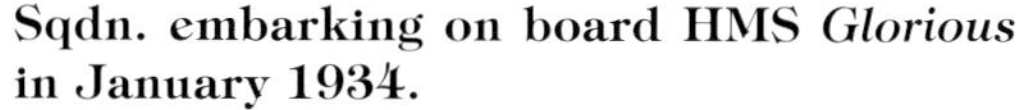Sqdn. embarking on board HMS *Glorious* in January 1934.

Trials were carried out aboard HMS *Nelson* during 1935 of the new Supermarine Seagull V operated by No. 444 Flight. This aircraft was a metal hulled seaplane with a pusher engine, which had been specifically designed for catapult launching and was to become known as the Walrus. The Swordfish may be the most known naval aircraft but not far behind in reverence is this amphibian (affectionately known as the Shagbat) entering into FAA service as the Fleet's standard amphibian-boat reconnaissance aircraft.

It was the first British military aircraft with a retractable undercarriage and the first FAA aircraft with the cockpit fully enclosed. It also achieved the status of being the first aircraft in the world to be catapulted from a ship with a full military load and was to operate from capital ships for over ten years, seeing service in every ocean and theatre during these years.

De Havilland modified some Tiger Moths into special radio-controlled aircraft known as the Queen Bee. These aircraft entered service during 1935 for use as target aircraft during Fleet gunnery exercises being catapulted from capital ships, flying at a height of 5000ft at 48 knots. HMS *Argus* was modified in 1937 for the role of anti-aircraft target service ship, acting as tender for the aircraft.

No. 820 Sqdn. began receiving the Blackburn Shark during August 1935, less than two years after accepting the Seal into service. The aircraft was the last Blackburn designed biplane torpedo bomber aircraft. Two Cierva C30 autogyros were operated aboard HMS *Furious* during 1935 resulting in five two-seater C40s being ordered, two of which had been received before W.W.II began.

MEDITERRANEAN ALERT

Abyssinian troops clashed with Italian troops over a disputed zone on their border with Somali-land in December 1934. Tension was building between the two nations which indicated that the Italians were on the verge of invading the country. The British Government sent HMS *Glorious* and HMS *Courageous* to Alexandria during August 1935 in preparation for an escalation of the confrontation. Glorious was stationed in Malta whilst Courageous, who was in home waters, set a record by reaching Alexandria in $5^{1/2}$ days arriving on station on 5th September.

De Havilland Queen Bee

Italy invaded Abyssinia (now known as Ethiopia) on 3rd October deposing Emperor Haili Selassie (Ras Tafari) who went into exile in Britain. Although total control was not gained until May, it was apparent that the Italians would keep the conflict within the borders of the country, thus Courageous returned home during February 1936.

With this invasion, Mussolini signed a pact with Hitler and thus the Axis power was instigated which caused discontent throughout the rest of Europe. The British Government was alerted to the inference of this power and began a study of the British Forces resulting in a re-arming programme.

NAVAL ESTIMATES OF 1936

The disposition of the current aircraft strength of 144 aircraft shared amongst the Fleet carriers was:- HMS *Courageous* and HMS *Glorious* - 48 aircraft (Baffin, Nimrod, Osprey, Seal and Swordfish); HMS *Furious* - 33 aircraft (Baffin, IIIF, Osprey and Nimrods); HMS *Hermes* with nine Seals aboard and HMS *Eagle* with six Ospreys. There were 34 aircraft embarked on board 29 Capital ships.

The FAA was to be strengthened by an extra 1½ squadrons and the pride of the Fleet, the new HMS *Ark Royal*, eventually to be the thorn in Hitler's side, was laid down (16th Sept) - the previous Ark Royal now bearing the name Pegasus. Four Illustrious class carriers were ordered - HMS *Illustrious* and HMS *Victorious* in 1936, with HMS *Formidable* and HMS *Indomitable* following on in 1937, all four being laid down in 1937. It was intended that these five ships would be the strength of the Fleet for the next two decades, however only one did not make it - Ark Royal.

SQUADRON STATUS FOR THE CATAPULT FLIGHTS

After the front line squadrons were formed in April 1933, it was now the turn of the catapult ships' flights to take up squadron status. This event occurred on 15th July 1936, after the assessment of the strength of the FAA, when the following flights were redesignated (albeit that they did not all actually achieve full squadron status immediately):-

No. 701 Sqdn. - from No. 447 Flt. - Ospreys - 1st Cruiser Squadron (three detachments for Med. Fleet)

No. 702 Sqdn. - from No. 444 Flt. - Walrus/Seals - 2nd Cruiser Squadron (three detachments for Home Fleet)

HMS Ark Royal

No. 705 Sqdn. - from No. 444 Flt. - Swordfish - Battle/Cruiser HMS *Repulse* (Med. Fleet)

No. 711 Sqdn. - from No. 447 Flt. - Walrus/Osprey - 1st Cruiser Squadron (four detachments for Med. Fleet)

No. 712 Sqdn. - from No. 407 Flt. - Ospreys - 2nd Cruiser Squadron (three detachments for Home Fleet)

No. 713 Sqdn. - from No. 445 Flt. - Ospreys - 3rd Cruiser Squadron (three detachments for Med. Fleet)

No. 714 Sqdn. - from No. 406 Flt. - Ospreys - 4th Cruiser Squadron (three detachments for East Indies Fleet)

No. 715 Sqdn. - from No. 403 Flt. - Ospreys - 5th Cruiser Squadron (three detachments for China Station)

No. 716 Sqdn. - from No. 443 Flt. - Osprey - 6th Cruiser Squadron (HMS *Amphion* on South Africa Station)

No. 718 Sqdn. - from No. 443 Flt. - IIIF and Ospreys - 8th Cruiser Squadron (four detachments to West Indies and America station)

No. 720 Sqdn. - new unit - Walrus - for New Zealand Division, HMS *Achilles*.

RAF Mount Batten in Plymouth was now the parenting base for the Home Fleet ships' flights, although the Mediterranean Fleet's aircraft were shore based at Kalafrana and Seletar in Malta. Kai Tak in Hong Kong was the base for the China Station and Bermuda for the West Indies station.

NEW ARRIVALS FROM FAIREY'S

The first Swordfish aircraft were received by the Torpedo Development Squadron at RAF Gosport on 19th February 1936 for trials and acceptance, which resulted in delivery of the type to front line squadrons

Hawker Osprey

Supermarine Walrus from HMS Southampton

and two catapult flights (No. 701 and 705 Sqdns.). Until the outbreak of W.W.II, all Swordfish pilots would receive their conversion courses at Gosport.

July saw their acceptance into front line service (FLS) by No. 825 Sqdn. who received twelve MkI aircraft to become the first Torpedo Spotter Reconnaissance (TSR) Squadron, and went to sea aboard HMS *Glorious*. This was the first of 29 front line squadrons or ships' flights and 26 training squadrons to use the aircraft in its nine years of operational duties. The RAF had two squadrons using the type; No. 202 Squadron (Oct 1940 - Jan 1942) and No. 119 Squadron (Oct 1944 - May 1945).

Fairey had been awarded the contract for building a spotter-reconnaissance seaplane to operate from the Capital ships' catapults. The aircraft had an enclosed cockpit for the observer, and Catapult flights began receiving the Fairey Seafox in April, replacing the last Fairey IIIFs of No. 714 Sqdn. and the Fairey Seals. The aircraft was to serve in this role until 1943. The Home Fleet flights were once again on the move and were relocated from Mount Batten back to Lee-on-the-Solent, whence they came, at the end of the year.

'BATS'

A new innovation in aircraft landing procedures aboard the carriers was the introduction during 1936 of the deck landing control officer, more affectionately known as 'Bats'. The approach speed of the aircraft was increasing so it was deemed that the pilots required a helping hand when landing, thus it was that 'Bats' appeared.

He had a precarious job positioned on the port side of the aft end of the flight deck using a bat in each hand with which he would indicate the altitude of the aircraft as it approached the ship. At the last moment

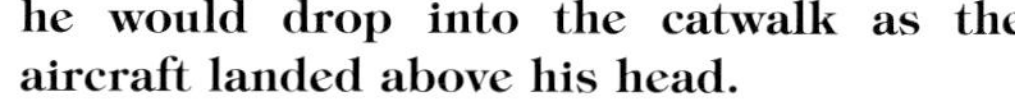
he would drop into the catwalk as the aircraft landed above his head.

THE ADMIRALTY REGAINS CONTROL

With the build-up of the British Forces, the Admiralty again harangued ministers for control of the Fleet Air Arm with enough force that a Government arbitration body was established under Sir Thomas Inskip in 1937. His report to the Cabinet on 21st July 1937, entitled 'The Navy and its Relation to the Fleet Air Arm and shore based aircraft' recommended that the RN regain full control of its aviation elements, training, equipping and organisation as the Air Branch of the Navy. The only concession for the RAF was retaining control of Coastal Command and the initial training of FAA pilots.

The handover began with the relinquishing of the air stations at Donibristle near Dunfermline, Evanton in Ross and Cromarty, Eastleigh, Gosport, Lee-on-the-Solent (which was to become the FAA Headquarters for nearly 40 years) and Worthy Down in Hampshire and Ford in West Sussex. These bases were the nucleus of the infantile Air Branch (still referred to unofficially until 1953). The construction of two new airfields at Arbroath and Yeovilton was authorised in 1938.

With the threat from the German Chancellor Adolph Hitler and his party increasing daily, the British services were busy training for the eventuality of conflict. The FAA was no exception, and new equipment was being put through its paces, the changes being brought about as a result of the Inskip report advising additional requirements were necessary to ensure the Fleet and its air force would be ready.

The ships and squadrons had little excitement during this period, only hard work. HMS *Eagle* was deployed to the South China Seas during 1937 to oppose the piracy which once again was rife, with many British (and Commonwealth) merchant men being targeted by the pirates. Once the safety of the shipping in the area was again established, the ship returned to perfecting its operations.

FLAGSHIP OF THE ROYAL NAVY

One of the most famous ships ever to serve in the RN, HMS *Ark Royal,* was commissioned on 16th November 1938 as the largest ship in the Fleet with a length of 780ft displacing 27,000 tons capable of 31 knots. It could carry up to 60 aircraft, had three lifts serving the two fully enclosed hangars (this was the first British carrier to have three lifts), there were two hydraulic catapult tracks forward of the island,

Fairey Seafox

Fairey Seal

athwart ship arrestor wires and the American designed mechanical crash barrier. Although the ship was to have a short life, it was eventful and honourable and will always be remembered as 'THE' British aircraft carrier of W.W.II.

Two days later the Royal Navy Volunteer Reserves (RNVR) was formed and many outstanding airmen (and other naval types) were to serve in the Navy as reservists during the twenty years of the RNVR (known affectionately as the Wavy Navy). Captain Bell Davies VC became the first Flag Officer Naval Air Stations with its HQ at Lee-on-the-Solent.

At the same time as the latest ship was being commissioned, the FAA's latest aircraft was delivered to Worthy Down for operation by two squadrons both bound for Ark Royal. The Blackburn Skua was received firstly by No. 800 Sqdn. during October 1938 followed by No. 803 Sqdn. during December. The aircraft was the first British aircraft designed for the role of dive bomber and the first British ship-borne monoplane.

The aircraft with variable pitch propeller, retractable undercarriage and multi-purpose flaps (necessary for the dive bombing role) was an excellent dive bomber, but the Air Ministry declared that its role was to be that of fighter/dive bomber. However it proved to be totally ineffective as a fighter and this role was eventually dismissed.

Another 'new' ship, HMS *Albatross*, was to join the RN prior to the arrival of Ark Royal. This ship was originally built for service as a seaplane carrier for the Royal Australian Navy (RAN) but, having paid off from the RAN, it was purchased by the RN as an additional carrier.

THE ROYAL NAVY AIR BRANCH

The Admiralty regained full control of the Royal Navy Air Branch on 24th May 1939. On this date the Air Branch shore establishments were renamed as a true member of the Navy with the title HMS followed by its given name (that of a species of bird except for Lee-on-the-Solent):-

ARBROATH* - HMS CONDOR

EVANTON - HMS FIELDFARE

CRAIL* - HMS JACKDAW

FORD - HMS PEREGRINE

DONIBRISTLE - HMS MERLIN

WORTHY DOWN - HMS KESTREL

EASTLEIGH - HMS RAVEN

YEOVILTON* - HMS HERON

LEE-ON-SOLENT - HMS DAEDALUS II (LATER ARIEL THEN DAEDALUS AGAIN)

* Air stations under construction

Also with effect from this date, all of the naval aviation training schools were redesignated as squadrons in the '700' series. The RN observer school was formed into three squadrons, Nos. 750, 751 and 752 Sqdns. under the umbrella of No. 1 Observer School, all based at Ford in West Sussex equipped with Sharks and Ospreys, Walrus

Blackburn Skua

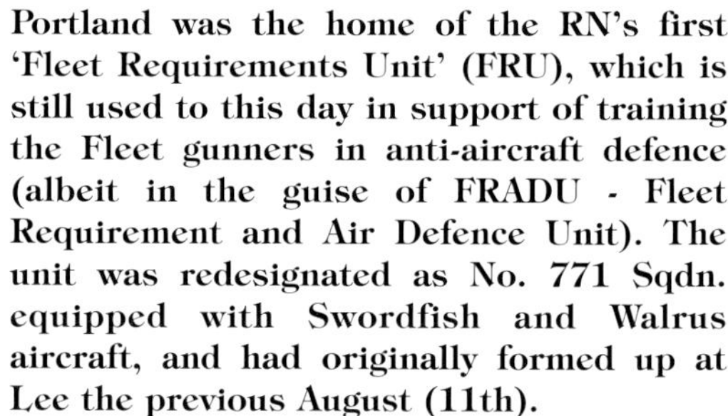

Fairey Swordfish

and Proctors and Albacores respectively.

The School of Naval Co-operation became No. 2 Observers School at Lee-on-the-Solent with Nos. 753 and 754 Sqdns. operating Seals, Sharks, Seafox, Walrus and Vega Gulls (the school had been resident at the airfield since its inception in 1920). The Seaplane School also formed up at Lee, No. 765 Sqdn. with Swordfish, Walrus and Seafox aircraft.

Worthy Down became the home of the No. 1 Air Gunners School equipped with Ospreys and Sharks operated by Nos. 755 and 757 Sqdns. A second Air Gunners School was formed at Eastleigh when No. 758 Sqdn. was commissioned with the same aircraft types on 1st July.

Gloster Sea Gladiator

Portland was the home of the RN's first 'Fleet Requirements Unit' (FRU), which is still used to this day in support of training the Fleet gunners in anti-aircraft defence (albeit in the guise of FRADU - Fleet Requirement and Air Defence Unit). The unit was redesignated as No. 771 Sqdn. equipped with Swordfish and Walrus aircraft, and had originally formed up at Lee the previous August (11th).

HMS *Merlin* at Donibristle became the base for deck landing training with the formation of two squadrons, both originally front line squadrons. No. 801 Sqdn. (Skua, Roc and Sea Gladiators) became No. 769 Sqdn. - Fighter Deck Landing Training Squadron, and No. 811 Sqdn. (Swordfish, Sharks and DH60 Moths) became No. 767 Sqdn. - Deck Landing Training squadron. Both of these squadrons had been 'employed' in this task since joining HMS *Courageous*, the Fleet's training carrier earlier in the year. The base communications flight was made up of the entire crew of Jersey Airways Company who 'joined' the FAA when the Germans took control of the island.

World War II 1939-42 Containment

HMS Eagle

HITLER'S EXPANDED GERMANY

Adolph Hitler, as Chancellor of Germany, had planned the taking of neighbouring countries by force to expand the country's territory. Austria, Czechoslovakia, Poland and Russia were to be the targets and he announced his plans to a select band of military leaders and ministers on 5th November 1937. Five months later he annexed Austria, taking control of the country in two days (12th/13th March). Unease in Czechoslovakia was increased due to three million Germans living in the country's Sudetenland on the Austrian border, and Hitler succeeded in gaining control of the country by 16th March 1939.

His attentions then turned to Poland and he began by demanding annexation of Danzig. This prompted Britain and France to agree, on 31st March, that they would aid the Polish in the event of aggression from the Germans. This deterred Hitler for a few months but the inevitable invasion of Poland began on 1st September. Britain demanded an immediate withdrawal but to no avail and announced war with Germany on 3rd September 1939.

THE ASSETS OF THE FAA

At the outbreak of W.W.II the FAA, although now an autonomous element of the RN, had not fully thrown off its chains of the RAF. Many of the incumbent aircrew and engineers were ex-light blue personnel. At the few FAA air stations and aboard the eight carriers, RAF ground crews could be found operating alongside their FAA counterparts.

There were seven full-time bases in use with eight more and one repair yard to become operational within the first twelve months. The sixteen carrier (front line) and eleven training (second line) squadrons were operating mostly outdated aircraft against a large mass of superior types in the Luftwaffe. This was overcome by the skill, enthusiasm and dedication of the aircrews who were to fight against bitter conditions, matched by the same qualities of the maintainers, ground support staff,

Supermarine Walrus

instructors and administration personnel on the ground.

The eight aircraft carriers were deployed to various stations and Fleets around the world:-

HMS *Albatross* (seaplane carrier) despatched to Sierra Leone for operations out of Freetown, protecting allied shipping. No. 710 Sqdn. formed with Walrus aircraft specifically for operations from the ship.

HMS *Argus* in reserve (soon to be reactivated as a training carrier).

HMS *Ark Royal* and HMS *Courageous* with the Home Fleet.

HMS *Eagle* with the Far East Fleet.

HMS *Furious* in the Forth as the training carrier (to be relieved by HMS *Argus*).

HMS *Glorious* with the Mediterranean Fleet.

HMS *Hermes* working up (despatched to operate in the Atlantic).

Besides the carriers, there were eleven squadrons operating flights of either Fairey Swordfish, Fairey Seafox or Supermarine Walrus aircraft from battleships and cruisers. These flights were the eyes of the Fleet, spotting for the big guns directing shell fire as required, used as reconnaissance aircraft and for search and rescue of downed aircrew. They were also to go into battle on some occasions and although they were not designed for the role, they did have some successes against the enemy.

Blackburn Skua / Gloster Sea Gladiator

FIRST OPERATIONS AND LOSSES

The First Sea Lord, Mr Winston Churchill, had strong misgivings about the German Navy submarines and the damage they could inflict on the shipping crossing the Atlantic. He proposed an idea of using the Fleet in attack units of an aircraft carrier supported by four destroyers to combat this threat.

The Home Fleet was divided into two units and sent to carry out anti-submarine duties. Their task was to use the carrier's aircraft to search for and initially attack U-boats, then the escorts loitering in readiness would continue the attacks and hopefully destroy them. HMS *Ark Royal* and her escorts were to patrol the South West Approaches, whilst HMS *Courageous'* group would patrol the North West Approaches (to be joined by HMS *Hermes*). Unfortunately these operations were soon to be seen as an expensive tactic when Courageous was torpedoed by U29 on 17th September but it could have been worse! U39 had unsuccessfully attacked Ark Royal three days earlier on the 14th.

Some senior officers saw these operations as an ill-conceived and costly idea which was not the case. If the Fleet had had more carriers at its disposal, it would have saved thousands of lives as well as many thousand tons of shipping. The idea was 'shelved' after this loss as a means of preserving the few carriers in the Fleet, however it was reactivated on the arrival of the escort carriers.

FIRST SINKING OF HMS ARK ROYAL

On 26th September the Germans reported the loss of HMS *Ark Royal* which they said had been successfully bombed by the Heinkel HeIII flown by Lance Corporal Adolphe Franke, who was promoted to Lieutenant and awarded the first Iron Cross of the war. Indeed he had bombed and strafed the ship in the first aerial attack on an aircraft carrier but had failed to inflict any damage. (The ship was evidently 'sunk' many times by the Germans before it was eventually to become a casualty in 1941).

Ark Royal was proceeding on 26th September to the aid of the damaged British submarine, HMS *Spearfish*, when she was spotted by three Dornier DO18 flying boats. The ship launched nine Blackburn Skuas of No. 803 Sqdn. which damaged two aircraft and the third was shot down by Lt. B McEwen and PO B Seymour, the first successful attack on a German aircraft in the war.

With the loss of Courageous and the two attacks on Ark Royal, the carrier force was redeployed. Ark Royal was deployed to Freetown (Force K) joining Albatross, Furious became the only carrier in the Home Fleet, Hermes went to Dakar (Senegal) and Glorious moved to Aden, whilst Argus was being prepared for service as the training carrier based at Toulon.

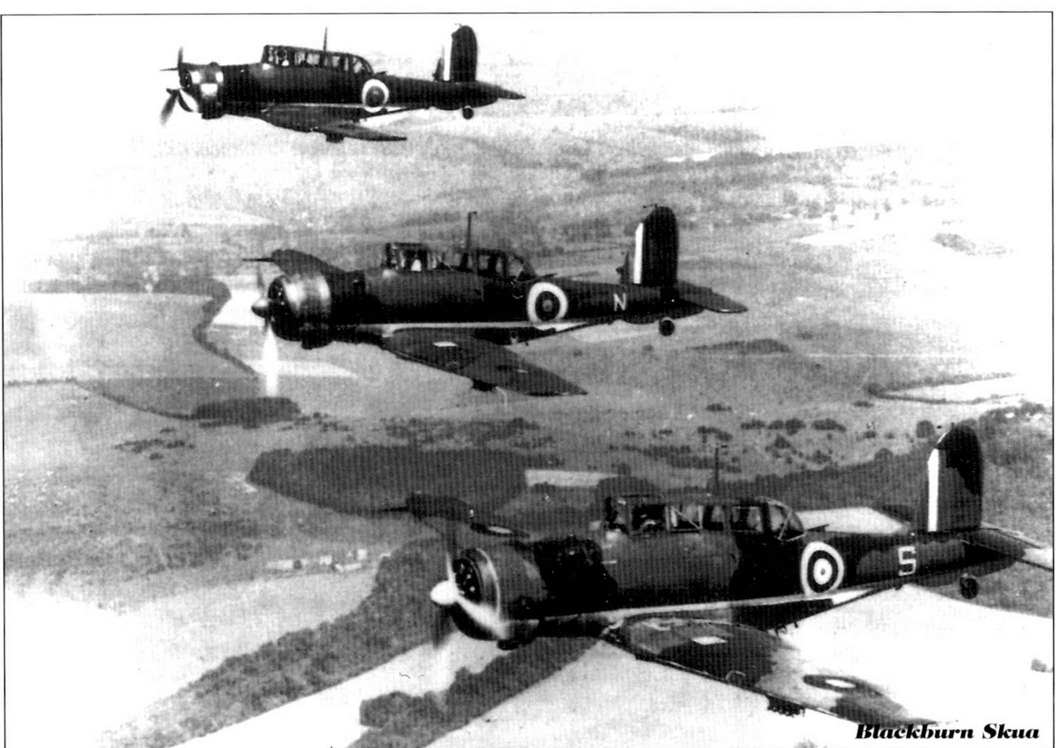

Blackburn Skua

BATTLE OF THE RIVER PLATE

The role of Force K was to hunt down and destroy the pocket battleship, the Graf Spee, which had been attacking shipping off the African coast. The German ship fled on hearing that the Force was on its way, only to be found by HMSs *Achilles, Ajax* and *Exeter* on 13th December off the mouth of the River Plate on the South American coast.

After a short engagement which resulted in severe damage to Exeter (and the Walrus on board) and Achilles, and damage to one of Ajax's Seafox aircraft, the ship escaped and headed for the neutral port of Montevideo in Uruguay. The remaining Seafox flown by Lts. Lewin and Kearney continually reported on the cruiser's actions in what became known as the Battle of the River Plate.

Force K was ordered to head across the South Atlantic to intercept the German ship and arrived at Rio de Janeiro on 17th to take on fuel. Whilst refuelling, the action at Montevideo reached a conclusion when the Captain of the Graf Spee, Captain Hans Langsdorff, believing that Force K had arrived to support the cruiser squadron, decided to scupper the ship.

Lewin and Kearney were airborne above the harbour when they witnessed the event reporting back to Ajax "Spee has blown herself up". For their flying throughout the episode, Lewin was awarded the DSC whilst Kearney was mentioned in dispatches, these two awards being the first of many received during W.W.II.

THE 'SHIP'S FLIGHT' SQUADRON

On 21st January 1940 a new squadron was born, No. 700 Sqdn. commissioned at Hatston under the command of Lt. Cdr. A Fleming, who was previously in command of No. 711 Sqdn. ships'

HMS Courageous

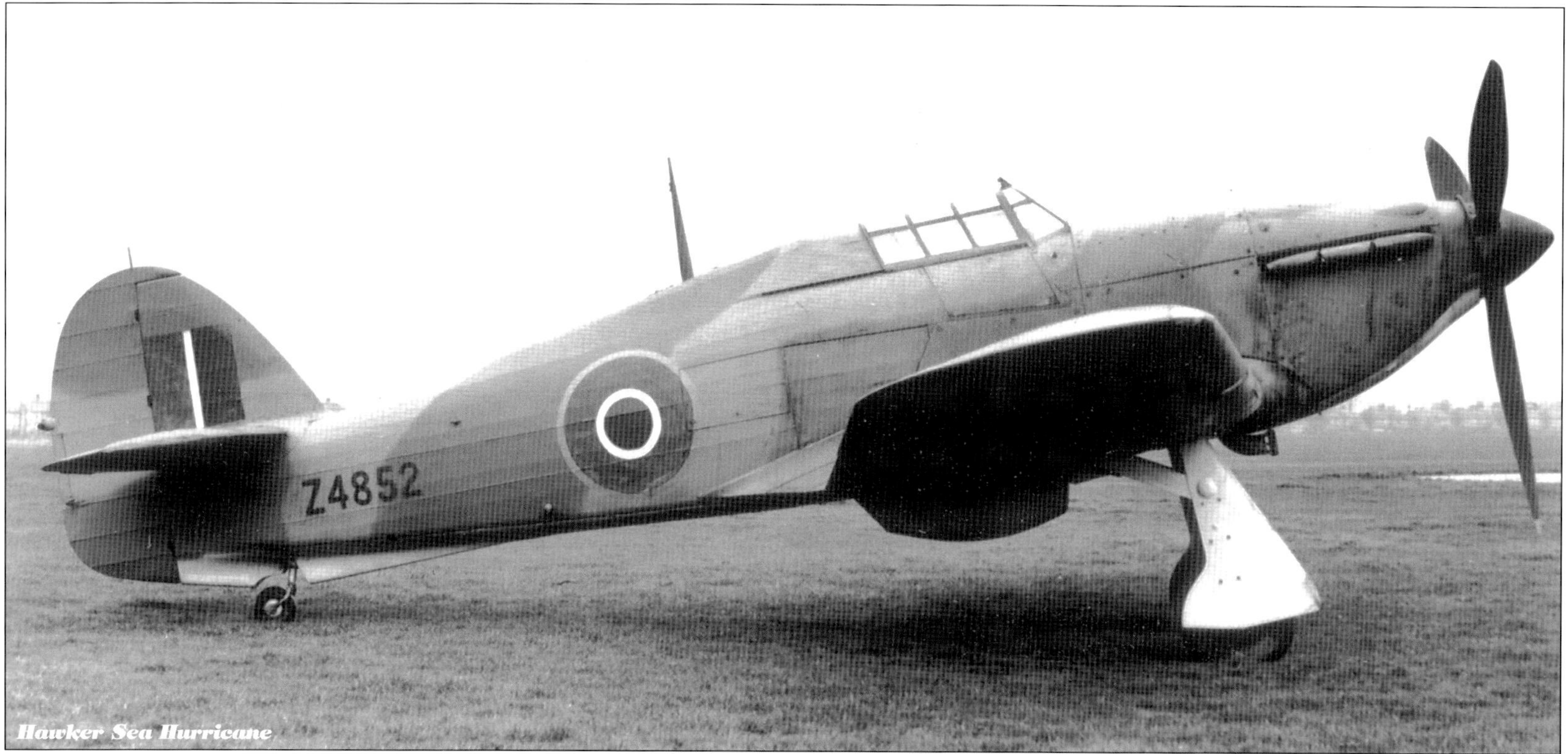

Hawker Sea Hurricane

flights. The squadron was formed with the amalgamation of the eleven squadrons currently operating aircraft on the battleships and cruisers, as the parent and training squadron for these flights.

On forming, the squadron had 65 aircraft borne of the three different types. Before disbanding in March 1944 (the need for these flights was removed with the arrival of escort carriers and armed merchant ships), seven support bases for the different Fleets and a special flight for operating on board HMS *Fencer* for the occupation of the Azores were to be established. Its compliment was to be surpassed by No. 836 Sqdn. later in the conflict.

NORWEGIAN CAMPAIGN

The next major actions by the Fleet Air Arm began with the German invasion of Norway beginning on 8th April 1940. The Home Fleet with HMS *Furious* sailed from its base at Scapa Flow to assist the Danes and Norwegians. However the first FAA actions were carried out by Nos. 800 and 803 Sqdn. using Skuas based at HMS Sparrowhawk (Hatson in the Orkneys) which were sent to attack the German cruiser Konigsberg in Bergen harbour.

HMS Glorious

Both squadrons launched with their eight aircraft on the morning of the 10th armed with 500lb bombs. On arrival at Bergen, the ship was sighted alongside the mole and Lt. W Lucy (No. 803 Sqdn. C.O.) led the attack which resulted in three direct hits, one of them between the ship's funnels, and many near misses including one which blew a large hole in the side of the ship. The ship's magazine exploded before she rolled over and sank in the deep fjord becoming the first capital ship to be sunk by air attack. All but one aircraft returned home safely.

The following day, Swordfish (Nos. 816 and 818 Sqdns.) from HMS *Furious* launched another attack on the harbour only to find the other German ships had sailed and only a couple of small torpedo boats remained. These were duly attacked by torpedoes in the first air launched torpedo attack of the war but unfortunately, due to the shallowness of the harbour where these boats were moored, the torpedoes ran aground causing no damage.

Further North at Narvik, the 2nd Destroyer Squadron was having its own battle against the Germans. On 13th April, HMS *Warspite* launched its Swordfish (No. 700 Sqdn.) to proceed the Fleet up the Ofot and Herjangs Fjords, piloted by PO F (Ben) Rice. Lt. Cdr. Brown, the aircraft's observer, reported back the positions of the seven enemy destroyers and directed the British guns firing at the Germans. He also informed the British destroyers of torpedoes launched at them so evasive action could be carried out. U64 was spotted in the Herjangs Fjord and

Rice carried out a successful bombing attack which resulted in the U-Boat's demise.

The 'After Battle' report from Vice Admiral Whitworth included the following passage - '*The enemy reports made by the Warspite's aircraft were invaluable. I doubt if ever a ship-borne aircraft has been used to such good purpose as it was during this operation. In addition the aircraft attacked and sank an enemy submarine.*'

During the campaign the FAA aircraft bombed enemy airfields, troops, docks, coastal shipping and railways and gave the Army air cover during their landings and land operations. This was initially provided by Swordfish aircraft (Nos. 816 and 818 Sqdns.) on board Furious. These were later supplemented by Sea Gladiators (Nos. 802 and 804 Sqdns.) which arrived with HMS *Glorious* hastily redeployed from the Mediterranean, and the four squadrons of aircraft, Swordfish of Nos. 810 and 820 Sqdns. and Skuas of Nos. 801 and 803 Sqdns, which were embarked aboard HMS *Ark Royal.*

The campaign however proved to be fruitless due to the lack of men, equipment, aircraft and operating bases. The allied forces were eventually overrun and the Home Fleet had the task of evacuating the Forces. At Narvik, Glorious gave air cover to the retreating forces and was also tasked with the recovery of the RAF aircraft that the FAA had ferried to Norway.

Glorious had previously delivered the RAF Gladiators of No. 263 Sqdn. to the theatre and, on 24th April, the squadron flew off the ship and landed on the frozen Lesjanskog Lake near Andalsnes. During this withdrawal, No. 263 Sqdn. re-embarked her Gladiators safely and although advised to ditch the eight Hurricanes of No. 46 Sqdn. RAF, the aircrew volunteered to try to land these aircraft on board the ship. Taking off from Bardufoss with deflated tyres all the aircraft successfully recovered on board, a tremendous feat as the pilots had not seen a carrier's deck before, yet alone land on one.

HMS GLORIOUS vs THE SCHARNHORST

After successfully evacuating the RAF from Norway, Glorious was dispatched to deliver its valuable cargo of aircraft and aircrew back to the UK, escorted by the destroyers HMS *Acasta* and HMS *Ardent*. Unfortunately on 8th June, they ran across the German battleships, Scharnhorst and Gneisenau, which engaged the British ships sinking all three.

Fairey Swordfish

During this confrontation, Scharnhorst was struck by a torpedo, resulting in her being out of action whilst repairs were carried out in Trondheim Fjord. Five days later, she was attacked by the Skuas of Nos. 800 and and 803 Sqdns. whilst in the fjord but no hits were achieved.

September and October saw further attacks aimed at sinking Scharnhorst in the fjords off Tromso and Trondheim. Swordfish of Nos. 816 and 825 Sqdns. embarked on board Furious carried out sorties on shipping in the fjords, including the first night attack torpedo droppings of the war.

With the fall of the Low Countries, Denmark, Norway and France, there was little naval activity in the immediate waters around Great Britain and emphasis moved to the escorting of convoys across the Atlantic, where the German U-Boats were gaining the upper hand due to the distinct lack of aircraft protection available, and to actions in the Mediterranean.

After the loss of Courageous and Glorious, the RN and FAA were eagerly awaiting the arrival of the four armoured Illustrious class aircraft carriers. Three were commissioned in less than twelve months; HMS *Illustrious* (25th May 1940); HMS *Formidable* (24th Nov 1940) and HMS *Victorious* (15th May 1941). The final ship,

HMS Illustrious

Fairey Swordfish

HMS *Indomitable*, was commissioned on 10th October 1941.

THE UNHAPPY OPERATIONS

With the capitulation of France, the majority of their Fleet were either disarmed or taken over by the RN. There were however four capital ships still under the control of French Admirals (and their escort ships) in Wharan Oran (Algeria) and Dakar (French West Africa). The British Government approached the French C in C, Admiral Gensoul to either join forces or intern his Fleet in British ports or Martinique to prevent them falling into the enemy's hands.

Force H had formed on 28th June in Gibraltar, tasked with the protection of the areas left unguarded by the immobilisation of the French Fleet and to oppose the Italian Fleet's operations, the defence of the Gibraltar Straits and the escorting of convoys in the Western Mediterranean. The Force consisted of HMS *Ark Royal*, the battleships HMS *Hood*, HMS *Valiant* and HMS *Resolution*, and thirteen ships.

The Force's first operation was to either escort or attack the French naval ships post their immobilisation, arriving off Oran on 3rd July 1940 to await the answer from Admiral Gensoul which was received the following day, the answer being 'non'. That night the French battleship Strasbourg and six destroyers slipped out of the harbour to be pursued by Swordfish from Ark Royal,

Fairey Albacore

Hawker Sea Hurricane

whilst the ships of Force H bombarded the remainder of the French Fleet. The Strasbourg and her escorts successfully escaped but two destroyers and the battleship Bretagne were sunk. The battleship Dunkerque was beached, then was later put out of action (on the 6th) when Swordfish attacked her with torpedoes.

Whilst Force H was entertaining the French at Oran, HMS *Hermes* was carrying out a similar operation on the 8th against the Richelieu which was at Dakar. Swordfish from No. 814 Sqdn. had the unfortunate task of disabling the ship, with their attack on the Richelieu resulting in four torpedo strikes causing considerable damage putting her out of action.

ENTER THE ITALIANS

The first Allied strike at the Italians after joining with the Axis Powers was carried out by the training squadron No. 767 which was training at Hyeres. The squadron bombed Italian installations and the city of Genoa on 12th June 1940. Lt. Cdr. G Dickens led the 'non-operational' Swordfish aircraft which had been armed with French bombs attached to the aircraft by spun yarn and fused before take-off.

A detachment of three No. 824 Sqdn. Swordfish from HMS *Ark Royal* were operating from Maarten Bagush to oppose enemy ships along the Libyan coast. These three aircraft, flown by Capt. O Patch RM and Lts. J Wellham and N Cheeseman, later moved to Sidi Barrani for a mission at Bomba Bay between Tobruk and Benghazi on 23rd August. Using three torpedoes, the flight successfully destroyed four enemy ships; two submarines, a destroyer and a depot ship.

Upon receiving confirmation of this attack by RAF reconnaissance aircraft, the Mediterranean Commander, Admiral Cunningham, praised it as a 'phenomenal result'. The operations from Maarten Bagush and Sidi Barrani were to be the prelude to some superb operations in the Western Desert by FAA squadrons during the battle with Rommel's Africa Corps.

BATTLE OF BRITAIN

On 16th July 1940, Hitler launched 'Operation Sealion' (Directive No. 16), the invasion of Great Britain, the first part of this operation being the elimination of the RAF - the Battle of Britain. Records show that the battle in the skies over Britain began officially on 10th July although the first few days prior to the signing of Directive No. 16 were probing missions to check out the RAF. On 8th August, the RAF promulgated that the battle was about to begin, then the German Commander, Herman Goering, announced that the full air assault (Adlertag - the day of the eagle) was to commence on the 10th. The main battle lasted 114 days until 31st October.

Fleet Air Arm pilots were loaned by the Admiralty to fly in RAF squadrons during the battle, and one course of trainee pilots at the fighter school at HMS Raven (RNAS Eastleigh) volunteered for temporary

Fairey Fulmar

HMS Ravenger

service with the RAF. They were re-assigned further training in Operational Training Units flying Spitfires and Hurricanes.

The pilots eventually served in a total of thirteen RAF squadrons, including three pilots who flew in No. 242 Sqdn. under the command of Douglas Bader - Sub. Lt. Cork being his wing man. These pilots were not the only FAA pilots seeing action against the Luftwaffe. No. 804 Sqdn. under Lt. Cdr. Cockburn (Sea Gladiators and Buffaloes) and No. 808 Sqdn. under Lt. Cdr. Tillard (Fulmar MkI) assisted their RAF allies. During the battle a total of 58 FAA pilots fought with the loss of nine lives.

TARANTO - THE FAA's BATTLE OF TRAFALGAR

One of the FAA's most famous raids took place on 11th November 1940 when the Italian Fleet was attacked in Taranto Harbour. This attack had been seen as a possibility even before the Italians joined the war, conceived when Mussolini's Forces invaded Abbysinia, by Capt. A St. G Lyster whilst in command of HMS *Glorious*. As early as 1938, attacks were being practiced on Malta's Grand Harbour and upon Italy entering the conflict, the plan was reactived when Capt. Lyster proposed a moonlight attack on the harbour. Swordfish aircrew began intensive night flying exercises including the practice of dropping night lighting flares, and special long-range fuel tanks were sent to HMS *Illustrious* to be fitted to the Swordfish.

The original proposed date for this attack was to be 21st October, Trafalgar Day, but the operation was postponed due to a hangar fire aboard Illustrious. The ship eventually sailed from Alexandria on 6th November. HMS *Eagle* was also to take part but due to contamination of her fuel tanks, she could only send six aircraft and crews from Nos. 813 and 824 Sqdns., 4a/c and 2a/c respectively. These aircraft joined up with Illustrious' Swordfish units Nos. 815 and 819 Sqdns. The twenty-one aircraft were fitted with the long-range fuel tanks giving the aircraft a range of over 400 miles which meant that the aircraft could only carry a crew of pilot and observer.

The first wave of twelve aircraft launched at 2030 hours at a distance of about 180 miles from the harbour led by Lt. Cdr. K Williamson C.O. of No. 815 Sqdn. Two of the aircraft were fitted with flares and bombs, and these arrived at 2300 hours dropping their flares lighting up Taranto Harbour for the main body to attack the Italian Fleet. The aircraft then went on to bomb the fuel tanks. Williamson led his flight into attack and the crews successfully launched their torpedoes (6 a/c) and bombs (4a/c). Only one aircraft was lost, that of the leader who, along with his observer Lt. N Scarlett, were taken prisoner.

The second wave of eight aircraft led by Lt. Cdr. Hale (C.O. of No. 819 Sqdn.) were launched an hour after the first one, with another aircraft following an hour later. One aircraft returned to the ship with problems, but the remaining eight aircraft successfully attacked the ships, again only losing one aircraft. Of these eight aircraft, five successfully attacked the battleships with their torpedoes whilst the remaining three dropped bombs.

The outcome of this attack, the first ever aerial assault using flares to illuminate the target, resulted in three battleships (INS *Cavour, Duillio* and *Italia*), the cruiser INS *Trento*, two destroyers (INS *Libeccio* and *Pessango*) and two other vessels all being hit. Shore facilities including the fuel tanks and seaplane hangars were all destroyed. This effectively removed the threat from the Italian Fleet, altering the balance of power in the Mediterranean in favour of the RN.

The successful use of flares to illuminate the target for other aircraft was proven during the Taranto raid. It was further used for many operations in the Mediterranean and North African theatres, especially in support of the Army, for illuminating enemy coastal shipping and ports, enemy ground force positions and armoured divisions for attack by the RN ships and RAF bombers. It was later adopted as a standard tactic by the RAF Bomber Command.

COASTAL COMMAND

Throughout the war, the convoys were given protection from the aircraft of the RAF Coastal Command whose headquarters

Supermarine Seafires and Grumman Martlets aboard HMS Stalker

RAF Coastal Command Catalina

were at Northwood, whilst each naval air station involved in coastal protection had a group headquarters. At these 'outstations', Officers from both services worked together to ensure operations utilised their limited resources with maximum efficiency.

Bases were set up in Gibraltar and Iceland for aircraft to operate from for convoy escort. This gave the Command a large area to cover but there was still an area of the Atlantic not covered where the U-Boat packs were to be found. To cover this area, a base in the Atlantic was necessary and the Portuguese allowed a base to be established in the Azores. Thus coverage for all of the Atlantic under British patrol was provided.

The areas of operation for the Liberators, Hudsons, Catalinas and Sunderlands covered the convoys across the Atlantic from the Azores, Ireland and Iceland. The Russian convoys were covered with aircraft operating from the Orkneys and detachments in Northern Russia, whilst Mediterranean convoys were escorted from Gibraltar and Malta. The first submarine destroyed was on patrol in the latter theatre, when a Catalina of No. 210 Sqdn. RAF flown by Flt. Lt. E Baker sank the INS *Marcello* with two depth charges on 6th January 1941.

During April 1941 the Admiralty was given full control of the Command, although it remained an element of the RAF. With this came a change in tactics, not only giving the crews more duties but more opportunities to directly strike at the enemy. This resulted in the surrender of I-570 off Iceland on 27th August, by a Hudson of No. 269 Sqdn. RAF. The U-Boat had been spotted by the aircraft which then attacked it with four depth charges. After assistance by a Catalina of No. 209 Sqdn. RAF, the submarine was taken in tow by British trawlers.

Coastal Command aircraft attacked enemy convoys which sailed along the European coasts, initially with Hudsons but later with torpedo equipped Beaufighters. The Command's units were also given the task of photo-reconnaissance and escort duties, and it was common to see FAA squadrons operating alongside their units in joint operations and support when they were stretched.

THE CATAPULT ARMED MERCHANT (CAM) SHIP

With the loss of the two aircraft carriers, the Atlantic convoys were easy prey for the German U-Boats and Fockewulf FW 200 Condor long-range bombers. This shortage was addressed by an idea conceived by Captain M Slattery who devised the Catapult-Armed Merchantman (CAM) Ship.

Four naval vessels and a Merchantman were selected for fitting with a catapult on their forecastle; Ariguani, Maplin, Patia,

Fairey Swordfish and HMS Ark Royal

Fairey Fulmar

Springbank and SS *Micheal E*. The ships were to be equipped by specially modified Fulmars and Sea Hurricanes operated by No. 804 Sqdn. The squadron was trained in the art of catapult launching and moved to its home base of Sydenham near Belfast whilst the ships were to be based in nearby Belfast docks.

Only four of the ships reached operational status as Patia was sunk in the North Sea. SS *Micheal E* sailed with a convoy to the USA on 27th May 1941 equipped with two Sea Hurricanes to be flown by S/Lts. M Birrell and E Clark, Birrell having the distinction of being the first pilot to carry out a launch from a CAM ship. Unfortunately the ship was sunk after only four days into the journey. June saw the Springbank accompany a convoy from Halifax Nova Scotia, with one of her aircraft intercepting an FW200 which escaped in cloud. Springbank was later sunk at the end of September.

There was one successful destroying of a Condor during August (3rd) when Lt. R Everett was launched from the Maplin to intercept the enemy aircraft. He chased the aircraft before setting it on fire causing it to crash into the sea and for this action he was awarded the DSO. Everett was, however, better known as the Grand National winning jockey after riding Gregalash to victory in 1929.

Early in 1941 HMS *Pegasus* (formally Ark Royal), in use as the catapult training ship, was pressed into operational status during May. Equipped with Fulmars, she was used for escort duties but this task was short lived after one of her aircraft crashed killing both crew. The ship unloaded the remaining aircraft on 12th July and returned back to her role as a training carrier.

HMS Argus as a training carrier

The task of operating catapult flights was taken over by the RAF Merchant Ship Fighter Unit (MSFU) in 1942. During their short term of operations as the FAA Catapult Fighter Unit, No. 804 Sqdn. carried out ten launches, all of which resulted in the shadowing FW 200 being chased off and one destroyed.

Although the catapult flights from the RN's capital ships also carried out operations during convoy duties, the ships were operating aircraft which were primarily used for spotting, reconnaissance and SAR duties and were equipped with floats so they could be recovered back to the ship after a sortie. The fighter catapult aircraft (both No. 804 Sqdn. and the RAF's MSFU) were mainly standard fighters equipped for catapult launching but not fitted with floats. The brave pilots had to ditch the aircraft in the sea near to one of the convoy ships if land was beyond their range.

THE NEXT STEP - THE ESCORT CARRIER

Captain Slattery's idea of operating catapult fighters had limited success but it did show that the concept was feasible. He then developed the idea of converting merchant ships into small aircraft carriers by fitting them with flight decks and hangars. The captured German passenger ship Hannover was decided on as the first ship to be converted. Meanwhile this concept was seen by Winston Churchill as a superb answer to the problem of convoy escort and he approached President Roosevelt to assist in the building of suitable ships in the American shipyards.

Conversion work began on the Hannover in January 1941 when the ship was fitted out at Blyth shipyard in Northumberland with a flush deck but no hangarage, to be commissioned six months later as HMS *Audacity.* The ship proved to be the new beginning in the escorting of convoys, effectively reducing the submarine threat by eliminating the ability of the German FW 200 Condors to spot and report the position of the convoys for the U-Boats to attack.

Tasked with operating from the ship, No. 802 Sqdn. equipped with Martlet Is was embarked in September and the ship was to sail in company with Gibraltar bound convoys. During three months on these convoys, the squadron successfully destroyed five FW 200s, damaged three and chased off one, and attacked three submarines.

Two of these Condors were destroyed by Sub. Lt. Eric Brown (later known as Winkle Brown, the famous test pilot), one when his aircraft had a bent propeller. Whilst returning with a convoy on 21st December, the ship became a target for U-751 and was sunk by two torpedoes. Audacity was a sad loss but the ship had proved the effectiveness of these small lightweight carriers.

Five more ships were converted as escort carriers from British ships and 39 were supplied from the USA (affectionately known as 'Woolworth' carriers). The ships saw service in every theatre and some were eventually used in the role of attack carriers once the submarine threat had been eliminated.

The first of the escort carriers supplied by the Americans was HMS *Archer*, commissioned in November 1941, but unfortunately the ship was plagued with mechanical problems and only completed three operational missions before being placed in reserve in August 1943. It was during one of her few convoy escort patrols on 23rd May 1943 when a Swordfish of No. 819 Sqdn., flown by Sub. Lt. Horrocks, successfully sank U-752 with rocket projectiles. This was the first kill of a submarine by this weapon.

Of these ships, only two were sunk by submarines; Audacity by U-751 and Avenger by U-155, both off Gibraltar. Two others, Nabob and Thane, were struck by torpedoes but made the safety of port. Slinger was struck by a mine whilst another, Dasher, was lost when she exploded after suffering a fire caused by a leaky fuel valve. This resulted in all remaining US delivered ships being modified to prevent a reoccurrence.

FORCE H - THE MEDITERRANEAN

After the successful mission at Taranto, the Luftwaffe sent its best Ju87 Stuka units to operate from Sicily with instructions to sink the British aircraft carriers serving with Force H. If they could achieve this feat, it would deter the British shipping from sailing in the Eastern Mediterranean and therefore be denied the use of the Suez canal.

Every time any carrier approached the Stukas range from Sicily, they would attack in force and were eventually to succeed on 10th January when HMS *Illustrious* was taken out of action, bombed by the Luftwaffe Stukas. The ship was hit by five 1000lb and three 500lb bombs blowing holes in her flight deck causing severe fires below decks and many of her defensive weapons smashed. The severe damage would have been enough to sink other ships but Illustrious carried on as her name implied.

With a list from the amount of water used for the fire fighting and her steering gear out of action she limped towards Malta and the safe haven of Grand Harbour. During this passage she was attacked another four times but she was saved from further hits by the action of the fighters providing cover and the anti-aircraft fire from her remaining guns.

So determined was the resolve of the enemy that they continued their attacks on the ship whilst in Grand Harbour. Four attacks were made by over 200 aircraft, Italian Air Force SM 79s and the Stukas, but the ship survived. Minor repairs were effected and she then moved to Alexandria to be prepared for passage to Norfolk Virginia where extensive repairs and rebuilding could be safely carried out. This kept the ship out of operation until May 1942.

CAPE MATAPAN

The loss of Illustrious was relieved by the arrival of HMS *Formidable* to the Mediterranean Fleet, arriving in Alexandria on 10th March. She was in action three weeks later during the Battle of Cape Matapan (28th March), an attack on the Italian battle Fleet. The enemy Fleet had been sighted in three groups, including the main battle group with the INS *Vittorio Vento*, attempting to catch a squadron of British cruisers in a 'pincer' manoeuvre.

Fortunately their plan had been discovered so Formidable's squadrons (Nos. 826 and 829 Sqdns.) operating Albacores and Swordfish were tasked to attack the Italian battle Fleet. The FAA attack consisted of two strikes. In the first, six Albacores led by Lt. Cdr. W Saunt attacked the battle squadron scoring a hit on the flagship Vittorio Veneto and the ship was forced to reduce speed and turn for home. A second strike of three Albacores and two Swordfish led by Lt. Cdr. J Dalyell-Stead successfully attacked the battleship and scored three hits with their torpedeos. She was now slowed to thirteen knots and called for her cruiser squadrons to form a defensive screen around her.

A third strike led by Lt. Cdr. Saunt was launched but as the cruisers put up a large barrage of anti-aircraft fire, the six Albacores and two Swordfish were unable to reach the battleship. They were however successful in striking the cruiser INS *Pola* bringing her to a dead stop. The ship and

HMS Tracker

Fairey Barracuda

two more, INS *Fuime* and INS *Zara*, were later sunk by gunfire from the Mediterranean Fleet but the battleship was able to reach the safety of her home port to effect repairs.

It is recorded that the captain of the Pola said that he had never seen such courage as that displayed by the crew of the attacking aircraft flown at point blank range in the face of withering fire. A tribute to the brave aircrew of the torpedo attack aircraft.

The Stuka units in Sicily were again successful when they were able to remove Formidable from operations. They bombed her on 26th May, scoring two direct hits with 1000lb bombs, inflicting severe damage which resulted in the ship joining her sister ship in the Norfolk Navy Yard. Her squadrons were sent to operate from the desert in support of the RAF until she returned to operational status eight months later in December. The successes by the Stuka units had the desired affect, reducing the RN's operations in the Mediterranean theatre until the balance of power could be reversed later in the war.

MASSAWA STRIKE

HMS *Eagle* was still making her presence felt in the conflict even though she was a small ship only capable of operating seventeen Swordfish. The aircraft from Nos. 813 and 824 Sqdns. were disembarked to Port Sudan on 25th March 1941, under the control of Cdr. C Keighley-Peach whilst the ship was in Alexandria. The aircraft were tasked with patrolling the waters off the enemy port of Massawa.

Whilst eight of the aircraft were on patrol on 3rd April, a squadron of Italian destroyers were spotted trying to run from the harbour. After two aircraft attacked without scoring a hit, Keighley-Peach returned to base to bring back the remaining aircraft whilst the first patrol aircraft shadowed the ships. Upon returning, the Swordfish attacked the ships with their bombs and after dropping their load, returned to base to reload and return for another strike.

The attacks were one of the most successful of the campaign. Two ships were sunk - INS *Nazario Sauro* and INS *Daniele Manin*, and two were forced to beach - INS *Pantera* and INS *Tigre* which were then destroyed by naval gunfire. The Nazario had been struck by a complete 'stick' of six bombs dropped by Mid. E Sargeant sinking her in six minutes. The surviving destroyer was eventually to be scuttled when the British forces captured Massawa.

IRAQ OPERATION

HMS *Hermes* was seeing little action East of Suez so whilst on station in the Persian Gulf, she loaned No. 814 Sqdn. for operations against Iraqi rebels led by Raschid Ali. The twelve Swordfish controlled by the RAF at Habbaniya were tasked to patrol the River Tigris and attack any rebels in the area. During one of the patrols, one of the aircraft crashed and its crew were then troubled by some of the rebels. Lt. J Dundas, flying another aircraft, landed and picked up the crew, flying back to Shaibah with five on board.

SINK THE BISMARCK

The German Navy received its latest Battleship, the Bismarck, early in 1941 and after sea trials the ship was ready to cause havoc amongst the Atlantic convoys. The ship put to sea from Kiel in company with the new cruiser Prinz Eugen and an escort squadron on 20th May with this exact task coded Operation Rheinbung.

The ships were spotted off Denmark and the battle squadron were ordered to sail from Scapa Flow in pursuit whilst the RAF were tasked with a large bombing attack. Unfortunately the weather was against the attacking forces so no attack was possible. In the worsening weather, a Maryland of No. 771 Sqdn. was launched from Hatston with a volunteer crew to search for the German Fleet. The only thing that could be confirmed from this mission was that they had sailed and were now in open waters.

The first ships to make contact were the destroyers HMS *Suffolk* and HMS *Norfolk* on the 23rd who, with the aid of Norfolk's Walrus, shadowed the German Fleet relaying their position so the squadron could intercept them. The British Fleet was led by HMS *Hood* and HMS *Prince Of Wales* who engaged the Germans the next day. This was to prove to be a setback to the British as the Bismarck sank the Hood with its first salvo, then the German Fleet inflicted severe damage on the Prince of Wales which had in fact shelled the Bismarck causing damage to her fuel supply which needed repairs.

As the Bismarck headed for St. Nazair, the

Brewster Buffalo

Home Fleet (HMS *Victorious*) and Force H (HMS *Ark Royal*) were despatched to intercept them. Victorious, a new aircraft carrier commissioned only nine days before (15th May), had two squadrons on board - No. 800Z Sqdn. with six Fulmars, and No. 825 Sqdn. with nine Swordfish, and they were tasked to carry out air attacks on the Bismarck. On the evening of the 24th, No. 825 Sqdn. was launched, led by Lt. Cdr. Esmonde and directed by HMS *Norfolk*, attacking the ship in three sections. One torpedo launched by Lt. P Gick struck the ship's armoured belt, possibly causing the damage by the Prince of Wales to be aggravated. The Fulmars continued to shadow the ship but lost contact the following morning.

Grumman Martlet

The RAF joined the hunt and a Coastal Command Catalina sighted the ship heading for Brest on the 26th. Shortly after, Swordfish of No. 810 Sqdn. from Ark Royal also picked up the ship and began following her. Ark Royal launched fourteen Swordfish from Nos. 810, 818 and 820 Sqdns. but unfortunately due to a mix-up, they attacked HMS *Sheffield* by mistake, launching eleven torpedoes. No damage was inflicted on the cruiser by a combination of the torpedoes blowing up on contact with the sea, and those that did not were evaded by the crew of the ship.

It was fortuitous that this attack had taken place (not in the eyes of those on board Sheffield) as it enabled the weapons to be changed from Duplex-headed torpedoes to contact type. Another fifteen aircraft led by Lt. Cdr. T Coode C.O. of No. 818 Sqdn. found the Bismarck and the formation split into its three squadrons and attacked from all sides. All the aircraft launched their 'tin fish', at least two making contact, causing damage to her rudder and steering gear which enabled the Home Fleet to catch the battleship and engage her. The Coup de Grace was given to HMS *Dorsetshire* which fired her torpedoes into Bismarck's port side. It should be noted that all these actions were carried out in atrocious, although typical, Atlantic conditions.

THE RELIEF OF MALTA

Throughout the year, Force H had been heavily involved in escorting the Malta Convoys. Four carriers were involved; HMSs *Argus, Ark Royal, Furious* and *Victorious.* Within the escort duties the ships, Argus and Furious in particular, were busy ferrying

HMS Victorious

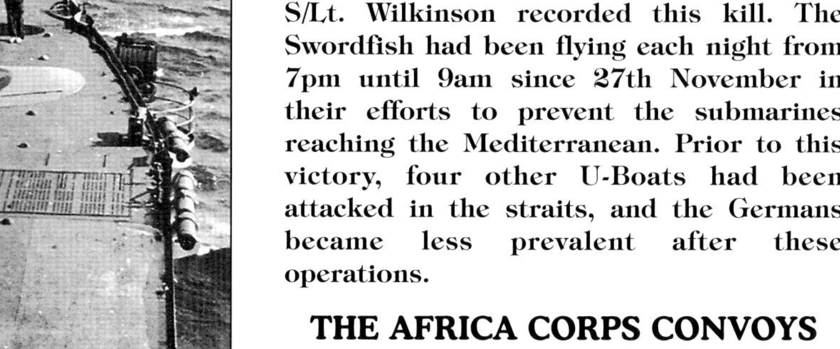

HMS Eagle / Sea Hurricanes

RAF aircraft to the beleaguered island. Between the months April to November the Force had escorted five supply convoys and eleven aircraft ferry supply convoys.

The old carrier Argus recommissioned at the outbreak of the war as a training carrier with a secondary role of ferry carrier. During 1941, she carried many aircraft to Gibraltar for onward passage to Malta, but she did however have another ferry passage during the summer when she was a member of the 'Fleet' for Operation Benedict, the first Russian convoy during August. Her 'cargo' was the Hurricanes of Nos. 81 and 134 Sqdns. RAF and the aircraft were delivered to Vaenga near Murmansk on 7th September. On completion, she returned to ferrying aircraft to Gibraltar before replacing Ark Royal in Force H.

Whilst returning to Gibraltar on 13th November after escorting a convoy, Ark Royal was struck by torpedoes from U81. The ship was recovering some of her Swordfish about 30 miles east of Gibraltar when she was hit. Within three minutes she assumed a twelve degree list but her damage repair teams fought well to keep her afloat. Tugs arrived from the naval base to attempt to tow her to safety but within sight of 'the Rock' she sank to the bottom of the Mediterranean Sea at 0613 hours on the 14th with the loss of only one life. During the conflict, Ark Royal had taken part in 32 major operations, had many near misses and, according to Lord Haw Haw, this thorn in Hitler's side had been sunk many times.

THE GIBRALTAR STRAITS - STOP THE U-BOATS

After the loss of Ark Royal, the ship's Swordfish squadron No. 812 was tasked with anti-submarine patrol duties at RAF North Front Gibraltar. The year ended with S/Lt. Wilkinson successfully sinking U-451 with depth charges on 21st/22nd December during a night attack on the submarine near Tangiers whilst it was transiting the Gibraltar Straits. This was the first night attack 'Kill' against the German U-Boats using air launched depth charges.

The Squadron had been operating from RAF North Front for nearly a month when S/Lt. Wilkinson recorded this kill. The Swordfish had been flying each night from 7pm until 9am since 27th November in their efforts to prevent the submarines reaching the Mediterranean. Prior to this victory, four other U-Boats had been attacked in the straits, and the Germans became less prevalent after these operations.

THE AFRICA CORPS CONVOYS

No. 830 Sqdn. had been formed on 1st July 1940 out of No. 767 Sqdn. after its attack on Genoa and was based at Hal Far in Malta, with the task of attacking convoys supporting Rommel's forces. All these attacks were carried out at night and resulted in successful strikes on 25 ships, thirteen of these being sunk. On one mission the Squadron completely decimated and broke up a complete convoy of twelve ships, two were sunk and the same amount were damaged, one being beached. This was achieved using nine swordfish aircraft, one of which was fitted with Air-to-Surface Vessel Radar (ASV).

The actions by this Squadron and those of the RAF had a serious affect on the amount of convoys resupplying the Africa Corps. Between them they sank well over 100 ships, reducing Rommel's supply line to less than 40%. The Germans did retaliate in early 1942 by attacking their base in Malta and destroying all but one of their aircraft which were then replaced with Albacores.

A major success was the sinking of the Italian liner the Victoria, one of four Italian liners in a large convoy of troops and supplies bound for Tripoli. The convoy was sighted by an RAF reconnaissance flight on 23rd February 1942, and a flight of two Albacores and seven Swordfish set off in search led by Lt. Cdr. F Hopkins. The Swordfish were forced to return to Malta due to a storm, but the Albacores sighted the convoy and were able to determine their direction. After arriving back at Hal Far, Hopkins arranged a second strike of six aircraft. Four of these aircraft made it to the convoy and attacked it in line astern scoring two hits on the 24,000 ton liner, slowing it down. Hopkins, who had been airborne for nearly twelve hours, was awarded the DSO.

Another force of five Albacores of No. 826 Sqdn. arrived from Libya in support of the

Fairey Albacores

attack. Lt. H Ellis attacked the Victoria releasing his torpedo which hit the ship amidships finally sinking it, whilst he himself was being attacked by two defending Ju.88s. The Victoria had a complete panzer division on board. For his actions, Lt. Ellis received the DFC.

THE WESTERN DESERT

An unlikely theatre of operation was that of North Africa and the Western Desert supporting the RAF and British Army. Operations by No. 824 Sqdn had previously been carried out during 1940 from the desert airfields. Three squadrons - Nos. 815, 821 and 826 Sqdns. were tasked with anti-submarine patrols, target illumination dropping of flares (path finding), spotting for bombardments and the attacking of targets and shipping with their Albacores and Swordfish aircraft. These operations were to last from June 1941 with the arrival of No. 826 Sqdn at Maaten Bagush until it was disbanded in August 1943.

The flare dropping technique used by the FAA Albacores resulted in a joint FAA/RAF tactic of lighting up targets by flares dropped by Albacores so the RAF Wellington bombers could successfully bomb the target. This was used to great effect from the first joint operation in April 1942 when two Albacores dropped 36 flares at intervals over the German desert airfield at Matuba, followed by the ten Wellingtons bombing the target causing considerable damage.

All three squadrons participated in the Battle of El Alamein. No. 821 Sqdn. was responsible for identifying the build up of the Africa Corps for its final push against the 8th Army on 1st September 1942. After raising the alarm, they directed the RAF Wellington bombers to the target and the damage inflicted resulted in the withdrawal of the enemy from the theatre and the defeat of Rommel. Nos. 815 and 826 Sqdns. continued to support the Army as it progressed its scourge of the Germans into Algeria.

Three more squadrons, Nos. 803, 805 and 806, became the Royal Navy Fighter Wing with the role of protecting the British convoys sailing to Tobruk, supporting British ground forces, escorting RAF bombers and attacking German forces. Operating under the control of the RAF, the unit's headquarters were at Sidi Haneish. However they also operated their Martlets, Hurricane and Sea Hurricane fighters from Sidi Barrani, El Gubbi, Maddalena and Tobruk.

The unit formed in Alexandria, at Dekhelia before moving to Mersa Matruh on 17th August, disbanding on 10th February 1942 after operating for nearly six months. In that period, the unit was responsible for the possible destruction of seventeen enemy aircraft for the loss of eight of its own aircraft.

Grumman Avenger

OPERATION CERBERUS - THE GERMAN NAVY'S CHANNEL DASH

After the sinking of the Bismarck, the cruiser Prinz Eugen reached the safe haven of Brest to join Scharnhorst and Gneisenau. These ships were under constant attack from the RAF but at the beginning of the year they were being prepared for sea. The FAA sent Lt. Cdr. Esmonde and his Swordfish squadron (No. 825) to Manston in Kent to prepare to intercept them when they eventually sailed.

The ships left Brest for a dash through the English Channel in abysmal conditions on the evening of 11th February 1942. The following day Esmonde led six aircraft on a suicidal attack on the ships. All the aircraft were shot down by the barrage of flak put up by the German Fleet or by the FW190s and Me109s which were giving air cover to the Fleet. The RAF had promised 50 Spitfires to support Esmonde's aircraft but only ten were in attendance.

Esmonde's aircraft was the first to be shot down by one of the FW190s whilst flying at 50ft above the Channel. Only two aircraft were able to launch their torpedoes at the battle Fleet but neither reached their target in this extremely brave but futile strike. Of the eighteen crew only five survived, three from one aircraft and two from another. Four of these survivors received the DSO and Leading Airman D Bunce, who had successfully destroyed a fighter during the attack, received the Conspicuous Gallantry Medal. Esmonde was posthumously awarded the VC (the FAA's first of the war) - he had been presented with his DSO only the day before. All the remaining crew members were mentioned in dispatches.

This heroic act by the members of No. 825 Sqdn. resulted in the first time when the complete crew involved in an attack were all honoured for their selfless act of courage. Vice Admiral Ramsay, Flag Officer Dover reported '*In my opinion, the gallant sortie of these six Swordfish constitutes one of the*

Grumman Wildcat

Supermarine Seafires

finest exhibitions of self sacrifice and devotion to duty that the war has yet witnessed'.

The operation raised many questions by the public, press and in Parliament as to why the FAA were still operating with such antiquated equipment. Priority was now given to the design and supply of modern aircraft for the FAA including the Supermarine Seafire. Aircraft manufacture was centred around the build up of the heavy bomber force for strikes against the enemy. It can be noted that during the main bomber offensive, 40 FAA pilots flew RAF Whitley and Wellington bombers - just as they had flown during the Battle of Britain.

THE FAR EAST FLEET

After joining the war with their infamous attack on Pearl Harbour, reportedly copied from the FAA attack at Taranto, the Imperial Japanese Navy and its carriers were beginning to take hold in the Far East. HMS *Hermes* was based at Trincomalee in Ceylon when word was received that the Japanese were intending to attack the island.

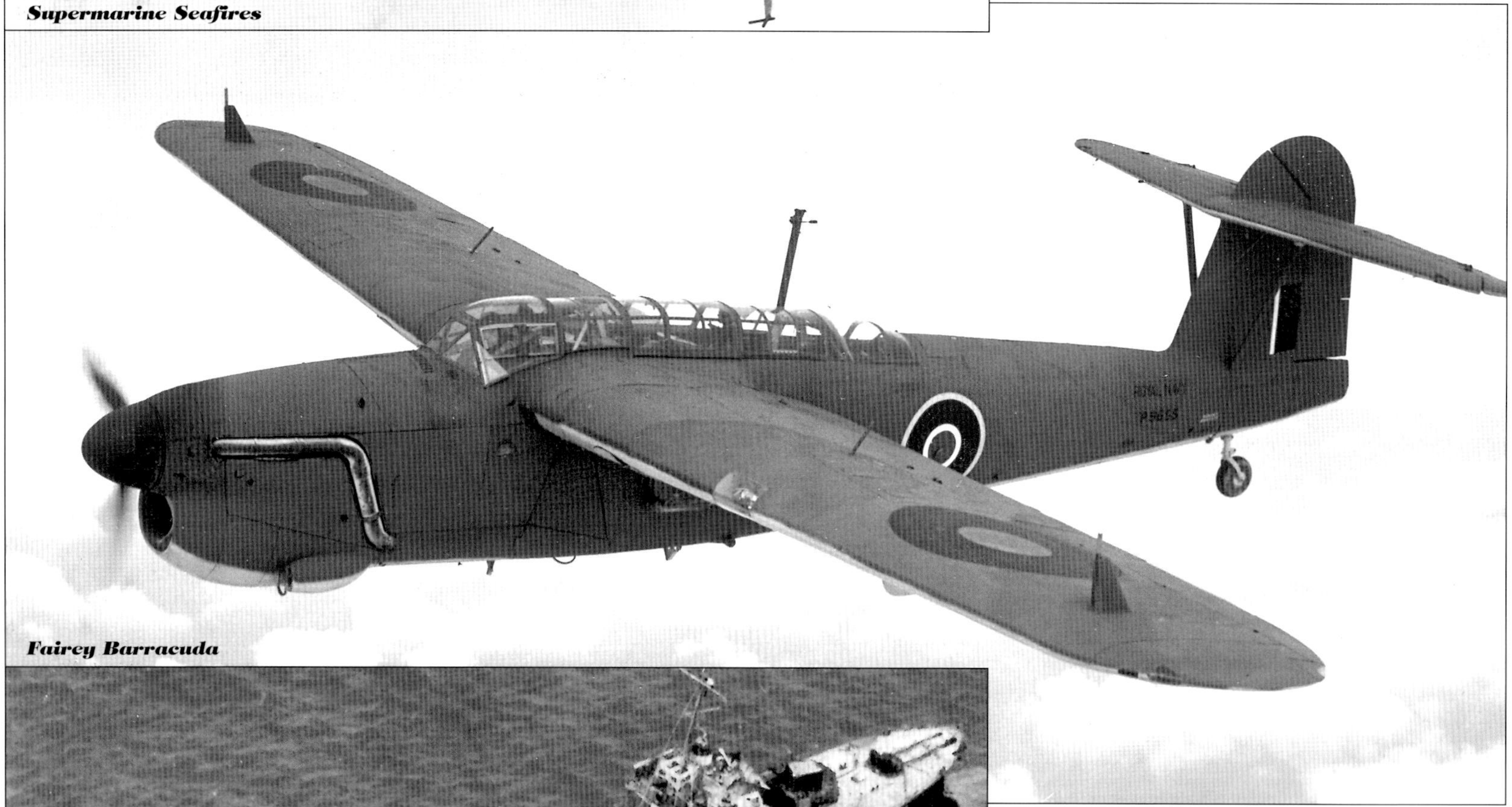

Fairey Barracuda

The ship put to sea leaving her aircraft ashore in an effort to save the ship from attack. This failed when she was attacked by Japanese dive bombers from the carriers IJS *Akagi, Hiryu* and *Soryu* and sunk on 9th April 1942, the only RN aircraft carrier to be sunk by air attack. This was a sad loss of the world's first true aircraft carrier which had first commissioned nineteen years earlier.

Diego Saurez Harbour

World War II 1942-45 Success in Europe - on to Japan

HMS Victorious

OPERATION IRONCLAD - THE TAKING OF MADAGASCAR

With the loss of Hermes, HMS *Indomitable* and HMS *Illustrious* were on station in the Indian Ocean operating from Cape Town and Durban in South Africa. These two ships took part in the operation to take control of the island of Madagascar from the incumbent Vichy-French forces.

The initial Operation Ironclad involved the capturing of Diego Saurez harbour and its surrounding airfields in the North. During the three days of the successful operation (5th -7th May 1942), HMS *Indomitable's* air group attacked the airfields whilst HMS *Illustrious'* air group provided air cover for the landing forces and attacked the French Fleet sinking the submarines FNS *Bevezieres* and *Le Heroes*, and the armed merchant ship Bougainville, damaging the sloop D'Entrecasteaux. Further operations in the south were successful in September when the island was finally taken. Illustrious supplied air cover for the invasion whilst Albatross, now fitted with a catapult, assisted with spotting duties.

OPERATION PEDESTAL - THE RELIEF OF MALTA

The largest Malta convoy, a Fleet of fourteen fast merchant ships and HMS *Furious* with a cargo of 38 Spitfires, sailed from Gibraltar on 9th/10th August 1942 escorted by three aircraft carriers; HMSs *Eagle*, *Indomitable* and *Victorious*, two battleships, seven cruisers and 24 destroyers. Operation Pedestal (Force Z) was under constant attack by enemy aircraft for the duration of the passage.

The biggest reward for the enemy was the sinking of Eagle by U-73 on the 11th after four torpedoes struck the ship 80 miles off the coast of Algiers, sinking her in less than eight minutes with the loss of only 250 lives. This was the last British Fleet carrier to be lost in W.W.II.

The first major air attack was from 36 Ju88s on the evening of the 11th, followed by constant attacks the following day when both remaining carriers, Indomitable and Victorious, were bombed. Victorious was hit by two bombs which fortunately did no damage, but the fate of Indomitable was much worse. Struck by two bombs on the flight deck, a further bomb exploded close to the ship blowing a 30ft hole in her side totally disabling her. This left only Victorious as an operational deck for the remaining few hours before the convoy was in range of the RAF's fighters in Malta, who would then take on the responsibility of air cover for the convoy and the two carriers could return to Gibraltar.

During 36 hours of air battles, the 126 FAA carrier based aircraft (70 fighters - Sea Hurricanes, Martlets and Fulmars, 56 Swordfish and Albacores) fought against over 500 enemy attackers destroying 30+ for the loss of thirteen aircraft. Lt. Cork, in his Sea Hurricane IC of No. 800 Sqdn. aboard Indomitable, shot down five of these aircraft.

When the carriers departed on the 12th, only one merchant ship had been damaged (later sunk off Tunisia), Eagle had sunk and Indomitable was out of action. So intense was the Axis resolve to destroy this convoy that repeated attacks by surface vessels and U-Boats had success during the night. Italian

Grumman Wildcat

torpedo boats sunk four ships and a cruiser and U-Boats hit three more cruisers sinking one of them. Air attacks the following day resulted in the bombing of six more merchant ships, four sinking and two limping into Grand Harbour.

Although this operation had been costly with the effective loss of two carriers, the sinking of two cruisers and a destroyer, five of the merchantmen made it to the island including the oil tanker Ohio, bringing much needed relief to the island. This was the last and most important Malta convoy to sail the Mediterranean and it was imperative that it got through to ensure the island's survival against the Axis powers.

THE HARSH RUSSIAN CONVOYS

At the same time as the operations for the relief of Malta, the British navies were suffering losses on the Russian convoys across the North Atlantic. The U-Boats operating in packs were having many successes culminating with the disastrous PQ17 convoy when 22 of the 36 ships were lost to the action of U-Boats and long-range bombers. At this time, only five of the escort carriers had been delivered and of these HMS *Audacity* had been lost and HMS *Archer* was unreliable, leaving only three operational.

Grumman Martlet

The next Russian convoy PQ18 was to include HMS *Avenger* equipped with Nos. 802 and 883 Sqdns. with Sea Hurricanes and a detachment of three Swordfish from No. 825 Sqdn. The convoy was first attacked on 12th September 1942 by enemy bombers from Luftflotte V which, due to lack of experience from the Sea Hurricane pilots, were able to press home their attack and sink eight ships. The two fighter squadrons reassessed their tactics in defence of the Fleet from attacking aircraft. The result was for two aircraft to remain airborne on Combat Air Patrol (CAP) with the remainder at readiness to launch on arrival of the enemy. This system of maritime protection is still in operation to this day.

Further attacks prevailed over the next two days. One ship was lost on the 13th during one of the two enemy forages. The first attack involved 22 aircraft whilst the second consisted of 27 aircraft, as well as some high level bombing from the enemy. The following day the enemy attacked over a prolonged period of three hours when more than 70 aircraft attacked the convoy. During these two days, the revised tactics resulted in the destruction of about 40 aircraft for the loss of only four Hurricanes.

During one attack, the Luftwaffe concentrated their efforts on Avenger with many bombs and seventeen torpedoes being released at her but she escaped unharmed after considerable seamanship by the ship's helmsman and the actions of the fighters. Three more ships were sunk by U-Boats, a small amount thanks to the patrols by the Swordfish aircraft who shared the destruction of U-589 with HMS *Onslow*. The convoy delivered 30 of its original 41 merchantmen to the Kola inlet before returning across the Atlantic escorting PQ13. The outcome of escorting the convoy resulted in the Germans reducing the scale of air attacks on future Russian convoys although they did increase the U-Boat operations, which were dealt with by aircraft from the escort carriers now entering service.

OPERATION TORCH - THE INVASION OF NORTH AFRICA

November saw the invasion of Vichy-French held North Africa by a combined British and American force coded Operation Torch. This was to be the largest gathering of aircraft carriers in a single operation to date with seven British and five US Navy ships. The carriers had a combined strength of over 300 aircraft and all of them wore US Navy markings and special Operation Torch roundels which were applied over the RN markings and British roundels.

The British Force began sailing from the Clyde on 22nd October 1942 joining with the US Force, grouping together fifteen convoys of ships with 70,000 troops and 160 British warships divided into three Task Forces; the Central Naval Task Force (HMSs *Biter, Dasher* and *Furious*) with the task of attacking Oran; the Western Naval Task Force (HMSs *Argus* and *Avenger*) tasked with operations at Algiers, plus Force H (HMSs *Formidable* and *Victorious*) providing air cover, and an American Western Task Force with their target being Casablanca.

The landings began on 8th November with the carriers' aircraft providing air cover for the amphibious landings, attacks on airfields, harbours, forts and enemy forces, distributing leaflets and reconnaissance flights. The French base commander at Blida surrendered his airfield to the attacking aircraft and Lt. B Nation, leading a formation of No. 882 Sqdn. Martlets, landed to take the surrender.

During the operations, which were so successful that the landings were completed within five days resulting in the withdrawal of the ships, Argus and Avenger were dive bombed off Algiers on the 10th by Ju88s, damaging three Seafires aboard Argus whilst minor damage to Avenger needed repairs which were carried out in Algiers harbour once it had been secured by the allied forces. Avenger suffered again five days later whilst escorting a convoy home, when she was hit by a torpedo from U-155 which sank her and most of her crew.

THE MERCHANT AIRCRAFT CARRIER (MAC) SHIPS

Nineteen merchant ships were converted from grain carriers (six ships) and oil tankers (thirteen ships) known as MAC Ships (Merchant Aircraft Carriers), seventeen for the British merchant Fleet and two Dutch merchantmen. These ships flew under the Red Ensign and Dutch Ensign, manned by merchant crews except for the aircraft detachments. The two Dutch MAC ships were manned by Dutch crews, both ships' company and the Swordfish aircrew.

The MAC ships differed from the escorts by actually being part of the convoy, carrying their cargo of grain or oil below decks. They were equipped with Swordfish aircraft in flights from Nos. 833, 834, 838 and 840 Sqdns. until they were all amalgamated into the FAA's largest squadron No. 836 equipped with over 80 Swordfish in flights. Three flights belonging to the Royal Dutch Navy's No. 860 Sqdn. (F.O. and Z Flights) operated within the auspices of No. 836 Sqdn. from its home base of Maydown, Londonderry.

Grumman Avenger

The first MAC ship to enter service was Empire MacAlpine commissioned on 14th April 1943, sailing with her first convoy the following month. The final convoy duty by a MAC ship was by Empire MacKay in June 1945. At the end of this convoy on the 28th, she launched her Swordfish aircraft not only for her last time, but also for the FAA's last operational biplane sortie of the war. During these two years, MAC ships sailed in 217 convoys without the loss of a single ship due to U-Boat action.

THE PACIFIC HEATS UP

HMS *Victorious* sailed to the Pacific to join up with the USS *Saratoga* arriving at Noumea in New Caledonia in May 1943. The first operation by this Task Force (TF14) 'Toenail' was the following month when the two ships headed the attack on the island on New Georgia leaving Noumea on 27th June. The air groups were to combine missions, Victorious operating all the fighter aircraft and the Saratoga all the strike aircraft, until the successful completion on the 27th July.

DEFEAT OF THE ITALIANS - OPERATION AVALANCHE

HMS *Indomitable* meanwhile returned to operations in support of the largest invasion force ever assembled (at that time) when 450,000 Allied soldiers were to invade the island of Sicily. The invasion began on 10th July 1943, with the ship providing patrols for the assembled Fleet against enemy U-Boats and surface ships, and air cover was supplied by RAF fighters in Malta. Six days into the month long operation, Indomitable was on the receiving end of a torpedo launched by a Ju88 which necessitated repairs in the USA (like her sister ships before her), a loss to the RN for twelve months.

After Sicily the Allies moved on to mainland Italy, with the port of Naples being the main target, and initial landings began on 3rd September six days before the main invasion at Salerno. The supporting naval forces were in two Fleets; Force 'H' with HMSs *Formidable* and *Illustrious* with the role of CAP for both Fleets and over the beach head; and Force 'V' with HMSs *Attacker, Battler, Hunter, Stalker* and *Unicorn* on her first operational mission, with the task of supporting the Army.

The landings began on the day the Italians surrendered - the 9th September 1943,

SS Empire MacAlpine

Sikorsky R4 Hoverfly

however the British Fleet was still required to provide defence against the Italian Fleet if they were to materialise. The main tasks were to provide fighter cover for the landings and attack shore targets, airfields and enemy troops.

The FAA's role in the operation was planned to last for two days as it was envisaged the airfield at Monte Corvino would be captured by this time, thus allowing land based aircraft to operate. However this was not the case and cover was required for four days then, when the airfield was captured, it was beyond use so an emergency landing strip had to be constructed, something which had not been expected. During these operations only two aircraft were lost and four damaged due to enemy action. However 42 Seafires were lost due to landing accidents aboard the carriers, a result of the aircraft recovering on deck with little or no wind assistance.

ESCORTS IN THE INDIAN OCEAN

There was to be no respite for the escort carrier HMS *Battler* and she was despatched to the Indian Ocean directly after Operation Avalanche for anti-submarine patrols and convoy protection duties. She was joined by HMSs *Atheling, Ameer, Begum* and *Shah* operating from Trincomalee and Durban, their air group disembarking to the local naval air stations. This small group of escorts successfully protected the Allied shipping during their twelve months on station and no ships were lost.

OPERATION TUNGSTEN, MASCOT AND GOODWOOD - TIRPITZ

The next mission to destroy a major element of the German surface Fleet was an attack on the Battleship Tirpitz at 'home' in the Norwegian waters from where she operated in her attacks on Arctic convoys. The ship had been damaged on various occasions whilst operating in the Northern Atlantic, but never to the extent that she was permanently removed from the war.

On 9th March 1942, the first attack of many on the ship had taken place. Albacores of No. 817 and 832 Sqdns. operating from HMS *Victorious* attacked the ship but unfortunately were unsuccessful and the ship sought refuge in Vestfjord. The following year an attack was launched using midget submarines whilst she was in Kaa Fjord, again causing damage which kept her out of action for a few months.

The battleship was scheduled for more attention as it was still causing casualties amongst the Russian convoys. Her tactic was to sail from her base amongst the Norwegian fjords, attack a convoy then retreat back to the fjord. Since the first attack by aircraft from Victorious, the ship had been regularly attacked by aircraft from the RAF then, in 1943, she was attacked by midget submarines which put her out of action. However the ship was still afloat in Kaa Fjord and still a threat to the convoys, a threat that had to be removed.

It was decided an attack on the ship would be carried out using a large force of aircraft from the Fleet carriers HMSs *Furious* and *Victorious,* and the escort carriers HMSs *Emperor, Pursuer* and *Searcher* whilst the ship was in Altenfjord. Air defence and U-Boat patrols would be the role of HMS *Fencer* and the carriers had a combined force of twelve squadrons with 168 aircraft,

Operation Tungsten began with the 42 Barracudas of Nos. 827, 829, 830 and 831 Sqdns. practising bombing techniques to perfect their skills for diving at angles from 45 to 60 degrees, which would be needed to affect the attack on the ship. Loch Eriboll was used as it was a remote area away from prying eyes and bore similar resemblance to Kaa Fjord.

This training completed, the two carrier attack groups sailed two days later on 30th March 1944, taking different routes but meeting up on 2nd April before joining the escort carriers. Both attack carriers had two squadrons of Barracuda aircraft; Nos. 827 and 829 Sqdns. on Victorious and Nos. 830 and 831 Sqdns. on board Furious.

The aircraft attacked the ship in two waves; the first led by Lt. Cdr. R Baker-Falkner (C.O. No. 827 Sqdn.) achieving nine direct hits whilst Lt. Cdr. V Rance's (C.O. No. 831 Sqdn.) group achieved five hits causing major damage. Three Barracudas and one Hellcat failed to return back to their ships.

Fairey Swordfish

Grumman Hellcat

Further raids during April and May had to be cancelled due to inclement weather. However another major attack involving three attack carriers, HMSs *Furious, Formidable* and *Indefatigable* using Barracudas fitted with 1600lb bombs did occur in July, code name 'Mascot'. A ramp was fitted at the front of Furious to aid the aircrafts' take-off with this heavier bomb, but the strike was without success due to warnings received by the ship which was able to put up a smoke screen.

The final missions against the ship 'Goodwood' were carried out in August 1944 involving the three Fleet carriers and two escort carriers, HMSs *Nabob* and *Trumpeter.* Four strikes were launched but only two hits were scored, one of the bombs penetrating down eight decks but unfortunately the 1600lb bomb failed to go off. The ship was finally sunk by the action of Nos. 9 and 617 Sqdns. RAF who were successful with their Tallboy bombs.

During the two years of operations against the battleship, ten aircraft carriers with nine different FAA aircraft types, midget submarines from the RN and bombers from the RAF had attempted to sink her. Probably no other warship has been targeted for so long and with so much enthusiasm and determination.

THE ESCORTS TURN THE TIDE

Tirpitz and her escorts were not the only problem to the convoys. Luftflotte V and the Atlantic U-Boat packs were still having success, and more and more of the escort carriers were entering service and joining in the battle against these raiders. The carriers were aided by the squadrons of Coastal Command carrying out their long patrols over the Atlantic searching for the U-Boats.

The tide was slowly turned with the aid of these ships and aircraft. In three convoys alone, eight U-Boats were sunk and another five damaged and at least six aircraft were shot down. By the end of the convoys, ten of the escort carriers had taken part in these harsh sailings, limiting the effectiveness of the U-Boat packs until eventually beating them, exactly what these Woolworth carriers and the MAC ships had been designed to do.

THE FAA LOOKS TO HELICOPTERS

After ordering the Cierva C40s in 1935 (delivered from 1939), the FAA was to continue developments in autogyros. During 1942, further deck handling trials were held using the US derivative, the Pitcairn PA39, in HMS *Ranger* and the SS *Empire Mersey* which had a platform fitted for the trials. These were to evaluate the feasibility of using autogyros for anti-submarine (AS) patrols with convoys.

In the States, Sikorsky was developing the flying machine which eventually would become the helicopter, making the autogyro obsolete. The R4 helicopter was ordered by the Admiralty in 1943 for use against submarines and, by ordering 25 machines (called the Gadfly), the RN became the world's first military organisation to order helicopters. The first pilots were sent to learn to fly this new aviation machine in 1943, as the nucleus of the world's first operational helicopter unit.

The first R4s embarked aboard the SS *Daghestan* for an east bound convoy during 1944 tasked with patrolling for U-Boats. However the crossing was plagued with bad weather and only limited operations were conducted. It was felt more development flying was required before the helicopter could be looked on as a reliable asset. The need for these R4s to return to convoy duties was alleviated with the ending of hostilities with Germany. They were now to be used for communications, radar calibration and photographic flights.

FAR EAST AND PACIFIC

The war in the Far East and Pacific was intensifying and the Allies were now on the offensive after recovering from the Japanese initial onslaught. April 1944 saw the beginning of continuous battles against Japanese forces in the Far East. Many British carriers were to be involved, not only the modern armour plated ships HMSs *Illustrious, Indomitable* and *Victorious*, but also the faithful escort carriers now relieved from Atlantic and Mediterranean convoys. These operations were to last six months with attacks on military installations, harbours, airfields, oil refineries and shipping at Sumatra, Java and Car Nicobar.

Illustrious joined the Far East Fleet during January 1944 after her repairs and combined forces with the USS *Saratoga* for

504 Sqdn Hellcat

the offensive. The first operation was attacking the port of Sabang on 19th April destroying the oil installations and at least 24 aircraft on the nearby airfield. The oil installations were rebuilt, requiring further attacks in July by aircraft from Illustrious and Victorious resulting in their destruction once again.

Operations intended to disrupt the Japanese supply lines began in June when Illustrious's air group attacked targets in the Adaman Islands. Strikes by Victorious and Indomitable's air groups were busy attacking Sumatra during August and September, then the Nicobar Islands were the targets during October attacking Japanese ships and airfields. These successful missions were diversionary to distract the enemy from the US Forces assault on the Philippines.

At the end of the year, the size of the RN in the Far East and Pacific had increased significantly. With the end of hostilities in Europe, more ships were available for the theatre which was reorganised into two Fleets - the Pacific Fleet with the large Fleet carriers and the East Indies Fleet with the escort carriers.

Supermarine Seafire

OPERATION OVERLORD - D DAY LANDINGS

The most important military operation in Europe was the liberation of mainland Europe and the ultimate defeat of the Germans. Plans were formulated between the Allies under the code name 'Overlord', the landings to take place in the summer of 1944. The FAA had an important role to play not only in the actual event, but also in the build-up. Many operations under the code name 'Channel Stop' were held during the months of April and May with the intention of luring Hitler and his generals into believing that the impending invasion was going to be at Calais.

At Culmhead, Lt. Cdr. N Hallett commanded the 24th Naval Fighter Wing (NFW) operating Seafire IIIs in Nos. 887 and 894 Sqdns., whilst the torpedo bomber Squadrons of the FAA were amalgamated into Coastal Command wings to carry out operations from RAF bases across to

France. Nos. 819 Sqdn. (Swordfish) and 848 Sqdn. (Avengers) moved to Manston with No. 155 Wing, joining No. 156 Wing located at Harrowbeer - No. 838 Sqdn. (Swordfish) and Perranporth, No. 816 Sqdn. (Swordfish) and Nos. 849 and 850 Sqdn. Avengers. Incorporated into No. 157 Wing at Hawkinge were the Avengers of Nos. 854 and 855 Sqdns. These Squadrons were involved in strikes against enemy positions, anti-shipping strikes, night operations against 'E' and 'R' boats, anti-submarine patrols and reconnaissance flights.

The most active airfield for the landings was Lee-on-Solent where the 3rd NFW was established, operating Seafire and Spitfire aircraft. This unit comprised of Nos. 808 (Seafire and Spitfire LF.Vb), 897 (Spitfire LVb), 885 and 886 (Seafire) FAA Sqdns., Nos. 2 (Mustang), 26 and 63 (Spitfire), 268 (Mustang and Typhoon) and 1320 Flight (Typhoon) RAF Sqdns., No. 414 Sqdn. (Mustang) RCAF and VOS-7 (Spitfire) US Navy Sqdn. This became the 34th Tactical Reconnaissance Wing of the 2nd Tactical Air Force. The USN Squadron comprised of pilots from the USS cruisers and destroyer flights using borrowed Spitfires for the role of Naval Observation flights.

This was the largest gathering of military might ever to assemble in European waters, with Forces from fifteen nations involved in the operation. Ships were located along the British south and south-west coasts, the majority off the Isle of Wight. An unprecedented act by King George VI was the review of 800 of these ships on 5th June, the eve of the operation.

The landings began on the morning of 6th June 1944 with the launching of two No. 808 Sdqn. aircraft from Lee-on-Solent at 0441 hours to spot for the armada of ships and landing craft at the Normandy beaches. The airfield was active throughout the day continuously launching aircraft as fighters and reconnaissance aircraft and, by the end of the day, 435 sorties had been launched from the airfield. During the initial phase of the landings No. 819 Sqdn., now operating from Manston, was tasked with the important role of setting up a smoke screen along the beaches with their Swordfish aircraft.

From the first take-off by the Seafires of the 3rd NFW until its disbanding on 15th July, 1,230 sorties had been achieved for the loss of only fourteen aircraft. During the main phase of the liberation of Europe, 6th-30th June, Lee-on-Solent was the busiest airfield with 2,223 operational sorties being achieved.

During "Overlord" there was limited carrier support, air support being flown from land.

804 Sqdn Hellcats

HMSs *Searcher* and *Emperor* provided anti-submarine warfare (ASW) patrols, and HMS *Albatross* was available for use as a repair ship for landing craft. However she was torpedoed in August and although she made it safely back to port, she was not repaired but put in reserve.

MEDITERRANEAN OFFENSIVE OPERATIONS

Operation Dragoon, the liberation of Southern France, began with troop landings at St. Raphael on 15th August 1944, with the Force of 90,000 troops (mostly American) supported by two US escort carriers and seven British - HMSs *Attacker, Emperor, Hunter, Khedive, Pursuer, Searcher* and *Stalker.* Operations consisted of bombing, close air support, strafing of enemy vehicles and trains and a few combat air patrols. During the two weeks the carriers were involved, over 1500 sorties were flown. The following month the Force was involved in the final operations in the Mediterranean, with the removal of German Forces in the Aegean and Balkans. Attacks were made on enemy positions and shipping being used for evacuation of German troops, reconnaissance, bombing and general harassing of the enemy. The final FAA operations in the Mediterranean theatre were carried out by Emperor's Hellcats from No. 800 Sqdn on 5th November when they flew patrols over Milos in the Aegean.

AS EUROPE SMOULDERS, THE FAR EAST RAGES

The war with Japan was continuing throughout the Pacific and East Indies, with the RN operating the majority of its assets in the theatre alongside the Americans with a concentrated effort to defeat the enemy and restore peace. The British Pacific Fleet (BPF) was to establish its base at Sydney with a 'theatre' base at Manus in the Admiralty Islands where the support carriers HMSs *Unicorn* and *Pioneer* were based.

Because of the large expanse of the Pacific Ocean combined with the large area of operations, a requirement for keeping the BPF at sea long enough to complete operations had to be devised. The 'Fleet Train' was established consisting of a large convoy of assorted ships carrying fuel, spares, fresh water and provisions, clothing, mechanical support services and repair

Chance Vought Corsair

facilities for the ships should they be damaged (the forerunner of today's Royal Fleet Auxiliary). This train would be at sea a safe distance from the immediate action but near enough to supply the requirements of the Fleet as and when necessary.

In support of the large amount of aircraft that would be operating in the theatre during the impending long battle against the Japanese, a series of self-contained mobile aircraft facilities were established. These Mobile Operational Naval Air Bases (MONABs) were all initially established at HMS Flycatcher at Ludlam in Norfolk and all were commissioned as 'ships'.

Ten were commissioned but, unlike the fixed air bases, these would not bear the names of birds but all their names would begin with 'Nab'. Operating alongside them would be Transportable Aircraft Maintenance Yards (TAMYs), of which only one was completed before the requirement for these two types of support unit ended.

By December, HMS *Indefatigable* had joined the BPF to give it its fourth armoured strike carrier and a combined air strength of over 200 aircraft. The deck of these carriers was soon to show the resilience of the armour compared to the frailty of the wooden decks on the USN aircraft carriers.

NEW TACTICS

A significant tactic developed by the Carrier Air Group was to send in a preliminary force to suppress Japanese anti-aircraft defences and fighter cover prior to the main attacking force arriving. This flight of aircraft was known as 'Ramrods'.

This was to be supplemented with an Air Operations Co-ordinator who would remain aloft during each strike to direct the aircraft to their targets thus ensuring maximum results from each strike. This role was similar to that of Master Bomber in the RAF Bomber Command, and it is a practice that is in use today with the Air Co-ordinator operating from Command and Control aircraft.

Major R Hay R.M. was appointed to the role of Air Co-ordinator, an experienced fighter pilot who would have to orchestrate the many different squadrons to their targets and photograph the results for interpretation as the strikes were in progress. He was assisted by other experienced pilots who would pass on results to him. The unit operated in a special flight of Corsairs aboard HMS *Victorious* from January 1945.

A special Photo Reconnaissance (PR) Unit was seen as a requirement for the strikes in the Far East and Lord Mountbatten insisted that such a Unit be instigated. No. 888 Sqdn., under the leadership of Lt. Cdr. R MacCaw, was given the task of becoming this PR Unit which was commissioned at RNAS Burscough on 10th June 1944 with six modified PR Hellcats.

The Squadron moved from its Lancashire base to its new home of Colombo racetrack, Ceylon for training during October 1944. It

Grumman Hellcats

was then dispersed to the carriers to act as flights operating over the targets at altitudes of 30,000 to 42,000, photographing strategic targets and also the results of the carrier strikes. This was the FAA's only specialised PR squadron throughout the war.

The first operation to use the 'Ramrod' tactic was the strike on the oil fields at Pangkalan Brandan and the port of Pangkalan Soe Soe, Western Sumatra on 4th January involving more than 100 aircraft. The mission was a complete success with the loss of only two aircraft, one due to engine failure, the other due to fuel shortage - both crews were rescued.

OPERATION MERIDIAN - SUMATRAN OIL REFINERIES

Whilst the BPF was relocating from Ceylon to Sydney (16th January - 10th February 1945), it carried out attacks on the Eastern Sumatra oil refineries at Pladjoe and Songei Gerong in Palembang, using aircraft from Illustrious, Indefatigable, Indomitable and Victorious (the 1st Carrier Sqdn.). Coded Operation Meridian I and II respectively, these two strikes were the largest British carrier operations of the war and probably the best planned and implemented.

These oil installations supplied the Japanese with the majority of their oil requirements and aviation fuel in particular so it was vital that the strikes were effective. Rehearsals were practised over Ceylon on the 13th January with each aircraft given a specific target to attack. The first strike was planned for 22nd January but this was delayed for two days due to weather conditions. Over 130 aircraft took part in the first attack, with the 'Ramrod' engaged in heavy fighting against the Japanese with about 65 aircraft possibly destroyed for the loss of nine FAA aircraft. Oil production was reduced by approximately 50% and the oil storage sites destroyed. The PR photos of the area showed the damage to the eleven known airfields and revealed six hitherto unknown enemy airfields in the area (which were later attacked).

The second strike on the 29th was expected by the Japanese and they fought valiantly against the strike force of 120 aircraft. Many aircraft were lost but the attack stopped the production at Songei Gerong and destroyed stored fuel. The result of the combined exercise was such that production was down to 25% and the stock of oil in storage was down to 20%.

Although the enemy attempted to strike at the carriers, the CAPs by Seafires prevented all but seven bombers from attacking the ships. All seven Sally's were shot down

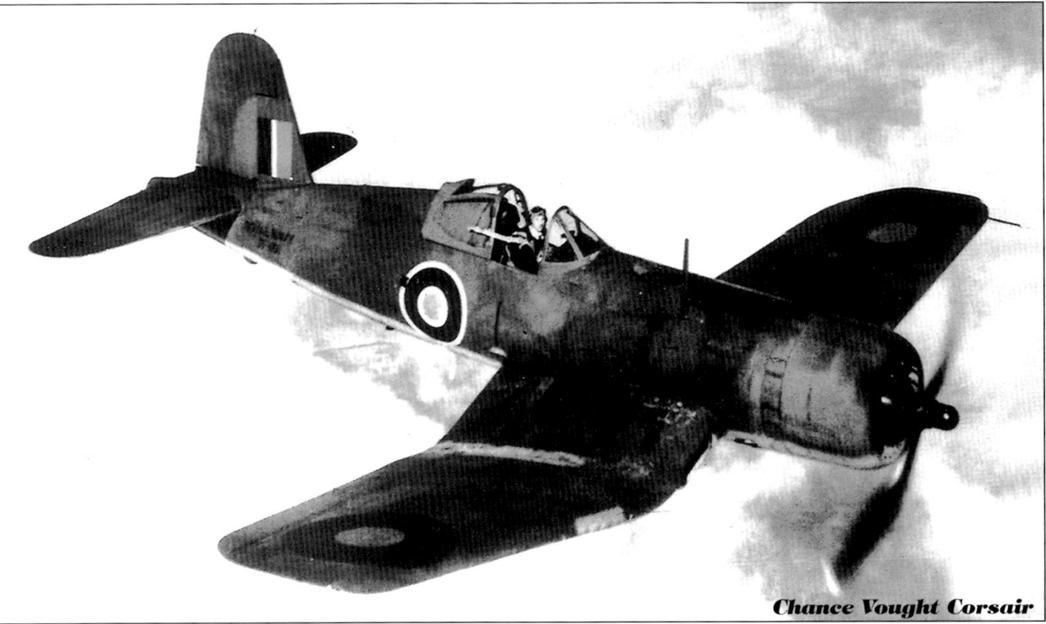

Chance Vought Corsair

bringing the total number of Japanese aircraft destroyed or damaged to 150+, for the total loss of 52 from the Task Force.

The success of the two strikes on these oil refineries was the result of meticulous planning, execution and dedication, producing possibly the best operational results of the theatre.

THE EAST INDIES FLEET

The 1st Carrier Squadron operations were not the only carrier operations going on. The escort carriers of the East Indies Fleet - HMSs *Ameer, Emperor, Empress, Hunter, Khedive, Shah* and *Stalker,* were busy supporting the 14th Army in its actions in Burma. The aircraft were involved in attacking enemy installations, shipping, harbours, supply lines and oil refineries. No. 888 Sqdn. detachments were kept busy with their PR tasks, not only with the action in Burma but also in Malaysia and Singapore in preparation for forthcoming operations for their liberation.

January 1945 saw aircraft involved in supporting the landings at Ramree and Cheduba Islands. On 28th February No. 845 Sqdn. dropped 40,000 leaflets over Malaya informing the populace of the impending assault. The Japanese attacked the East Indies Fleet on 1st March, and three enemy aircraft were shot down by Hellcat aircraft from No. 804 Sqdn. from Empress. These were the last Japanese aircraft to be destroyed during air combat by escort carrier squadrons.

OPERATION ICEBERG - OKINAWA

The US invasion of Okinawa was supported by the ships and aircraft of the 1st Carrier Squadron joining up with the US Fifth Fleet as Task Force 57. This was the largest Fleet ever assembled, with 400 warships and 800 assault craft all assembling at Ulithi Atoll.

Beginning on 26th March and continuing through to 25th May, they were the longest

Grumman Avenger

Fairey Firefly

continuous operations of the RN for over 100 years, with only one week of respite available from 23rd April to 1st May in the Philippines. The BPF's task was to prevent the Japanese replenishing their Forces in Okinawa by staging through the Sakishima Gunto islands in the Philippine Sea.

Aircraft continuously attacked the island's airfields at Ishigaki Shima and Miyako Shima, but after each attack the Japanese filled in the bomb craters and reused them. The Force would attack for two days before replenishing, then carry out another two days of attacks, a sequence that would continue throughout this operation. Damage was caused at the airfields of Kiirun, Matsuyama and Shinckiku in Formosa, but these were again repaired quickly. The Japanese maritime resources, both military and merchant, were severely decimated during these missions, the policy being that any ship in the area which was not allied was sunk.

KAMIKAZE ATTACKS

On 1st April the Japanese revealed their newest weapon - the kamikaze. Indefatigable was 'bombed' by a stricken Mitsubishi A6M3 Zeke which had been attacked by a Seafire flown by Lt. R Reynolds of No. 887 Sqdn. Fires started in the hangar, fourteen men were killed and the ship was out of action for 30 minutes. The ship's armoured deck saved it from serious damage, as did that of the other British armoured Fleet carriers that received kamikaze hits.

Five days later Illustrious was hit by a D4Y Judy kamikaze attack. The aircraft struck the deck prior to falling over the side and exploding causing damage to the ship's side and some aircraft on deck. The ship remained operational until the 15th when she was relieved by Formidable whilst repairs were carried out to her hull.

A change of plan was effected on 9th April when the BPF was diverted to attack the airfields in Formosa in place of the USN whose wooden decked ships had suffered considerable damage by kamikaze aircraft. During these missions (12th -14th April), a flight of about 50 Sonia bombers attempted to reach the Fleet but at least sixteen were destroyed or damaged and the attack failed. After 29 days of intensive operations, the BPF sailed to Layte in the Philippines for a well earned but brief respite.

During the second phase of the operation, Kamikaze aircraft were able to penetrate the fighters defending the ships on 4th and 9th of May, inflicting damage on two carriers on both days. Formidable was on the receiving end of these suicide bombers on two occasions. In the first attack on the 4th, a Zeke penetrated the deck making a two foot hole, but the resulting fires and damage put the ship out of action for only six hours. In

504 Sqdn Hellcats

the second kamikaze attack five days later, eighteen aircraft were destroyed making the deck inoperable for a mere fifteen minutes.

Indomitable was also hit by a Zeke during the attack on 4th May, with the aircraft breaking up on impact and falling over the side of the ship. Only superficial damage was sustained with little effect on operations. Then, on 9th May, two kamikaze aircraft crashed onto the flight deck of Victorious, one making a small hole, the other destroying four aircraft, but the ship remained operational whilst temporary repairs were affected.

Formidable suffered major damage during this second phase of 'Iceberg' when a Corsair, landing on deck whilst the after aircraft lift was down to hangar deck level, missed the arrestor wires and crashed into the hangar. As it hit the hangar deck its guns began firing. The ensuing fire engulfed the hangar destroying another 30 aircraft and damaging the hangar beyond repair by the ship's crew. Four days later the ship withdrew back to Sydney.

The remainder of the BPF completed operations on 25th May after achieving 5335 sorties for the loss of 203 aircraft during the 62 days in the theatre. Replacement aircraft were delivered to the armoured carriers by HMSs *Chaser, Ruler, Slinger* and *Speaker* throughout the operation. It had succeeded in its task of preventing the Japanese from resupplying its Forces in Okinawa and, whilst the BPF suffered some damage to its ships by the Kamikazes, only Illustrious needed major repairs. The American Navy, however, suffered considerable damage by these aircraft.

7TH MAY 1945 - PEACE IN EUROPE

Whilst the German armies were being defeated across Europe, the FAA was still busy supporting allied actions. The last aerial success against the Luftwaffe was the shooting down of four Bf109s by No. 882 Sqdn. on 26th March. The squadron was with HMS *Searcher* for the final operations off Norway.

The last European action for squadrons of the FAA was in this theatre and involved three of the escort carriers; HMSs *Queen, Searcher* and *Trumpeter.* On 4th/5th May, in a combined operation against the port of Kilbolton near Halstad used as a base for U-Boats, the ships' Avengers and Wildcats attacked the German vessels destroying a U-Boat and a depot ship.

In the early hours of 7th May (at 0241 hours), Field Marshall Jodl of the German High Command signed the surrender document bringing peace to Europe 335 days after the liberation of Europe began with the D-Day landings, ending 68 months of fighting.

Mitsubishi A6M3 Zeke.

THE 21ST CARRIER SQUADRON

The ships and aircraft of the East Indies Fleet were active from the beginning of the year through to the Japanese surrender in August. They were busy in the role of supporting actions amongst the islands in Borneo, Burma, Indonesia, Malaysia and Singapore providing air cover for beach assaults, attacking oil fields, installations, shipping and strategic targets, combat air patrols, spotting for the guns of the warships and reconnaissance. The carriers became the 21st Aircraft Carrier Squadron in April.

With the exception of HMS *Ameer,* the Squadron took part in the landings at Rangoon during May, providing air cover for the troops and preventing any intervention from the enemy forces in Singapore and the Adaman and Nicobar Islands. Strikes were made on their airfields and shipping. and the following month attacks were made on the installations in Sumatra which had previously been attacked during the Meridian operations, destroying about 50% of the enemy's available aircraft and airfields.

For the PR missions mapping the enemy positions, No. 888 Sqdn. was operating aboard Empress in the Bay of Bengal 100 miles away from their target areas. The sorties lasted more than six hours photographing from altitudes up to 36,000ft. Whilst carrying out one of the sorties, Lt. J Tomlinson RNVR (an American) was forced

HMS Victorious

Fairey Firefly 1

to bale out after his engine failed and it is reported that he was captured by the Japanese and was later beheaded. The Squadron's final missions were flown in June with reconnaissance over Malaya and Singapore whilst operating from Ameer, disembarking back to Ceylon on the 25th.

The final operations by the aircraft of the 21st Carrier Sqdn. were in July, with more strikes in Sumatra and the destruction of airfields in the Kra Isthmus, and supplying air cover for the Fleet of minesweepers clearing away the Japanese mines from the sea ways around the islands. The last day of operations, 26th July, ended with a kamikaze attack which sank the minesweeper HMS *Vestal* and inflicted damage on Ameer but not disabling the vessel.

At the time of the ceasefire, the aircraft from the escort carriers were responsible for the destruction of about 40% of all enemy aircraft destroyed in that arena, and had successfully kept the sea lanes open and free from enemy ships.

THE FINAL OPERATIONS

After the costly but successful attacks on Okinawa and Formosa, attention was turned on mainland Japan and the defeat of this tenacious enemy. Operations along the Japanese coastline began on 17th July, the day after the 1st Carrier Squadron sailed from Manus as Task Force 37 comprising of HMSs *Formidable, Indefatigable, Implacable* and *Victorious.* A second British Task Force, No. 112, was in company responsible for resupplying the Fleet and for its protection. It included the 30th Aircraft Carrier Squadron - HMSs *Arbiter, Chaser, Ruler, Speaker* and *Striker.*

The first days of the operations were affected by the bad weather although some strikes against airfields, shipping and railways were achieved. Resuming on 24th July, the only enemy aircraft carrier to be bombed by the FAA was the IJS *Kaiyo* in Shido Wan by Sub. Lt. Cawood in his No. 849 Sqdn. Avenger. He scored two direct hits which broke the ship's back and she was beached.

Chance Vought Corsair

The BPF concentrated its attacks in the Inland Sea between Shikoku and Honshu, continuing its attacks on airfields, dockyards and naval bases on the main islands of Japan. Attacks on Japanese warships at Harima and Maizuru on 28th and 30th resulted in thirteen warships sunk or damaged and several merchant ships ended up in the same condition.

During the final attacks of the war, the second and last VC for the FAA in the war was awarded to Lt. R 'Hammy' Grey RNVR from No. 1841 Sqdn. aboard Formidable. Lt. Grey, a Canadian, was leading a formation of eight corsairs on a 'Ramrod' mission when they came across the destroyer IJS *Amakusa* in Onagawa Wan. Leading the attack, his aircraft was hit by defensive fire from shore batteries and five

Chance Vought Corsair in the markings of Ft. Lt. R Grey VC.

other ships setting his aircraft on fire. He continued the attack, scoring a direct hit which sank the destroyer, before crashing into the bay.

The main body of the BPF withdrew from the theatre after its final operations on 10th August. During the 25 days of these final operations, the 225 aircraft had completed 2615 sorties for the loss of 39 aircraft during combat. They had destroyed or damaged at least 347 aircraft and had sunk or damaged over 350,000 tons of Japanese ships. Indefatigable was to remain on station for the remaining few days of the war.

Indefatigable then sailed with the British and American ships to accept the Japanese surrender in Tokyo Bay, but during transit the Fleet was attacked by Japanese aircraft on the 13th. The Japanese then surrendered at 0700 on 15th August but, a few hours prior to this, Seafire aircraft from Nos. 887 and 894 Sqdns. shot down eight aircraft. Unfortunately Sub. Lt. F Hockley was also shot down and was taken prisoner before being executed by three Japanese Officers. The Officers were later tried as war criminals and found guilty, two were sentenced to hang and the other was imprisoned for fifteen years.

The last action of W.W.II was on 31st August and 1st September when aircraft from HMSs *Indomitable* and *Venerable* attacked suicide boats in Hong Kong harbour. These boats were manned by Japanese who refused to accept their country's surrender. Venerable was one of four new carriers which had arrived in the Pacific too late to see action, the others being HMSs *Colossus*, *Glory* and *Vengeance*.

The surrender of the mighty Imperial Japanese Forces was signed by the Japanese Foreign Minister, Mr. Shigemitsu, on the 2nd September onboard the USS *Missouri* in Tokyo Bay, although other areas of their Forces were still to acknowledge their defeat. HMS *Glory*, stationed off Rabaul, New Britain was the scene for the signing of the Japanese surrender of their Forces in New Britain, New Guinea and the Solomon Islands by General Imamura on 6th September. At the end of the confrontation with the Japanese, there were 34 operational carriers in the theatre supported by the MONABs and repair facilities.

Supermarine Walrus

Fairey Firefly Mk 5

THE END OF THE CONFRONTATIONS

At the end of the war the FAA had 72,000 officers, men and women, 74 front line squadrons with 3700 aircraft operating from 56 bases and 59 aircraft carriers. Twenty-eight carriers were under construction with three more on order. Of these, only twenty-one would be completed, some of them for other navies.

During the war with Germany, Italy and Japan, the RN had lost five Fleet carriers and four escort carriers. Of the original carriers from 1939, only three still remained, all in reserve after sterling service during the campaigns. These were HMS *Furious* (commissioned June 1917), HMS *Argus* (Sept 1918) in reserve as an accommodation ship, and HMS *Albatross* (Sept 1938), in reserve after being struck by a torpedo.

The older aircraft types had all been replaced by faster, more agile and adaptable aircraft albeit the Swordfish served in all theatres until 28th June 1945. The men and women of the FAA, supported by the men of the RN and Merchant Navy, worked together to achieve the results and respect which they earned.

The brave aircrew recorded some truly remarkable achievements, particularly during the Atlantic and European battles using old equipment against heavy odds with many casualties. The first and last aerial combat by British Forces were by aircraft of the FAA who had proved from the earliest days that naval aircraft and their aircraft carriers are the principal weapons of war.

HMSs Vengeance & Venerable

Not seeking glory, FAA personnel do not receive the credit that is due for their part in the Battle of Britain, Battle of El Alamein, D Day, Norwegian and Mediterranean operations and especially Convoy duties. Without the participation of these Units, the RAF and British Army may have had a harder struggle and longer battles. As for the war with the Japanese, the majority of credit for the fall of the Japanese might is placed on the shoulders of the USA, but an equal amount should be given to the British servicemen (and women) without whose courage and determination it would possibly have gone on for longer, costing more lives than were already lost.

During the six years of conflict, the RN and FAA had participated in every theatre and had, once again (as in the first world conflict), demonstrated that these two military elements need each other and fit together like hand and glove. They are also depended upon by the other two services without which their task could not be completed. Unfortunately, as will be seen, once a conflict is over, the FAA bears the brunt of Government defence cuts.

New Developments in Aviation Jets and Helicopters

Supermarine Seafire F XVII

PEACE BRINGS DEMOB AND DISMANTLING OF ARMS

With the end of hostilities in the forgotten war (the Far East), the majority of the carriers returned home to the UK, some used for the repatriation of the British and Commonwealth servicemen who had been kept prisoner by the Japanese. As the lend-lease hardware was now finished with, the carriers were returned to the Americans, most of the aircraft were ditched over the side of the ships or buried at the airfields and much of the manpower was demobbed and returned to civilian life.

The requirement for a large military force was no longer needed, ships were either scrapped or sold off, squadrons were disbanded and airfields were either closed down or reduced to care and maintenance. Within a year of VJ Day, the remaining NFWs were disbanded with no fewer than 59 FLSs disappearing from the FAA compliment. Of the eighteen Carrier Air Groups which were proposed for operation in the Pacific theatre, eight were cancelled at the end of hostilities, and four of the remaining ten were disbanded.

Of the 59 carriers that were in service in 1945, the escorts were returned back to merchant use except for HMS *Pretoria Castle*. The US 'Woolworth' ships were returned to America except for HMS *Thane* which was broken up and HMS *Biter* which became the FNS *Dixmude*. HMS *Nairana* became the Dutch Navy's Karel Doorman whilst HMS *Colossus* joined the French as the Arromanches. Five of the Majestic Class were sold to other navies (HMS *Leviathan* was scrapped), the four Malta Class ships were cancelled and only two of the proposed Eagle Class were to be completed along with four (of eight) Centaur Class.

The Fleet could call on the remaining thirteen carriers (four Illustrious, two Implacable and seven Colossus Class) as the backbone of the post war Royal Navy. HMS *Pretoria Castle* was still in use as a training and trials carrier (until 1947), whilst HMS *Unicorn* and HMS *Campania* were in reserve. HMS *Venerable* would soon depart for service as the new Karel Doorman but this would be replaced by HMS *Warrior* which had been operated by the Royal Canadian Navy (RCN).

Many shore bases and airfields were closed down, 32 at home and 27 abroad, including the MONABs which had become permanent bases. The peace time FAA now had 28 establishments including Bramcote, Brawdy and Lossiemouth handed over by the RAF, and were soon to operate from the new base of Culdrose in Cornwall. Overseas only four bases were to be operated; Hal Far and Ta Kali in Malta, Changi in Hong Kong and Sembawang in Singapore.

Of the manpower, the majority of the pilots during the war were from the RNVR (94% of the officers) and most returned to their pre-war occupation. This left a shortfall in experienced pilots resulting in many observers retraining as pilots, the NCO pilots either left the service or took up commissions. The maintenance personnel were only lightly affected as many of the artificers and senior maintenance ratings were career servicemen. Combined with the reduction of operational aircraft, it was not so drastic.

POST WAR FAA EQUIPMENT AND DEVELOPMENT

Since 1943 when No. 1770 Sqdn. formed with the Fairey Firefly, the type had been in continuous service as the mainstay of FAA Fighter-Reconnaissance (FR) operations, and many more years of service were to be given by this aircraft in its upgraded series. During 1945/46, eleven squadrons were to re-equip with the Firefly. Of these, ten were replacing its stablemate the Fairey Barracuda.

The much modified clipped-wing FR.4 began entering service during 1947, to be followed by the FR.5 the following year sporting a streamlined engine cowling, four-bladed propellor and incorporating a fairing on each wing, one for fuel and the other for the radar scanner. The Mk5 was developed into various specialised roles for either day fighting (the FR.5), night fighting (NF.5) and finally anti-submarine patrols

Blackburn Firebrand

(AS.5). The final operational variants of this remarkable aircraft were the unarmed AS.6 and AS.7 which entered service with No. 814 Sqdn. during January 1951 and No. 824 Sqdn. in 1952.

The type was finally retired from front line service in 1955 although it did continue in use as a training aircraft with No. 796 Sqdn. who retired its aircraft in December 1957. This was not the end of the type in FAA use as it was to soldier on until November 1961 as a pilotless drone - the Firefly U.9 with No. 728B Sqdn. at Hal Far, Malta. The 40 aircraft converted to drones were the last of over 1700 Fireflies to see service during eighteen years which saw the type in action during W.W.II in Korea and Malaya.

THE SEAFIRE

Another type to see action in the same theatres as the Firefly was the Seafire, also substantially modified to continue in service. The first of these was the navalised MkXVII (developed from the FAA's MkXV) which entered service in September 1945 with No. 883 Sqdn. Two versions were built; the Fighter (F.XVII) with a fuel tank in the rear fuselage to extend its range, and the fighter reconnaissance (FR.XVII) which had four cameras mounted in the same space.

Three more derivatives were to be developed for the FAA. First was the Mk45 with various modifications, the most significant being the fixed-wings, four 20mm guns and initially the Griffon 61 with a five-bladed propellor. A Seafire Mk45 reached a speed of Mach 0.88 whilst carrying out diving trials, which is claimed to be the fastest speed attained by a Seafire. Although not used as a front line aircraft, trials were carried out on board HMS *Pretoria Castle* in 1946, and the reliability of the new strengthened undercarriage resulted in only two failures during 239 landings.

Next came the Mk46 which came as both a fighter and fighter reconnaissance version fitted with an oblique camera behind the pilot. As with the Mk45 the type was initially fitted with the Griffon 61 engine and five-bladed propellor, but eventually both the Mk45 and Mk46 were to receive the more powerful 2,375-h.p. Griffon 85 fitted with contra rotating propellors. Neither type were operated by front line squadrons but used by training units.

The final Seafire was the Mk47, entering service with No. 804 Sqdn. during February 1948, and like the two previous models it was also supplied as both FR and fighter versions. These Seafires saw action in Malaya and Korea whilst serving aboard HMS *Triumph* with No. 800 Sqdn. Seafires were finally retired from service when the last unit operating the type, No. 764 Sqdn. at Yeovilton, stood down their Seafire 17s on 23rd November 1954 after twelve years of sterling service for the FAA.

THE FIREBRAND

The first Blackburn Firebrand was flown as far back as February 1942 in answer to an Admiralty requirement from 1939 for a four gun single-seat monoplane fighter. The early marks of the aircraft were superseded even before they were delivered thus the 48 production aircraft did not see combat service. The type was eventually to see front line service when No. 813 Sqdn. was commissioned at Ford on 1st September 1945 with Firebrand TF.IV (torpedo strike fighter), the day before world peace was declared. Only two FLSs operated this aircraft; No. 813 Sqdn. both TF.IV and TF.5, and No. 827 Sqdn. with the TF.5.

The original design requirement of a fighter was changed to a torpedo fighter after the first twelve F.1s had been produced, becoming the first single-seat aircraft designed to deliver torpedoes since the Blackburn Dart of 1921. These sturdy aircraft were able to carry two 2,000lb bombs or sixteen 3' rocket projectiles beneath the wings, a 1,850lb 18' torpedo beneath its fuselage and had four fixed 20mm cannons. They remained in service for eight years until replaced by the Westland Wyvern.

THE LAST PISTON FIGHTERS

The first 'new' aircraft types to enter service with the FAA after the war were still developments of aircraft originally designed for use by the RAF. The Sea Mosquito TR33 was the first twin-engined carrier borne aircraft ordered. It became the first British twin-engined type to land aboard an aircraft carrier when Lt. Cdr. Eric 'Winkle' Brown RNVR landed a modified Mosquito VI aboard

De Havilland Sea Mosquito

HMS *Indefatigable* on 25th March 1944. This resulted in the production of the TR33 with folding wings, improved undercarriage, deck hook and nose radar plus a larger diameter four-bladed propellor to increase the thrust from the Merlin engine. No. 811 Sqdn. received the type during 1946.

Another de Havilland type designed for the RAF was to become the FAA's first twin-engined single-seat fighter. The Sea Hornet F.20 entered service in July 1947 with both No. 703 Sqdn. and the only FLS, No. 801 Sqdn. The type was also developed into a two-seat Night Fighter operating with No. 809 Sqdn. and a Photo-reconnaissance version PR.22 used by No. 801 Sqdn. alongside its F.20s. The PR model was equipped with both day and night cameras, and the two fighter models could carry bombs, mines or rocket projectiles to supplement its four 20mm cannons.

The last piston-engined aircraft to be received in service was the Hawker Sea Fury, a naval variant of the Tempest II/Fury Light Fighter. Three prototypes were constructed, the first flying on 21st February 1945. The first deck trials had been carried out during October 1945 when this prototype operated from HMS *Ocean.* The aircraft was a redesigned Fury I without folding wings. The production aircraft would have power folding wings, the first aircraft in the service so fitted.

Further trials on board HMS *Victorious* during 1946 showed the need to modify the

De Havilland Sea Hornet

Hawker Sea Fury

deck hook prior to the aircraft being received in service, thus delaying the first squadron deliveries. The first production F.MkX aircraft entered service with No. 778 Sqdn., the Service and Carrier Trials Unit based at RNAS Ford, during February 1947. The first front line unit was from the RCN, No. 803 Sqdn. during August 1947 to be followed by the FAA's own No. 807 Sqdn. on 29th September.

Following the normal FAA tradition, all aircraft can do more than originally designed for, and the F.MkX fighter was soon modified as a fighter bomber (the FB.11) with provision for external stores, namely two 1,000lb bombs, depth charges, rocket projectiles and fuel or napalm drop tanks. The Sea Fury was the standard fighter bomber in the FAA's inventory and proved to be instrumental in supporting the United Nations' operations in Korea, as the mount of six fighter squadrons.

THE FAA's 'OWN' PISTON-ENGINED AIRCRAFT

Only one piston-engined aircraft, not previously designed for use by the RAF, was to see regular service aboard aircraft carriers. This was the Shorts Sturgeon, initially ordered in October 1943 as a long-range twin-engined strike torpedo-reconnassiance-bomber for the task of attacking the Japanese. It was the first twin-engined aircraft specifically designed for use from the decks of aircraft carriers and would have a range of over 1,000 miles with an endurance of nearly 6hrs 30mins at a cruising speed of 200 Knots. Before any of the prototypes were completed, it was redesignated as a reconnaissance-bomber, therefore the need for carrying a torpedo was deemed unnecessary.

The first flight took place as late as June 1946. As it had not flown before the war ended, it was again redesignated as a target tug capable of carrier operations, having been replaced by the Sea Mosquito in the role of long-range bomber. Successful trials were completed aboard HMS *Victorious*

Shorts Sturgeon

before it entered service with No. 771 Fleet Requirement Sqdn. at RNAS Ford in September 1950, used mainly for high speed gunnery practice and air-to-air firings.

At the time of the steam catapult trials aboard HMS *Perseus* during July 1951, the aircraft was the largest carrier aircraft in the FAA inventory and so was an active participant in the trials with an aircraft from No. 703 Sqdn. embarked. The third squadron to use the type was the Hal Far based No. 728 Sqdn. who operated the type from 1951 until its retirement in October 1958.

Development in aircraft types had been rapid during the war with piston-engine development reaching its pinnacle with the 2,480-h.p. Bristol Centaurus Mk18 and Rolls Royce Griffon Mk85 producing 2,375-h.p. Gas Turbine engines were now the engines being developed to power the aircraft of the 50's and beyond.

THE HELICOPTER AND ITS FUTURE

As has already been mentioned, the FAA was the first military establishment to realise that helicopters were going to play an important part in aviation of the future. Not to be deterred by the poor results from trials held during the war, the FAA took delivery of the Sikorsky VS-316 R-4 Hoverfly I. These were encompassed into No. 771 Sqdn. as a helicopter flight based at Portland, thus becoming the world's first helicopter squadron upon receiving the helicopter in February 1945. At the end of the year, the Hoverfly I was joined by an improved version, the Hoverfly II.

The helicopters and those allocated to RNAS Gosport Station Flight were tasked with experimenting, carrying out trials and developments and proving the operational ability and roles of the fledgling machines. Other trials were performed including hydrographic surveying, gunnery spotting and torpedo operations, most of which were successful in proving the 'worth' of these new machines.

Some of the trials included operations from the decks of warships. Lt. A Bristow landed aboard the escort vessel HMS *Helmsdale* in September 1946 for the first landing of a helicopter on a warship at sea, and Lt. K Reed landed his R-4 onto the forecastle of HMS *Vanguard* off Portland on 1st February 1947 for the first landing of a helicopter onto a battleship. He later demonstrated the technique to the Royal Family when landing on the ship two days later as it sailed for South Africa - this after taking off in a blizzard.

Sikorsky Hoverfly

As No. 771 Sqdn. was a busy composite Fleet Requirements Unit (FRU), it was realised that a full squadron should be formed to carry out the demanding task of evaluating and operating helicopters within the Fleet. This encouraged the reforming of No. 705 Sqdn. as the Helicopter FRU responsible for aircrew and maintenance staff, developing operating techniques, helicopter trials and evaluations. The squadron commissioned at HMS Siskin Gosport on 7th May 1947 operating the FAA's R-4 helicopters.

THE FIRST CARRIER 'JET' LANDINGS

The Fleet Air Arm has the distinction of being the first service in the world to carry out trials with jet powered aircraft on board an aircraft carrier. Winkle Brown was again given the honour, taking a converted De Havilland Vampire I prototype (known as a Sea Vampire 10) on board HMS *Ocean* on 5th December 1945.

The aircraft was modified for these trials by having a deck hook fitted, the oleos were lengthened and the flaps were increased by 40%. Winkle carried out assorted landing approaches at RAE Farnborough and at RNAS Ford prior to his 'real' landing on board the ship. However, the flaps created a problem when they were damaged by the ship's arrestor wires, resulting in their having to be remodified to allow the trials to continue.

The Sea Vampire successfully launched and recovered fifteen times, thus proving the feasibility of operating jet types from carriers. What was determined by the trials was that the aircraft's limited endurance would not be sufficient for operating at sea and that the turbojet had a slow response to its controls, making it suspect to accelerating from the deck in the event of a 'go round' if the aircraft missed the wire.

These trials, combined with the delay of the arrival of the Supermarine Attacker, resulted in the ordering of the Sea Vampire F.Mk20 for advanced training purposes with no intention of it reaching operational squadron status. The aircraft were modified FB5s fitted with enlarged dive brakes and flaps, clipped-wings, 'A' type deck hook, 'long travel' oleos and fuselage strengthening. Three prototypes and

DH Sea Vampire

DH Sea Vampire F20

eighteen production F.Mk20s were ordered for use by No. 702 Sqdn., the Naval Jet Evaluation and Trials Unit based at Culdrose, and No. 787 Sqdn., the Naval Air Fighting Development Unit (NAFDU) at West Raynham.

The first aircraft were received in February 1949 by No. 787 Sqdn. then in April by No. 702 Sqdn., and both units were tasked with proving trials for the operation of jet aircraft. Carrier trials were carried out on board HMS *Implacable* during September and October, with more trials taking place on board HMS *Theseus* during May and June 1950. The aircraft were involved in two exercises. The first 'Exercise Sunrise' saw two aircraft from No. 702 Sqdn. complete over 200 successful landings and launches, whilst the second involved taking part in interception flights in the North Atlantic and Arctic operating areas when HMS *Vengeance* provided the deck.

THE RNVR REFORMED

With the running down of the Forces after the war, when everlasting peace was seen to be over the horizon, the wartime RNVR was disbanded and its members either took on full-time commissions or returned to civilian life. By 1947 however it was apparent to both Europe and the Americans that the Russians were not content and were intending to spread their communistic policies across as much of the world as they could.

Fortunately the Government accepted that the British Forces would not be strong enough to counter this threat without some form of backup, so the RNVR was re-established under the command of Captain R Armour RN. The volunteers who joined would be weekend airmen and they would be required to take part in an annual operational training period of two weeks during the summer at an operational base or on board a carrier.

The first unit to commission was No. 1831 Sqdn. at Stretton on 1st June 1947 equipped with Seafires as a fighter squadron. Two more fighter squadrons were to be established; No. 1832 Sqdn. at Culham on 1st July and No. 1833 Sqdn. at Bramcote on 15th August, both equipped with Seafires. The final founding squadron was also formed on 15th August as a fighter anti-submarine unit equipped with Seafires and Fireflies. This unit, No. 1830 Sqdn. based at Abbotsinch, would eventually relinquish its Sea Furies and become a dedicated anti-submarine unit.

DH Sea Vampire

The first annual camp held aboard a carrier was when No. 1832 Sqdn. embarked their Seafires on HMS *Implacable* on 9th July 1949. Seven years later, Cdr. R 'Mac' Rutherford landed his Sea Hawk on HMS *Bulwark* for the first RNVR jet aircraft carrier landing. The Squadron took part in the RNVR's first NATO exercise at Hal Far during 1952 where they proved to be an efficient unit resulting in Mac earning his promotion to Commander, presented to him by Admiral Lord Louis Mountbatten of Burma. Not all the firsts go to this unit - No. 1831 Sqdn. at Stretton began equipping with Attacker FB2s on 14th May 1955, the first RNVR unit with jet aircraft.

THE COMING OF THE 'JET AGE'

Even though piston-engine types were still entering front line service, the development of gas turbine engines (more colloquially referred to as jets) meant the inevitable obsolescence of

Supermarine Attacker

the types and the arrival of the jet powered types. The Admiralty ordered their first of these, the Supermarine Attacker, a development of the Spiteful aircraft powered by a Rolls Royce Nene turbojet, on 7th July 1945 when 24 pre-production aircraft were approved.

DH Tiger Moth

Due to problems with the Spiteful's flying characteristics, the building of the Attacker was suspended in February 1946. Eventually the first prototype flew on 27th July 1946 as a non-naval variant, followed by the first navalised aircraft on 17th June 1947 which began sea trials on board HMS *Illustrious* four months after this first flight. The contract for the Navy's first operational jet fighters was placed in September 1948, a significant step in FAA aviation.

The initial test flying of the aircraft was carried out by Lt. Cdr. Mike Lithgow RN. Rtd., who was now Supermarine's chief test pilot. Flying the prototype Attacker, he achieved a speed of 564.882 mph on 26th February 1948 to win the International 100km Closed Circuit Record. Two years later the aircraft, flown by Lithgow, won the SBAC Challenge Cup. This was the second year in succession that a naval prototype aircraft type had won this coveted trophy (it was previously won by the Hawker P1040 Sea Hawk prototype).

The production Attacker fighter aircraft first flew on 5th May 1950. It had folding wings, four 20mm cannons in the wings, and the fighter bomber variant could carry rocket projectiles or 1,000lb bombs below the wings. They were also fitted with Martin Baker ejection seats as standard, and Lt. P McDermott became the first pilot to use an ejector seat in an operational aircraft when he ejected from his No. 787 Sqdn. Attacker on 21st March 1951.

The first aircraft were delivered to the NAFDU No. 787 Sqdn. at RAF West Raynham during January 1951. The squadron was part of the Central Fighter Establishment and operated alongside its equivalent RAF development units. The first operational FAA jet fighter squadron was commissioned at RNAS Ford on 22nd August 1951 with No. 800 Sqdn. having eight Attacker F1s. The squadron embarked on the navy's newest carrier, HMS *Eagle*, on 4th March 1952 to begin its work with the ship's air group.

AIRCREW GRADING FLIGHT

A need to evaluate the flying potential of aircrew candidates was addressed in 1949 by using two Tiger Moth aircraft. These were RN aircraft operated and serviced by Western Airways at Plymouth's Roborough airport. The candidates would be at the British Royal Naval College (BRNC) at Dartmouth and would then go to Plymouth for grading.

Eventually, however, these two aircraft could not cope with the amount of flying required for the task. HMS *Thunderer* at nearby Manadon engineering college also had two aircraft which were utilised, as were aircraft owned by the Plymouth and District Aero Club. This was still not satisfactory so a further seven Tiger Moths were delivered during 1950. The contract with Western Airways was taken over by Airworks during 1960.

Supermarine Attacker

Hawker Sea Hawk

HAWKER JET AIRCRAFT ORDERED

The Admiralty was eager to follow in the RAF's support for jet propelled aircraft and following on from the Attacker order, they ordered three prototypes of the Hawker P1040 (to become Sea Hawk) interceptor in February 1946. The first prototype, which was purely a development aircraft, flew on 2nd September 1947, followed a year later by the first true naval prototype complete with deck hook, catapult spools, folding wings and four 20mm cannons. The development aircraft won the SBAC Challenge Cup with a speed of 510 mph on 1st August 1949.

The Navy ordered 151 of these lightweight fighters, the first production aircraft taking to the air on 14th November 1951. They entered service with the Service Trials Unit No. 703 Sqdn. at Ford the following September, and No. 806 Sqdn. became the first operational squadron commissioning at RNAS Brawdy with eight F.Mk1 Sea Hawks on 2nd March 1953. The aircraft set a trend in RN carrier-borne aircraft being equipped with tricycle undercarriages. With the exception of the Wyvern and Sea Harrier, all front line aircraft following on would also have tricycle undercarriages.

DH Vampire landing onboard HMS Warrior with a rubber deck

The aircraft was developed into a fighter bomber FB3 and its final mark was that of fighter ground attack FGA 6. A total of 434 Sea Hawks were delivered to thirteen front line squadrons, eight training squadrons and one RNVR squadron, making it the largest quantity of jet fighter aircraft produced for the FAA. After taking part in the Suez crisis of 1956, it was finally retired from FLS when No. 806 Sqdn. relinquished its final aircraft in December 1960. However it did continue as the Indian Navy's front line fighter until replaced by the Sea Harrier in 1983.

NEW AS STRIKE AIRCRAFT

The Fairey Gannet, an anti-submarine strike aircraft, was ordered on 1st August 1946, powered by an Armstrong Siddeley Double Mamba turbo-prop engine. This engine consisted of two Mamba engines operating through a single common gearbox driving two contra-rotating propellors, either of which could be shut down in flight increasing the aircraft flight duration. This was an idea proposed before the war specifically for carrier borne aircraft by Faireys and resulted in the Fairey Prince double engine. However, the idea was not developed due to the urgent work developing existing engines.

The Gannet was the first British naval aircraft designed to combine search and strike missions, incorporating a retractable radar scanner (the world's first), and to carry its weapon load internally except for rocket projectiles. When the prototype flew for the first time on 19th September 1949, it became the world's first aircraft to fly with a double turbine-propellor arrangement. This was followed by recording the first carrier deck landing and take-off of a turbo-prop aircraft when, on 19th June 1950, Lt. Cdr. G Callingham landed aboard HMS *Illustrious.*

JET AIRCRAFT DEVELOPMENT CARRIER TRIALS

A novel approach to jet operations onboard aircraft carriers was the feasibility of landing on rubber decks with undercarriage-less aircraft. For these trials three Vampire aircraft were given strengthened undersides - two F.Mk20s and an F.Mk1 which were designated Sea Vampire F.Mk21s. The initial trials flown by Winkle Brown were held at Farnborough, with the first attempt at landing on the rubber deck on 29th December 1947 coming to grief, seriously damaging the aircraft. Winkle was approaching in the former F.Mk1 but the approach speed dropped too much and, upon opening the throttle, the engine response was not good enough to prevent the aircraft hitting the forward edge of the deck and bouncing off.

The trials restarted during March 1948 and Winkle successfully landed 40 times on Farnborough's deck - next was to try it on an actual carrier deck at sea. For these trials, HMS *Warrior* was fitted out with a flexible deck in Portsmouth dockyard during the summer of 1948. The ship had been serving with the RCN for two years before returning to Portsmouth and, after the fitting of the new decking, she commissioned in the RN and immediately began 'Flexideck' trials.

The first landing on her deck was successfully achieved by Winkle on 3rd November 1948 but the trials were to prove that the handling of aircraft without undercarriages was not satisfactory, creating many operational problems on the deck. As far as ships were concerned, the trials were terminated although they did continue at Farnborough as late as 1953.

Winkle Brown, who rose to the rank of Captain, was the foremost test pilot in the Fleet Air Arm. His achievements can be placed on a parity of Wing Commander Samson some thirty years earlier. Both these intrepid aviators were paramount in developing, testing and proving ideas to better increase the safety and role of aviation in naval operations.

THE DRAGONFLY ARRIVES

In December of 1946, the Westland Aircraft Company at Yeovil arranged with Sikorsky in the USA to build their latest helicopter, the S51, under licence. The first S51s were supplied by Sikorsky and one of these was evaluated by No. 705 Sqdn. during 1948 and 1949, including the first sea trials aboard HMS *Vengeance.*

The S51 Dragonfly as it was to be known, was a much improved helicopter after the Hoverflies, and delivery of the HR.Mk1 helicopter commenced on 13th January 1950. The main role of the helicopter was deemed to be that of search and rescue (SAR), with the aim of each coastal air station and each aircraft carrier having helicopters for SAR, replacing the last amphibian in FAA service, the Supermarine Sea Otter, in this role. Its first 'operational' SAR mission was during September 1951 when the submarine HMS *Affray* was in difficulties and Dragonflies were sent to assist in the rescue of its crew, although unfortunately no crew were saved from the stricken submarine.

More trials were being carried out to prove helicopter operations from smaller ships, beginning in 1951 in RFA *Fort Duequesne*. The results were to suggest that this was a feasible operation and it was put forward

Fairey Gannet

Westland Dragonfly

that larger warships and supply ships be fitted with an operating deck.

The ocean survey ship HMS *Vidal* was the first ship to have limited helicopter facilities fitted to operate a Hiller HTE-2 helicopter specially fitted with floats. It began operating the type from August 1954, and twenty Hillers were supplied to No. 705 Sqdn. in May 1953 under the Mutual Defence Assistance Programme (MDAP) for training helicopter pilots.

The first carrier to receive a Dragonfly for its SAR flight was HMS *Indomitable* in January 1951. The helicopter was soon to replace the destroyer 'plane guard' which kept station behind the ship during launches and recoveries in case an aircraft should ditch in the sea. Once the S51s were attached to each carrier, it was seen that it would be better for it to hover alongside the ship during these operations, thus providing a more expedient method of rescue in the eventuality of a ditching. This is a practice still used today on conventional carriers.

SWEPT-WING AIRCRAFT

Swept-wing aircraft evaluation was proceeding rapidly across the Atlantic, so in 1946 the Air Staff embarked on a policy of redressing the balance. One of the aircraft used for these evaluations was a swept-wing variant of the Attacker known as the Supermarine Type 510, which was the first British jet aircraft with both swept-wings and tail surfaces. The aircraft's first flight was on 29th December 1948 and during its trials it reached speeds up to a maximum of Mach 0.93.

The aircraft was eventually to receive the name Swift and was proposed as a naval swept-wing fighter after being fitted with deck hook and Rocket Assisted Take-Off Gear (RATOG) in preparation for sea trials. The aircraft, flown by Lt. J Elliot, embarked on HMS *Illustrious* on 8th November 1950, thus achieving the status as the first swept-wing aircraft to operate from an aircraft carrier. Although the trials were a success and fifteen launches were achieved, the aircraft was not to enter the FAA. Neither was the swept-wing development of the Hawker Sea Hawk, the P1052; this aircraft was to carry out trials on HMS *Eagle* during May 1952.

It had been proposed as early as 1945 for Gloster Meteors to be modified for trials on board HMS *Pretoria Castle* (these were eventually carried out by the Sea Vampires). Meteors were not to go on board a carrier until 1950 when two specially modified RAE Meteor IIIs from Boscombe Down carried out 32 landings on HMS *Implacable*. It was found that the Meteors, fitted with strengthened undercarriages and V-frame arrestor hooks, had the best deck landing characteristics of any type previously landed on an aircraft carrier, but no decision was made to develop a navalised Meteor.

Hiller HTE-2

Gloster Meteor III

The Korean War

THE POTSDAM PROCLAMATION

The Potsdam Proclamation on 26th July 1945 reaffirmed the promise made by the Allies in December 1943 to grant Korea freedom from the Japanese. With the Japanese surrender, the Allies agreed that the Russians would liberate the north of the country whilst the Americans the south, the 38th Parallel being the dividing line for the operation. The Russians took this dividing line as their boundary and refused to allow the country to be rejoined as one.

After two years of failed negotiations, the United Nations organised nationwide elections which established an independent government and the South was declared a Republic (ROK) on 15th August 1947. The Russians however refused to either accept the Government or the UN mandate on the country, setting up another Government in the north. Three years later the North Korean Army invaded the Republic, advancing on the capital Seoul on 27th June.

The UN Security Council immediately sat in an emergency session and declared North Korea's actions as illegal, calling for an immediate end to the hostilities and withdrawal of its Forces. The Americans took action against the North Koreans two days later, supplying air support for the South and blockading the northern coastline.

The RN was immediately made available to the UN. The Eastern Fleet (two cruisers, two destroyers and three frigates) accompanying HMS *Triumph* was soon in the area, arriving on 30th June 1950, joining forces with the US Fleet led by USS *Valley Forge* operating in the Yellow Sea. The combined task force (TF77) could call on 60 strike aircraft (Seafires, Fireflies, Corsairs, Panthers and Skyraiders).

THE FAA's KOREAN OPERATIONS

The air operations began at 0545 on the 3rd July when Triumph's aircraft carried out the first attack. Seafire Mk47s of No. 800 Sqdn. and Firefly FR1s of No. 827 Sqdn. attacked bridges, railways and Haeju airfield 25 miles north of the 38th Parallel and 75 miles north of Seoul. The mission was a success with all aircraft returning safely albeit some with flak damage. The operations continued for two days before the ships withdrew to replenish.

Supermarine Seafire 47s

The next major strikes were carried out on the 18th/19th July, when attacks by the strike aircraft on airfields at Onjong-ni, Pyongyang and Yonpo resulted in a total of 45 enemy aircraft either destroyed or damaged. Other targets included oil refineries, bridges, railways and factories around Hamhung, Hungham, Numpyong and Wonsan.

Unfortunately the serviceability, range and weapon capability of the British aircraft was restrictive on the strike role required of the two squadrons, and it was decided that they would be more suited to CAP and anti-submarine patrols (ASP) whilst allowing the US strike aircraft to push forward with the attack missions.

Supermarine Seafire 47

Fairey Fireflies on HMS Triumph

The final recovery of the 19th July was the landing of the ship's SAR Sea Otter which had completed the last rescue mission by this, the last biplane type in front line service. The aircraft, flown by Lt. P Cane with Aircrewman G O'Nion, had been sent to rescue a downed USN Corsair pilot (Lt. W Muncie). The sea state was outside the aircraft's operating limits and although visibility was poor, the aircraft alighted on the sea. After recovering Muncie, the aircraft was able to take off and return to Triumph.

OPERATION CHROMITE

During late August 1950, intelligence reported that the Chinese Communist Forces were being assembled on the Korean borders, with the obvious intention of supporting the North Koreans. In an attempt to bring the war to a quick end, operation 'Chromite' was planned - a US Marine Corps (USMC) assault on Inchon and the liberation of Seoul. The British Eastern Fleet became TF91 with the role of blockade and covering Force.

Supermarine Sea Otter

The first stages commenced on 13th September, with the main offensive beginning two days later. There was very little resistance and little action although the air operations continued until the arrival of land-based aircraft on the 19th. The operation was a success, liberating Seoul and pushing the communist forces north, returning the land south of the 38th Parallel back to the ROK.

Triumph withdrew from the theatre after this operation. Of her 24 strike aircraft, less than half were serviceable mainly due to the lack of spares for these obsolete aircraft types. During this period of operation, the ship lost only one aircraft due to enemy action although the Firefly flown by Lt. Andrews made it back to the ship. One Seafire was also shot down by a USAF B29 but the pilot, Commissioned Pilot Mr. White, was rescued.

The American aircrews were having trouble identifying the FAA aircraft so, after the Seafire had been erroneously shot down, it was decided that FAA aircraft were to wear black and white stripes similar to the D Day invasion stripes. It was also decided that the US carriers would operate off the west coast in the Sea of Japan, and the Commonwealth Forces would patrol the eastern coast in the Korean Bay area of the Yellow Sea.

SUPPORT FACILITIES

Bases in Japan became the 'home' for the UN Forces with the carriers operating from Sasebo, Kure and Iwakuni. Aircraft support was at the nearby air base at Iwakuni where an Air Engineering Department (AED) had been established as an aircraft repair and support facility.

The main support facility was established at Sembawang in Singapore, from the AED previously on board HMS *Unicorn*. The week prior to the invasion of the Republic, the ship disembarked its aircraft support facilities to the new base of HMS Simbang before returning to the UK and decommissioning.

The invasion brought a new lease of life for Unicorn. She was employed as support ship delivering replacement aircraft and returning damaged aircraft to the repair facilities, as well as being used as a 'spare' deck for deck landing practice and for the transportation of ground forces to and from the area. An AED was re-established on the ship tasked with minor repairs, the transfer of aircraft and supplying personnel for a Forward Working Party - a team of NCOs and ratings who operated from air bases in Korea tasked with salvage and minor repairs of aircraft that would make emergency landings. HMS *Unicorn* was joined by HMS *Warrior* for the ferry run from the UK to Singapore and on to Sasebo.

THE SEA FURY ARRIVES FOR ACTION

HMS *Triumph* was replaced by HMS *Theseus* which arrived at Sasebo on 5th October 1950 with an air compliment of Sea Fury FB11s and Firefly AS5s. She began her operations in the Yellow Sea four days later attacking shore installations, boats, ports and bridges, enemy defences and lines of communication, achieving a good success rate.

During one of the sorties on 10th October, Lt. S Leonard was shot down in his Sea Fury 90 miles behind enemy lines, suffering a broken arm and two broken legs trapping him in the aircraft. Aircraft from No. 807 Sqdn. patrolled over the area whilst waiting the arrival of the rescue Sikorsky H-5 from the 3rd Air Rescue Squadron USAF. On arrival at the scene the pilot and the doctor extricated Leonard whilst keeping the enemy at bay with their machine guns. This was the longest rescue mission by a helicopter at that time, a distance of 125 miles from its base at Pusan near Seoul.

Further operations were carried out around Chinnampo and Pyongyang, the aim being to secure the area and develop Chinnampo as a port for the UN ships. Whilst in the area continuing missions along the coast supporting the advancing UN Forces, Theseus embarked a US Navy S-51 helicopter for mine spotting within the estuary, the first time a helicopter had carried out operations from the deck of a British aircraft carrier.

Fairey Firefly crash on HMS Triumph's deck

ENTER THE CHINESE

The success at Inchon resulted in the US Forces hoping to completely defeat the North Koreans and thus unite the country under President Rhee. President Truman had given General MacArthur the go ahead to advance into North Korea. However, neither the UN nor the US President were aware that advancing beyond the 38th Parallel was the signal the Chinese had laid down as the criteria for joining in the war on the side of the North Koreans.

The war was to see a dramatic change at the end of November when the Chinese Army joined the North Koreans on 25th November 1950, bringing with them a strong force of men, materials, military hardware and the new Russian Mig 15 jet fighter.

FAA TASKED WITH PR MISSIONS

Theseus was operating in the Yellow Sea flying supportive strikes against the communist forces until Boxing day. The ship's Sea Furies and Fireflies also carried out strike sorties, CAP operations and ASPs in search of two North Korean submarines believed to be in the Yellow Sea.

After a short break at Kure the ship was back in operation and the Fireflies were tasked with flying armed reconnaissance missions at 1500ft or less, whilst aircraft from the US 5th Air Force provided air cover. The quality of the photos from these

Hawker Sea Fury FB II

HMS Theseus

missions enabled accurate strike missions to be carried out against targets to prevent the enemy from re-supplying its front line. The aircraft were vectored to their targets by USAF forward air controllers 'Mosquitos', similar to the Air Co-ordinator during the Pacific campaign.

The ship had been equipped with a Sea Otter Flight for the role of SAR, but this was replaced by a Sikorsky S-51 of the US Navy when the Sea Otter was disembarked for an engine change. The S-51 embarked on the 3rd April 1951, the first time a British aircraft carrier had been equipped with a helicopter for SAR duties. Nine days later it was to carry out the first SAR mission from the deck of a British carrier, successfully rescuing Commissioned Pilot F Bailey after he ditched his Firefly 40 miles from the ship.

The last operation for HMS *Theseus* began on 9th April when she combined with the USS *Bataan* in the Sea of Japan continuing with the reconnaissance, anti-submarine, strike and bombardment missions. On completion of her final operation, the ship sailed for home on 25th April after nearly 3500 operational sorties, mostly in winter weather conditions. She was relieved by HMS *Glory* who arrived at Sasebo on 23rd April with Sea Fury FB11's and Firefly AS 5's plus a SAR S-51 flight on loan from the US Navy. She began her first patrol on the 27th April and then joined USS *Bataan* on 2nd May for continued joint operations.

Operation 'Strangle' was the UN counter-offensive to cut off the enemy's front line from the rest of North Korea. All lines of communication were to be destroyed by a combined air assault attacking roads, railways, bridges and tunnels. Much of the CAS and attacks on enemy troops and store depots were carried out acting on information supplied by 'Leopard' groups - non-communist guerilla groups operating behind enemy lines. The periods of operations lasted nine days - two four day periods of action separated by one day replenishing.

Fairey Firefly Mk 4

In June the British 'Mosquito' aircraft, the Auster AOP.6's of No. 1913 Light Liaison Flight, were delivered to the theatre by HMS *Unicorn*, followed in October by No. 1903 Independent Air Observation Post Flight. Although RAF units, they were manned by Army personnel and were the only two British aviation units to operate from Korean soil.

THE END OF HOSTILITIES - OH REALLY!

A ceasefire was proposed on 23rd June 1951 by the Soviet UN Ambassador with talks being held at Kaesong. It eventually appeared that it was a delaying tactic by the communists to regroup and recover from the mauling received by the UN Forces. Talks were in progress throughout July and into August breaking down late in the second month. As a show of force for the communists at the peace talks, the combined air groups from HMS *Glory* and USS *Sicily* provided CAP and bombardment spotting for operations in the Han Estuary, whilst the UN Forces resumed actions against the now regrouped communist forces before the end of August.

THE SECOND KOREAN WAR ENTER THE ROYAL AUSTRALIAN FAA

HMAS *Sydney* with three squadrons embarked, two with Sea Furies and one with Firefly AS5 and 6s, relieved HMS *Glory* (who was to refit in Sydney) for an agreed three-month period beginning on 30th September. The air group's missions were a continuation of her predecessors, CAP, ASP, CAS and strike missions, gunfire spotting and supporting the UN guerilla groups.

The historic first RAN FAA mission was by Lt. Cdr. M Fell (RN) who launched from the ship on 5th October, on an operational mission from a commonwealth aircraft carrier. Five days later, the air group was involved in a series of strikes and spotting of naval bombardments during an intense period of operations in the Kojo area.

November 1951 saw the beginning of the next round of peace talks at Panmunjoy, a village in no-man's land. The protracted ceasefire began on the first day of the talks (12th) and initially only reconnaissance and defensive operational sorties were flown. Again the communists regrouped, stalling over the repatriation of POWs, and the talks eventually broke down in October 1952, after nearly twelve months. This time, however, the UN Forces had resumed operational missions early into the talks when it was obvious the communists were once again regrouping.

During this period, Sydney's air group were busy along the west coast of North Korea, attacking railways, trains and bridges, supplying CAS for the ground troops and Leopard operations, attacking shipping and junks and carrying out reconnaissance and ASP missions. The ship was tasked to operate on the east coast during Operation Athenaeum, the attack on the shore batteries at Hungnam. The operation began on 20th November and, during the two days of action, the air group was responsible for CAP and strike missions in a successful operation which rendered the town out of action and of no use to the enemy.

After a short spell escorting troop convoys, Sydney returned to the normal patrol areas with the added task of providing defence for the UN 'friendly islands' off the Korean west coast, prior to a rest at Kure. After the break, the ship was back on patrol around the islands until she left the theatre on 27th January 1952 relieved by HMS *Glory* following her refit in Sydney.

The ship recommenced operations on 7th February. The rotation of operations between RN and US carriers was proving to be an effective way of ensuring the enemy was continuously harassed, preventing them from building up a strong force along the west coast of the country. Embarked aboard Glory was the FAA's first operational Dragonfly SAR flight, replacing the USN flight which had been invaluable during its period on loan.

NEW MANDATES FOR THE RN/FAA

New priorities had been drawn up for the British and Commonwealth naval forces and, as well as retaining the target combat air patrols (TARCAP) and bombardment spotting roles, strike missions were resumed. The bombing and strafing of enemy positions, railway tunnels and bridges were now a defined objective. However, 'strike' targets were to be clearly identified as 'hostile military targets' before any attacks could be carried out and this restricted the effectiveness of the UN strikes.

Auster AOP6

April saw the arrival of HMS *Ocean* with its two strike squadrons who brought with them the beginning of a new era. Squadrons were no longer formed into Air Groups but were now acting as independent units responsible to the ship Commander Air. Additionally, early in June, Sub. Lt.'s B Randall and N Cook, the first RNVR aircrew to see action in Korea, arrived aboard the ship to join No. 802 Sqdn. Ten more were to see service in the theatre before the cessation of hostilities, supplementing the full-time aircrew on operational squadrons which was exactly what the RNVR had been established for.

AT LAST - THE UN REVISES OPERATIONS

After eight months of negotiations, the UN delegation concluded that the communists were not intent on unconditional peace, so the restrictions on operations were removed during June. The Joint Chiefs gave permission for a combined Naval-Air Force attack on the country's four main hydro-electric plants. They carried out a joint attack on the main stations at Suiho and Fusen, then the USAF would attack Choshin whilst the Naval Force would strike at Kyosen.

The attacks began on 23rd June and continued the following day. A combined total of 1654 missions were flown, and 90% of North Korea's electricity supply was destroyed, at a cost of two aircraft brought

HMAS Sydney

Fairey Firefly Mk. 5

down by ground fire (both pilots were rescued). The role played by the FAA squadrons was to increase CAPs by the Sea Furies against communist reprisals whilst the Fireflies attacked the power stations in Changyon and Haeju.

The next major operation, named 'Pressure Pump', was on targets in the North's capital Pyongyang and the combined operation on 30 specific targets began on 11th July. Ocean's air group, led by Lt. Cdr. C Roberts No. 825 Sqdn. CO, was tasked with attacking the railway yards with the Fireflies using rockets, whilst the Sea Furies were to bomb the target. A second strike was carried out later in the day, again led by Roberts, and both strikes were successful with all 39 aircraft returning safely. As a continuation to this operation, the next targets were the power stations at Chinnampo, which were attacked the following day when two strikes were launched achieving good results.

BEWARE - MIGs IN THE AIR

The ship was dispatched further north to strike at railway targets around Chongju 50 miles south of the Chinese border. Operating within the area known as 'MiG alley', the air group was regularly opposed by the enemy, however the MiG's best adversary was the USAF F86 Sabre Jet Fighter. The communist forces had built up a strong air contingent whilst regrouping, amassing a strength of at least 1800 aircraft of which many were MiG 15 jet fighters. During July and August, the MiGs began venturing south where they could oppose UN Forces.

Ocean's air group faced serious opposition along the west coast, the only carrier to do so during the war. During an early morning mission on 9th August 1952, eight MiGs attacked the air group which included a flight of four No. 802 Sqdn. Sea Fury FB11's led by Lt. P 'Hoagy' Carmichael. Lt. P Davies and Sub. Lt. B Ellis fired at two MiGs and were seen to get good hits on one aircraft which began smoking before breaking away (unfortunately no kill was confirmed). Hoagy meanwhile achieved a good hit on another MiG which went down and crashed resulting in the first kill of an enemy jet by a piston-engined fighter. Another flight also scored hits on a MiG when Lt. H McEnery hit the tail on one of three aircraft attacking Lt. R Clark (RNVR) but again no kill could be confirmed.

The following day, the same flight was again attacked by eight MiGs. Lt. Davies fired at one aircraft which broke away after receiving some hits and then, accompanied by Ellis, he successfully destroyed another in a head-on attack. Over the two days the Squadron had destroyed two MiGs with at least three more damaged, for no loss or damage to their own Sea Furies.

These 'dog fights' proved the fighting characteristics and efficiency of the last piston fighter in the FAA, and the professionalism, skill and team work of the FAA pilots. There was however some concern with regard to the true safety of the FAA aircraft if attacked in force by the MiGs. As a means of reducing the possibility of being attacked, it was decided to remove the 'D Day' stripes from the aircraft.

Much support was centred on assisting the non-communist Guerrilla landings in the Ongjin peninsula throughout Ocean's time on station. Directed by the Leopards, many strikes were made on villages where the enemy was hiding out or had mortar and gun positions. HMS *Unicorn* joined on 1st September supplying CAP flights with crews from Ocean, but this was the only time the support ship flew operational sorties until after the cessation of hostilities.

THIRD TIME ROUND

Ocean completed her operations on 30th October when she was replaced by HMS *Glory* who began her third tour of operations which would last until 10th November 1952. The operational routines were still the same; nine day operations rotated between the USN and RN carrier in the theatre. The squadrons were tasked with the continued destruction of bridges, lines of communication, transportation (trains, vehicles, junks and ox-carts), attacking enemy troop concentrations, gunfire spotting and TARCAPs. During the second patrol, the squadrons were specifically tasked with the attacking of troop concentrations along the coast around and south of Chinnampo where the enemy was building up a strong force, with the intention of attacking the UN islands off the coast.

Korean MiG 15

The peace talks at Panmunjom had broken down after it was not possible to agree to the communist's demands that all prisoners held in the south be returned, irrespective of their own wishes. The UN's attacks on the North Koreans recommenced causing much damage on the enemy positions and infrastructure but unfortunately the resolve of the communists was still not broken, thus the fighting continued.

The operations entered their third Korean winter and, as before, the weather affected the amount of operations flown. The two operational periods either side of the new year (1953) were to be costly. Eight aircraft were lost, including one of the ship's SAR Dragonfly helicopters which was blown over the ship's side with the loss of two crew. Four other pilots were lost, one was taken prisoner and another four aircraft had to make emergency landings on the beach at Paengjong-do

Further operations in the new year centred around assisting the Guerrillas in their war against the North Korean/Chinese Forces. The Sea Furies were especially successful in attacking the enemy on their behalf whilst the Fireflies were busy with ASPs and in supporting the defence of the UN islands off the coast. The TARCAP operations were reduced to being in support of minesweepers and landing craft when operating close to the enemy shores, and when deemed necessary if the enemy shore batteries fired on the other ships operating in the area.

IN SIGHT OF PEACE

The Russian leader Stalin died on 5th March, bringing unrest within the communist countries as he had been the whip hand in controlling the communist 'empire'. The Premier of North Korea, Kim Il Sung, backed by the Chinese General P'eng Teh-Huai, suddenly agreed on 28th March to the exchange of sick and wounded Prisoners of War. This was in answer to a proposal made by the Red Cross some four months earlier.

The talks resumed on 11th April when an agreement was reached for the exchanging of these POWs. The talks were then put on hold until the completion of the transfer and then resumed on 26th April. Again the stumbling block as far as the communists were concerned was the repatriation of all the POWs held by the South Koreans as they wanted them all returned. Finally, on 16th June, a solution to ending the conflict was formulated.

However this was thrown into confusion two days later when President Rhee set free 27,000 North Korean POWs who had indicated they did not wish to be repatriated. The communists broke off negotiations and launched an offensive on the 25th attacking ROK Forces but talks were again re-established after this episode in order to draw up another agreement for an armistice.

North American F-86 Sabre

PEACE IS AROUND THE CORNER

HMS *Glory's* final operational mission on 14th May brought to an end the ship's Korean operations, after a total of fifteen months involvement in the war where 9500 operational sorties had been flown by her squadrons.

HMS *Ocean* returned for her second stage of action in the war. Her two embarked squadrons, Nos. 807 and 812 flying Sea Fury FB11s and Firefly FR5s respectively, had been involved in the conflict whilst aboard HMS *Theseus*. Included in the aircrew of No. 807 Sqdn. were three members of the Royal Netherlands Navy, the first time Dutch exchange officers had been in the theatre. She relieved the US carrier USS *Bairoko* on 20th May and was tasked with the continuation of the missions carried out by her predecessors.

June saw the evacuation of some of the islands where the aircraft carried out TARCAP sorties above the evacuation Fleet. The Chinese had pushed forward so the two carrier task forces were tasked with support for the UN Forces against these attacks, with the FAA aircraft supporting the Commonwealth Division. Other CAS missions continued after the communists had been driven back, attacking the usual targets.

On the 16th July, No. 810 Sqdn. led by the CO Lt. Cdr. A Bloomer, disembarked three of her Fireflies to Pyongtaek airfield 40 miles south of Seoul to assist the US 5th Air Force in defeating low flying enemy aircraft which were operating in the hours of darkness. The Fireflies became night fighters and, after a short period of training, completed 31 missions before the war ended. Although no enemy aircraft were destroyed, the use of these aircraft deterred the enemy from continuing their operations.

The aircraft continued to operate from the airfield on night policing duties preventing the violation of the demilitarised zone after the armistice was signed. The final patrol commenced on 15th July but sadly the crew of a Firefly were lost when their aircraft failed to gain height after a RATOG takeoff and crashed into the sea. These were the last two FAA personnel to lose their lives in

Hawker Sea Fury

DH Dominie

the war. The CAS missions continued as did the strikes on bridges, enemy positions and gun emplacements. The final operational landing was on 23rd July ending the active 'war' tasks of FAA aircraft, although further missions were to be flown after the signing of the armistice in support of the security forces.

HMS *Unicorn* sailed from Hong Kong on 25th July to return to the theatre but the following day she received word that a Dutch merchant ship, SS *Inchkilda,* was being attacked by three Chinese gunboats off Ockseu Island. Unicorn went to the ship's assistance driving the three gunboats away allowing the Inchkilda to continue on her journey.

THE ARMISTICE

The peace negotiations resumed on 10th July after the US assured the communists that the South Koreans would honour the agreement. A final armistice was thus agreed with the demarcation boundary being the existing battle line. However a final twist to the signing of the armistice on 27th July 1953 was that President Rhee refused to sign it, whilst the communist commanders would only sign it at their headquarters, not with the delegates at Panmunjom. It was eventually signed at 10.00am (Korean time) by the UN delegates and the Communists, led respectively by Lt. Gen. William Harrison and Gen. Nam Il. The war ended twelve hours later after three years and 33 days. It was the first confrontation involving the UN with fifteen member nations assisting in the fight in support of the South Koreans.

MOPPING UP OPERATIONS

Whilst the UN Forces withdrew from the theatre, HMS *Ocean* and her USN partner USS *Bairoko* continued with air patrols outside the North Korean three mile limit. This was to remind the communists that the UN Forces had not fully withdrawn and were still active and to monitor the cease fire. These operations continued until September.

The first patrols by Ocean (1st-12th August), were in company with Unicorn. Both ships patrolled the Yellow Sea and pilots would be loaned to the Unicorn from Ocean for the flying. The same arrangements were used during the next patrol when Unicorn again operated alongside Ocean for a five day period (August 25th-29th). On 31st August 1953, Unicorn sailed from the Yellow Sea for the last time, heading for Hong Kong and ultimately home via Singapore.

She was the only carrier active in the theatre throughout the conflict and although not as a 'fighting' carrier, she did provide a deck for squadron pilots to carry out deck landing practices. Her guns fired at the enemy in a bombardment action against enemy positions at Chopekki Point (22nd September 1951) and she carried out CAPs in company with Ocean twelve months later. It is true to say that without the support of this ship, the operations of the light Fleet carriers would have been hard pushed to sustain their operational capacity.

HMS *Ocean* eventually sailed for home during November when she was relieved by HMAS *Sydney* who was herself relieved by HMS *Warrior* during April 1954 for the last RN aircraft carrier patrol. The monitoring operations were completed in the summer of 1954 bringing to an end the UN operations in Korea. The five Light Fleet Carriers and thirteen squadrons who had taken part in the conflict had completed 23,000 operational sorties with the Seafires, Sea Furies, Fireflies, Sea Otters and Dragonflies (all except the latter were originally designed during W.W.II).

Although many aircraft were damaged or lost, the FAA lost a total of 31 aircrew (including Flt. Lt. D Guy RAF with No. 810 Sqdn.) and the RAN FAA three aircrew. However their lives were not lost in vain, as the conflict was to show the solidarity of the United Nations in its role of defending the rights of a country against aggression from another.

THE LIGHT FLEET'S LAST OPERATION OF THE CONFLICT

Unrelated to the Korean War, but linked by the communist forces' attempts to be a dominating force in the Far East during the last aircraft carrier patrol in 1954, HMS *Warrior* was to receive a unique Presidential Citation from the President of Vietnam. Upon completion of her UN duties, she was sent to the North Vietnamese port of Haiphong to evacuate refugees to the south, successfully transferring more than 3,000 and earning the citation.

Percival Sea Prince C2 VIP Aircraft

British Inventions Lead the Way

Gloster Meteor first delivered in 1952

BRITISH NAVAL AVIATION STILL NUMBER ONE

The 1950's were to be the best ten years of the FAA's history. Six new modern advanced aircraft carriers were to be commissioned and operating from them would be equally modern equipment. The RN would introduce safety designs to its aircraft carriers, designs that were to revolutionise aircraft carrier operations worldwide.

The FAA was to develop the tactics and procedures in the important role of anti-submarine warfare (ASW), both with fixed and rotary wing aircraft. The Helicopter itself was going to prove the most valuable asset the modern FAA would possess, capable of many roles, more than could ever have been envisaged when this mode of flying was first conceived.

The FAA would be at the front of the RN's operations in Korea, Suez, Malaya and the Middle East in the role of world peace, supporting and protecting friendly nations against oppression and terrorist actions. Roles that were, and still are, the primary function of both the RN and FAA.

As we have already seen, the RNAS and RN have been at the forefront of naval aviation, development of the aircraft as a fighting weapon, aircraft carrier designs and the operation of aircraft at sea. This was to continue after the war, with aircraft getting bigger, heavier, faster and more complex both in their design, servicing and operation.

To allow these aircraft to work at sea, major changes were to be sought to ensure that maximum safety and operational status could be achieved. Three British designs were developed that would revolutionise naval aviation throughout the world, namely Cdr. C Mitchell's (RNVR) steam catapult, Lt. Cdr. N Goodhart's mirror landing sight (MLS) and Captain D Cambell's angled flight deck.

THE STEAM CATAPULT

An idea patented as long ago as 1938 by Mr. C Mitchell, steam catapults would be the solution for the launching of these heavier aircraft. He designed a relatively simple slotted catapult driven by steam from the ship's boilers, which drove a piston down the track pulling the aircraft along. This gave the aircraft a smooth constant acceleration down the deck.

During 1950, HMS *Perseus* was fitted with a steam catapult to conduct system trials, initially alongside the wall at Belfast then at sea. Using the catapult built on a superstructure along the centre-line of the forward half of the ship, the initial trials used aircraft which, after launching, were recovered at the nearby Sydenham air station then craned back on board to start again. Trials then moved to Rosyth Dockyard in Scotland to allow modifications to be implemented more quickly - the design company, Brown Brothers, were from Edinburgh.

During the sea trials, pilot-less Seafire aircraft were launched with a minimal fuel load, sufficient to allow the aircraft to fly off the ship once accelerated down the deck. The trials proved a great success, and the system was ordered to be installed in HMS *Ark Royal* during her construction. From then on, it was to be used by the RN and all other navies with conventional carriers.

NEW MIRROR LANDING SIGHT

The main hazard of operating aircraft on board aircraft carriers is the successful arresting of them when they land on board. Since the first landings by Dunning in August 1917, it is true to say it was never 'safe' landing aboard a pitching moving deck. During the Korean War, the FAA lost or damaged far more aircraft in landing accidents than by enemy action, with many brave aviators also losing their lives.

Help was at hand when, in 1951, Lt. Cdr.

Percival Sea Prince T1

Nick Goodhart devised a landing system that would alleviate the role of 'Bats' (although Landing Sight Officers {LSOs} were to replace them). This system allowed the pilot to concentrate on his landing, correcting his approach by watching a series of lights. The Mirror Landing Sight consisted of a gyro stabilised horizontally concave mirror which reflected a ball of light relative to datum lights. This indicated to the pilot his relative position to the flight deck.

The operating height of the mirror was adjustable so it could be set for the different aircraft types. Aircraft were eventually fitted with an Audio Air Speed Indicator system to assist the pilot in controlling his approach speed and a Head Up display, thus allowing him to constantly look at the mirror on approach. The mirrors were set for the aircraft to catch the No. 3 arrestor wire.

The first trials were conducted at the Royal Aircraft Establishment (RAE) at Farnborough, followed by sea trials aboard HMS *Illustrious*, the training and trials carrier in 1953, until she was placed in reserve at the end of 1954 and HMS *Bulwark* took over. These trials were to be the last operations of the W.W.II veteran and the first for the new carrier.

It was decided that there would be two sights fitted to the ships, either side of the deck. The portside sight would be the normal sight used with the starboard sight as a secondary back up system. Exercises were frequently carried out utilising this secondary sight to familiarise the pilots with it.

HMS *Ark Royal* was again the first British ship fitted with the device, however, the USS *Bennington*, an American Essex class ship, was the first to use the system operationally with an FJ-3 Fury jet fighter landing on the ship on 22nd August 1955.

THE ANGLED DECK

Captain Dennis Cambell, who had first-hand experience of flying from a carrier's deck as he had been aboard HMS *Courageous* in 1933 flying the Nimrods of No. 800 Sqdn., was now Assistant Chief Naval Representative at the Ministry of Supply. He suggested a modification to the flight deck layout which would revolutionise carrier aircraft operations.

Whilst discussing the operation of aircraft on the flexi-deck at a conference on 7th August 1951, he suggested the deck be angled 10 degrees to starboard so the aircraft could be pulled forward ready for catapulting off. Working with Mr. Lewis Boddington (from the RAE), it was realised that this feature would work on all conventional carriers and that by positioning the 'runway' in such a way, if aircraft missed the wires, they could take-off again without fear of hitting other aircraft on the deck.

The first trials were held using HMS *Triumph* as the deck and a revised runway was painted with a 10 degree angle. Unfortunately no landings were made as the arrestor wires would have to be repositioned across the deck but this did not prevent 'touch and go' being performed, proving the concept.

Lewis Boddington suggested at the outset that the design be incorporated in the build of the new Fleet carrier HMS *Ark Royal*, thus the ship became the first in the world to commission with an angled deck fitted during its build. It has subsequently been incorporated into the build of all conventional aircraft carriers throughout the world.

Fairey Gannet T5

The first ship in service to be modified with an angled deck was to be the USS *Atietam,* another Essex class carrier which was fitted with a prototype 10.5 degree deck during September 1952, carrying out her first trials in April 1953. The FAA's Service Trials Unit, No. 703 Sqdn., operated on the ship's deck during May 1953.

DH Sea Heron C20 'Admirals Barge'

THE DECADE OF THE NEW CARRIERS

The largest aircraft carriers to be operated by the RN were to enter service during 1951 and 1955 - HMS *Eagle* and HMS *Ark Royal* respectively. There were to be four of these large ships built but two were cancelled, the original HMS *Eagle* and HMS *Africa.* HMS *Eagle* was completed prior to the new inventions being developed whereas Ark Royal had all three installed during build hence the longer time in build. Both ships were the first in the RN to be fitted out with cafeteria style messing replacing the previous system where the sailors ate in their mess deck.

After commissioning on 1st October 1951 as the then largest ship with a displacement of 36,800 tons, HMS *Eagle* began her aircraft trials on 4th March 1952 with No. 800 Sqdn. (Attackers, the first FAA jet squadron to go to sea), No. 826 Sqdn. (Fireflies) and No. 827 Sqdn. (Firebrands).

When her sister ship was commissioned on 25th February 1955 weighing in at 37,200 tons, she was the most modern warship in the world. As for carrier operations she had a 5.5 degree angled deck, full mirror landing sight, a new arrestor wire system, steam catapults and three aircraft lifts (the only British carrier to have three although one was removed later). For crew comfort, besides the cafeteria messing, hammocks would no longer be needed as bunks were fitted and she was also equipped with an internal television system - the first of its kind in the RN. She began her sea trials in June 1954.

THE CENTAUR CLASS

Designed as an improved Colossus class light-fleet carrier during the war, the Centaur class were due to enter service during this decade. Originally eight were to be built but at the end of the war they were cancelled and the four already on build were to be broken up but were later reprieved. HMS *Centaur* was commissioned on 1st September 1953 and had the honour of being the first British carrier to operate with an angled deck, albeit only a realigning of the deck's runway.

The next two of the class, HMS *Albion* and HMS *Bulwark*, were to follow over the next fourteen months. The former began her first operations accompanying Centaur in the Mediterranean, whilst Bulwark relieved HMS *Illustrious* as the trials and training carrier with an angled deck. The last of the class, HMS *Hermes*, was to be built with all the new carrier innovations but did not commission until the end of the decade.

The redesigned Colossus class were model tested to provide the best combination of sea worthiness, stability, endurance, range and speed, and were the first British ships to have an electrically welded hull giving better rigidity and strength. They were to provide their ship's company with untold comfort; they had refrigeration compartments for fresh provisions, cafeteria style messing, a ship's laundry and a full sickbay complete with operating theatre, X-ray facilities and a dentist. The best comfort though was the mess deck bunks replacing the hammock as in Ark Royal.

SUPPORT MANPOWER TRAINING

The training of the manpower to maintain and operate the aircraft was dispersed to airfields and establishments across the UK. After basic naval training, the different branches were to continue their respective training at these establishments before joining either a training squadron, ship or air station. Mechanical engineers were trained at Bramcote, radio and electrical ratings at a mix of HMS Collingwood, Lee-on-Solent and Worthy Down, whilst Lossiemouth was the home for the aircraft handlers. Survival equipment servicing was taught at RN Establishment Seafield Park, with meteorology at Kete and photography at Ford.

COMMUNICATIONS FLIGHTS

All the air stations were equipped with communications aircraft and after the war most used a variety of different types (Ansons, Havards, Expeditors and Dominies) until a standardisation of this facility was established. The Navy ordered Hunting Percival P66 feeder liners to fulfil the role, and the Sea Prince C1 was delivered in July 1950 for use as an "Admiral's Barge" with No. 781 Sqdn., the FAA Communications Squadron based at Lee-on-Solent, the HQ of the FAA. The Sea Prince was to operate alongside the DH Dominies, already the mainstay of communications aircraft in the service.

The range and endurance (plus comfort) of these aircraft was not adequate with a shrinking air arm, and the distance between

DH Sea Devon C20

Westland Dragonfly

bases was increasing outside of the range of the Dominie and Sea Prince. The FAA took delivery of its new communications aircraft, the DH Sea Devon C20, conversions of civil Doves, arriving at the squadron in April 1955. Eventually most of the bases were equipped with a Sea Devon as the standard station 'Hack'.

The development of the twin-engined Dove was the DH114 Heron four-engined feeder liner and delivery of the first Sea Heron C2 was in July 1961. The five aircraft received were all ex-civil airline aircraft and all, except for one aircraft which was allocated to Hal Far, were operated by No. 781 Sqdn.

SAR TECHNIQUES AND OPERATIONS

The Dragonfly was the 'vehicle' which would seriously develop the role of helicopters but it was limited by its size and range. It was however instrumental for the development of rescue techniques using helicopters including use of the 'Sproule Net' to rescue personnel. This was a device developed in 1951 by CPO Lock and Lt. Cdr. Sproule. It was a net attached to the helicopter's rescue winch which was lowered into the sea, and the helicopter would then manoeuvre so that the winch man could position the net to pick up the body or disabled person.

CPO Lock was instrumental in the development of SAR equipment and techniques during these early days in rescuing airmen (and the public) from the sea. After developing the 'Sproule net', he next devised a strop that would be lowered down to the person in the water, who would then place the strop over their head and arms before pulling down a 'locking band' to secure themselves in. The cable would then be raised and the body would be pulled into the helicopter. This became known as the standard rescue strop, and its first use was in the rescue of Lt. W Davis on 4th August 1953 when he ditched in his Sea Fury off HMS *Theseus*. This is now an international SAR 'tool'.

The helicopters of No. 705 Sqdn. were to gain heralded fame when they led the rescue of British and Dutch people from the flood waters of Norfolk and Zealand in Holland after the storms on 31st January and 1st February 1953. Nine of the squadron's Dragonflies rescued 810 people during the eighteen days of the operation. During one mission, seven people were carried in one helicopter which was a record at that time. Twice Queen Juliana of the Netherlands was flown in the helicopters to see the flooded low land and witness the rescue work. The squadron had the honour of leading the massed flypast at the Queen's Coronation Fleet Review four months later.

NEW FAA FIGHTERS UNDER DEVELOPMENT

De Havilland were developing two twin boom aircraft for the FAA, the first being the Sea Venom F20 taking to the air on 19th April 1951. The first ten Sea Venom aircraft were used for trials and evaluations by both the Aircraft & Armament Experimental Establishment (A & AEE) at Boscombe Down and the De Havilland Company at Christchurch. These

DH Sea Venom

DH110

trials included sea trials aboard HMS *Illustrious*, initial deck trials on 9th July 1951 and later night trials at the end of 1953, prior to them entering squadron use the following year.

The DH110 all-weather fighter was ordered for evaluation as a swept-wing, twin jet engined day and night all-weather fighter (FAW) for both the RAF and FAA. The prototype flew for the first time on 26th September 1951 and exceeded the speed of sound in a shallow dive on 9th April 1952. However the RAF chose the Gloster Javelin after the prototype DH110 broke up during its display at Farnborough on 6th September, killing its crew and 29 people in the crowd.

The project was continued for the FAA and carrier deck touch and go's were performed with HMS *Albion* on 23rd September 1954. The first true deck trials were held aboard HMS *Ark Royal* on 5th April 1956 which included arrested landings with catapult and free launches. The FAA ordered the type as its next generation FAW aircraft now known as the Sea Vixen, the last British fighter to operate from conventional aircraft carriers.

The first flight of the single-seat naval fighter Supermarine Type 508 flew at Boscombe Down on 31st August 1951. This aircraft was developed from an original 1945 specification for a fighter without an undercarriage to operate from the flexidecks (the Type 505). After modifications and trials, it was to enter FAA service as the Scimitar fighter.

The Type 508, which was to conduct sea trials aboard HMS *Eagle* during May 1952, was built with straight wings and a 'V' tail plane, and these were replaced with a swept-wing and tail plane with a fin in the Type 525. This type was also fitted with 'blown flaps', high pressure air from the engines forced over the flaps to increase the lift from them whilst reducing landing and stalling speeds, the first such system to be built into a high performance aircraft.

AIRBORNE EARLY WARNING (AEW)

A new conception was introduced to the FAA operational roles in 1951, that of Airborne Early Warning (AEW) with the arrival of the Douglas AEW.1 (AD-4W) Skyraider. These large American aircraft were equipped with a large ventral radome below the aircraft used for tracking aircraft and vectoring the fighters to intercept them, extending the range of the ship's radar

DH110

Douglas Skyraider

capability. No. 778 Sqdn. took delivery of its first aircraft during November.

The squadron was responsible for the operational training of the aircrews and maintainers with the aircraft until the unit was recommissioned as No. 849 Sqdn. on 7th July 1952, the only front line operator of the type. The squadron was divided into five flights; the HQ training flight and four flights for operations on the carriers. When it finally retired the type, it was the last piston-engined aircraft in front line service with the FAA, replaced by the Gannet AEW3 in December 1960.

The American invention was a significant development in naval aviation warfare (and later all military aviation), allowing Fleets to operate in 'deep water' areas of the world's oceans, whilst having a good picture of aircraft within the range of the AEW's radar. Prior to this, the Fleet would have to operate using the ships' radars which could only give limited range. This new concept gave beyond horizon range including 'look down' blind areas. It was initially installed on Grumman Avengers in the USN before progressing to the Skyraider, and was eventually further developed such that future large airliner types would be developed with rotating search radar above their fuselage operated by air forces worldwide.

THE FINAL FIREFLY VARIANTS

January 1951 saw the arrival of the Firefly AS6 unarmed anti-submarine aircraft when they joined No. 814 Sqdn., replacing the unit's FR1s. The squadron had formed two months earlier as part of the 7th Night Air Group of the FAA's first all-weather group, the other unit in the group being the Sea Hornets of No. 809 Sqdn. Its role was to develop the type as a night ASW aircraft, and training exercises were held in both HMS *Vengeance* and HMS *Illustrious,* with over 900 hours being flown during these training missions.

The AS Mk6 introduced the carriage and use of the British designed Sonobuoys for submarine detection. These buoys were dropped into the water where they would automatically lower a listening microphone whilst floating on the surface. The signal from the buoy would be picked up by the operator who would listen for the sound of a submarine below the surface. The RNAS had used an audio listening device during W.W.I in its search for German submarines. The buoys would be dropped in a 'pattern' thus covering a large area, and each buoy would be individually identified so the exact location of the submarine could be determined. This system, though much modified, is still used by navies worldwide.

The Mk6 became the standard ASW aircraft for the FAA equipping FLS, training units and RNVR squadrons, until replaced by the Grumman Avenger AS4 and 5s which were used as a stopgap until the arrival of the Gannet from 1955 onwards. The delay in receiving the Gannet resulted in a much modified Firefly Mk7 being developed which had been initially intended as the stopgap aircraft.

This Mk7 was redesigned to have a crew of three, an extra observer being required to operate the equipment used in the detection of submarines. The first modified aircraft

HMS Eagle

flew on 22nd May 1951, a month later than it should have been in service, the delay being due to the major design changes required. The aircraft was to use the Griffon Mk59 necessitating a larger radiator, needing a larger fin and rudder to counter the de-stabilising effect caused by this new radiator fit. The wing had an increased span and the rear cockpit area was enlarged and fitted with a bubble type canopy.

The type was not very successful when operating from the deck of carriers, hence the acquisition of the Grumman aircraft, and it was relegated to training squadrons for a variety of roles. Some of the aircraft were later converted to the U Mk8 pilot-less drones, later joined by the last variant of this aircraft, the U Mk9s which were conversions of AS Mk5 aircraft. The last Firefly was retired by No. 728B Sqdn. in November 1961 after eighteen years service with the FAA.

HMS Eagle during exercise Mainbrace

HMS EAGLE SAILS AT LAST

After nine years and one week building, HMS *Eagle* sailed from Belfast for her first sea trials on 31st October 1951. Ordered on 19th May 1942 and laid down on 24th October as HMS *Audacious*, progress was halted on the build at the end of the war. The ship was renamed Eagle on 21st January 1946 and launched three months later by HRH Princess Elizabeth on 19th March.

After the success of these trials, she carried out her flying trials during February 1952 with a Firefly of No. 703 Sqdn. being the first aircraft to land on her deck on the 14th of the month. She had been completed before she could be fitted with an angled deck so operated with the original axial deck as designed.

After commissioning she entered service in March equipped with Attackers of No. 800 Sqdn. and Firebrands with No. 827 Sqdn. for initial operational trials, followed by trials with the Supermarine Type 508 and Hawker P1052 during May, finally reaching operational status in August.

During 1953, trials were held on board to assess the operational capability of the new Bristol tandem rotor Type 173 helicopter on board an aircraft carrier. The trials resulted in an order for the helicopter although design changes were required (designated Type 191), but this order was subsequently cancelled after transmission and engine problems delayed the arrival of the type in service.

Her first commission began with the ship and squadrons working up, followed by the NATO (North Atlantic Treaty Organisation) exercise 'Mainbrace' and cold weather trials in the Arctic. She took part in the Coronation Fleet Review at Spithead in 1953, and Mediterranean exercises before entering her first refit in June 1954.

MORE NEW TRAINING TYPES

No. 750 Sqdn. was reformed on 17th April 1952 tasked with the training of the FAA Observers using Barracudas and some ex-RAF Avro Ansons. Ten months later the squadron began operating Fireflies and the new Hunting Percival Sea Prince T1 flying classroom. This aircraft was a development of the Sea Prince C1 aircraft in service as a communications aircraft, and these aircraft were to give nearly 30 years service until being retired in 1979.

The Meteor first flew on 5th March 1943, but it was to be another nine years before the FAA received its first Meteor aircraft. Although the RAF was operating the type as front line fighters, the FAA operated various marks in the support role. Meteor T7s arrived in September 1952 to No. 759 Sqdn., the Naval Air Fighter School's No.1 Operational Flying School at Culdrose, joining the School's Vampire T11s for jet conversion courses.

The Hal Far based No. 728 FRU Sqdn. received the T7 in 1955 joined by the target tug TT20 in 1958. For the RN's Sea Slug trials in the Mediterranean during 1959-1961, the squadron operated twenty-one U15/U16 drones from the RAE. No. 728 Sqdn. was finally retired in May 1967 but the Meteor continued in FAA service with Airwork at Hurn until as late as March 1971.

RETURN OF THE AVENGER

With the delay in the arrival of the Gannet as the FAA's main ASW platform, an alternative short term aircraft was required to replace the ageing Barracudas and early marks of Fireflies and also to supplement the AS6 Fireflies. The redesigned Firefly AS7s,

Supermarine Scimitar

Gruman Avenger AS4

designed to fill the gap, were unsuitable for carrier operations and the answer was found by reintroducing the Grumman Avenger, seven years after first retiring the type. This involved acquiring the USN TBM-3E model which was later modified for the FAA becoming the AS4 and the AS5.

The aircraft began their service with No. 815 Sqdn. which commissioned in May 1953 and No. 824 Sqdn. in July, both with the unmodified TBM-3E. These were replaced with modified AS4s early in 1954, and four FLSs operated the type until replaced during 1955, the last being No. 814 Sqdn. which retired the type on 4th November. Four aircraft were modified for the role of electronic warfare (EW) operating in No. 831 Sqdn. 'A' Flight for just over a year from May 1958, the last operational users of the type.

WESTLANDS LAST FIXED-WING AIRCRAFT

Originally designed in 1944 as a piston-engined long-range naval strike aircraft, the Westland Wyvern S4 eventually entered service during May 1953 with No. 813 Sqdn. at RNAS Ford, now as a turbo-prop strike aircraft. The first prototype aircraft flew on 12th December 1946 as the TF Mk1 with large contra rotating propellors driven by a Rolls Royce Eagle piston-engine. This and the second prototype were not navalised and were built for development and handling trials. The first sea trials using the navalised third prototype were held on HMS *Implacable* on 9th June 1948, however these were cut short due to propellor bearing failures. They resumed on 13th July and, after this first series, the trials continued the following May and June in HMS *Illustrious.*

The Wyvern TF Mk2, fitted with an Armstrong Siddeley Python turbo-prop engine, flew on 22nd March 1949. A lengthy development programme took place to prove both the aircraft and engine including carrier trials in June 1950, again in Illustrious. The TF Mk3 was the next development, but only one example of this two-seat aircraft was built, first flying on 11th February 1950. It was not developed further and remained with Westlands.

None of these three marks were to reach squadron service. This was left to the Wyvern S4, but even after entering service there were still problems with the aircraft. These were eventually ironed out by Westlands and sea trials were initially held in June 1953 aboard USS *Antietam* which had been fitted with the British designed angle deck. Further trials were held in both HMS *Eagle* and HMS *Illustrious,* completing in November.

The Wyverns of No. 813 Sqdn. embarked in HMS *Albion* on 24th September 1954 for the type's first operational deployment. It was disembarked to Hal Far upon arriving in Malta and remained there until embarking for the return journey. However it was found that the aircraft was unsafe for catapult launches due to enforced fuel starvation needing the aircraft's fuel system to be modified. Because of this problem, Lt. B MacFarlane entered the record books when he successfully ejected underwater from his aircraft which ditched on take-off. To compound the ditching, the ship then ran over the aircraft with MacFarlane still in the cockpit.

The second front line squadron equipped with the Wyvern, No. 827 Sqdn. commissioned at Ford on 1st November 1954. Both these squadrons became part of Eagle's compliment embarking in her in the summer of 1955. Upon disembarking to Ford in November, both squadrons

Westland Wyvern TF1

Westland Wyvern TF2

disbanded and two replacement squadrons were commissioned - No. 830 Sqdn. to operate from Eagle and No. 831 Sqdn. destined to serve on HMS *Ark Royal.*

Three second line units, all trials units, were to receive the aircraft: No. 787 Sqdn. (the Fighter Development Unit), No. 703 Sqdn. (Service Trials Unit) and eventually No. 700 Sqdn. which reformed when these two units amalgamated in August 1955 as the Trials and Requirements Unit. The last unit operating the type was No. 813 Sqdn., which had re-commissioned at the end of 1956 to replace No. 830 Sqdn. but then disbanded on 22nd April 1958. The Squadron had re-commissioned at the end of 1956 to replace No. 830 Sqdn.

Westland Wyvern 4 over HMS Ark Royal

DH Sea Venom

Douglas Skyraider

Helicopters to the Fore

THE WHIRLWIND JOINS THE FAA

The primary FAA helicopter squadron, No. 705 Sqdn., had carried out much development work with the early helicopters but these were very limited in their capabilities. Sikorsky then developed the S55 Whirlwind, a larger more able helicopter which was to be licence-built by Westlands. The FAA was to receive many examples of this machine from Westlands but the first helicopters were supplied direct from Sikorsky.

Designated Whirlwind HAR Mk21, No. 848 Sqdn. commissioned with ten of these helicopters on 29th October 1952, being the first FL helicopter squadron in service with the British military forces. The company would also deliver fifteen HAS 22s for anti-submarine warfare (ASW) before Westlands were ready to supply the helicopter from its Yeovil factory.

The role of the HARs was soon to be that of troop transportation and support, and the squadron was despatched aboard HMS *Perseus* to the Far East six weeks after commissioning for operations against the insurgents in Malaya - thus the role of 'Commando' helicopters was born. With the arrival of its HAS 22s, without the sonar fit, the squadron was titled the Amphibious Warfare Trials Unit eventually to become the Royal Marine Commando Squadron.

Three of the original HAS 22s were modified as VVIP 22s and were operated by No. 781 Sqdn. for communications until 1970. The aircraft were painted VIP green/white and were affectionately known as 'Green Parrots'. One of the aircraft was used as the personal helicopter for Prince Philip and regularly landed in the grounds of Buckingham Palace.

The sonar equipped Whirlwind HAS 22s were ordered to establish the helicopter in the ASW role, the helicopter being fitted with a dipping sonar that could be lowered into the sea. No. 706 Sqdn. was commissioned on 7th September 1953 at Gosport as the Anti-Submarine Helicopter Trials Unit equipped with eight HAS 22s and two Hiller HT1s.

The squadron, although based at Gosport, had most of its six months trial period at Belfast with sea trials aboard HMS *Perseus.* It was redesignated as No. 845 Sqdn. on 15th March, the FAA's first FL ASW squadron, and pioneered the role of ASW tactics, procedures and the dropping of air launched torpedoes by helicopters. The development work was carried out whilst the squadron was based at Hal Far in Malta with detachments to the carriers stationed in the Mediterranean during this period.

Sikorsky HAS 22

The trials proved the concept of using helicopters in the role, although the operational capability of the Whirlwind in its present version was restricted due to a lack of both power and endurance. Fixed-wing aircraft would continue as the front line ASW squadrons and the Gannet, although delayed, was soon to enter service, albeit only for a short period until superseded by the helicopter. No. 845 Sqdn. continued to develop the helicopter ASW techniques.

Westlands' first example of the Whirlwind flew on 15th August 1953 as a Series 1 helicopter. Ten were delivered to the FAA the following July as HAR Mk1s, followed by the HAR Mk3 which arrived in September 1955. Both these types were powered by US engines and were used for SAR and communications roles. A few

Westland Whirlwind HAR Mk 1

Coronation Fleet Review 15th June 1953

airframes were converted to the HAR Mk5 powered by a British Alvis Leonides Major engine, and these aircraft were used for development trials for the ASW Whirlwind HAS Mk7.

THE MALAYAN OPERATIONS

Since the end of the second war, the Far East had been unstable with the communist support for terrorist and guerrilla factions. The Federation of Malaya was established on 1st February 1948, with the joining of British colonies in the peninsular causing an uprising by the Chinese population. A state of emergency was declared on 16th June and Commonwealth troops began opposing the rebel forces.

The first FAA operations against the bandits and insurgents began in October 1949 when the Seafires (No. 800 Sqdn.) and Fireflies (No. 827 Sqdn.) on HMS *Triumph* were used as support for the ground forces. However the use of the carrier borne fixed-wing aircraft was not sufficiently successful for the operations to continue.

The real beneficial role played by the FAA came about with the arrival of the ten Whirlwind HAR21s from No. 848 Sqdn., the squadron having been commissioned specifically for anti-terrorist operations in the theatre. The squadron arrived at Sembawang on 8th January 1953 (ferried by HMS *Perseus*), to begin a period of area familiarisation.

During this period the squadron was tasked with the transportation of troops to a remote location in the jungle, and the mission on 24th January 1954 saved the troops days of hard slog through dense jungle. The following day, the first casualty evacuation (CASEVAC) operation was successfully completed when three injured soldiers were transferred from the jungle to the British Military Hospital at Kiurara. These were the first operations for the squadron and Whirlwind, and were to be the forerunners of many more such operations from then on.

Operating in flights of three aircraft, one at Sembawang the other at Kuala Lumpur, (the remaining four aircraft remained at Sembawang), the squadron began their support operations the following month operating from Forward Operation Bases (FOBs). The flights carried troops and equipment to remote areas lowering them down by rope if the area was not suitable for landing, then picking the troops up after they had completed their operations. Other missions included CASEVAC flights, leaflet dropping and prisoner transfers.

Two major missions were to prove the worth of the helicopter in supporting commando operations. The first, 'Bahadur', involved the transportation of 75 Gurkas and their equipment to a landing zone using four of the helicopters. The second was the transfer of a complete brigade of 650 men and equipment by the squadron to an area in Western Pahang during operation 'Cato'. The ten HAR21s were supplemented with five Westland HAR1s for SAR duties, allowing the Sikorsky aircraft to concentrate their efforts in commando operations.

The communist High Command withdrew to Indonesia in February 1954 and their support for the terrorists in Malaya diminished. The crisis was declared over with the cessation of the rebel actions at the end of 1956 and the squadron disbanded after its last operation on 18th December. The Malayan Government awarded the squadron a silver Kris Dagger as a token of its appreciation for the work carried out during its three years in the theatre.

CORONATION FLEET REVIEW

The Fleet was assembled in the Solent for the Coronation Fleet Review by Her Majesty Queen Elizabeth II at Spithead on 15th June 1953. The ships were headed by HMS *Eagle* accompanied by eight more RN and Commonwealth aircraft carriers; Illustrious, Implacable, Indefatigable, Indomitable, Perseus and Theseus, HMAS Sydney and HMCS Magnificent. Thirty-seven squadrons with 350 aircraft flew above the assembled Fleet, led by the helicopters of No. 705 Sqdn. The aircraft represented all the types in service, including the Flag Officer Flying Training R.Adm., W Couchman in a Sea Vampire F20.

THE LAST BOULTON PAUL AIRCRAFT

Originally designed as an RAF advanced trainer after the war and first flying in May 1947, the Balliol was ordered for the FAA as the Sea Balliol. Thirty navalised examples were ordered differing from their RAF cousin by having a smaller propeller, folding wings, deck hook and strengthened undercarriage. The FAA order was the last order for operational aircraft to be produced by the company.

The Balliol entered service at Lee-on-Solent in September with HMS *Triumph's* Flight equipped with three aircraft which were intended to give pilots deck handling training. The Flight was the only one formed for attachment to a designated carrier, embarking for the first time on 18th January 1954. Their role as training aircraft was limited due to the arrival of jet aircraft although it did serve with six RNVR squadrons in the training role replacing their Harvards.

It was then used as a communications aircraft with No. 781 Sqdn. and many air stations had examples as the station 'hack'. Whilst with No. 781 Sqdn., it was used as the flying acquaintance aircraft for the Junior Officers' Air Courses (JOAC). These were officers who were not going to be FAA aircrew but were to receive flying experience. This role was taken over by No. 702 Sqdn. which commissioned on 30th September 1957 specifically for JOAC flights.

CARRIERS OLD AND NEW

The first three Centaur class ships were all to be commissioned in the short period of fourteen months; HMS *Centaur* on 1st September 1953, HMS *Albion* on 26th May 1954 and HMS *Bulwark* on 4th November 1954. All three were laid down during the war (as was HMS *Hermes*, the fourth of the class) and launched between April 1947 and June 1948. The ships were then laid up whilst decisions were made as to their 'need' in the Fleet. They were to reach operational status mainly because they had deeper hangar deck spaces capable of taking the aircraft coming into service, and would replace the Illustrious class. This was a more economical solution to the Fleet's carrier requirements as it would cost too much to alter the hangars of the Illustrious class.

Centaur was the first British carrier to operate with an angled deck. When she entered service, she had an axial deck with an angle runway painted on it, and she is in the record books as being the ship to go into a refit after the shortest time from commissioning - four months. She went into Portsmouth dockyard for a complete angle deck and the realignment of the arrestor wires and crash barrier.

The remaining two ships were commissioned with interim 5 degree angle decks. HMS *Albion's* deck was used for the touch and go deck landings by the DH110 prior to sailing for the Mediterranean, while HMS *Bulwark* replaced HMS *Illustrious* as the trials and training carrier giving the training facilities an angled deck to practice landings.

With the arrival of the modern aircraft

Boulton Paul Sea Balliol

HMS Centaur

Fairey Gannet

carriers, the streamlining of the RN and the reduction in the defence budget combined with the new aircraft being larger, heavier and faster, the present carrier Fleet's future was obvious. These carriers would need extensive rebuilding to permit them to operate the jet aircraft as their operating equipment, lifts and hangars were designed to operate the piston aircraft of the 1940s, and were not capable of working with these new aircraft.

Only one of the armoured Fleet carriers, HMS *Victorious,* was to be refitted for the operation as a jet aircraft carrier. Of the remaining three Illustrious class, HMS *Formidable* was mothballed after the war and scrapped in 1953, HMS *Indomitable* continued operations in the Home Fleet as the Flagship during 1951, then as flagship in the Mediterranean Heavy Squadron the following year before paying off for scrap after a petrol fire (3rd February 1953), and HMS *Illustrious* operated as the trials carrier before going into reserve in 1954. The two Implacable class ships, HMS *Implacable* and HMS *Indefatigable,* were both used as training carriers in the early part of the 1950s, both being retired in 1954 before eventual scrapping.

Of the remaining W.W.II carriers, HMS *Pretoria Castle* had been returned to the merchant fleet in 1947 after her spell as the trials carrier, and HMS *Campania* was loaned as a floating display for the Festival of Britain for two years (1949-1951) then acted as flagship for the first British Nuclear Tests in the Pacific during 1952. She was put in reserve upon her return, finally going to the breakers in 1955. The last to go, HMS *Unicorn,* was placed in reserve upon returning from Korea in 1953 until eventually being scrapped six years later.

The Colossus class light fleets served well in Korea but their days were numbered after the conflict. HMS *Glory* carried out some operations against the Malayan insurgents during 1953 on her way home from Korea, and was then used for a troop and ferry ship prior to being paid off in 1954. HMS *Perseus*

and HMS *Pioneer* were both sold for scrap.

HMS *Ocean* and HMS *Theseus* were utilised in training roles although they were both used as helicopter and troop carriers during the Suez Campaign in 1956, then put into reserve awaiting their disposal. The latter had been used prior to Suez as the deck for the Joint Experimental Helicopter Unit operating Whirlwinds and Sycamores.

HMS *Triumph* was converted as the RN's Heavy Repair Ship after a spell as a training ship. This reconfiguration took seven years to complete, and she served in this role for ten years until paying off in 1975. She was eventually to go to Spain for scrap in late 1981, just months before the outbreak of the Falklands War (1982). She would have been an important asset to the British Fleet if she had not been one of Mr John Knott's casualties, as no such service was available those 8,000 miles from home.

The remaining two were to become ships of the major South American powers. HMS *Vengeance* was loaned to the RAN, eventually becoming the Minas Gerais in the Brazilian Navy in December 1956. HMS *Warrior* was used for Post Korean War UN peacekeeping duties before being refitted in 1956 with an angle deck, MLS and upgrading of her catapults (they remained hydraulic type) and took part in the British Hydrogen bomb tests in the Pacific in 1957 before becoming the Argentinean Independencia.

INTENSIVE FLYING TRIALS UNITS - THE GANNET

As already mentioned, the Gannet anti-submarine search and strike aircraft had first flown in 1949. No. 703 Sqdn. received the FAA's first aircraft in January 1954 but this was only in preparation for the first unit to operate the aircraft. It entered service with No. 703X Sqdn. on 15th March 1954, and this unit was formed as the Gannet Intensive Flying Trials Unit (IFTU) using the first four AS Mk1s delivered. This was the first IFTU to form, after this all new aircraft would be accepted by an IFTU, mostly as an individual No. 700 Sqdn.

The role of the unit was to carry out intensive flying with the new type to prove its capability and operational efficiency, and to train the first operational pilots, crew and maintenance staff on the type. The members of these units eventually formed the backbone of the first FLS and the training squadron that would continue with its training role once the IFTU disbanded.

The Gannet IFTU was to operate for nine months until disbanding in December 1954. It received the first four aircraft into service but unfortunately two of these were to have

HMS Triumph as a Heavy Repair Ship

Fairey Gannet

accidents due to compressor stall in the engine. One aircraft was ditched on take-off during trials aboard HMS *Albion* in August, but after minor modifications the remaining aircraft completed the trials aboard HMS *Illustrious*. By the time the unit had completed its task, it had flown 1,700 hours testing the aircraft.

NAVAL AIR DEPARTMENT

After the war, the Naval Aircraft and Carrier Equipment Departments were established at RAE Farnborough to evaluate aircraft and equipment for service use by the FAA and RN for the development of naval aviation. Located at RAE Bedford was the Flight Division of Aerodynamics which was involved in testing the aerodynamics of aircraft intended for military service including naval aircraft.

The two units at Farnborough were amalgamated in 1954 as the Naval Air Department (NAD) and, due to the lack of space at Farnborough, moved to the airfield at Bedford which was being expanded. The airfield had carrier deck equipment test facilities built into it for the work of assessing and developing aircraft and ships' systems compatibility. The NAD was tasked with designing, testing and proving the systems for both fixed and rotary wing aircraft.

A 200ft steam catapult track was constructed at the end of a 3,500ft runway, the launcher was raised 6ft above the deck and two arrestor wires were located at the end of the runway to stop the aircraft after launch. This was used for assessing the steam pressure requirements for launching of aircraft in all configurations and loads permissible.

An arrestor hook landing deck was built for aircraft to fast taxi on, with deck hook down to catch the wires, for proving the aircraft's deck hook system. Finally a safety barrier base was used for firing aircraft at speeds of up to 150 knots. The aircraft were launched along a 200ft cordite catapult system firing the aircraft into the barrier. The equipment was to be used for nearly twenty years for all RN carrier aircraft and systems, until the demise of conventional fixed-wing carrier operations.

THE 'COMPLETE' ASW AIRCRAFT ENTERS SERVICE

The Gannet entered FLS with No. 826 Sqdn. at Lee-on-Solent on 17th January 1955 to operate in HMS *Eagle*, first embarking in May. The following month saw two squadrons form; No. 824 Sqdn. for HMS *Bulwark* and the training squadron No. 737 Sqdn., part of the Anti-Submarine Training School. This training squadron also took delivery of the first T2 dual control aircraft, a conversion of the AS1.

Within a short time the AS1 and T2 were to be joined by the next two versions, the AS4 and T5 which were fitted with a more powerful uprated engine. The first AS4 replaced No. 824 Sqdn.'s AS1s in the summer of 1956, while some of the AS4s were also converted for ECM roles with No. 831 Sqdn., the FAA's EW squadron, and these were redesignated AS6-ECM aircraft. Another six were converted for taxi service aboard the carriers with the designation Mk4 COD (Courier Onboard Delivery), one being allocated to each ship.

A total of eleven front line squadrons, two RNVR and five training squadrons of the FAA eventually operated the type, the last fixed-wing ASW aircraft to serve before being replaced by helicopters. It was also to serve with the Australian, the West German and Indonesian Navies. The type was only to last in FLS for some 65 months, the last FAA operator being No. 810 Sqdn. which disbanded on 12th July 1960 after serving aboard HMS *Centaur*.

ALL WEATHER JET FIGHTER

The FAA's first two-seat jet aircraft for FLS, the DH Sea Venom FAW 20, entered service with No. 890 Sqdn. on 20th March 1954, the first All Weather Fighter (AWF) squadron to be equipped with jet aircraft. The aircraft was a navalised version of the Venom NF2 night fighter for the RAF, as a replacement for the Sea Hornet NF21s. The naval flight of the A & AEE at Boscombe Down had taken the prototype on board HMS *Illustrious* on 9th July 1951. No. 890 Sqdn. took its aircraft on board HMS *Albion* on 19th July 1955 for the squadron's first deployment (it had carried out trials aboard HMS *Bulwark*, the training carrier, two months earlier on 15th May).

The type was only to have a short front line use, being replaced by the DH110 Sea Vixen in 1959, but in its short career it had been instrumental in proving the new Firestreak Air-to-Air guided missile. Three modified aircraft joined the Trials and Requirement Unit, No.

Sea Venom F20

700 Sqdn. for the trials, then on completion they joined No. 893 Sqdn. embarking in HMS *Victorious* to carry out the first firings by operational aircraft. Some Sea Venoms were modified for the role of EW operating with No. 831 Sqdn., joining the Gannets.

THE HEAVYWEIGHTS

HMS *Eagle* entered Devonport dockyard during June 1954 to be fitted with an interim 5.5 degree angle deck and redesigned crash barrier and MLS. It had been intended to fit a side lift similar to that fitted to her sister ship HMS *Ark Royal*, but this was cancelled and the ship returned to service in February 1955.

Steam catapults were installed during a short modernisation programme in 1956, and another short refit was carried out in early 1957 before the ship was to commence its next phase of operations, mostly in the Mediterranean. She was to operate with HMS *Victorious* for the first time at the end of 1958, meeting up with her in Grand Harbour Malta on 14th October. The last time Victorious had been in the Mediterranean with Eagle was when the previous ship was sunk (11th August 1942).

Taking longer than Eagle to complete, the fourth HMS *Ark Royal* was commissioned into the Fleet on 25th February 1955 with Captain Dennis Cambell (of angle deck fame) in command. The ship was laid down in the Cammell Laird yard at Birkenhead on 3rd May 1943, and she was launched by Queen Elizabeth seven years later on the 3rd May 1950.

One of the main reasons for her completion taking nearly twelve years was the decision to incorporate the three carrier developments mentioned earlier. She was the first carrier in the world with all three built into her during initial build and she was also to feature a deck edge lift, the first to be installed in a British carrier, giving the ship three aircraft lifts.

She was accepted by Captain Cambell on 25th February 1955 and the first aircraft to land on her decks was a Dragonfly helicopter flown by the Captain on 4th March. She began aircraft flying trials during June before starting an operational tour in the Mediterranean in September. During the trials, however, problems kept reoccurring with the new steam catapults and hydraulic arrestor wires and these problems were reported on in the British press. To prove to the public that this was no major problem, the Seahawks of No. 800 Sqdn. were launched whilst the ship was in Portsmouth Harbour with all the aircraft departing the catapults safely.

AIR EXPERIENCE FLIGHT REBORN

At the end of the war, it was decided that non-flying junior RN and RM Officers would be given experience of flying and, to provide this service, the Tiger Moths of No. 799 Sqdn. B Flight at Gosport were used. This was reformed as No. 727 Sqdn. on 23rd April 1946, still at Gosport, and was to remain operating in this role until disbanding on 17th January 1950. The task of providing this flying then passed to the

DH Sea Venom F20

Communications Squadron at Lee-on-Solent.

Re-established at Brawdy six years later on 4th January 1956, it was then tasked with providing air experience flights to the cadets at Britannia Royal Naval College (BRNC). This Dartmouth Cadet Air Training Squadron, No. 727 Sqdn., was equipped with a variety of aircraft and helicopters during its five years existence; Sea Balliols, Sea Princes, Sea Vampires and Dragonflies. The squadron took over the tasks of No. 702 Sqdn., the JOAC flight, and received its aircraft.

The squadron disbanded in December 1960 when the fixed-wing element was retired. The helicopter flight was to operate at the college from Norton airfield situated on Townstall Hill overlooking the college, and was tasked with providing helicopter flight experience to non-flying officers under training. The Dragonflies were replaced with a Wasp in 1967 which served until 1982 when the aircraft was needed for Operation Corporate.

No permanent flight exists. Instead a detachment supplies experienced flights each term, still operating from the heliport at Norton. The airfield remains operational with full hangar and office facilities supporting a variety of military helicopters which call in for a stopover.

SUPERMARINES LAST FIGHTER

The first flight of the Scimitar was at Boscombe Down on 19th January 1956, and this was the final redesign of the undercarriage-less fighter first proposed in 1945. The aircraft was now designated as a low level strike aircraft - a considerable difference to its original conception. The aircraft was equipped with a low altitude bombing sortie (LABS) system which allowed it to fly at high subsonic speeds below radar height, the first FAA aircraft with this ability. It was to retain its fighter designation and its four 30mm Aden cannons remained as a standard weapons fit.

The type made its first deck landing on HMS *Ark Royal* in April 1956, followed by trials in July 1957 when 148 landings/launches were achieved, with the aircraft operated by the A & AEE. When the IFTU No. 700X Sqdn. was commissioned on 27th August 1957, one of its major proving tasks was the delivery of the British tactical nuclear weapon, and the Scimitar was the first FAA aircraft to be armed with the weapon. The squadron eventually became No. 803 Sqdn. in June 1958 for operations as part of HMS *Victorious'* air group.

GRANGE AIRFIELD CLOSES DOWN

HMS Siskin at Gosport was one of the country's first five military airfields established in 1914 as an RNAS base. It had been the base for the formation of many of the fledgling RNAS squadrons before and during W.W.I and for flying training. The basics of flying training now used worldwide were developed at the base when the flying school was under the leadership of Major Smith Barry, and the first form of in-flight communication, 'the Gosport Tube', was devised under his term in command.

Between the wars, it was the training school for catapult flights and became the RN Observer Training School in 1921. It was home to the Torpedo Training School and two torpedo squadrons, with Swordfish pilots being taught at the school. Upon the official forming of the FAA in 1924, Gosport became the FAA's principal base. During W.W.II it was an RAF base but was still used by FAA units and, during D-Day operations, it was a standby airfield for the squadrons at nearby Lee-on-Solent. After the war, it was given over to the FAA where it became the centre of helicopter flying and the post entry aircrew training. It was to close on 31st May 1956 after more than 40 years continued service.

Located at the airfield since 1914 was the torpedo development flight involved in airborne depth charge and torpedo trials. It was responsible for the design and development of

HMS Ark Royal

Supermarine Scimitar

Supermarine Scimitar

the Gosport mirror torpedo sight which allowed the pilot to line up his aircraft prior to releasing it at the target. This unit was to become the Advanced Torpedo Experimental Establishment after W.W.I, becoming the Aircraft Torpedo Development Unit (ATDU) during W.W.II, with the added task of investigating the art of airborne mine-laying.

After the war, the unit was to become a joint RAF/RAE unit remaining at Siskin until locating to Culdrose on 28th May 1956. Many famous pilots served with the unit and one of these, Rex Warneford, was a member of A Flight when he earned his VC in June 1915.

Its aircraft were regularly seen dropping weapons along the length of Gosport's Stokes Bay in the Solent until 1949 when it then used the ranges at Weston Super Mare and the Isles of Scilly. Three years after moving to Culdrose, the unit was to lose its aircraft, and future trials would be conducted borrowing aircraft from either the FAA or RAF as required. The unit was eventually to close on 27th August 1993 (now as a unit of the Admiralty Underwater Weapons Establishment) after 80 years service, mostly benefitted by the RNAS and FAA in their ASW operations.

OPERATION MUSKETEER THE SUEZ CRISIS

During July 1956, the fragile relationship between Israel and its Arab neighbours was deteriorating with many border clashes taking place. Egypt was to be given financial aid for the building of the Aswan Dam from the USA and Britain, but this was withdrawn by the Americans on 18th July because of the country's poor economic condition and its friendliness with the Communist Bloc. This move resulted in President Gamal Abdel Nasser declaring nationalisation of the Suez Canal (26th July), and the revenues raised would be used to build the dam.

Britain and France objected to this and raised the issue with the UN Security Council on 3rd August. During the debate on the 5th October, the Council agreed that the canal should be internationally controlled but this was vetoed by the Russians. Britain and France were planning a military operation to regain control of the canal but to succeed, assistance was needed from the Israelis. This was secured as the Israel-Jordan/Egypt confrontation was developing into a war scenario.

A joint operation was planned. Israeli troops began moving into the zone on 29th October which resulted in the British and French making an ultimatum for a ceasefire the following day and to be given control of the canal. Already knowing that the Egyptians

HMS Bulwark

DH Sea Venom

would not yield to the Israelis, the Anglo-French forces were being prepared to invade Egypt.

The RN had five carriers in the Mediterranean; HMSs *Albion, Bulwark, Eagle, Ocean* and *Theseus,* and the French had two; FN *Arromanches* and *Lafayette*. Ocean and Theseus were being used in the role of amphibious carriers operating helicopters for the landing of troops, CASEVAC and support missions, whilst the remaining five ships were all tasked with strike missions against military installations, airfields and troops. The aircraft were adorned with yellow and black stripes to ensure they would not be identified as enemy aircraft.

The first strikes were carried out by RAF Canberra and Valiant bombers attacking the Egyptian air bases before dawn on 31st October, followed by operations by the FAA aircraft. Sea Hawks, Sea Venoms and Wyverns carried out attacks, and the Skyraiders controlled the operations whilst the Gannets were busy on ASW patrols. The missions, to attack and destroy the airfields at Abu Suier, Cairo West, Dekheila, Fayid, Kabrit and Kasfareet, were successfully completed. The Egyptian Air Force was destroyed before it could mount a counter attack.

HMS *Eagle* led the British Fleet during the operation. Even though her starboard catapult had broken down, she was still able to launch 621 sorties, losing only two Wyverns and one Sea Hawk (all three pilots were safely recovered) whilst one Sea Venom was damaged but recovered to the ship.

The land warfare was being conducted by the Israelis, advancing down the Sinai coast, and the strike missions were now aimed at the support of these troops, destroying transportation, bridges, railways, military forces and installations as the Egyptians retreated. The UN was against the action and called for a ceasefire which Egypt accepted on 2nd November. Initially the Israelis agreed the following day but were pressurised by the British and French to continue.

Anglo French paratroops dropped into the zone around the cities of Port Said and Port Fuad on the 5th, followed by the amphibious assault from the two carriers the following day when No. 845 Sqdn. and the Joint Experimental Helicopter Unit landed the 500 men of 45 Commando Royal Marines (RMC) and all their equipment. This was the first such mission for launching an amphibious assault with helicopters.

However, due to increased political pressure, the operation was called to an abrupt end when a ceasefire was called at midnight on the

Hawker Sea Hawks aboard HMS Eagle

Hawker Sea Hawk wearing Suez stripes

6th and the British and French troops were withdrawn back to the ships. The operation had cost sixteen British servicemen their lives, and the FAA had lost four aircraft although they launched over 1400 sorties from the five ships in the six days.

SMALL SHIPS' FLIGHTS

Helicopters had carried out trials from RN frigates and destroyers as well as RFAs since convoy trials in W.W.II. During 1954, the Ocean Patrol Ship HMS *Vidal* operated a Hiller HT1 of No. 705 Sqdn. fitted with floats, and a small flight deck was constructed at the ship's stern for the helicopter to operate from. The helicopter was seen to be a useful addition to the ship's assets so plans were made for more permanent arrangements to be installed in ships for helicopter operations.

The first unit to be formed for independent operations from non-aircraft carriers was attached to HMS *Protector*, the Falkland Islands and Antarctic patrol ship. The unit, formed from No. 701 Sqdn. on 11th July 1955 with two Whirlwind HAR1 helicopters, was to be the forerunner of the now well known term "small ships' flight". This was to be the model for all future flights which were to be autonomous units of a squadron as a permanent part of the ship's compliment.

Small ships' flights were to be an integrally designed weapon for all ships of frigate size or above commencing with the County Class destroyers and Leander Class frigates of the 1960s. Other ships already with the Fleet were to be refitted with helicopter operating and support facilities. Ships of the Royal Fleet Auxiliary were also fitted with landing decks, and later designs of support ships were also fitted with hangars and support facilities for helicopter operations.

THE UNLUCKY SEAMEW

A new lightweight ASW aircraft, the Shorts Seamew ASMk1, was received into service with No. 700 Sqdn. during November 1956 for service aboard all the current RN aircraft carriers. It was conceived as a cheap, easy to operate and maintain ASW aircraft which could fulfill the requirements of the increasing need for NATO to counter the Russian submarine threat. It had first flown

Westland Whirlwind

on 23rd August 1953 and had attended the Farnborough Airshow in 1954 before commencing sea trials in HMS *Bulwark* on 12th July 1955.

After successful operational sea trials were held aboard HMS *Warrior* by two aircraft from No. 700 Sqdn., it was decided to equip ASW squadrons of the RNVR with the type, replacing the Grumman Avengers. After the delivery of seven aircraft, the RNVR was disbanded so the aircraft were put into storage before eventually being scrapped. The aircraft did not enter service with the regular squadrons due to the delivery of the Gannets and unfortunately no orders were received from the European NATO countries. The contract for the remaining aircraft (from an order for 30) was therefore cancelled.

HMS Protector's Westland Whirlwind HAR9

THE RNVR DISBANDS AGAIN

Unfortunately the defence cuts of 1957 called for the immediate disbanding of the RNVR. During their ten years of supporting the FAA, they had carried out exercises aboard the Fleet aircraft carriers HMSs *Bulwark, Illustrious, Implacable, Theseus, Triumph* and *Vengeance,* and many annual camps at bases both at home and overseas, especially at Hal Far. During the Korean War (1950-1953), thirteen RNVR pilots flew with the operational squadrons in the theatre.

At the height of activities the RNVR had thirteen squadrons based within five divisions around the country:-

Channel-Ford 1840 & 1842 anti-submarine

Midland-Bramcote 1833 fighter

Honiley 1844 anti-submarine

Northern-Stretton 1831 fighter

1841 anti-submarine

Scottish-Abbotsinch 1830 & 1843 anti-submarine

Southern-Culham/Benson 1832, 1834, 1835 & 1836 fighters

The RNVR operated 30 marks of aircraft of sixteen different types in all roles that their full-time counterparts operated, giving a large population of trained reservists experience in some of the more modern types. Their operations included fighter, anti-submarine, photo-reconnaissance and basic flying training. All divisions also had communications aircraft at their disposal.

Squadrons from the RNVR had taken part in the Coronation Fleet Review and had held a Jubilee Flypast over Windsor Castle in the presence of Her Majesty the Queen the following year. Admiral Sir Casper John attended the RNVR's last parade at Stretton where he took the final salute, after which the eleven remaining squadrons disbanded on 10th March 1957.

WHIRLWIND HAS Mk7

The HAS Mk7 ASW development of the Whirlwind helicopter replaced the Gannet as the front line ASW weapon, equipped with both radar and sonar capable of carrying either a torpedo, bombs or depth charges. The IFTU squadron No. 700H commissioned on 18th March 1957 for six months of proving trials. The squadron carried out night sonar trials whilst aboard HMS *Bulwark* during September, continuing the trials when disembarked to Lee-on-Solent during October. No. 845 Sqdn. began receiving the aircraft in June to replace their HAR3s but, after the loss of some of the aircraft due to engine overheating problems, the HAS Mk7 was grounded for six months in late 1958 whilst the problem was resolved.

One of the development Mk5s was to become the prototype gas turbine powered Whirlwind when it was modified in 1958 with a General Electric T-58 (later to be a licence built DH/RR Gnome) engine, first flying on 28th February 1959. Some seventeen of the HAS Mk7s were converted to become the unarmed HAR Mk9s for SAR and station flight duties fitted with this jet engine.

THE HELICOPTER SHUTTLE

The first time that the helicopter was to show its usefulness in transferring men and equipment from one ship to another was when the Sea Hawk Squadron, No. 898 Sqdn., was moved from HMS *Ark Royal* to HMS *Bulwark* on 28th June 1957. Both ships had two SAR helicopters, and these four machines transferred the 85 men and twenty tons of squadron stores from one ship to the other in 55 minutes.

The ships were steaming side by side whilst the loads were shifted. The under-slung loads were carried in nets and with slings, and only one mishap occurred when one load dropped into the catwalk (and some in the sea) as the helicopter moved off Ark Royal's deck. The operation was seen as a time saving method of embarking a squadron, and it was to be the

Shorts Seamew

Westland Whirlwind load lifting

Westland Whirlwinds on board HMS Eagle at Istanbul

first of such moves and is still used today.

THE GYRODYNE AND SARO P531

Fairey Aviation aircraft had been serving in the FAA for over 40 years when the company moved into the helicopter 'field'. Development of the 'Gyrodyne' family of helicopters led to the design of an Ultra Light Helicopter as an intended helicopter for the Army. It was fitted with jet thrusters on the rotor blade tips, and first flew on 14th August 1955.

Two of these helicopters were to carry out trials with the FAA to assess the practicality of small helicopters operating from the frigates and destroyers of the RN. Trials were held aboard HMS *Grenville* in the English channel during Autumn 1957 when over 70 landings and take-offs were achieved, successfully demonstrating the future small ships' flight concept. The practicality of operating from the decks of frigates was demonstrated to the public at the 1958 SBAC Airshow at Farnborough. A flatbed lorry driven down the runway substituted for the flight deck with the Ultra Light Helicopter launching, recovering and hovering over the rear of the lorry. This display was re-enacted with its successor, the P531, in 1961.

However the design was not pursued after the trials were completed, and the type was to be superseded by the Saunders Roe P531 which was developed by Fairey Aviation as a helicopter for both the Army and Navy, the first purpose designed helicopter for operations from small ships. Initial designs of the type, a turbine development of the SARO Skeeter, began in November 1957. It was flown by Ken Reed (of HMS *Vanguard* fame) for the first time on 20th July 1958 from the Hayes factory, only four days after the engine had been delivered.

As early as 1948, Lt. Cdr. J Sproule had submitted an idea to the Admiralty which suggested fitting helicopters with suction pads to aid their safe operation from the decks of ships. The pads were to be operated by the pilot who controlled an engine driven vacuum pump. Sproule also designed a harpoon system which could be used in combination with a grid fitted to the ship's deck (trials were conducted with a Dragonfly during March 1955). This system was further developed to use a winch down system and was tested at Farnborough during 1960 but not progressed until over ten years later. It is now commonly used by navies worldwide.

The P531 joined No. 700X Sqdn. in October 1959 for development trials, carrying out trials aboard HMS *Undaunted* during November and December when more than 300 landings had been performed including 30 night landings. One of the prototypes was fitted with the suction pads for trials aboard Undaunted during late 1961 and HMS *Ashanti* during August 1962.

The trials proved the suction theory but were not conducive to easy handling of the helicopter once on the deck. Three prototypes were used for nineteen different undercarriage arrangements tested to find the best design, and it was finally decided that a wheeled castoring undercarriage was the best solution. The success of the P531 trials resulted in the Westland Wasp helicopter complete with the castors.

FAA ELECTRONIC WARFARE

The FAA started to show an interest in electronic warfare at the end of 1951 when No.

Fairey Gyrodyne after restoration (1998)

751 Sqdn. formed at RAF Watton as a radio warfare unit initially with Mosquitos. This was later to be officially recognised as an EW unit in 1957, carrying out trials and exercises with electronic equipment and the jamming of radars both ashore and on ships of the RN, with a base move to Culdrose. By then, two flights were operated; A Flight with Sea Venom 21 ECM and B Flight with Avenger AS4s.

Further trials work was being conducted by other units and No. 744 Sqdn. commenced airborne radar jamming trials with Avenger AS5s during July 1955. This resulted in the commissioning of No. 745 Sqdn. on 23rd April 1956 as the specialised radar jamming unit with modified Avenger TS5s. It was disbanded at the end of 1957, its work being passed to No. 751 Sqdn. as the only FAA EW squadron.

So important was the role becoming that the squadron was redesignated as a front line squadron becoming No. 831 Sqdn. on 1st May 1958 operating with the two flights still at Culdrose. It was to move to RAF Watton for operations alongside No. 97 Sqdn., the RAF's EW squadron, before both were disbanded to become one RAF/RN unit in 1966.

Saro P531

THE WORLD'S FIRST JET POWERED HELICOPTER - THE WESSEX

Following the cancellation of the Bristol Type 191, the FAA needed a replacement for the Whirlwind in the ASW role. It was decided to order the Westland WS58 Wessex, a turbine powered licence built Sikorsky S58. Westlands received one of the Sikorsky piston powered examples in June 1956, and this aircraft was modified with the fitting of a Napier Gazelle jet engine, first flying on 17th May 1957. Although the Fairey Ultra Light Helicopter was powered by a turbine engine, it was not a true helicopter in the sense that the blades were driven directly by the engine without the use of a driven gearbox.

The first Westland built Wessex HAS 1 flew thirteen months later on 20th June 1958 as the FAA's first purpose built ASW helicopter, fitted with an automatic flight control system giving the helicopter all-weather and night operational capability. The Wessex IFTU No. 700H Sqdn. commissioned on 1st April 1960 becoming the Helicopter Advanced Flying Training Squadron (No. 706 Sqdn.) on 4th January 1962, and was tasked with training pilots on the type, supporting airborne trials for the ATDU and eventually the training of future commando helicopter pilots.

The first FLS was No. 815 Sqdn. commissioning on 4th July 1961. The squadron was to be part of HMS *Ark Royal's* air group replacing the Gannet in the ASW role, embarking for the first time on 13th November. However, the aircraft had to return home to Culdrose shortly after due to engine problems, resulting in modifications being carried out to all the HAS Mk1s.

The eight new guided missile destroyers of the 'County Class' were all to be equipped

Grumman Avenger EW6

Westland Wessex Mk 1

with a single Wessex helicopter. These were the world's first non-aircraft carrier warships to be built with integral helicopter operating facilities including hangar, maintenance facilities and storage for aircraft spares. The first flight was commissioned on 14th March 1964 for service aboard HMS *Devonshire*.

The Wessex was to become the helicopter work horse of the FAA, operating as a SAR helicopter on the aircraft carriers, ASW helicopters aboard aircraft carriers, destroyers and two converted Tiger Class cruisers (HMSs *Blake* and *Tiger*), in the commando role on the commando carriers, assault ships, logistic support ships and in RFAs carrying out transfers between ships.

THE TROUBLED ISLAND OF CYPRUS

The British protectorate of Cyprus in the Eastern Mediterranean has always been unstable due to the distrust of the other by the Greeks and Turks who both claim sovereignty of the Island. The Greek population (roughly 80%) would like union with Greece (Enosis) but this is opposed by the Turkish 20%.

Action in support of Enosis was supported by Archbishop Makarios resulting in him being exiled by the British. Rebel forces led by Colonel Grivas carried out guerrilla warfare against the British and terrorism against the Turkish minority. These actions intensified until it was decided the FAA would supply anti-shipping patrols to prevent the shipment of arms to the terrorists and guerrillas.

A special flight of three Gannet AS1s was formed from No. 812 Sqdn. at Eglinton on 17th March 1956. Known as the Cyprus Maritime Patrol Squadron, No. 847 Sqdn. was given the task of providing daily patrols around the island. Arriving at Nicosia on 5th April, the squadron remained on the island until November 1959 flying nearly 1700 operational sorties with their three aircraft, maintaining at least one aircraft available throughout their tour of duty. The AS1s were replaced with AS4s during June 1958.

THE RED HAWKS

No. 738 Sqdn. was tasked with demonstrating FAA flying skills at the 1957 SBAC show with their Sea Hawk aircraft, and a formation team of five aircraft was established painted red and christened as the 'Red Hawks'. After training, the team had a routine of loops and rolls in diamond formation and demonstrations were given at Woodford, Manchester and Squires Gate, Blackpool. During the Woodford display, however, two of the aircraft were to clip wings after getting too close but both aircraft landed safely.

Sikorsky HAR22 of No. 728C Sqdn at Malta

THE AMPHIBIOUS WARFARE TRIALS UNIT

The decision to form a Trials Unit for the development of amphibious operations with the Royal Marines was to have a profound affect on both the future operations of the RN and FAA. The Amphibious Warfare Trials Unit (AWTU), No. 728C Sqdn., was formed on 7th January 1958 with four Whirlwind HAS 22 helicopters at Lee-on-Solent, but was to operate out of Hal Far in Malta, home to its parent squadron.

The Unit was to develop the role of the helicopter in support of commando operations and in particular when being disembarked for landings ashore from the Fleet's amphibious ships. It carried out exercises in Malta with the Royal Marines of

HMS Victorious' busy flight deck

the 3rd Commando Brigade (3CB) including troop embarking and disembarking, stores lifts and the lifting of vehicles (this included a Citroen 2CV). Once the techniques and operating methods were established, beachhead landings were exercised.

Embarked in the landing ship HMS *Striker*, the squadron and 3CB set off for the deserts of Libya. Disembarking in Tripoli, Exercise Tarhina was conducted in the desert where the squadron set up an operating site, the first of many sites to be established by FAA Commando Units worldwide. During the exercise, the squadron developed the techniques for troop transport, CASEVAC and reconnaissance missions, stores re-supply flights, parachute drops and machine gun firing trials. Operations were conducted both during the day and night, and further exercises were held using the deck of HMS *Bulwark* which was later to become the RN's first commando assault carrier.

The trials were to develop into an 'active' mission against the Greek fundamentalists in Cyprus, before disbanding and reforming as the first Commando Squadron, No. 848 Sqdn. The AWTU had proved the concept and from now on the FAA would have units operating in support of the 3rd Commando Brigade.

The operations of No. 847 Sqdn.'s Gannets in Cyprus certainly reduced the flow of arms to the rebels but their attacks continued so, during 1958, it was decided to increase the opposition to their attacks. No. 728C Flight, the AWTU, was sent to support the Forces against the guerrillas. The unit was at Malta working with 45 RMC in perfecting the role of helicopters in the transfer of troops and equipment from ships for assaults on beachheads. Their four Whirlwinds HAS 22s were craned on board HMS *Bermuda* and transferred to Cyprus, along with the 3CB on 16th June 1958.

The squadron was called upon to join forces with No. 284 Sqdn. RAF operating Bristol Sycamores, to transfer the Commandos and men of the Royal West Kents to capture terrorists who were operating from a hide in the mountain village of Akanthou. The operation coded 'Operation Springtime' began on 11th July with an early morning launch from Nicosia to transport the men to Lefkoniko. The Whirlwinds and Sycamores transported the troops to the village two days later, with one Whirlwind disembarking its load of marines 50 yards from the hide located on a slope below a rock face. Unfortunately the terrorists had moved on.

This was the first time a second line unit had been in action since W.W.II, albeit limited (only two others would see action with Wessex Flights during the Falklands war of 1982 - No. 737 Sqdn. and No. 772 Sqdn.). A ceasefire was agreed on 13th March 1959, with the establishment of an Independent Republic. Makarios was elected as the Republic's first president in the December elections.

THE RN's CAPITAL SHIPS

The Fleet carriers HMSs *Ark Royal* and *Eagle* were to operate off Malta in combined exercises. The two ships had also delivered the four Whirlwinds for the AWTU to the island and, on 7th February 1958, their Sea Hawks and Venoms were to combine for a flypast over Valetta. Sixty-two aircraft in total, and both ships, were to enter Grand Harbour after recovering the aircraft.

Whilst in the harbour the ships were to demonstrate that aircraft launching capability was not restricted whilst at anchor in a harbour. On the 14th, seven Gannets and three Wyverns were launched from the steam catapults on Ark Royal, whilst two of Eagle's Skyraiders carried out a free take-off (the first time this had been done by this large aircraft).

After a refit in Portsmouth, HMS *Victorious*, the last of the Illustrious class armoured aircraft carriers, was recommissioned after seven years (October 1950 - January 1958). The ship emerged extended by a 30ft insert into the ship's hull, with the lengthened flight deck angled at 8.75 degrees, steam catapults, MLS, the latest arrestor wires system and the new aircraft early warning radar system.

This system was the largest radar system to be fitted to an aircraft carrier. Referred to as

Hawker Hunter T8 of Heron Flight

the 'Dustbin', the Type 984 three-dimensional radar was capable of tracking, fighter direction and surveillance operations within one system. It had the ability to identify all aircraft within its range giving clear positioning and height, information which provided the defending aircraft with a positive interception track.

She began her work-up and sea trials on 3rd February 1958 with two helicopters of No. 701C Flight embarked for helicopter delivery service (HDS) duties. Her aircraft operation and handling trials were held in June, and during the trials a Scimitar was successfully launched after a free take-off. Her air group embarked for the first time on 25th September with No. 803 Sqdn. Scimitars (the type's first deployment), No. 824 Sqdn. Whirlwind helicopters, No. 849 B Flight Skyraider AEWs and No. 893 Sea Venom FAW21s. Unfortunately, on embarking, the CO of No. 803 Sqdn. was killed when his Scimitar crashed on landing, an inauspicious beginning to the type's operational career.

SWEPT-WING TRAINER ARRIVES

To carry out training of pilots for the future swept-winged aircraft, the FAA ordered the Hawker Hunter T Mk8, a development of the RAF's T Mk7 fitted with an arrestor hook and brake parachute. The first aircraft were delivered to No. 736 Sqdn., the Naval Air Fighter and Strike School, at Lossiemouth in July 1958. These aircraft were then passed on to the Air Warfare Instructor Training and Swept-Wing Conversion Unit No. 764 Sqdn. also at Lossiemouth.

This trainer was to remain in service until retired by the Fleet Requirements and Air Direction Training Unit (FRADU) in 1996 after 38 years service. During this time, revised versions of the Mk8 were introduced fitted with equipment used by Buccaneers, Sea Harriers and Sea Vixens. Two Advanced Flying Training units, No. 759 Sqdn. at Brawdy and No. 738 Sqdn. at Lossiemouth, used the type.

The FAA ordered single-seat GA.Mk11 aircraft as weapon trainers which were operated by No. 738 and No. 764 Sqdns., the former receiving the type in June 1962. The last two second line squadrons disbanded at Lossiemouth in 1970 and their aircraft were passed to Airwork Ltd for use with the FRADU.

MIDDLE EAST TROUBLES

On 22nd March 1946, Britain granted independence to Transjordan and, three years later on 2nd June 1949, the Hashemite Kingdom of Jordan was established reigned by King Abdullah. He was assassinated by an Arab extremist in 1951 and was eventually succeeded by the seventeen year old King Hussein. The other ruling Arab leaders, led by President Nasser, tried in vain to have the young king assassinated due to his friendliness and liberal attitude, especially towards peace with Israel.

The amalgamation of Egypt, Syria and the Sudan as the United Arab Republic (UAR) on 1st February 1958 threatened the stability of the Middle East. Syria and Lebanon had formed a military defence treaty in 1956, but Lebanon did not wish to join the UAR who insisted on an insurrection in the country. Fighting began in April reaching the capital Beirut in June and continuing for a further month, when the country's President, Camille Chamoun, appealed for help on 14th July.

The Americans immediately despatched troops stationed in Europe to assist, and the British Government despatched HMS *Eagle* from its exercises to lend air support. Its three fighter squadrons, No.'s 802 and 898 Sqdns. with Sea Hawks and No. 894 Sqdn. with Sea Venoms, operated over the country until the ship was withdrawn on 22nd August. No action was encountered by UAR aircraft.

The UAR was becoming a threat to the Kingdom, so Jordan and Iraq formed the Arab Federation in March 1958 with King Feisal II as head of the state. Five months later, on 14th July, a coup in Iraq resulted in the death of King Feisal and his son and thus King Hussein was declared the new Head of

Hawker Hunter T8 used as an "Admiral's Barge"

Hawker Hunter GA11

the Federation. Realising his position was insecure, he dissolved the Federation after only two weeks as its Head.

Pressure from the communist supported UAR and the revolt in Iraq encouraged King Hussein to request assistance from Britain in maintaining the safety of his Kingdom. An air lift was established from Cyprus to Jordan, with HMSs *Eagle, Bulwark* and *Albion* all involved in the operations, the first two keeping stray Arab aircraft clear of the airlift routes whilst the latter was used as a troop transporter.

Around the clock CAP was maintained by the Sea Hawks and Sea Venoms controlled by the Skyraiders, and the squadrons from Eagle operated in the Mediterranean whilst Bulwark's aircraft operated from Aden and the Red Sea. The Gannets of No. 814 Sqdn. carried out AS patrols around the Mediterranean Fleet. The initial operations were relaxed at the end of July, but there was a further alert at the end of September when the three ships were again called to show support for Jordan when there was signs of another confrontation. However this did not materialise.

Whilst Britain gave Jordan support, the Americans were supporting the Lebanese who were also being threatened by the UAR and Iraq. The support of these two powers for these countries was a significant factor in peace in the region, and relationships with the other Arab nations was re-established (albeit precariously). The British Forces withdrew from the area on 29th October 1958.

ENTER THE SEA VIXEN FAW Mk1

The DH110 was officially named the Sea Vixen on 4th March 1957 and entered service with the IFTU No. 700Y Sqdn. on 4th November 1958. This heavyweight fighter had taken seven years to reach squadron level after much development work. It was the first British aircraft with an integrated weapons system and the first British fighter aircraft without guns, using air-to-air guided missiles as its main attack weapon.

The first flight having been in September 1951, the type was ordered in February 1954 and the first production aircraft was to go to the Test and Evaluation Units at Boscombe Down and Bedford in 1957, embarking on HMS *Ark Royal* for handling trials during July 1957 (18th-25th) when the aircraft completed 50 landings/launches.

The IFTU was equipped with eight of the aircraft to train up the crews and maintainers which were eventually to become No. 892 Sqdn. on 1st July 1959. During its eight months, it operated three aircraft aboard

Hawker Sea Hawk

DH Sea Vixen FAW Mk 1 used for trials

HMS *Victorious* in May for operational carrier assessment flying, completing 244 landings including 55 at night. A further IFTU was established on 2nd November with four aircraft from No. 892 Sqdn. identified as B Flight, tasked with evaluating the Firestreak missile. The trials were to last until August 1960 when the flight was disbanded.

The Sea Vixen training squadron was established as B Flight of No. 766 Sqdn., the All Weather Fighter Training Squadron, on 22nd October 1959. This squadron was to be the Sea Vixen Training Squadron until disbanding on 10th December 1970, and also created a display team ('Fred's Five') during 1963 using five of the squadron's aircraft. Operating alongside this squadron was No. 899 Sqdn. as the Sea Vixen Headquarters Squadron, the first time a second support squadron had been formed for an aircraft type which was given front line status.

A new concept was to be developed using the Sea Vixen, that of 'Buddy Buddy' refuelling, the idea being that one of the unit's Sea Vixens would act as a tanker aircraft, fitted with extra drop tanks and a drogue and hose refuelling tank, tasked with refuelling its 'buddies' from the squadron. The aircraft was fitted with a nine foot refuel probe on the port wing which would locate into the basket of the hose and fuel would be transferred from the tanker aircraft.

The aim would be that the buddies could be launched with a low fuel load but full weapons load or their range could be extended. The trials proved a success and the system was to become a standard operating method used not only by the FAA but many other air arms worldwide.

BLERIOT AIR RACE

The Daily Mail London-Paris air race was to include two FAA aircraft - a Sea Vixen with the observer Lt. Cdr. W Carter as the competitor, and a Scimitar with Cdr. I Martin competing. The latter was to succeed in winning the fastest single-seat aircraft race in a time of 43 minutes 11 seconds from the Arc De Triumphe to Marble Arch on 19th July 1959. The first run was on the 13th but many problems caused delays and, after finding solutions, the winning run was cleverly devised with the help of many people, both military and civil. The race began with Martin as a pillion passenger on a motor bike ridden by the French world champion, Georgs Hovels, and witnessed by many of his adoring fans, the supporters stopping traffic so that it was a clear run to the heliport at Issy.

He was then flown by FAA Whirlwind to the air base at Villacoublay where he was strapped into his Scimitar which had been started up, pre take-off checked and cleared for take-off prior to his arrival. To gain entry to the cockpit without danger from the intakes as both engines were turning, a special gantry was erected. The ground crew had his passport stamped by the French Authorities and, once in the cockpit (with his passport), it was an immediate take-off for Wisley.

Upon landing, the engines were cut to reduce stopping distance, the cockpit canopy was opened on approach, Martin got out of the cockpit and, using a slide designed by Vickers, he slid to the ground and ran to the waiting helicopter. Again his passport was in the possession of a member of the team. Flying to a helipad constructed by the Albert Bridge, he ran down to the river to a waiting speed boat which took him to a jackstay at the pier.

The jackstay had been erected by the RN gunnery school at Whale Island and he was pulled up the river bank by students of the school, then a waiting Royal Marine motor cycle took him to the finishing point at Marble Arch. A good team effort by the RN, RMs, FAA, Vickers and civilians from both sides of the channel resulted in a win for the team.

DH Sea Vixen FAW Mk 1

Supermarine Scimitar

BRITAIN'S ONLY HELIBASE BECOMES OPERATIONAL

RNAS Portland, HMS Osprey, the only helicopter base to be constructed in the UK, was commissioned on 24th April 1959 by Admiral Sir Manly Power, the Commander in Chief Portsmouth. Portland Harbour had been home to many FAA and Coastal Command Units since before W.W.I, and it was decided that with the arrival of the R4B Hoverfly helicopters operating with the anti-submarine School, a base for helicopter operations should be constructed.

Two hangers were erected and a landing pad was built on the RN playing fields located in front of the fleet canteen, which was taken over as the helibase headquarters, operations centre, control tower and workshops. The base was to have a runway added to its layout in 1966 which was 400ft long by 100ft wide, complete with ground control approach equipment.

The first 'based' helicopters arrived on 14th April 1959, when the twelve Whirlwinds of No. 815 Sqdn. arrived at 16.00 hours. The heliport was to remain an important base for helicopter training for nearly 50 years, with all the front line squadron helicopter types operated from its runway. It was eventually to become the main base for the parenting of the small ships' flights until its closure in March 1999 (days short of its 50th anniversary).

GANNET AEW3

The FAA's AEW Gannet entered service with No. 700 'G' Sqdn., the Gannet AEW3 IFTU, on 17th August 1959, with its aircraft joining No. 849 Sqdn. when it disbanded on 1st February 1960. This model of the aircraft had many differences from the ASW and training aircraft - a redesigned tail with increased fin area, a streamlined fuselage with an internal cabin for the two radar operators, repositioned engine and exhausts, and the large ventral radar below the fuselage. To accommodate the radar, a longer stroke undercarriage was fitted. The prototype had first flown twelve months earlier, on 20th August, and carried out sea trials aboard HMS *Centaur* (November 1958) and HMS *Victorious* (May 1959).

The type replaced the Skyraiders with No. 849 Sqdn. continuing as the only AEW squadron in the FAA, the final operator of the last pure Fairey type in FAA service. The squadron was to continue with an HQ flight and three flights of four aircraft for carrier operations. Each flight was to be augmented by a single AS4 version that was converted for COD (Carrier Onboard Dispatch) duties by removal of all its weapons systems and associated electronics.

It was basically the ship's communications 'hack', and many sailors were carried ashore for 'compassionate' reasons by these aircraft giving some of them their first experience of flying, let alone from a carrier. The last COD deployment was HMS *Ark Royal's* COD flight which disembarked for the last time on 17th July 1972 after sixteen years of carrier operations. The COD role was to be operated by an additional Sea King for No. 824 Sqdn., quite fitting as the squadron had been the first recipient of the AS4 Gannet.

SCIMITAR STEALS THE SHOW

Once again it was the FAA's turn to show its

Westland Whirlwind

Fairey Gannet AEW 3

aircraft off at the SBAC show at Farnborough, with the aircraft from HMS *Ark Royal* chosen to do the flying displays and the Scimitars of No. 807 Sqdn. performing some formation aerobatics. However two manoeuvres were to show the professionalism of naval aviators. One was the landing of one aircraft which touched down and then accelerated between two aircraft taxiing in the opposite direction with their wings folded. The other was the picking up of the Dart Target which it then towed around the airfield. The tow rope for the target was mounted between two 12ft poles, the aircraft approached with its hook down, picking up the 2000ft rope followed by the dayglo red 140 lb target.

HMS Hermes

HMS HERMES COMPLETES

The decade finished on a high when, after taking fifteen years to build, the Navy's latest most modern aircraft carrier, HMS *Hermes,* at last joined the Fleet and was accepted on 18th November 1959 after her trials, being commissioned one week later on the 25th. Laid down in the Vickers-Armstrong Barrow-in-Furness shipyard during W.W.II (21st June 1944), this ship took longer to complete than any aircraft carrier in the history of the RN. Although conceived as a Centaur class light-fleet carrier, she bore no resemblance to her three sister ships having a 6.5 degree angled deck, MLS, Steam catapults, a deck-edge aircraft lift, radiation protection system, the 984 '3-D' radar system and a larger redesigned island superstructure. The first aircraft to land on her deck was a Seahawk of No. 700 Sqdn. touching down on 10th May 1960 at the start of three weeks of flying trials. Her squadrons embarked for her first commission on 6th July 1960, namely No. 804 Sqdn. Scimitars, No. 814 Sqdn. Whirlwind HAS 7s, No. 849C Flight Gannets and No. 890 Sqdn. Sea Vixens.

THE COMMANDO CARRIER

The 1958 Defence White Paper announced that HMS *Albion* and HMS *Bulwark* were to be converted as dedicated helicopter/troop carriers, with both ships entering a refit and modernisation programme. The latter began conversion in January 1959 and the refit took just twelve months to complete, with the ship re-commissioning as a Landing Platform - Helicopters (LPH). The conversion was not to the full standard she would eventually reach, mainly due to the urgent requirement of the ship in its new role. Albion's conversion would be more extensive on the initial reconfiguration.

Bulwark re-commissioned on 19th January 1960 as the first dedicated commando carrier. The ship was devoid of catapult and arrestor gear, air conditioning had been

HMS Bulwark

installed, as had four landing craft on gun sponsons (after the removal of the 40mm guns). There was accommodation for up to 750 Royal Marines and soldiers as standard which could be increased in emergency conditions to two commando units (1200+ men). The ship was reconfigured to operate a squadron of Whirlwind troop carrying helicopters, a new role which was to last 22 years, outliving her sister by nearly ten years.

After initial trials in the Portland areas, she embarked her Whirlwind helicopters of No. 848 Sqdn. on 10th March as she sailed to Devonport to embark 600 commandos of 42 RMC for a tour in the Far East. She would be called upon to prove her worth fifteen months later in support of the Sheikhdom of Kuwait which was under threat from the Iraqis.

After de-commissioning as a conventional carrier in February 1961, HMS *Albion* recommissioned on 1st August 1962 as the second commando carrier. The ship's conversion was more extensive than that of her sister ship, the main visible difference being the complete removal of the angle deck. She was fitted out to carry 900 men as standard and also to operate the Wessex helicopters which were replacing the Whirlwinds.

The RN's intention was that the two ships would alternate in operations, with one ship operational in the Far East at all times. Eventually joining these ships would be a couple of specially designed assault ships which would carry the supporting heavy vehicles and tanks used in assaults. The two ships, HMS *Fearless* and HMS *Intrepid*, would be based on an American design and were to be ordered in 1962.

THE BLACKBURN BUCCANEER

Blackburn submitted their B103 as a tender for the FAA strike aircraft in the Admiralty requirement NR/A.39 for a low level, subsonic, carrier borne strike aircraft. The aircraft was to feature a rotating bomb door to ease the loading and delivery of its bombs, and was to be the world's first specialist low level high speed bomber capable of carrying a nuclear weapon. This was taken into account when twenty prototype and development aircraft were ordered in July 1955. The first of these flew on 30th April 1958 which was the date specified when ordered. It was a tremendous feat by Blackburn to keep to the designated programme, and it was probably the only military aircraft to fly on the date required when ordered.

Carrier trials were held aboard HMS *Victorious* on 19th January 1960, with 30 landings/launches successfully achieved. Much of the development work was carried out at the A & AEE and Blackburns, whilst one aircraft was used by De Havilland for

Blackburn NA 39 Buccaneer Prototype

Blackburn Buccaneer S1 wearing the anti-radiation white colour scheme

Gyron Junior engine development. The RN Test Flight at Boscombe Down carried out further deck trials during 1961 aboard both HMS *Ark Royal* and HMS *Hermes.*

The IFTU was formed on 7th March 1961 as No. 700Z Sqdn. using six pre-production aircraft and during the Farnborough Airshow of 1962, four of the aircraft displayed as an FAA display team. The first front line squadron was to be No. 801 Sqdn. commissioned on 17th July 1962 carrying out its workup aboard HMS *Ark Royal*.

Due to the poor performance of the Gyron Junior, the Mk1 was severely handicapped. The aircraft had to take-off with a light fuel load and then be refuelled in flight to allow them to continue their mission. However, this problem was overcome by re-engining the aircraft with the Rolls Royce Spey engine which produced 40% more thrust, which meant that the dimensions of the engine intakes had to be increased to allow for the greater airflow required by the engine.

The redesigned model was ordered on 8th January 1962 as the Buccaneer Mk2, and the first prototype was a rebuilt Mk1 prototype which first flew on 17th May 1963. Five aircraft were used for development trials using the deck of Ark Royal during March 1965 for handling and operational trials. The type entered service in April 1965.

FIRST RN PILOT FLIES THE F4 PHANTOM II

Whilst serving with the British Naval Staff at the Embassy in Washington during 1961, Cdr. P Chilton was given the opportunity to fly some evaluation sorties in the new F4H Phantom II being developed for the USN. Flying out of the McDonnell Douglas test facility at Edwards AFB in California, Chilton flew in three of the pre-production aircraft, and later flew in a production model from the factory at St. Louis. At that time there was no indication that the RN was interested in the aircraft - little did Chilton know that the FAA would operate the type as its last conventional fixed-wing aircraft.

Blackburn Buccaneer S1 wearing standard colour scheme

THE KUWAIT CRISIS

The Sheikhdom of Kuwait asked for assistance from the British when their independence was threatened by Iraq after the Iraqi Prime Minister, General Kassim, announced that the tiny country was an annex of his country, rejecting the 1899 Anglo-Kuwait agreement. The British Forces were put on alert on 29th June 1961, and HMS *Victorious* was sent to the Gulf from the Far East to join up with HMS *Centaur* which was already on station to supply air defence requirements. The commando carrier, HMS *Bulwark*, which was exercising in the Persian Gulf arrived off the Kuwaiti coast 24 hours later.

The commandos of 42 RMC were put ashore by the helicopters of No. 848 Sqdn., securing an airstrip ten miles outside the city for use by both the FAA and RAF aircraft. Air support for the landings was supplied by the fighters from the other two carriers, Sea Vixens FAW Mk1s from Nos. 890 and 893 Sqdns.

The support from the British had its desired affect. The Iraqis backed down promising that no attack on the Sheikhdom would be attempted by her Forces, although the claim to the ownership was still legally theirs. The British Forces were withdrawn from 8th July after these assurances were announced, but the Iraqis did eventually invade the country in 1990 when Saddam Hussein sent his Republican Guard across the border. This resulted in the nearest conflict to W.W.3 when a united force liberated the country in a war known as the Gulf War.

After the Kuwait operations, HMS *Bulwark* was to enter a short refit in Singapore dockyard before re-commissioning on 7th October 1961. This was significant as it was the first time since W.W.II that a British aircraft carrier would be commissioned into service in an overseas port. During her two month refit, over 900 crew were to be flown from the UK to Singapore, with an equal amount returning home from the ship and squadron.

HOVERCRAFT DEVELOPMENT

The Inter-Service Hovercraft (Trials) Unit (IHTU) was formed at HMS Ariel Lee-on-Solent in September and was tasked with evaluating the potential of the new invention of Christopher Cockerell. The foundation of this Unit can be traced to the actions of Lord Louis Earl Mountbatten of Burma who, in 1956, when serving as the First Sea Lord, instructed the Admiralty that the practical use of the hovercraft should be investigated at once.

After a delay, he was to have further input which resulted in Saunders Roe in 1958 being contracted to produce the SRN-1 (Saunders Roe Number -1), a man-carrying hovercraft. After the machine was demonstrated at Lee-on-Solent, the decision was made to form the IHTU to evaluate the machine and two were ordered for the Unit. In effect the world has Earl Mountbatten to thank for the further development of Cockerell's invention.

The first SRN-1 39ft 3.5 ton hovercraft was loaned to the Unit, arriving on 28th February 1962 to begin pilot training, sea keeping and performance trials. As the Unit was for all three services to evaluate, the hovercraft trials were held at Lee, RAF Thorney Island and the Browndown Ranges between Lee-on-Solent and Gosport. The Vickers Armstrong VA1, a hovercraft of similar size to the SRN-1, arrived for trials during May and was followed by the SRN-2 in December. This was a much larger and heavier machine which, after initial handling and training trials in the Solent, saw further trials in the Portland areas before returning to the Solent.

Vickers loaned their 30ft 4 ton VA-2 for trials in the Libyan desert in the spring of 1963. This craft had an undercarriage fitted with two wheels allowing it to operate from heavily cambered roads, and the trials were to evaluate the problems of dust, abrasive conditions and operations across sloping ground.

Two sets of trials were carried out using the 25 ton Denny D2 hovercraft. This 84ft machine was capable of carrying 70 passengers but had unreliable power units so the trials were inconclusive. The hovercraft was used for drag assessment trials in the Firth of Clyde which involved being towed by the Fast Patrol Boat HMS *Brave Borderer* in February 1963. All of these craft were loaned by their manufacturers, and it was now time to purchase outright the Unit's own hovercraft.

HMS Bulwark approaching Singapore prior to her refit

EAST AFRICA FLOODS

Severe rain in the Rift Valley of East Africa gave way to the flooding in Kenya during November 1961, and relief flights were supplied by the eight Whirlwind HAS 7s of No. 825 Sqdn. which were disembarked from HMS *Victorious* to the airfield at Port Reitz near to Mombasa on 22nd November. The squadron detached two aircraft to Malindi 80 miles North of Mombassa and another two to Lamu a further 80 miles North.

The helicopters provided much needed supplies to the nation's population who lived on the Yatta Plateau, and carried out CASEVAC flights and were tasked to reconnoitre the area. One interesting rescue was when 140 cattle were transferred across the swollen Subaki River to dry land. After sixteen operations, the squadron was replaced by No. 824 Sqdn. aboard HMS *Centaur,* which was relieving Victorious on the Far East station. Most of No. 825 Sqdn.'s aircraft were transferred to their sister unit to continue the relief operations.

BORNEO/BRUNEI OPERATIONS

Support for the commando squadrons operating in the Far East stations was stepped up, and the air station at Sembawang in Singapore was developed providing all the facilities which could support the aircraft. A support unit was established on the base supplying replacement helicopters when necessary and recovering aircraft 'down birds'. The base was re-commissioned on 4th September 1962 with Lt. Col. M Wilberforce RM in command, the only time a Royal Marine Officer has assumed command of a FAA station.

As a continuation of the communist

Blackburn Buccaneer S1

Westland Whirlwinds operating in Jungle terrain

Westland Wessex Mk 1 carrying out drills with RMs

Wessex HUM Mk 5s of No. 700V Sqdn

harassment of ex-British colonies which had become the Federation of Malaya in 1948, the Indonesians were causing problems in Borneo and Brunei. The Island of Borneo was under divided rule, with the northern third under the British as part of Malaya, and the remainder as part of Indonesia.

A rebellion in the British Sarawak region was instigated by the Indonesians on 8th December 1962, and the guerrillas also invaded the small independent state of Brunei resulting in a request by the Sultan for assistance against the aggressors. Soon into action delivering 40 RMC ashore on 14th December were the Wessex HAS 1s of No. 845 Sqdn. and the Whirlwind HAS 7s of No. 846 Sqdn., arriving in Kuching aboard HMS *Albion* on her first deployment as a commando carrier.

FAA commando squadrons were to operate in the area for a further three and a half years during the undeclared war with Indonesia, the result of the forming of the Federation of Malaysia in September 1963 (the union of Malaya, Singapore and Northern Borneo). This Federation was refuted by Achmed Sukarno, the Indonesian leader, who declared that it would be destroyed. Supporting the FAA units would be RAF Belvederes, Whirlwinds and Pioneer aircraft, and Beavers and Austers of No. 656 Sqdn. AAC. These aircraft were regularly seen on the flight decks of the commando carriers.

No. 846 Sqdn. operated mainly from Lubuan and Kuching during its eleven months of operations before withdrawing from the theatre in November 1963, after completing over 3750 sorties with its Whirlwinds. The Wessex HAS 1s of No. 845 Sqdn. were to operate from the FOBs, the detachment at Nanga Gaat becoming an integrated member of the local Iban community during its time at the base.

DEVELOPMENT OF THE WESSEX

The Wessex HAS Mk1 was developed into further types, two of which were to serve in the FAA. Some of the early HAS Mk1s were used as troop carriers, having their ASW equipment removed, equipping No. 845 Sqdn, and their success in Malaya resulted in a requirement for the RAF to receive an improved version, the HC Mk2 powered by two smaller Gnome engines. The FAA version was designated the Wessex HU (Helicopter Utility) Mk5, an armed assault helicopter. It first flew on 31st May 1963 and joined the IFTU No. 700V Sqdn. on 29th October, eventually becoming No. 848 Sqdn. seven months later. They replaced the Wessex Mk1s of No. 845 Sqdn. at Nanga Gaat on 23rd June 1965.

The Ministry of Aviation loaned No. 771 Sqdn.

Wessex HAS Mk 3

one of their Wessex Mk1 helicopters for Sonar 195 trials. This aircraft was fitted with four large floats, two either side of the fuselage, and the helicopter landed on the sea for the dunking and retracting of this new equipment which was to be fitted to the new HAS Mk3.

This new ASW helicopter was powered by an uprated single Gazelle, and improved systems included a radar scanner housed in a radome behind the gearbox. The helicopter first flew on 30th November 1964 although it did not reach the FAA until No. 700H reformed on 9th January 1967, entering FLS with No. 814 Sqdn. nine months later.

THE SHAPE OF THINGS TO COME

During a six day period, 8th -13th February 1963, the Hawker company test pilots Bill Bedford and Hugh Merewether conducted trials with the revolutionary Hawker P1127 aboard HMS *Ark Royal.* Bill Bedford landed the type, later to become the Harrier, for the first time on the 8th whilst the ship was in Lyme Bay. After conducting take-offs and landings both vertically and with a short take-off, no problems were encountered. However the trials failed to produce any significant response from the Admiralty, and the aircraft was not seen as a potential naval fighter.

The next RN ship to carry out trials was HMS *Bulwark* when the next development of the P1127, the Kestrel, was operated from the ship on 18th-20th June 1966 during an amphibious operation. The aircraft, which was again flown by Bill Bedford, was to operate alongside the Wessex helicopters without any problems. The Defence White Paper of 1966 approached the idea of V/STOL operations aboard British warships but concluded that a specialised ship would be needed.

A FAA CONCEPT USED WORLDWIDE

Probably the most wisely named helicopter, the Wasp, entered into service with the commissioning of No. 700W Sqdn. on 4th June 1963. The Wasp was the final naval development of the SARO P531 and looked similar to its real life namesake. It buzzed like a wasp and its flying characteristics resembled it, especially with its four legs dangling below it as if laden with pollen. With its introduction into FAA service, it was to give the RN the lead in the operation of small helicopters from the stern of 'small ships'.

The small ships' flight was a concept in naval aviation bred by the FAA with the forming of HMS *Vidal* Flight in 1954. With the forming of No. 829 Sqdn. as a dedicated small ships' flight squadron, the standards were set that would be copied by the world's navies who also formed these flights for their ships.

It consisted of a team of normally six maintainers led by a CPO who was titled as the Senior Maintenance Rating (SMR) with

Hawker P1127 wearing a Sea Harrier colour scheme whilst in use as a training aircraft at Yeovilton

Saro P531

the powers of an Air Engineering Officer (AEO) whilst aboard his respective ship. The pilot was the flight commander and the last member was his crewman. The crewman was initially a sailor (from all branches of the RN) who had volunteered for the role and had passed a training course which included navigation, survival and the art of missile aiming. Upon completing this course, he received his wings and the title Missile Aimer.

The Wasp was carried aboard the ships to increase their anti-submarine capability and was capable of carrying both depth charges or a torpedo. It only had a short range as it was required to operate close to the flotilla giving immediate attack capabilities if an enemy submarine was able to get near to it. It was later developed to carry anti-ship wire guided missiles to counter the soviet fast patrol boat threat.

The RN's tribal class and some of the Rothesay class ships were modified to carry a flight, and all of the Leander class and subsequent class of frigates and destroyers were designed to operate helicopters, a trend which has been copied by all navies operating ships large enough for a helicopter flight. The first flight was formed on 11th August 1963 to operate from HMS *Leander*. In all, 58 ships were to operate the helicopter in the FAA during its service life which was bought to an end when the type was withdrawn at the end of May 1988.

It was to be a superb helicopter whose service aboard frigates of the Tribal, Leander, Rothesay, Amazon and Broadsword class, Sheffield class destroyers, survey, ocean and ice patrol ships brought the FAA into the lives of the sailors who served on these ships. No longer were the 'Airey Faireys' confined to aircraft carriers, an unknown quantity to the majority of the senior service.

The IFTU was re-commissioned as No. 829 Sqdn. on 4th March 1964, tasked with the training of both aircrews and maintenance personnel in the new role of 'small ships' flights'. The squadron was responsible for 'parenting' the ships' flights which were all individual units within the squadron, and eventually took responsibility for the Wessex flights in the County class destroyers and RFAs, and the ice patrol ship Whirlwinds, ie all the flights on non-aircraft carriers were passed to the squadron.

At Culdrose, No. 706 Sqdn. was tasked with converting pilots to the Wasp. This was later taken up by No. 703 Sqdn. when it commissioned at Portland on 22nd January 1972. The squadron also took on the responsibility of training the crews for the flights, operating in difficult confined conditions located at the stern of these ships.

This was particularly evident in the Tribal class frigates which had a hangar whose deck was a lift becoming the flight deck when raised. To complete the exercise, heavy wooden covers had to be manually removed to uncover the helicopter prior to the lift deck being raised and replaced on completion of the day's flying - no fun in rough seas.

With the need for training helicopter crews for small ships' flights, HMS *Undaunted* was fitted with a landing platform on its stern for use as the Fleet's deck landing training ship during 1961. Based at Portland, the ship began operating as a trials deck before supporting the Wasp helicopter training requirement as the flights began forming.

The ship had a dual role of a deck for training pilots and that of training the deck landing officers who came from all branches of the navy. Deck lashing crews were also trained using the visiting helicopters. This was a major facility for small ships' flight flying training and was a constant scene of helicopters landing and launching, with the ship completing its 1000th landing on 4th December 1967.

Westland Wasp

A World Force - Looking Good

HMS Eagle

SUPER CARRIER ANNOUNCED

Designs for the replacement of the current aircraft carriers were first conceived in 1959, with the final design announced on 30th July 1963. The CVA-01, a 53,000 ton super carrier was to be constructed along with purpose built escort ships. Bids for the build of the ship (and its four sisters) were to be submitted by April 1966 with completion by 1973, when they would enter service replacing the five ships presently in the Fleet (HMSs *Ark Royal, Centaur, Eagle, Hermes* and *Victorious)* as each ship was completed.

The carrier was to have a flight deck of 925ft with an island structure amidships which was to split the deck into two - the port side as an angled landing deck area whilst the starboard forward deck would be a launch deck. This would allow both launching and recovery to be in operation simultaneously. The angle deck was reduced to three degrees keeping the ship's beam within manageable dimensions, and it was fitted with four arrestor wires and a steam catapult thus allowing it to be a combined launch and recovery runway. The arrestor gear was to be operated by direct water jets instead of the present hydraulic type giving a more positive deceleration of the aircraft and a reduction in machinery required.

The flight deck had no overhang, instead the flight deck edge began some 40ft forward of the stern. Below was the quarterdeck fitted with a rear facing missile defence system, and this deck had a direct access to the hangar deck to allow aircraft to be positioned on the deck to carry out engine running tests.

There were two lifts serving the single hangar deck; one lift was positioned on the starboard after deck edge, the other amidships in front of the island. These lifts were to be a completely new design, moving away from the chain operated types, and were to be raised and lowered using scissor legs, thus reducing weight and space allowing access on three sides of the lift (this design was eventually to be incorporated in the Invincible class ships).

HMS Eagle pre-refit

The project was to be short lived, however, as the proposed five ships were cancelled in the February 1966 Defence White Paper. The building of these ships would have restricted other development projects, in particular the tactical nuclear strike aircraft of the RAF, thus it was that they were not to be built after all.

Further to the cancellation of the CVA-01, more bad news was to follow in the 1968 White Paper when the Government announced the phasing out of the RN attack carrier force. HMS *Eagle's* refit was cancelled, with only HMS *Ark Royal* being refitted to operate the F4 Phantom II.

ADEN AND TANGANYIKA

The British protectorate of Aden, a coastal area on the Arabian Sea in Yemen, was a strategic base for British Forces whose major role was ensuring the passage between the Gulf of Aden (Yemen and Djibouti) and the Red Sea remained open for access to the Suez Canal. The People's Democratic Republic of Yemen laid claim to Aden on 13th April 1956 and sporadic fighting occurred on the protectorates' borders until Britain finally withdrew in November 1967.

Many FAA squadrons were active during the period of 'conflict' supporting the locally based troops and RAF personnel. All carriers operating East of Suez regularly exercised in the waters off Aden including joint exercises with the RAF based aircraft. It was a regular stopping off point to and from the Far East station although it was not normal for FAA units to partake in the skirmishes. However this situation altered in the 1960s when Britain was preparing to leave the protectorate, and the anti-British South Arabians increased their harassment of the 'local' British.

Disembarking to Khormaksar from HMS *Ark Royal* on 19th December 1963 was the Wessex HAS 1s of No. 815 Sqdn. to support the British troops to quell the tribal disturbances in the protectorate. It was later to operate from Radfan during May and June of 1964, flying over 400 sorties ferrying 1300 passengers and stores to the barren mountains. During September and October 1965, aircraft from HMS *Eagle* carried out flights against the rebel forces.

During the early 1960s, independence was granted to British territories in East Africa - Kenya, Tanganyika, Uganda and the island of Zanzibar, all of whom remained in the Commonwealth and could rely on military support from Britain.

African Nationalists stirred up unrest in these countries. Many of the 'hard' nationalist forces had been trained by the communist Chinese who were instrumental in supporting the unrest. The Zanzibar Government was overthrown on 12th January 1964 with the troubles then spreading to the mainland states. Following a revolt by the Tanganyikan Rifles, British assistance was requested on 25th January by President Jomo Kenyatta of Kenya on behalf of the Presidents of the four countries.

The first support arrived in the form of No. 45 RMC who landed via the helicopters of No. 815 Sqdn. from HMS *Centaur*. The ship had been operating off Aden with Wessex HAS 1, Gannet AEW3 and Sea Vixen FAW1 Squadrons embarked, and was sent to Dar-Es-Salaam with all speed to assist in quelling the revolt. Prior to leaving Aden, she embarked two Belvedere aircraft of No. 84 Sqdn. RAF and the RMC.

The initial revolt was quelled within 36 hours of assistance being requested, but British Forces remained in the area to restore order in the region. Centaur remained on station until relieved on 7th February 1964 by HMS *Victorious*, whose air group was similar to that of Centaur with the added power of No. 801 Sqdn. with the new Buccaneer Mk1s.

The helicopters moved troops around whilst the Sea Vixens and Buccaneers provided air cover over the area (controlled by the AEW Gannets) required to cover the RAF transport aircraft bringing reinforcements to East Africa. Joined by these other troops, the uprising was completely suppressed and Zanzibar was returned to governmental control. (Zanzibar merged with Tanganyika to become Tanzania on 26th April). HMS *Victorious* withdrew from the area on 22nd February.

THE ROUGH DIAMONDS

The naval advanced flying training school at Brawdy consisted of No. 738 and 759 Sqdns., both equipped with Hawker Hunters. The instructors from these units were to form an aerobatics display team for the base open day in 1964 using nine of the aircraft, and were named the Rough Diamonds.

The display team was to reduce to four aircraft, all from the weapons training squadron No. 738 Sqdn., for subsequent air shows and were to perform at shows across the country. Their final display as the Rough Diamonds was allegedly at the Brawdy Air Day 1968, but they were however to reform with seven aircraft one last time for the final air show at Brawdy in 1970.

THE REBIRTH OF COMBINED SERVICES

The 1st April is always a significant date within the British services, as it seems to be the date used by successive governments to redevelop the management systems and military structures within the Forces (remember 1st April 1918 in particular). 1964 was to be no exception. With effect from 'All Fools Day', the organisations for the three services would amalgamate (the Admiralty, War Office and Air Ministry) under the umbrella of 'The Ministry of Defence' (MOD) run by civil servants.

This new ministry was to take away the autonomy of the three individual services in an attempt to control the overall resources and procurement of the military requirements of the country. It would also control the roles of the services and, as we shall see eventually 30 years hence, we would take steps backwards with the services combining with joint forces.

Each service was supposed to retain its own identity which in effect it did (until the 1990s), but it was to show over the years that whoever was the military head of the MOD (it is rotated between the services) at any one time, his service would benefit in defence spending budgets during their term in office. Basically, control had been taken from the military experts and gained by Government Civil Servants whose bias was to keep their political masters happy and not the services. At one stage during the 1980s, there were eight civil servants within the MOD to every serving person.

HMS EAGLE RETURNS

After its major refit lasting five years, HMS *Eagle* re-commissioned on 14th May 1964. She was in effect a rebuilt ship, so extensive was the refit that the complete flight deck armour plating had been replaced. The deck had been fitted with an 8.5 degree angle and the starboard side of the deck forward of and along the island was extended outboard. Two steam catapults were installed, both on the ship's port side (one along the angle deck, the other on the forward straight deck), and improved arrestor gear was also fitted.

The superstructure on the island was to include new radar masts and the new 'dustbin' type 984 radar above the bridge which was also enlarged. A 'Flyco' (Flying Control Position) extending 25ft over the flight deck was fitted on the port side to enable the approach to the new angle deck to be visible from the island. Most of the original AA and 4.5" guns were removed and replaced with the new Seacat anti-aircraft missile systems. Only the after 4.5" sets on both sides were retained.

There were substantial changes below decks. Secondary ships' controls were installed in the machinery control room, new displays were fitted to the operations room, the after end of the lower hangar was converted into mess decks, the initial mess decks were modernised and air conditioning was fitted throughout the ship.

The total refit was arguably the most extensive ever completed in one period to any ship in the RN. She emerged as the largest ship ever to be operated in the RN's history with a full load displacement (FLD) of 54,100 tons (her sister ship was to reach a final FLD of 50,786 tons). She would be capable of operating up to 45 aircraft and helicopters, less than when first commissioned, however the aircraft had increased in size many times since the ship was originally designed in 1942. It is anticipated that two super carriers, due in 2012/14, will be larger than HMS *Eagle.*

As the ship was in effect a 'new' ship, her operating trials were to be lengthy and she did not take on her air group until 2nd December (No. 800 Sqdn. Buccaneer S1 and Scimitar, No. 820 Sqdn. Wessex HAS 1, No. 849D Flight Gannet AEW3 and No. 899 Sqdn. Sea Vixen FAW1). She had carried out her aircraft operating trials with four Sea Vixens of No. 766 Sqdn. during October and November whilst on a cruise to Gibraltar. After embarking her full air group, she sailed for the Far East where the Gannets were used to patrol the Malacca Straits for Malaysian insurgents.

FAA SUPPORT SHIPS HMS BRINTON - A LESSER KNOWN FAA SHIP

Commissioned in May 1964 was HMS *Brinton,* a 'Ton' class minesweeper operated by a crew from the Royal Naval Reserve (RNR). She was tasked with supplying a safety boat for the rescue of any helicopter crews in the Culdrose exercise areas east of the Lizard Peninsular, and was required to operate during night flying periods mainly, but also took part in helicopter transfer training, supplying a deck for winching.

The need for a seagoing deck for helicopter deck training was raised with the withdrawal of a specific training aircraft carrier. The answer was to build a special ship for the role and so RFA *Engadine* was ordered in 1965, the ship being part of the auxiliary fleet and not a RN ship. To cover the need prior to the ship being delivered, one of the Fleet's tank landing craft, HMS *Lofoten,* was to be converted.

The conversion of Lofoten was completed in June 1964 with its commissioning as the Interim Helicopter Support Ship on 23rd with a Wessex of No. 737 Sqdn. onboard. She was capable of operating two Wessex helicopters and was fitted out with accommodation, stores spaces, workshops and 10,000 gallon fuel tanks to allow the operation of the helicopters. If needed for the transportation role, she could accommodate six Wessex helicopters on her deck. Her role was to transport ASW helicopters to deep water for training exercises in both the SW and NW Approaches supporting the helicopter squadrons.

THE HOVERCRAFT UNIT GETS ITS OWN CRAFT

After loaning the first hovercraft for this joint service unit to train pilots and carry out initial service trials, the service took delivery of its own first four hovercraft. The large SRN-3 (77ft/35 tons) was delivered on 2nd June 1964 followed by three SRN-5 (28ft/7tons) arriving in September. Two of these smaller craft were destined to be operated by a unit detached to the Far East.

The SRN-5s were used for pilot training as well as many trials which included rescue and fire fighting, mine counter measures, sea keeping and hovercraft navigator training. One of the craft was used to transport HM the Queen from Yarmouth on the Isle of Wight to RAF Thorney Island in July 1965, the first time HRH had been transported by hovercraft.

The larger SRN-3 proved to be exceptionally useful in a logistic support role transporting men, equipment and vehicles. The craft took part in this role during the NATO exercise 'Wooden Wagon' held in Germany during May 1966, transferring men and equipment across the River Weser. The SRN-3 could cross the river's mud flats thereby reducing the distance across from twenty miles (for the landing craft) to six miles.

The hovercraft was involved in ASW and fishery protection exercises and Dan Buoy operations during its working life. The craft probably holds the record for the fastest passage through the Kiel Canal when it travelled the 52 miles distance in 1hr 45mins reaching speeds of up to 40 knots when travelling to Copenhagen for

HMS Eagle post-refit

SRN3 Hovercraft

demonstrations in May 1966.

Its final task on 21st February 1972 was for the assessment of damage a hovercraft could sustain if struck by underwater mines. Stripped of unnecessary equipment (including two of its engines), explosives were detonated beneath the craft whilst afloat in the Solent. Upon completion, the craft returned under its own power back to Lee-on-Solent, proving the theory that hovercraft could sustain damage and shock forces to their hulls and still operate.

THE LAST HEAVYWEIGHTS
1 - THE SEA VIXEN FAW Mk2

The development of the DH Sea Vixen was to produce the last British 'Heavyweight' Naval Fighter, the Sea Vixen FAW Mk2. The aircraft was modified having extensions to the tail-plane booms and additional fuel tanks and equipment bays, and was equipped to operate the latest airborne missiles - the Red Top infra-red air-to-air homing missile and Bullpup air-to-surface missile. This version was slower than the Mk1 and took 30% longer to reach its operating ceiling, but it was a more capable multi-role fighter aircraft.

The first two aircraft were Mk1s diverted during assembly to begin the Mk2 production line, the first flight of the FAW Mk2 being on 1st June 1962. These aircraft were joined by the first two production aircraft for trials by De Havilland and the A & AEE at Boscombe Down, particularly with Red Top and Bullpup missiles.

This improved version of the Sea Vixen began its service life with the Aircraft Handling Unit at RNAS Brawdy during August 1963. The first squadron to receive the aircraft was No. 899 Sqdn., the FAW Mk2 IFTU. This squadron was given front line status on commissioning on 15th June 1964, eventually becoming the fighter element of HMS *Eagle* until the ship paid off on 26th January 1972.

2 - THE MIGHTY PHANTOM

With the cancellation of the Hawker P1154RN supersonic V/STOL interceptor fighter in the Defence White Paper of 13th February 1964, the RN was still seeking a replacement for the Scimitar and Sea Vixen. After a hard sell by the McDonnell Douglas team, the F4 Phantom II was chosen and this American aircraft was to be redesigned around the Rolls Royce Spey engine.

Two YF-4K prototypes were ordered on 1st July, the first foreign orders for the aircraft (eventually over 5000 would be built). The reasoning was that the aircraft was already in build so it would be a cheaper alternative and a more expedient solution to developing a British carrier aircraft. The RN saw a need for 143 of the aircraft to serve on the two fleet carriers and the new CVA 01 plus training squadrons.

The FAA Phantom required many modifications in order to operate from our

DH Sea Vixen FAW Mk2

McDonnell Douglas F4K Phantom II

carriers (small in comparison to US carriers), as did the ships. Stronger landing gear, high lift devices and an increased stroke nose undercarriage to increase the launch angle of attack of the aircraft were needed, as well as redesigned engine intakes, larger than their American counterparts, and a completely redesigned engine bay. Installation of British avionics and specialist equipment needed other design changes within the fuselage. The radome had to be capable of folding back (as with the Sea Vixen and Buccaneer) for compatibility with the aircraft carrier lift dimensions.

These alterations to the aircraft's design, plus the need to send the British components across the Atlantic, ruled out the reasoning for buying the Phantom. The aircraft became more expensive than the basic US model, its service entry was delayed and the operational performance was reduced.

3 - THE WORLD'S PREMIER NAVAL STRIKE AIRCRAFT

The first Buccaneer Mk2 aircraft were used for trials with the A & AEE before the second Buccaneer IFTU was formed, No. 700B Sqdn. on 9th April 1965. The first FLS was No. 801 Sqdn. which formed on 14th October and had the privilege of flying low over Nelson's column only one week later in celebration of the anniversary of the Battle of Trafalgar. Like the Sea Vixen, the Buccaneer was to have both a training squadron, No. 736 Sqdn., and a headquarter's squadron, No. 803 Sqdn.

The A & AEE continued development trials including some which were conducted at NAS Pensacola in Florida and aboard the USS *Lexington,* the USN's training carrier. On completion, one of the aircraft flown by Cdr. G Higgs and Lt. Cdr. A Taylor, flew the

Blackburn Buccaneer S2

SRN6 Hovercraft

first FAA non-stop transatlantic flight from Labrador direct to Lossiemouth, a distance of 1950 miles in 4hrs 16mins on 4th October 1965.

DETACHED HOVERCRAFT UNITS

The IHU (Far East) was established as an independent unit to carry out logistic support and naval patrols, as well as operations and trials, both day and night, overland, at sea and along rivers in Singapore, Malaysia and Thailand. During these trials in 1965, the craft carried out a 310 mile journey along the Rayong River in Sarawak including rapids. The total travelling time was eight hours - it normally took between eight and twelve days by conventional river craft.

Bell 47 Souix

On 6th June 1967, a detachment of personnel was to form Naval Party 8902, a unit for operations in support of the RMC detachment on the Falkland Islands. The detachment of ten men to operate the single SRN6 craft established a base at the redundant whaling station of Moody Brook, complete with hangar, workshops, offices and an ops room.

The islands consist of two main islands and 200 smaller islands, with the population spread out throughout the islands, and the only town is Port Stanley - with a harbour. There are no roads, transportation is by land-rover or horses although there are two Government-owned Beaver aircraft which were used for transport when required, and the main link between inhabitants is two-way radios. The task of the hovercraft unit was to operate as a liaison between the communities and the transferring of the garrison RMs to carry out exercises.

ROYAL MARINE PILOTS

The first four Royal Marine officer pilots since W.W.II were to receive helicopter pilot training during 1965. After successfully completing the course, they formed the nucleus of the 3CB Air Squadron (3CBAS) flying Army helicopters in support of the brigade. These officers would receive military training at RM barracks at Deal, Lympstone and Eastney before moving to the BRNC Dartmouth for some naval training and to complete their grading flights at Roborough.

Once graded they would complete the courses as the FAA pilots, with basic flying training at RAF Linton-on-Ouse and would then move to Culdrose for basic helicopter flying training with No. 705 Sqdn. and advanced flying training with No. 707 Sqdn. From here, the pilots would move to the Army Air Corps base of Middle Wallop to receive operational training on the Bell 47 Souix and Scout helicopters which they would be flying. By the time they became operational, these officers would have received training by all branches of the British Forces.

As the unit was basically a department of the AAC attached to the 3CB, they would be flying AAC helicopters (albeit with Royal Marine markings). As with the AAC, the officer pilots would be flying alongside Royal Marine NCO aircrew and the unit would borrow Army aircrew personnel. The helicopters would be serviced by members of REME under army servicing schedules. Eventually the 3CBAS aircraft would move to Yeovilton and become an FAA squadron, the RM pilots wearing FAA wings and not the blue wings of the AAC.

Westland Wessex HUMk5

HMS CENTAUR PAYS OFF

Arriving in Portsmouth on 20th August 1965 to pay off, HMS *Centaur* was to become an accommodation ship for the crews of aircraft carriers in refit. The first crew to join were those of HMS *Victorious* and, upon moving

HMS Intrepid & HMS Fearless

onboard, the captain of Victorious, Capt. D Davenport, assumed command of Centaur becoming the first RN captain to command two ships at the same time. The ship was to remain an accommodation carrier for the next seven years, moving between Portsmouth and Devonport as required until eventually going to scrap in 1972.

THE ASSAULT SHIPS

HMS *Fearless,* the first of two ships ordered in 1962 especially designed as heavy armoured vehicle transport ships, was commissioned on 25th November 1965 and its sister ship, HMS *Intrepid,* would commission on 11th March 1967. These two ships were ordered to supplement the two commando carriers, for embarking all the heavy artillery and armoured vehicles required during an assault. The ships were built with a flight deck capable of operating five Wessex helicopters although there were no hangarage and only limited support facilities. If these were required, support would be provided from the accompanying carrier.

Below the flight deck was a docking bay with four large landing craft which were capable of taking the vehicles and men ashore. There were two vehicle decks in the forward end of the ship accessed via ramps from the dock, and mess decks for 370 troops were built into the walls of the dock. The ship would flood the dock which would lower the stern of the ship into the sea where a rear ramp was lowered so the landing craft could leave the ship with their load to head for the beaches.

The ships alternated with each other in the East of Suez theatre as did the two commando carriers and therefore, until the RN pulled out of the Far East in 1971, there

Fairey Gannet AEW3

DH Sea Vixen FAWMk2 (BAE Systems)

was a permanent assault force in the theatre. The ships were not allocated specific squadrons to operate but carried detachments of aircraft from whichever commando squadron was involved in the exercise or operation. Often seen operating with the groups would be Army Air Corps Scout helicopters used as observation and spotting aircraft whilst the Wessex were used to transport troops and equipment.

BIERA PATROLS

On 11th November 1965, Mr. Ian Smith's Government in Rhodesia declared a Unilateral Declaration of Independence (UDI) from Great Britain, stubbornly refusing to relinquish power to the black majority. HMS *Eagle*, on its way to Singapore after operations in Aden, was diverted to the East African coast to provide any necessary air defence for Zambia but no need developed.

Following UDI, sanctions were put in place by the UN, a part of these sanctions being to prevent oil being delivered to the land locked country. Oil deliveries were made to the port of Beira in Mozambique and the RN was tasked with preventing tankers from delivering their cargos to the port. Carriers were a major contributor to this operation with HMSs *Ark Royal, Eagle* and *Victorious* all taking part.

HMS *Eagle* began the first patrol in the Mozambique Channel on 15th March 1966 which lasted for 50 days identifying some 770 ships. The aircraft were active 24 hours per day, with a total of nearly 1900 sorties being flown covering 200,000 square miles each day, mostly by the Gannet AEW3 with its powerful radar which would pick up any contact. Once detected, the Vixens and Buccaneers would be sent to photograph the target ship for identification.

A BRAVE PILOT

A sad but remarkable sortie during the patrol by HMS *Ark Royal*, which had relieved Eagle, occurred on 10th May 1966. A Sea Vixen from No. 890 Sqdn. was returning to the ship when it suffered an engine flame out accompanied by loss of fuel. A Scimitar tanker was launched to intercept the aircraft and refuel it but unfortunately the Sea Vixen's pilot, Lt. A Tarver, was unable to make contact with his flight refuel probe and the aircraft's other engine stopped due to fuel starvation.

The aircraft was in sight of the ship when Tarver ordered his observer, Lt. J Stutchbury, to eject but the ejection sequence failed. Attempting to bale out whilst at 3000ft, the observer became stuck in the escape hatch so the pilot inverted the aircraft even though it was only flying at about 200 knots. After a second attempt, the observer remained jammed. Not content with the situation, Tarver attempted to manually free his observer and was leaning out of his own cockpit as the aircraft struck the sea.

Unfortunately Stutchbury was lost but miraculously Tarver survived as he was dragged free by his parachute. He was picked up by the ship's Wessex and flown back onboard. For his heroic actions to free his crew mate, he was awarded the George Medal.

THE LAST WHIRLWIND

Entering service specifically for SAR duties during 1966 was the re-engined unarmed Whirlwind HAR9. Powered with the Gnome engine which also powered the Wessex HU5 and was to later power the Sea King, the aircraft first flew on 15th October 1965. The helicopter was the last in line of the type to enter service, the first being the Sikorsky HAR21s of No. 848 Sqdn. back in 1952 which says a lot for the helicopter's design and survivability. The seventeen Mk7s converted to the Mk9 continued in operation for another eleven years.

Ideally suited for SAR, it carried a crew of three; the pilot, aircrew man and SAR diver, and could carry a further five in the cabin. The SAR flight deployed aboard HMS *Hermes* was first to receive the type in January, the only ship board SAR flight to operate the type. It served at all the major air stations and as the SAR flight at Lee-on-Solent. The type was to see service in the Antarctic, with two replacing the Mk1s which had been serving aboard HMS *Protector* since she

Westland Whirlwind HARMk9

commissioned in 1955. The flight continued to operate the type after HMS *Endurance* commissioned in May 1968 as the replacement Falkland Islands' Guardship and Ice Patrol ship. The two aircraft remained as the flight until tension in the South Atlantic brought about the type's replacement in 1976.

It was deemed that the ice patrol ship, which worked usually for about seven months in the Antarctic region, needed helicopters which could be armed as protection for the ship. Two wasp helicopters were specially modified to replace the Whirlwinds for the ship's winter sailing in 1976, with the two HAR9s remaining at Lee-on-Solent for additional use by the station SAR flight, until finally retired in March 1977 when replaced with Wessex Mk5s.

BORNEO - CONTINUED COMMANDO SQUADRONS SUPPORT

The commando squadrons continued operations in Borneo until final withdrawal in 1966. Whilst operating in the theatre, they remained under the control of its parent commando carrier, although 50% of the aircraft were to remain permanently ashore with detachments at Nanga Gaat, Sibu and Simanggang in support of the troops in the Sarawak and on the island of Labuan off Brunei. Sibu was the region's capital and as such had an airport, but the other two sites were FOBs in the jungle, and the aircraft operated mainly in the mountainous and jungle regions transporting the troops and their equipment as required.

A military coup led by Lt. Gen. Suharto on 12th March 1966 deposed Sukarno and his communist supporters from power in Indonesia. Peace talks in Bangkok resulted in the announcement of the end of hostilities in the region on 1st June 1966, followed by the signing of a treaty with Malaysia on 11th August, bringing the Malayan/Malaysian confrontation to an end. The Wessex of No. 848 Sqdn. were to be the final FAA helicopters in the theatre, although they were handed over to No. 845 Sqdn. for embarkation in HMS *Bulwark* on the cessation of the hostilities with the Indonesians. No. 848 Sqdn. began the FAA commando operations in Malaya in February 1949 so it was fitting that the final anti-terrorist and guerrilla operations shoul also be by the squadron, albeit seventeen years later.

Westland Whirlwind HARMk9 carrying guided weapon on the forward fuselage

Top: Blackburn Buccaneer S2

Left: DH Sea Vixen FAW Mk2

Bottom: Fairey Gannet COD

A MORE CAPABLE SERVICE

HMS HERMES RETURNS

After two years in dockyard hands, the last major 'fixed-wing' refit of HMS *Hermes* was completed with the ship re-commissioning on 28th March 1966. She had been fitted with longer and more powerful catapults to enable her to operate the Buccaneer and Sea Vixen FAW Mk2 aircraft. The flight deck had been increased to the maximum width it was able to support, which included extending it on the starboard side to give the ship an Alaskan Highway around the back of the island.

The Bridge had an additional deck fitted which included a replacement 'Flyco', and internally the ship now had full air-conditioning throughout. She re-commissioned with the honour of being the RN's first all-missile ship as during the refit all her guns had been replaced with the Seacat missile systems.

The first aircraft to land aboard the ship was not to be a high powered heavyweight but a biplane Tiger Moth flown by the ship's Commander Air. The ship was to complete trials and operations in home waters prior to heading east. However, before deploying to the Far East, her air group would stage a demonstration of naval air power at the 1966 Farnborough Airshow in September.

THE SEA KING

A contract was signed on 27th June 1966 for Westlands to build 60 Sikorsky S61/SH-3D Sea Kings for the FAA powered by Gnome engines. Westland purchased four Sikorsky helicopters for developing and proving work, one for company trials, two for RAE and A & AEE development work, and one for Rolls Royce for engine proving. All were originally fitted with the standard US equipment which was then replaced by the British equipment. The first flight of a Gnome powered aircraft was on 8th September 1967.

The Sea King produced by Westland was a Hunter-Killer helicopter carrying four homing torpedoes, sonar, Doppler, automatic flight controls, power folding main rotor head with a rotor blade which would give a cockpit indication of an impending failure, retractable undercarriage and a boat shaped hull giving it the ability to float on the water. It was the most advanced ASW helicopter in the world at that time, with double the range of its predecessor, the Wessex HAS Mk3.

CHIPMUNKS FOR THE GRADING FLIGHT

The Tiger Moths had been in continuous use for pilot grading for sixteen years and, although a steady reliable aircraft, they were pre W.W.II vintage and were not representative of the monoplanes in service. To replace these, twelve ex-RAF Chipmunk T10s were delivered to the civil airport of Roborough in Plymouth during June 1966. Even though they were nearly twenty years old, they were a reliable cheap solid aircraft. The first flight of the aircraft was in 1946 and was designed to replace the biplane Tiger Moth as a military and civil trainer.

HMS Hermes

Westland Sea King HAS Mk1

The Chipmunks were used to give prospective FAA aircrew a chance to gain some flying experience whilst training at the college. It also gave the instructors the opportunity to grade the ability of the prospective pilot. Prospective aircrew cadets would have twelve hours of flying instructions to achieve a standard of preparation for an examination where they would be assessed on their ability as a pilot and their future potential in the FAA.

After nearly 30 years service, the aircraft were replaced in 1994 by a German built 'plastic' aircraft - the Grob G115 Heron. These composite aircraft are operated by Shorts on behalf of the RN so they are actually civil aircraft wearing civil registrations and not military colours or serials.

Chipmunks have also been used as station 'hacks' at Culdrose, Lossiemouth and Yeovilton, and were operated by two training squadrons, the communications squadron No. 781 Sqdn. at Lee-on-Solent for RNR pilot training and glider towing, and No. 771 Sqdn. at Culdrose for station flight use.

F4K FIRST FLIGHT

The first prototype F4K Phantom II flew on 27th June 1966 and was dedicated to engine development research. This and the next aircraft were powered by the Spey engine but the majority of equipment was US standard. The next four were built to full British naval standard and were to be used for systems and weapons development flights. It is sad to mention that the original prototype was burnt on the fire dump at RAF St Athan during 1982/83 after efforts by the author to save the aircraft for the FAA museum.

English Electric (BAC) Canberra T17

The first aircraft were all to be used for research and development flights, and the first FAA F4 deck trials were carried out aboard the USS *Coral Sea* on 18th July 1968. These trials were to show that the catapult and recovery approach performances were better than the USN F4B and F4J aircraft. The initial trials were held in the USA and flown by USN and company test pilots prior to the A & AEE test pilots reaching qualification on the type. The development aircraft were then to be operated by the A & AEE and Rolls Royce.

Due to the aircraft being heavier than any previous (or future) FAA aircraft, the steam catapults and arrestor gear needed improving before fitting to HMS *Ark Royal,* which was to be the only aircraft carrier fully modified to operate the type. The steam catapult gear was lengthened and had water cooled blast deflectors whilst the arrestor wires were to be rotary hydraulic types. The ship was also to be fitted with the new nylon emergency safety barrier, similar to that fitted to US carriers.

JOINT RAF/RN EW SQDN.

As the British EW squadrons (No. 831 Sqdn. equipped with Gannet ECM6s and Sea Venom 22 ECMs, and No. 97 Sqdn. the Signals Development squadron equipped with Varsity, Canberras and Hastings) were carrying out joint exercises with obsolescent aircraft, it was decided they would amalgamate to form a joint ECM squadron manned by aircrew and maintainers from both services.

This new squadron, No. 360 Sqdn., was to be equipped with a specially built version of the Canberra, the T17. The squadron began forming on 1st April 1966 with the Canberra B2s until the arrival of these much modified EW T17s. The other aircraft types used by the two squadrons were withdrawn from use.

DHC Chipmunk

McDonnell Douglas F4K Phantom II on first flight

The RN unit finally disbanded on 26th August with the official forming of No. 360 Sqdn. on 23rd September. The RAF's No. 97 Sqdn. retired on 2nd January 1967.

The squadron was eventually to relocate to RAF Cottesmore on 21st April 1969, where it operated for six years before moving to the RAF's Canberra base, RAF Wyton, on 1st July 1965. This was to be home for the specialised squadron until disbanding on 31st October 1994.

'HUMPHREY' THE HUMPBACKED WESSEX

Entering service with No. 700H Sqdn. on 9th January 1967 was the redesigned ASW Wessex HAS Mk3. Developed from the HAS Mk1, this helicopter was easily distinguishable from its predecessor by the hump on the spine behind the gearbox panels. The panels were also modified to direct the airflow away from the hump, which was the radar dome for the helicopter's search radar. The helicopter was equipped with an improved fully automatic flight control system which gave it much better stabilised flying characteristics.

The first FLS, No. 814 Sqdn., was formed in September and the following month it absorbed the IFTU, initially operating its aircraft aboard RFAs. Flights of single Wessex HAS Mk3s were to form the helicopter flights embarked on board the County class destroyers (two of these would see action during the 1982 Falklands Conflict). No. 819 Sqdn. at Ballykelly in Northern Ireland was equipped with the HAS Mk3 for exercises with the Londonderry based Joint Anti-Submarine School.

Two cruisers were to be converted as helicopter cruisers with flights of four ASW Wessex Mk3 helicopters on board, and these were introduced to make up for the shortfall in aircraft carriers. The 1966 White Paper announced that three of these W.W.II vintage ships would be modified and converted for the role, namely HMSs *Blake, Tiger* and *Lion,* although the latter was not converted mainly due to the costs incurred with the conversion of HMS *Tiger*.

ADEN WITHDRAWAL - OPERATION MAGISTER

The regular attendance of the carriers and their aircraft had the desired affect of showing the strength of British Forces in the area of Aden. No better was this power demonstrated than when the air groups of HMSs *Hermes* and *Victorious* joined up with the RAF aircraft for a 50 aircraft flypast of Sea Vixens, Buccaneers and Hunters over the protectorate during May 1967.

Passing carriers were always operating off Aden in support of the protectorates' resident units. During a visit in May 1967, No. 826 Sqdn. from Hermes operated from a small airstrip of Habilayn against dissidents, the last direct action by the FAA prior to the final withdrawal of British Forces at the end of November.

The main withdrawal began when HMS *Bulwark* arrived on 7th October with No. 848 Sqdn. to disembark 42 RMC for duties

Westland Wessex HASMk3

HMS Victorious

relieving the Army units who were returning to the UK. The fixed-wing aircraft from HMS *Eagle* took over from the RAF squadrons who also returned to the UK, whilst HMS *Albion* replaced Bulwark for the recovery of the commandos. The operations were to continue throughout October and November until only the detached squadrons and the RMC remained ashore plus a few civilian personnel with the staff of the High Commissioner.

Patrols were flown continuously from early morning until after dusk, and the commando helicopters were fully armed with guns and SS11 missiles in defence against Arab mortar sites. One Wessex was hit in the tail by bullets without causing too much damage, which was only detected once the aircraft had landed.

The High Commissioner was to review the assembled Fleet of 24 ships including the Assault ship HMS *Intrepid,* and witness a final flypast of FAA aircraft on 25th November prior to the final operations. The British flags were lowered on 29th November saluted by Col. D Morgan RM, the last British soldier in the protectorate who was flown out in the Wasp helicopter of the commando squadron.

The helicopters of No. 848 Sqdn. lifted 11,000 passengers and over 2.5 tons of stores and, on the final day (29th), lifted the remaining 500 members of 42 RMC, who were being harassed by hostile Arabs, from the RAF airfield of Khormaksar. During the withdrawal, Eagle's aircraft had supplied air cover and the last British military aircraft to leave the airfield, and thus the protectorate, was a Sea Vixen of No. 899 Sqdn. with the British flags on board. The ships Albion (Bulwark from 7th December), Eagle and Fearless and supporting ships remained off the Arabian coast until the end of the year.

A SAD END TO A FAMOUS SHIP

Due to remain operational until the end of the decade, HMS *Victorious* returned from the Far East on 21st June to enter a short refit. It had been announced in the year's Defence White Paper that she was to continue operations until HMS *Ark Royal's* 'Phantomisation' refit was completed. Unfortunately a small fire in the mess decks caused by a domestic water boiler catching fire resulted in about £20,000 worth of damage.

This was excuse enough for the continuation of the refit to be terminated by the Labour Government who announced that the ship would be withdrawn from use at that time and not in 1969. Thus the fine old lady of distinction was laid up in Portsmouth until being towed to Faslane for scrap. At the time (July 1969), she should have been entering Portsmouth with her paying off pennant flying proud. Victorious' career began with her aircraft attacking the German battleship Bismark, she suffered kamikaze attacks in the Pacific and served in all Fleets with most aircraft types over 30 years. She was the only carrier to be cut in half and receive a lengthening 'plug' in the longest refit in history. The final act of salute to this ship was the flypast of the last airworthy Swordfish aircraft operated by the RN Historic Flight as she left the Harbour for the last time.

HELICOPTER SUPPORT SHIP COMMISSIONED

Replacing HMS *Lofoten* at the end of 1967 was RFA Engadine, commissioned into the Royal Fleet Auxiliary as the first ship designed for the support of helicopter training. Entering service on 15th December, the ship was used as a seagoing deck for operational training of a variety of

The first McDonnell Douglas F4K Phantom II at Yeovilton

DH Sea Vixen FAW Mk2

units, however its main task was to support the helicopter training squadrons.

It could embark up to four Wessex (later two Sea Kings) or six Wasps (later six Lynx) helicopters. Operating mostly off the Portland exercise areas, the ship was also regularly used for the operation of the FAA's pilotless target aircraft for ships gunnery practice. These aircraft were launched using a small portable ramp, the targets being recovered after landing by parachute. The ship was also utilised for specific trials and was capable of operating worldwide.

THE SEA VIXEN IS STILL NO. 1

Two memorable episodes in the Sea Vixen FAW2's service life were to occur during 1968. The first feat was achieved when all twelve Sea Vixens of No. 893 Sqdn. flew non-stop from Yeovilton to Akrotiri in Cyprus on 18th April, a distance of 2,200 miles. This was the furthest distance the type was to fly non-stop, and the first time a complete squadron had transitted together to another base direct from their parent base, without embarking on board a ship.

The second was the display team established from No. 892 Sqdn. for the 1968 Farnborough Airshow. Led by Lt. Cdr. Simon Idiens, the six aircraft were displayed as "Simon's Circus". This was the largest aircraft used by any display team to the present day, and the routine flown by the team was considered to steal the show.

THE PHANTOM ARRIVES

The last conventional carrier type IFTU formed on 30th April 1968 when No. 700P Sqdn. was commissioned having three F4K Phantoms on its strength. The Phantom II was destined to become the last conventional fixed-wing carrier borne aircraft type to enter service with the RN. The first three aircraft had arrived at Yeovilton direct from the manufacturers the day before the commissioning.

The FAA Phantom was a Fighter Ground Attack aircraft with the designation FG1, and the IFTU were eventually to receive eight aircraft for its workup and trials programme. It was given the honour of displaying at Farnborough during the September 1968 Airshow, with the display aircraft producing sonic booms to impress the crowds. It was to be (and still is) the only fully supersonic aircraft to be operated by the FAA and the only type having engine reheat.

Even though the IFTU had been formed, much trials work was required to be completed by the A & AEE at Boscombe Down and the RAE at Bedford. All the new carrier facilities needed to be proved, and this was done at NAD Bedford where an aircraft was loaned to test the catapult, jet blast deflector and crash barrier. Its first catapult launch was completed on 16th December.

The A & AEE carried out the first deck trials onboard a British carrier, with HMS *Eagle* being used as HMS *Ark Royal* was still being refitted. The first trials during March 1969 comprised of 121 touch and go's before the first actual landings being made in June when three aircraft completed 61 arrested landings and take-offs. The ship's waist catapult was long enough for launching but special water cooling systems were installed in the deck and jet blast deflectors to compensate for the reheat from the aircraft engine.

Only two FAA squadrons were to operate the type; No. 892 Sqdn., the operational unit, and No. 767 Sqdn., the Air Warfare Fighter Training Unit. The training squadron was responsible for training all RN and RAF (air defence) aircrew on the type and the training of maintenance personnel for the FAA. Some of the aircraft used by the squadron were RAF aircraft which wore a camouflaged colour scheme with the squadron's codes and golden hawk motif on the tail.

The squadron commissioned on 14th January 1969, ten weeks before the FLS which was an unusual occurrence. However its survival was to be short lived due to the MOD's decision that all fixed-wing flying training would, in future, be carried out by the RAF. The squadron disbanded on 1st August 1972, six years before the Phantom was to complete its service with the FAA. Training of future FAA personnel was to be completed by the Phantom Training Flight at RAF Leuchars.

PROJECT ROYAL BLUE - THE TRANSATLANTIC AIR RACE

The operational Phantom squadron was commissioned on 31st March 1969 from the IFTU as the only FLS to operate the type in FAA service. It continued the work done by the IFTU from which it was formed, including the first operational carrier trials during October 1969, when the squadron embarked onboard USS *Saratoga* for a six day period.

The three competing aircraft in the Transatlantic Air Race

The squadron was to also gain a place in aviation record books when it had three aircraft participate in the Daily Mail Transatlantic Air Race, commemorating the 50th anniversary of Alcock and Brown's epic first crossing of the Atlantic. The race was from the top of the GPO Tower in London to the top of the Empire State Building in Manhattan New York, taking place between 4th and 11th May 1969.

Three crews took part actually flying between US Naval Air Station Floyd Bennett and the British Aircraft Corporation airfield of Wisley near Guildford. RAF Victor tankers were a major factor in achieving the best results, and meticulous planning ensured that they were in the rendezvous positions for in-flight refuelling.

The aircraft were flown across 'the Pond' on 24th April in preparation for their west to east crossings, the observers in each aircraft being the race entrant. The first crew attempted the race on the first day, completing the race in 5hrs 31mins, whilst the second crew took 12 minutes off the time on 7th May. Both crews had bettered the previous best for the west to east flight across the Atlantic, but the record was to be set during the third attempt.

On the last day the squadron CO, Lt. Cdr. B Davies, and Senior Observer, Lt. Cdr. P Goddard, took their turn. They crossed 'the pond' in a record time of 4hrs 46mins 57 seconds with an average true air speed of 1,100 mph, and completed the race from point to point in 5hrs 11mins 22 seconds to win both the overall fastest time and fastest time in their class, winning a total of £6,000.

HMS Tiger with No. 826 Sqdn Sea Kings

ASW CRUISERS COMMISSION

Commissioning on 23rd April was the first ASW cruiser, HMS *Blake,* now fitted with a flight deck and hangar capable of accommodating four helicopters. No. 820 Sqdn. Wessex HAS Mk3 aircraft embarked in her on 30th June 1969. The second ship, HMS *Tiger,* entered service during 1972 embarking No. 826 Sqdn. with Sea Kings on 22nd August. Both ships would operate the Sea King until they were paid of - HMS *Tiger* in 1978 and HMS *Blake* in 1980.

COMMANDO SUPPORT NORWAY - CLOCKWORK

An important NATO role was taken up by the Royal Marines, that of rapid deployment to NATO's northern flank, Norway, in the event of a Russian invasion. This was to support the Norwegian Forces until arrival of reinforcements. With the impending withdrawal from East of Suez, the amphibious assault assets would be increased, thus it was an ideal Force for sending to Norway if needed.

To support this new task, No. 846 Sqdn. formed on 29th July 1968 and after training with the commandos embarked in RFA *Engadine* on 9th February 1969 for transit to the Norwegian base of Bardufoss. This deployment and the subsequent exercises in the area were to be known as 'Exercise Clockwork' and were to become an annual deployment of the amphibious force. The FAA base at Arbroath, HMS Condor, was eventually to become the home to 45 RMC, the arctic marines, who would be moved to Norway and back by the ships and commando squadrons to hone up the amphibious force's skills. The RMC were regularly exercising with the Dutch Marines for combined NATO exercises, and these two Marine units were to form the NATO Combined Commando Force in 1973.

ATTACK FORCE WASP

The Caribbean island of Anguilla was in a state of unrest when assistance was sought by the Government to restore order. The West Indies Guardships of HMSs *Minerva* and *Rothesay* sent their Wasp flights ashore with 130 marines and equipment on 19th March 1969. The Wasps were then used for reconnaissance flights, leaflet dropping and logistic support. The British withdrew on 15th September after peace was restored.

NUMBER 142 PILOTS COURSE

The FAA took over the passing out parade at RAF Linton-on-Ouse on the last day of July 1969 when 36 fixed-wing front line aircraft were to overfly the parade. In the static were examples of FAA aircraft for the visitors and VIPs to view, including Tiger Moth, Sea Prince, Sea Vampire, Gannet, Sea Vixen and F4 Phantom II aircraft.

The occasion was the passing out of the last seven FAA fixed-wing pilots after successfully completing their flying training with No. 1 FTS. They had successfully completed their grading flights at Roborough, basic flying training at RAF Church Fenton and the jet course at Linton. They were now going to Brawdy for training with the Hunters then to either Lossiemouth or Brawdy for their type conversion, as the last fixed-wing pilots or so it seemed!

HARRIER GR1 TRIALS

HMS *Bulwark* was to carry out the first Harrier GR1 trials in 1969, this being the first production model of the Harrier. Operated by the Harrier Conversion Team, the aircraft landed and took off from the ship with under-wing drop tanks and rocket pods. These were followed with the most important trials to date which were held onboard the helicopter cruiser HMS *Blake* during August, with the aircraft embarking on the 8th.

The aircraft was operated with a wind speed of 35 knots across the deck (in all directions) and with the ship pitching and rolling through a 12 degree range without affecting the operational capability of the aircraft. These trials sparked the interest of the Admiralty in the aircraft and further proving trials by the RAF were to result in the FAA eventually having a version of the aircraft which would be ordered in May 1975.

WESTLAND SEA KING

The first Westland built Sea King helicopter flew on 7th May 1969 and carried out deck trials aboard the Helicopter Training Ship RFA *Engadine* on 2nd July whilst the ship was off Portland. The type's IFTU No. 700S Sqdn. formed on 19th August at Culdrose, specifically tasked to prove the ASW qualities of the aircraft, then February 1970 saw the first FLS No. 824 Sqdn. forming for

Westland Wessex Mk5 wearing "Arctic" camouflage

Westland Wasp HASMk1 onboard HMS Andromeda as used in the operation

RAF Hawker Harrier GR1 onboard HMS Bulwark

English Electric (BAC) Canberra T4 at Yeovilton

operating aboard HMS *Ark Royal.*

The IFTU was to set up a helicopter endurance record on 3rd December when one of its six aircraft piloted by the squadron CO, Lt. Cdr. V Sirrett, with Lt. Cdr's. R Millsdon and J Flindell as crew, flew for 4hrs 19mins 26 seconds flying 602 miles. When the IFTU disbanded on 29th May it had achieved 2700 hours with its compliment of six aircraft and proved all predicted spheres of operating modes for the type. This included its primary role of ASW, troop transportation, load lifting and SAR.

FLEET REQUIREMENTS AND AIR DIRECTION TRAINING UNIT

Fleet requirement duties had been performed by Airworks since the disbanding of the last FRU squadron No. 728 Sqdn. in August 1965. Operating out of Bournemouth airport, the company operated FAA Meteors as target tugs but their operational limitations were being surpassed by the aircraft and ships' AA weapons in service. Ten converted ex-RAF Canberra B2 bombers were used to replace the ageing meteors. The first Canberra TT18 was delivered to Airworks on 15th September 1969, and two B4 trainers were also used by the FRU for pilot training. The final Meteor TT Mk20s were retired eighteen months later after all the Canberras had been delivered.

These were not the first Canberras to be used by the FAA. No. 728 Sqdn., the FRU squadron which had been based at Hal Far in Malta, had previously operated six Canberra U Mk14s for Seaslug trials over seven months in 1961. The aircraft were unmanned aircraft drones which could safely be fired upon by the anti-aircraft missile. The trials were completed successfully on 2nd December and the remaining aircraft were passed to the A & AEE.

Westland Sea King HASMk1 of No. 824 Sqdn the first FLS

The Airworks unit was moved to Yeovilton on 1st December 1972 to amalgamate with the Air Directions Training Unit which operated Hunters and Sea Vixens, becoming the FAA's FRADU. Soon to join the TT18 was the last mark of the venerable British bomber, the Canberra T Mk22, easily identified by the long pointed nose housing the Blue Parrot radar system. The first of these aircraft, seven converted ex-RAF PR Mk7s, entered service in November 1973.

These aircraft replaced the Sea Vixens (which were finally retired from FAA service in 1974), tasked with the role of anti-missile ship simulators. They would fly in formation with Hunter aircraft positioned outboard of the aircraft and would then attack ships. At a point in the mission, if they had been armed with missiles, the Hunters would actually simulate a strike at the ship as if they were the missiles. The Canberras have been replaced with the Dassault Falcon 20 and the Hunters were replaced in 1996 with redundant RAF Hawk aircraft.

FAA's LAST STRIKE AIRCRAFT SBAC DISPLAY

The 1973 SBAC show was to be the last full FAA display at Farnborough which would include all the elements from the strike aircraft to the helicopters, including the two latest types. The static display contained all the types of aircraft operated in FLS plus ground displays, enticing would-be aviators

English Electric (BAC) Camberra T22

and engineers to join the premier air force.

There were two display teams; Simon's Circus displayed their six Sea Vixens (No. 892 Sqdn.), whilst No. 809 Sqdn., The Phoenix Five, put their Buccaneers through a routine, both performing low level strikes on the airfield. The Wessex Vs of No. 845 Sqdn. carried out a commando assault aided by 41 RMC, which included rescuing a downed Hiller HT2 of No. 705 Sqdn. Solo displays were given by Wasp, Gannet and the new Sea King helicopters, whilst a three ship F4K Phantom display was included in the airfield attack. Never again was such a display to be performed at an SBAC show.

DECADE ENDS ON A FALSE HIGH

The Queen reviewed the Western Fleet and presented it with new colours on 29th July in Torbay, when the assembled Fleet was headed by HMS *Eagle.* Eighty-nine aircraft took part in the flypast for Her Majesty, the 58 fixed-wing aircraft operating out of Yeovilton and the 31 helicopters from Culdrose.

It was a false dawn as the RN was about to enter the decade which would see the gradual reduction of the carrier Fleet. To accompany this reduction, the supporting surface Fleet was also to be reduced and the days of the Royal Navy being a force to reckon with were about to take a beating. Successive short-sighted defence cuts had, as usual, seen the FAA as the 'not so important' military arm - anything it can do, so can the RAF.

HMS HERMES BECOMES A COMMANDO CARRIER

Sailing from Portsmouth in January 1970, HMS *Hermes* embarked her squadrons on the 14th for its deployment to the Mediterranean. This was to be her last deployment as a fixed-wing carrier after twelve years operating as the lesser known Fleet attack carrier. Returning to Portsmouth on 22nd June for de-storing, she was then towed to Devonport to commence conversion to a commando carrier (replacing HMS *Albion*).

Hawker Hunter

HMS Eagle

Re-commissioning as a commando carrier on 18th April 1973, like the two other commando carriers she had all the fixed-wing operating equipment removed, as was the 'dustbin' type 984 radar. Areas of the flight deck were strengthened to allow RAF Harriers to operate from the deck and four landing craft were installed on the boat decks. Additional accommodation was fitted so she could carry a full compliment of 750 Royal Marines as standard with additional space for a second unit.

She was to differ from the other two ships in having ASW aircraft as standard compliment, thus she would normally embark sixteen Commando Wessex MkVs and four Sea King ASW helicopters. She carried out successful sea trials before embarking on her first operation - an ASW exercise!

HMS EAGLE'S FINAL COMMISSION

Trials for the new RAF Harrier were completed during March 1970 when two aircraft from A & AEE Boscombe Down embarked on board HMS *Eagle* for carrier deck type certification, the end result being that the type received its full deck operations clearance (this meant that RAF Harriers could be embarked aboard carriers). Her final deployment began on 26th May 1971, departing Devonport for a nine month cruise to Australia and New Zealand via the Far East. The main reason for the deployment was the withdrawal of the Flag Officer 2 Far East Fleet (FO2FEF), with the closing down of the RN facilities in Singapore.

The lowering of FO2FEF's flag and the White Ensign on the evening of 31st October was followed by the sailing of HMS *Eagle* accompanied by HMSs *Albion*, *Triumph* and *Intrepid* plus escorting ships from Singapore dockyard the next morning. The ships were then to sail in line astern past the island in salute to the Singapore Government. Overhead flew a massed flypast including Buccaneers, Gannets, Sea Vixens, Sea Kings, Wessex and Wasp helicopters. With the closing down of the Singapore dockyard, only Hong Kong was to remain as a base East of Suez.

Meanwhile, in the Far East, the Sea Kings from No. 826 Sqdn. were involved in a rescue of the 40-man crew of the SS *Steel Vendor* which had foundered on a reef in the

No. 826 Sqdn. Westland Sea King rescuing the crew of the SS Steel Vendor in the South China Sea

Fairey Gannet COD4 of No. 849B Flight, the last user of the type

South China Sea during a typhoon. Three aircraft were launched on 7th October in gale force winds and successfully winched the crew to safety, returning back to the ship with them on board.

THE PHANTOMISED HMS ARK ROYAL

After completing a three year refit and emerging as the most powerful warship the Royal Navy would ever possibly operate, HMS *Ark Royal* was re-commissioned into the Fleet on 24th February 1970. The refit was needed to enable her to operate the Phantom aircraft, and the original plan was to carry out a modernisation similar to that of HMS *Eagle* plus phantomisation. However, due to the Labour Government's plans to scrap the Fleet carriers, the minimum work required to operate the type was carried out.

During the refit, the ship's flight deck was redesigned, with the port side having an 8.5 degree angled deck and an after-parking area capable of accommodating two Phantoms. This extension was also to receive a waist catapult, and the starboard side had an extension aft of the crane position behind the island, built out to allow additional parking space.

Areas of the flight deck were strengthened to operate this new aircraft especially around the catapult and the jet blast area, a requirement necessary due to the aircraft's use of after-burners for launching. This also necessitated special water cooled blast deflectors to be fitted. The aft end of the deck was strengthened to receive the impact of this heavier aircraft during recovery and new direct acting arrestor wires were installed.

Until the refit the launch bridle, which was attached to the nose of the aircraft to pull them down the catapult track, was always discarded as the aircraft was launched off the deck. During the refit, however, a reusable bridle system was fitted, with the modification resulting in a protrusion over the edge of the flight deck. Trials had previously been carried out on HMS *Victorious* when the system was fitted at the end of her port catapult during her 1960 refit. An improved mirror landing sight was also installed, based on the USN system able to cope with the Phantom's approach speed.

The island superstructure was redesigned increasing its size to allow the fitting of the new radar and communications fits and to increase the Flyco as in Eagle. The 'Alaskan Highway' behind the island was to have two decks built onto it, thus preventing continuous access around the starboard side of the island. Emerging from the refit, she was the most potent fighting force in the Fleet and was to remain so for the next eight years.

The air group allotted to the ship was the Buccaneers of No. 809 Sqdn., Sea Kings of No. 824 Sqdn., Gannets of No. 849B Flight and the Phantoms of No. 892 Sqdn. These squadrons were to remain the ship's units until finally leaving the ship at the end of November 1978, the last conventional fixed-wing squadrons, plus the Sea Kings of No. 824 Sqdn. and the SAR Unit — the last operators of the Wessex Mk1.

HMS Ark Royal

McDonnell Douglas F4K and Westland Wessex HAS1 SAR helicopter

The first aircraft arrived in March 1970 for wire pulling trials followed by full flying trials between 30th April and 15th May, with the first F4 landing on board the ship on the first day. The full air group arrived on 14th June for workup, being declared available for NATO during September. The ship's first exercise was the NATO Autumn Northern Wedding off the Norwegian coast and was followed in November with Lime Jug 70 in the Mediterranean.

During the Lime Jug Mediterranean cruise the ship was to make the headlines twice, firstly for an international incident, the second when she made history. During the exercise, the Russian Kotlin 365 was shadowing the Fleet and the carrier in particular, with her Kamov Ka-25 Hormone helicopter flying over the ship. The Kotlin was eventually to get so close to the ship that the two collided when the ship commenced night flying operations on 9th November 1970 whilst south of Greece. The carrier attempted evasive action but it was not sufficient to prevent the two ships making contact. The carrier received a split in the for'castle, and a 4ft x 3ft hole four feet above the waterline in the boatswain's store which was repaired in only eight hours. The damage to the Kotlin is not known, but seven of her crew were thrown overboard, five being rescued but the other two were lost.

The second event made history when, on the 29th, she become the first RN warship to launch a hot air balloon. The Bristol Belle, flown by Lt. Adams from No. 849B Fight, took off from the flight deck bound for Malta with mail from the ship. The balloon landed in a field and became the first balloon to land on the island. The mail received special first day cover franking of the stamps.

Westland Sea Kings

THE RAF BACK AT SEA

After receiving clearance to operate from the decks of aircraft carriers following the trials aboard HMS *Eagle* in 1970, HMS *Ark Royal* was to embark the Harrier GR1s of No. 1(F) Sqdn. RAF for an exercise in the Moray Firth on 4th May 1971. The aircraft were to remain on board until the 19th, operating alongside the Buccaneers and Phantoms in a successful joint operations exercise.

This was to be the first time a full RAF squadron had embarked on board an aircraft carrier since W.W.II - there had been many detachments of helicopters and observation aircraft prior to this. It was to be the first of many such operations by RAF Harriers on RN aircraft carriers. The success of operating the Harrier onboard carrier decks in combined operations was to be the forerunner of future operations by RAF squadrons on decks of British ships.

It is now normal practice for the current Fleet to embark RAF Harriers when ships deploy, so much so that the current Invincible class have been modified with accommodation for these units. RAF Harrier aircraft have operated from RFAs, RN cruisers and amphibious ships, as well as ships from the British merchant fleet since this first deployment of the type, culminating in a combined joint RN/RAF Sea Harrier/ Harrier Force 30 years later.

THE LARGEST HOVERCRAFT ARRIVES

The IHU received its largest hovercraft when the BH-7 (British Hovercraft) was delivered on 28th September 1970. The machine was 77ft long, weighed in at 47 tons, and was capable of speeds in excess of 60 knots. This craft was to be used for the most comprehensive trials by the unit, including one whilst fitted with the world's largest propeller blade, the Hawker Siddeley 21ft diameter blade.

The majority of its work was in support of the Navy, with the Naval Evaluation Trials (NETs) being funded by the RN for evaluation of a possible squadron of hovercraft and their practical roles. Cold weather operations had been limited to those in the Falkland Islands, thus a series of intense cold weather trials were to be carried out in the Baltic Sea with the support of the Royal Swedish Navy. Hot and humid operations had already been completed with the smaller craft, and it was felt that as the Iranians had purchased these larger hovercraft, their operating data would be accessed by the RN.

Arctic exercises using the BH7 were to be held during the early months of 1972, and the hovercraft left Lee-on-Solent on 9th February, reaching the RSwN base of Galo five days later. After operating in the Stockholm Archipelago for twelve days, the craft headed further north into the Gulf of Bothnia, eventually reaching the town of Ranea about 50 miles south of the Arctic Circle on 9th March. Operating in the Gulf for two weeks, this phase of the exercise proved successful except for repairs being needed to the skirt. One problem did occur when the craft had to be freed by two tractors after becoming wedged in an ice ridge whilst on the return journey back to Galo.

Demonstrations were given in Stockholm prior to the return journey to Lee-on-Solent which included a series of further demonstrations to the Danish military at Copenhagen and the Germans at Wilhelmshaven, arriving back at Lee on 12th April after 64 days away. During the period of the trials, only four days were lost due to mechanical problems and 36 sorties across the ice were carried out reaching speeds of 70 knots across smooth ice and 50 knots over rough ice ridges.

The summer of 1972 saw the craft in the Portland areas completing NETs with Flag Officer Sea Training (FOST), tasked with a variety of operations ranging from passenger transfers, replenishment at sea, towing of other vessels and helicopter target exercises. More important exercises were held when the craft was used alongside the FOST fast patrol boats in simulated weapons attacks against ships operating in the training area.

BH7 Hovercraft

Another major exercise was searching for and locating a missing submarine, and all the tasks set by the FOST staff were successfully completed. The BH7 was tried out as a support vessel for HM Coast Guard patrolling the channel, intercepting 34 suspicious radar contacts during a six day period in September.

OPERATION EXIT

Admiral Nelson liberated the Maltese islands from French Occupation on 5th September 1800 and, since that time, it had been the Mediterranean home to British Forces and in particular the RN, known as the RN's unsinkable aircraft carrier in W.W.II. During 1971, however, the relationship became soured by the island's Prime Minister, Mr. Dom Mintoff, who was determined to drive the Forces from the island.

This ill-feeling threatened the position of the Forces at the end of 1971 such that HMSs *Eagle* and *Albion,* in the Indian Ocean on their way home from the Far East, were ordered to head for the Mediterranean to assist in the withdrawal. The threat was removed as Mintoff backed down albeit only for a short period.

The new year saw the threat reappear as diplomatic approaches were not resolving the situation. HMS *Bulwark* was having a refit and repairs after a fire in her boiler room, but it was decided that she should go to the island as a floating HQ for the now impending withdrawal. A supposed eight week period in refit was reduced to twelve days and the ship left Plymouth on 13th January with ten Wessex Vs of No. 845 Sqdn. plus four from No. 846 Sqdn., arriving in Grand Harbour on the 18th.

She was to remain in the harbour for ten weeks operating the helicopters from her deck in support of the withdrawal, however an agreement was reached for British Forces to remain on the island for a further seven years.

HMS Bulwark operating in Valetta Harbour Malta

Final disembarkation of the Sea Vixens of No. 899 Sqdn. Note the aircraft are all painted up with flowers and slogans

During the 72 day period, the squadron completed over 1100 sorties from the ship (including flying Mr. Mintoff over Floriana for an aerial view of the island), which was a remarkable amount of sorties considering there was a restriction on flying in the area. Embarking 41 RMC for their return to the UK, the ship left the harbour on 30th March with a nine aircraft flypast over Valetta.

HMS EAGLE'S LAST FAREWELL

The ship disembarked the fixed-wing element of her air group for the last time whilst on passage from Gibraltar to Portsmouth on 23rd January 1972, and the Sea Kings and Wessex SAR Flight to Culdrose the following day. All the units except for the Sea King squadron were disbanded upon the ship's return to the UK, leaving only the three fixed-wing squadrons aboard HMS *Ark Royal* as the front line fixed-wing aircraft in the FAA.

The Sea Vixen was retired from FLS with the disbanding of No. 899 Sqdn. after serving on FL Squadrons for nearly thirteen years, the longest serving fighter in FAA service up to this time (now surpassed by the Sea Harrier).

HMS Ark Royal passes her sister ship HMS Eagle in Plymouth Sound. Note the removal of the forward deck of the latter — now fitted to the former.

Blackburn Buccaneer S2 about to be launched from HMS Ark Royal

The squadron decommissioned on the same day as the ship, with the aircraft scheduled to fly over the ship as it entered Portsmouth Harbour for the last time. Unfortunately inclement weather in the Solent prevented this farewell flight taking place.

The Sea Vixens were flown from Yeovilton to RAF St. Athan at the end of the month, arriving in the condition that they had disembarked from HMS *Eagle*, all painted up in flowers, motifs and graffiti. Permission had been given for the aircraft to be so adorned so each of the fourteen aircraft was decorated by their respective crews whilst in Gibraltar (the ship's last port of call). It made for a colourful departure and the arrival at Yeovilton caused quite a stir as only the advance party were aware of the aircraft's condition.

The ship was to remain alongside in Portsmouth for de-storing, and a ramp was erected so vehicles could drive onto the ship for loading, thus speeding up the process. Completed by early August, the ship was to depart Portsmouth for the last time under tow for the journey to Devonport where she would remain as a 'source of spare' for HMS *Ark Royal*. She was finally to be towed to the breakers yard at Cairn Ryan in October 1978, after her sister ship left Plymouth for her last deployment.

After retirement from No. 899 Sqdn., the Sea Vixen was to continue in support of naval training. The final naval use of the aircraft was to be with the FRU operated by Airworks and later Flight Refuelling, who also used the aircraft to carry out trials on their refuelling pods.

Some were destined to become pilot-less target drones, the Sea Vixen D Mk3, three being converted by Flight Refuelling. The final two were retired from RAE Llanbedr in Wales in 1995, a twist of fate being that some 40 years previous the type had been initially ordered by the RAF as a long-range day-fighter and night-fighter but cancelled when the Gloster Javelin was chosen for the roles. The final flights of the type would be whilst wearing RAF roundels and flashes, not RN codes. (The Javelin was retired from the RAF in 1968 and from the A & AEE in January 1975).

FAA BUCCANEERS TO THE RESCUE

On the day that HMS *Eagle* sailed into Portsmouth with its paying off pennant flying, trouble was brewing in Central America with Guatemala threatening to invade British Honduras. The only Forces in the country was a detachment of an Army regiment without any aviation assets at it disposal. The Government diverted HMS *Ark Royal* from the North Atlantic to head south and launch a flight of aircraft to the capital Belize City.

Three days later whilst the ship was some 1300 miles from the country, a flight of Buccaneer tankers launched to support the two aircraft which were to overfly the city, refuelling them twice in both directions. The two aircraft, fitted with wing and bomb-bay fuel tanks, reached Belize and carried out two orbits around the city before returning back to the ship.

This show of strength had taken five minutes short of six hours flying time. Achieving its desired aim, the Guatemalans backed down. Once again the mighty Ark Royal had been seen as a powerful force in the South Atlantic without being in the area, the first was the supposed threat to the Graf Spree 32 years earlier. Another demonstration as to the importance of a strike carrier in the Fleet!

DARKNESS DAWNS

With the decommissioning of HMS *Eagle* upon its return to the UK on 26th January 1972, it was the real beginning of the run down of the FAA. HMS *Centaur* was in use as an accommodation ship after decommissioning in 1966, and she was to go to scrap in 1972 when no longer needed as a back up accommodation for the carrier force. HMS *Albion* was to operate in NATO exercises during 1972 but was paid off at the end of the year and sold in 1973 as a cable laying ship. This left the RN with one strike carrier, HMS *Ark Royal*, and two commando carriers, HMSs *Bulwark* and *Hermes*.

Due to there being only three front line fixed-wing squadrons and all pilot training for the Phantom and Buccaneer passing on to the RAF, the need for bases was reduced. The bases at Lossiemouth (HMS Fulmar) and Brawdy (HMS Goldcrest) were both handed over to the RAF in the early 70s.

Front line fixed-wing squadrons were to move to RAF bases after their autumn 1972

Westland/Aerospatiale Lynx pre-production aircraft used by the Air Engineering School

period on board Ark Royal, leaving their FAA bases for the last time on 4th September. The Buccaneers relocated to RAF Honington upon disembarking to operate alongside their RAF counterparts, and the F4s relocated to RAF Leuchars, also joining RAF counterparts. The Gannets had moved to Lossiemouth joining the RAF's AEW Shackletons during 1970 when Brawdy was handed over.

This left the FAA with four bases operating FL Squadrons; HMS Heron at Yeovilton, HMS Osprey at Portland, HMS Seahawk at Culdrose and HMS Gannet at Prestwick, all with helicopter squadrons. The remaining fixed-wing aircraft in service were all old types; No. 750 Sqdn. at Culdrose with Sea Princes, No. 781 Sqdn. (the communications squadron) operating aircraft at HMS Daedalus with Sea Herons and Sea Devons, and the Chipmunks at Roborough for the experience and grading flight, plus the electronic warfare Canberra T17s of the joint RAF/RN No. 360 Sqdn. at RAF Cottesmore.

Training was also streamlined and the mechanical engineering school at Arbroath, HMS Condor, was moved south to join the other engineering schools at Lee-on-Solent during the autumn of 1970 (the base became RM Condor, home of 45 RMC). The training school was re-titled as the Air Engineering School, now responsible for all rating FAA career engineering training and FAA specialised short courses in engineering, management and administration.

THE FLYING CAT

First designed as the Westland WG3 in 1963 as a replacement for the Scout, the Westland/Aerospatiale Lynx AH1 flew for the first time on 12th April 1972. This was followed by the FAA version, the Lynx HAS Mk2 on 20th May, and the Navy Lynx was to enter service as a replacement for the Wasp helicopter.

Like the Wasp before it, its pedigree can be traced to a requirement for the British Army which was subsequently redesigned for the FAA. It was a joint Anglo-French helicopter, one of three to be built for the Forces of both nations (the Puma and Gazelle being the other two).

The development of the helicopter had resulted in many roles available for the ship to operate the helicopter in; ASW, SAR, Anti-surface vessel search and strike, communications and liaison duties, gunfire spotting, vertreping and troop transportation. Many of these roles could be, and were, operated by the Wasp but not with the same payloads or radius of operations as the new helicopter would be capable of.

The first eleven Lynx helicopters (both variants) were built for development trials by Westlands with the first sea trials aboard RFA *Engadine* in the autumn of 1972. A long trials and evaluation programme was needed, the aircraft being a new design fitted with new unproven engines. The RR Gem Production aircraft began rolling out of the Yeovil factory in 1976 with the first flight on 10th February.

This new helicopter could carry a much greater payload than the Wasp, including two homing torpedoes with six marine markers or two nuclear depth charges in the ASW role, and four Sea Skua or four AS12 wire guided missiles in the anti-shipping role for which it was also fitted with the Sea Spray surface search radar so it could act independently from the ship. It could fly forwards at 140+ knots and backwards at 120 knots, fifteen knots faster than the Wasp was capable in forward flight! Possessing a rigid rotor head, the helicopter was capable of a full roll, demonstrated many times at air shows whilst flown by company pilots. It could carry seven passengers in the rear of the aircraft compared with three in the Wasp.

The Lynx was a tricycle undercarriage helicopter giving it better manoeuvrability on small decks, and one of the fundamental changes was the installation of two engines

Hawker Hunter T8 used by the Standards Flight

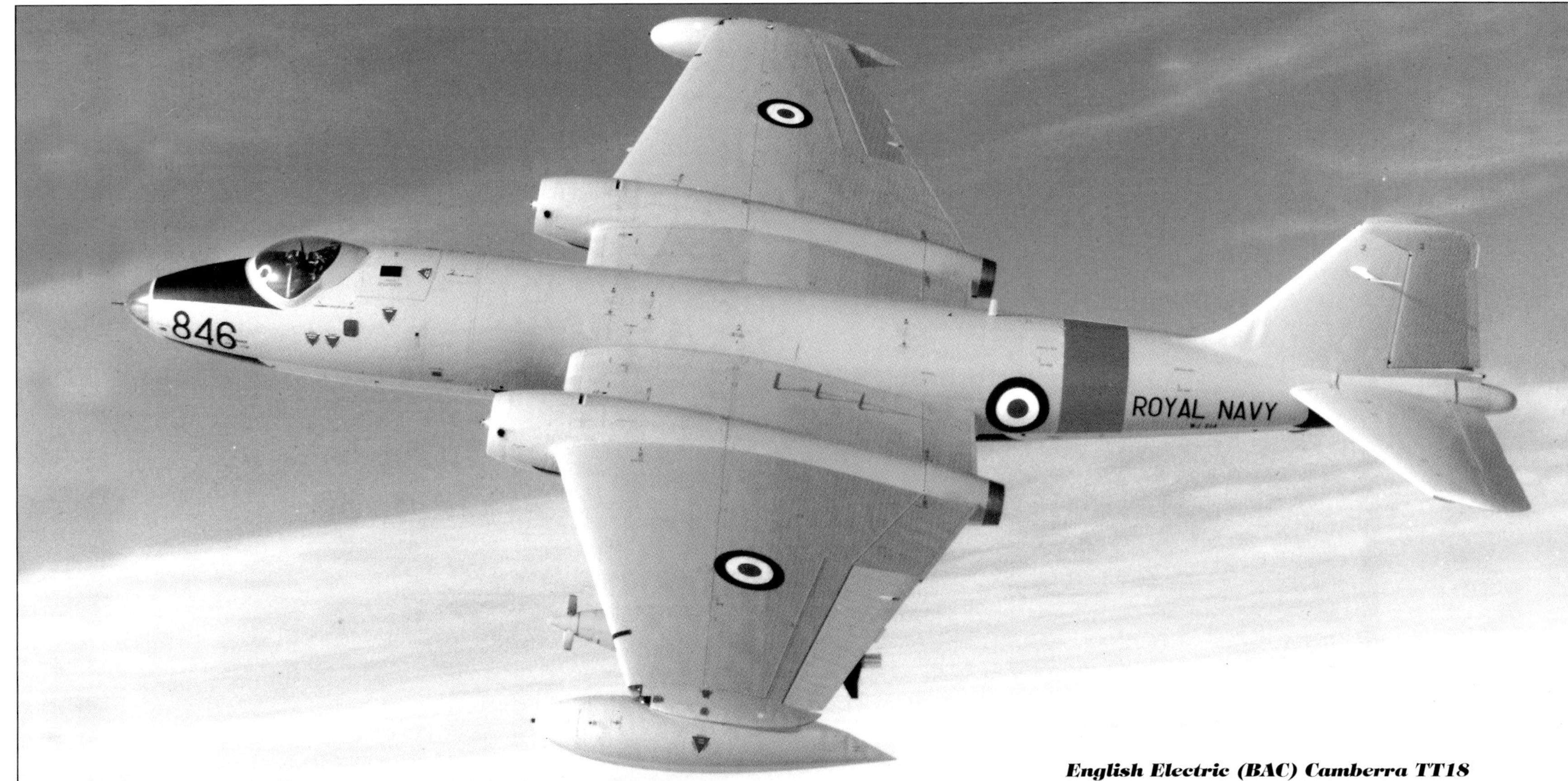

English Electric (BAC) Camberra TT18

instead of one as in the case of the Wasp. The helicopter was a more capable machine, operating over a longer range and duration with more weapons against both submarines and surface ships. It was to replace the Wasp on all flights except those embarked aboard the Rothesay class frigates which were to be phased out.

It was fitted with a harpoon system beneath the helicopter's underside which was released by the pilot when he was ready to take off, and upon landing he activated it so it would catch onto the ship's grid on the deck thus securing it safely on deck. This was another idea by Sproule who had the idea back in 1955 when it was tried on the Dragonfly helicopter.

This system required the centre of the ship to have a metal grid incorporated, and allowed the ship to operate the Lynx in greater sea states than was possible for the Wasp. It also allowed the helicopter to turn itself into wind for launching and recovery which alleviated the need for the ship to turn into wind when operating the helicopter.

FRADU - THE FAA's LARGEST FIXED-WING UNIT!

With the moving of the FRU from Hurn airport to join up with the Air Direction Unit during 1972, the FAA's largest fixed-wing unit was then the FRADU based at Yeovilton equipped with 24 Hunters, 12 Canberras and a handful of Sea Vixens. It was a vital asset both for the FAA and the Fleet providing a service which included target towing, gunnery and missile tracking, radar calibration, air interceptions and pilot evaluation and grading on behalf of the FAA's Naval Flying Standards Fixed-Wing Flight (NFSF{FW}).

This civilian operated unit had ex-RAF and FAA pilots flying the missions on behalf of the RN. During 1975 a display team was established with four of the Hunters, and this was to be the only civilian military jet

The Blue Herons

Hiller HT2

display team until disbanding in 1980. The team won the trophy for the best display team at the International Air Tattoo of 1977 when displaying and performing against such international teams as the Red Arrows and Patroulle de France

THE OTHER ANGLO-FRENCH HELICOPTER FOR THE FAA

Stablemate to the Lynx, the Gazelle HT2 training helicopter began life as an army helicopter. Its original design was an observation helicopter for the French Army. It was to bring a new innovation to helicopter design, that of a shrouded tail rotor called a Fenestron, a series of encapsulated blades replacing the tail rotor. It also had a rigid main rotor head which gave the helicopter much improved manoeuvrability.

The potential of the helicopter as a training helicopter was appreciated by both the RN and RAF. The RN ordered 35 aircraft for the training role, with the FAA examples differing from the RAF model by having a rescue winch and a stability augmentation system. The first aircraft flew in July 1972 and it was to be a major step up from the present training helicopters of the FAA, the Hiller HT2 and Whirlwind HAS 7.

HMS UNDAUNTED RETIRES

After six years of sterling service, HMS *Undaunted* was retired from the role of helicopter landing platform training ship. She was replaced by a converted aircraft lighter RNAL No. 50, which was to become the Flight Deck Training Unit floating deck operating in Portland Harbour.

The new deck was to take over after many small ships' flight FDO's, lashing numbers and flights had been trained on operating helicopters on small decks. Many thousands of deck landings had been completed on Undaunted in her time at Portland, and her nickname of HMS Unwanted was not meant to be derisory but more a name of affection by the thousands of ratings, officers and aircrew who were to gain valuable experience in her.

CYPRUS - 'THE FINAL CONFLICT'

During the fourteen years since 'peace' had been declared with the establishment of the Republic in Cyprus, the Greek population led by Makarios still sought Enosis and spasmodic fighting continued. The UN sent a Peace Force in 1964 and although the skirmishes continued there was not an overwhelming threat to the peace initially. However the build up of hostility towards the Turkish Cypriots continued unabated and eventually, on 15th July 1973, a military coup by the Greek Cypriot National Guard seized power and Makarios fled the island.

Twelve months later, the Turkish military invaded the north of the island to prevent the Greek Cypriots from succeeding with the union with Greece. The RN was called upon to evacuate refugees from the island, and HMS *Hermes* was in passage from the USA to Malta to disembark 41 RMC when it was re-tasked to go to Cyprus. It disembarked the commando unit ashore to support the British Forces whilst the ship sailed to the coastal town of Kyrenia in the heart of the Turkish invasion force.

Embarked were the Wessex HU5s of No. 845 Sqdn. and Sea Kings of No. 814 Sqdn. who, assisted by the Wessex HAS 3 from HMS *Devonshire*, rescued over 1500 evacuees from the beach, 20% of a total of 7526 rescued, transferring them to the sovereign base at Akrotiri. The RMC brigade were re-embarked and taken to their original destination, Malta.

The invasion resulted in a split of the island, eventually forming the Turkish Cypriot Federal State in the northern third of the island as an independent state, with the

Westland Aerospatiale Gazelle HT2

Greek Cypriots controlling the remainder of the island.

THE FAA's FIRST DEDICATED SAR UNIT

All the operational bases operated helicopters for search and rescue primarily of crews from crashed aircraft with some civilian support. The first unit tasked with supporting the civil rescue organisations was No. 771 Sqdn. in October 1961 whilst based at RNAS Portland, but this was secondary to its helicopter crew training role. During 1973, the FAA's first 24 hour 365 day SAR unit with the task of civilian SAR operations was established at Lee-on-Solent.

It was to replace the previous SAR cover provided by the RAF's No. 22 Sqdn. which had been located at Thorney Island prior to the base being reduced to 'care and maintenance' status. This Government funded unit was equipped with three Whirlwind HAR Mk9s to cover the rescue work as designated by HM Coast Guard Service along a 160 mile length of the English Channel from Beachy Head to Start Point.

The Whirlwinds known as 'Faith, Hope and Charity' were the last of the type to retire when replaced by four Wessex Mk5 helicopters in 1977. The flight maintained a round-the-clock SAR capability until the helicopters were required for use in the South Atlantic during 1982. Whilst the FAA aircraft were away, the commitment was covered by RAF SAR helicopters.

From 14th February 1983, the FAA SAR commitment was re-established with helicopters detached from No. 772 Sqdn. at Portland. These were to remain until 20th March 1988, when the flight was to operate from the helibase at RNAS Portland with an increase in SAR coverage area now from Beachy Head to Lyme Bay. This proved to be unsatisfactory so a contract was awarded to Bristows Helicopters to provide round-the-clock SAR coverage from Lee-on-Solent, and they still operate from this site providing 24 hour SAR coverage. For the short period before the two Bristows helicopters arrived, the RAF supplied Mk3 SAR Sea Kings to give coverage

THE COD WAR

An embarrassing conflict was to be 'fought' between Britain and its NATO partner Iceland over disputed fishing rights in its coastal waters. Iceland had increased its rights from four miles to 50 on 14th July 1973, and this was disputed by the British Government who were to win a ruling in the International Court of Justice on 17th August that it was an illegal move. Thus the Cod War was to be fought with RN Frigates against Icelandic Gunboats.

Lee on Solent Wessex MkV SAR

Westland Wessex HUMk5 of RFA Regent Flight as used in Cyprus

The argument was to escalate when the gunboats were deliberately sailed at the protecting British frigates and the trawlers they were protecting, culminating in contact with the ships, the first of these on 10th September. The Wasp helicopters were restricted in their role by being tasked with look-out duties, searching for the gunboats so that the trawlers could recover their nets before the 'enemy' arrived, allowing safe evasive action.

A specialised flight was formed in No. 737 Sqdn. using a Wessex Mk3 modified for operations in the Arctic, and 'O' Flight was commissioned on 14th November, days before an agreement was reached with Iceland. The agreement allowed British trawlers into the 50 mile zone for a two year period, but with a maximum of 130,000 tons of fish per year limit. The flight embarked in RFA *Olna* in the new year for a visit to South

Westland Wasp HAS Mk1 from HMS Eskimo

BAe Sea Harrier launching from HMS Ark Royal's 12 degree ramp

Africa before disbanding on 10th April 1974.

FAA MINE COUNTER MEASURES (MCM) EXERCISES

Early trials had been carried out using the SRN-5 hovercraft, but it was with the introduction of the SRN-6 Mk2 at the end of the 1960s that productive trials could be developed. After much development, both these methods were to demonstrate the hovercraft as an effective tool in detecting mines. Part of MCM operations is the recovery of 'disabled' ships within a minefield, and the hovercraft was seen to be especially useful in this role, successfully recovering ships during trials and exercises.

This resulted in the use of hovercraft in naval MCM exercises during 1973/74. The first was exercise 'Scotch Broth' in the Firth of Clyde from 29th January 1973 for three weeks when four hovercraft were used, three SRN-6s and the BH7. This was followed by operation 'Quick Shave' during September in the Plymouth area, but unfortunately bad weather restricted the use of the SRN-6 and other MCM vessels. Two more exercises were held which involved the BH7 and SRN-6 hovercraft; 'Whitebait' during March 1974 in the Humber Estuary, and 'Northern Merger' in the Firth of Forth during September 1974.

With the trials completed, the IHU was to disband at Lee-on-Solent on the last day of 1974. The last joint mission was carried out by an SRN-6 on 18th December in the Solent and a ceremony was held the following day when the unit's Inter-service standard was lowered for the last time. During its thirteen years in service, the unit had operated in all climates in 22 countries on land and at sea proving the vehicle is a useful component of a country's armament. The FAA continued operating hovercraft with the forming of the Naval Hovercraft Trials Unit (NHTU) on 1st January 1975, from the naval contingent of the IHU.

BAe Sea Harrier

NOT ALL BAD NEWS

NEW 'CRUISERS' ORDERED

After many years of discussion and design, the MOD ordered three new Through Deck Command Cruisers. These ships had been envisaged as early as 1966 and designed as cruisers in a shrewd move by the Navy to deceive the Labour Government, not as replacements for the current carrier fleet but as command ships that would be able to operate a small squadron of ASW helicopters.

Initially there was opposition to this through deck but because of the MOD holding its stance, the new Conservative Government upheld the concept. The final design was of a Sea Dart equipped cruiser having a flight deck of 600ft with a full hangar served by two lifts operated by 'scissor arms' and giving access on three sides.

The 19,000 ton ships were designed to be powered by four Rolls Royce Olympus marine engines as fitted to the new destroyers entering service, and would be capable of operating a squadron of nine ASW Sea King helicopters. The first, HMS *Invincible,* was ordered in April 1973 to be built by Vickers Shipbuilders in Barrow-in-Furness. All three were to be built in Barrow originally, but this changed when Swan Hunters in Newcastle was awarded the order for HMS *Illustrious* in May 1976 and HMS *Indomitable* in December 1978. The last one was renamed as HMS *Ark Royal (V)* after public pressure to keep the name alive when the fleet carrier paid off.

THE 'SKI' RAMP

The RN and its ship designers had, since the first aircraft carriers, led the way in developing equipment required for the safe operating of aircraft. This was to continue with the design by Lt. Cdr. D Taylor of the 'Ski' Ramp, a method of increasing the lifting capacity of Harriers when taking off from the deck of a carrier.

It was similar to the idea used on HMS *Furious* during 1944, when she had a small ramp built onto the deck to give fully loaded Fairey Barracudas added lift during attacks on the Tirpitz in Norway. The idea was first computer demonstrated during 1972 by BAe, and was continued by the RAE at Bedford and BAe at Kingston. After further computer studies and a thesis by Taylor, funding was provided to design and construct a ramp at RAE Bedford for trials.

This test ramp was designed to operate with ramp angles from 6 to 20 degrees, with the first trials conducted at the lower angle. A total of 116 launches were made with GR1 and T2 Harriers from this angle without incident and these trials continued over the next two years reaching 20 degrees in April 1979. It was found that the optimum angle was 12.5 degrees and this would be the angle for the ships of the RN. HMS *Hermes* was the first to be so fitted, followed by HMS *Ark Royal (V)*.

IMPROVED SEA KING ORDERED

The Mk50 Sea King helicopter for the RAN was an improved version for operating in the hotter climate of the Southern Hemisphere. The modifications included improved avionics equipment, installing more powerful Gnome engines, an improved gearbox and a six bladed tail rotor for improved stability. The aircraft was also fitted with an in-flight refuelling system which allowed the crew to refuel without actually landing aboard the ship supplying the fuel. It incorporated the refuel point to be fitted at the rear of the cabin door, where the nozzle would be winched from the deck and attached to the point.

The RN ordered the first of twenty-one Sea Kings built to this standard in November 1974, designated the Mk2, and put together a modification programme to upgrade the 48 Mk1s to the same standard as Mk2A helicopters. The upgrading work would be carried out at Fleetlands and the NASU (Naval Aircraft Support Unit) at Culdrose from the end of 1977 once the new build aircraft had been received.

The first flight of the Mk2 was on 18th June 1976, with the first deliveries to FLSs later in the year. No. 814 Sqdn. was to have an American passive sonar fit, Jezebel, to four of their aircraft to use for trials aboard HMS *Bulwark* during 1980. The Mk2/2As were also to be the first to appear with a modification for protection against FOD (foreign object damage) to the engines from ice particles when flying in cold operating areas. Known as the 'barn door', this panel was fitted above the cabin in front of the engines, now fitted to all ASW Sea Kings.

AIRCREW BRANCH ESTABLISHED

After a break of nearly 30 years, the Aircrew Branch of the FAA was established on 1st April 1974 formed with the nucleus of ratings used as 'temporary' aircrew with flights and squadrons. With the introduction of helicopters into the service, non-pilot crews were drawn from volunteers from the ranks of all branches of the RN. The observers in ASW helicopters

HMS Invincible fitting out in Barrow in Furness

BAe Sea Harrier FRS Mk1

were RN Observer Officers as with the fixed-wing aircraft although the helicopters still carried a volunteer crewman. The last TAG in service, Angus Donaldson, was serving with the aircrew school at Portland and became the first rating in the aircrew branch.

The Wasp helicopter introduced the missile aimer into the FAA, with volunteer junior rates again drawn from all branches of the service. The service was increasing its use of helicopters, thus there was an increase in ratings loaned from their respective branches for flying tasks. This brought about the reintroduction of the aircrew branch.

RED DRAGON FLIGHT

Already an accomplished pilot, HRH Prince Charles the Prince of Wales, was to receive 'junglie' training on the Wessex Mk5 before joining No. 845 Sqdn. The Wessex Mk5 training squadron, No. 707 Sqdn., formed a special flight of three helicopters for the task on 29th July 1974. These new helicopters were maintained and serviced in accordance with the rules for all royal aircraft, and wore distinctive colour schemes, with parts of the fuselage painted Day-Glo red for ease of identification. The conversion course included detaching to Lee-on-Solent for the Prince's wet dingy drills and to HMS *Hermes* during November for deck landing practice. The flight was disbanded as part of No. 707 Sqdn. on 12th December and moved to No. 845 Sqdn. with the Prince.

The Prince returned to the ship on 25th February along with the squadron for a four month deployment during which he completed 500 hours of Wessex Mk5 flying. Leaving the squadron upon disembarking on 26th June, the helicopters were returned to the standard green colour scheme for use with the junglie units.

SEA HARRIERS ORDERED

As early as 1971, the Navy asked for a study into the modifications required to produce a navalised multi-role Harrier for the designated roles of fighter, strike and reconnaissance. The designers eventually produced an aircraft based on the GR3, the major change being the front fuselage which had a raised cockpit and hinged nose accommodating the aircraft's Blue Fox radar. Other changes affected the liquid oxygen system, the stores pylons, redesigned hydraulic and electrical system, a modified air brake and a new ejector seat.

The Government announced the order for 24 Sea Harrier FRS.1s (Fighter Reconnaissance Strike) in May 1975, which later increased to 31 aircraft, to operate from the Invincible class cruisers and HMS *Hermes*. Squadrons of five aircraft would operate from each ship, alongside the ships' ASW Sea King squadron. Three development aircraft were also ordered to be used to complete the testing and clearance to operate flying by the A & AEE.

As an aid to introducing the radar fit to these single-seat pilots, three Hunter TMk8s were modified with the Sea

Hawker Hunter T8M

Harrier's nose and avionics fit. Two were initially operated by BAe at Dunsfold and the Royal Signal and Radar Establishment at Bedford for development and proving trials of the systems. These Hunters were the last development of the Hunter aircraft which had first flown in 1951 and had entered service with the FAA in 1958.

THE SECOND COD WAR

The agreement with Iceland secured after the first 'Cod War' of 1973 was coming to an end in November 1975. In July the Icelandic Government increased the fishing limit to 200 miles from the 50 mile limit agreed, and began arresting British fishing boats operating in the area. Four Wasp equipped frigates (later increased to six) accompanied by an RFA supply ship, a support ship and ocean-going tugs were despatched to protect the British fishing fleet and their rights once outside the twelve mile limit.

The Wasps operated with RAF Nimrods to locate the position of the Icelandic Coast Guard boats, and they would then alert the fleet so they could bring in their nets before they could be cut by the Icelandic boats. The tug boats, which were capable of inflicting much damage to the gun boats, would position themselves between them and the trawlers to stop them getting to the nets, whilst the Wasps would also hover over the nets so they could be pulled in, as the Icelandic boats would not be able to pass over the ropes.

Initially formed too late to be of effect during the first war, another specialised Wessex III flight was formed to operate in the disputed area. Oscar Flight of No. 737 Sqdn. formed on 19th February for operations aboard RFA *Tidepool* and RFA *Olwen*. The aircraft had its sonar equipment removed and was modified for operations in the Arctic.

Initially operating from Olwen, the helicopter embarked in Tidepool on 22nd April and carried out search patrols, SAR missions and Vertrep flights in support of the operations, before withdrawing on 25th May. By this time, talks were again productive with a renewed agreement being reached on 11th June. However the Flight remained at Portland, available for rapid deployment if required, until it was disbanded on 11th September 1975.

THE HOVERCRAFT CONTINUES TO SHOW ITS VALUE

Continuing to show its capabilities, the NHU was tasked to perform bomb disposal operations during October and an SRN6 was to deploy to Dengie Flats in Essex, the site of a bombing range, to clear the area.

Westland Wessex HAS Mk3

Vosper Thorneycroft VT2

Westland Aerospatiale Gazelle HT2 used as the 'Admiral's Barge'

Westland Aerospatiale Gazelle AH1 used by the Royal Marines

Lynx HAS Mk2 load lifting trials onboard HMS Birmingham

It was successful in clearing an area which would normally have taken four months in just four days and further operations were completed in January 1978 and March 1979.

Two hovercraft were hired for evaluation, an SRN4 from Hoverlloyd and the large VT2 for towing and noise trials. The BH7 was modified yet again for another series of MCM trials during 1976, taking part in exercise 'Roast Beef' in October 1977 when it completed 190 hours of operations.

THE NEW TRAINING HELICOPTER ARRIVES

Delivery of the first Westland Aerospatiale Gazelle HT2 to the rotary wing basic training squadron, No. 705 Sqdn. took place on 10th December 1975. They were to replace the Hiller HT2s and Whirlwind HAS7s which had been the primary training helicopters for thirteen and fifteen years respectively.

The type was to remain as the FAA's primary training helicopter until withdrawn from service in October 1997 after nearly twenty years service. Future helicopter training would be carried out using civilian Squirrel helicopters operated by a civilian organisation, as was the helicopter pilot training for the other services.

The last FAA training Gazelles were with Fleetlands as the station hack, and with Flag Officer Naval Aviation as his VIP helicopter. During service with No. 705 Sqdn., a display team (the Sharks) was formed, originally with six aircraft but later reduced to four and then the final team consisting of a Gazelle pair.

Originally a detachment of the Army Air Corps (AAC), the RM 3CBAS operate the type in the observation role. These are the Gazelle AH Mk1 helicopters similar to those used by the AAC which are operated with RMC companies. The brigade detached from the AAC and moved to Yeovilton initially remaining as its own unit, but it became No. 847 Sqdn. in 1997.

Westland Wessex HU Mk5

THE LYNX ENTERS SERVICE

After four years of development flying, the Lynx joined the FAA with the commissioning of the IFTU No. 700L Sqdn., a unique squadron as it was to be a joint Royal Navy/Royal Netherlands Navy unit. The FAA's first production aircraft had flown on 10th February 1976, and deliveries commenced just prior to the IFTU commissioning on 1st September at Yeovilton. The squadron's first deck landings were completed by the Squadron CO when he put down aboard HMS *Birmingham* the following February.

The squadron was to partake in the mass flypast over the Fleet for the Silver Jubilee Review at Spithead during June 1977 and, upon completion of its task, the squadron recommissioned as the Lynx HQ Squadron, No. 702 Sqdn., on 3rd January 1978. This new squadron was responsible for the training of pilots and observers for the type, which differed from its predecessor by having two officers as its crew. There was no missile aimer crewman, due mainly to the technical improvements and the mission weapons that were to be carried by the helicopter.

The squadron was also responsible for the training of the maintenance personnel for the flights. Like No. 829 Sqdn., it had responsibility for the parenting of the Lynx ships' flights until the FLS No. 815 Sqdn. commissioned in 1981.

HMS BULWARK TO RESERVE

After twenty-one years of service, HMS *Bulwark* was to be put on the reserve list and kept in a P by O state at Portsmouth, a reprieve from the original intention to dispose of the ship. Sailing into Portsmouth on 26th March 1976, she was prepared for long term reserve duties with a reduced crew of 200 men.

Interest was shown by Peru in acquiring the ship for a Harrier carrier, but it was announced in January 1978 that the ship would be refitted to operate as an ASW carrier for a five year period, to fill the gap between the retirement of HMS *Ark Royal* and the arrival of HMS *Invincible*. The refit began on 20th March and was completed with the commissioning of the ship on 23rd February 1979. She was now in her third role since first commissioning and, like HMS *Hermes*, she retained the secondary commando role.

HMS ARK ROYAL's LAST REFIT

Entering refit on 22nd November 1976 for the last time, HMS *Ark Royal* had to be

BAe Sea Harrier FRS Mk1 on board HMS Hermes

completed in time for the Fleet Review during June 1977. So tight was the programme that the refit had actually started whilst the ship was returning home from the Mediterranean in October, with dockyard workers joining the ship in Toulon. The refit was completed in time and the ship sailed for post refit trials on 9th June, followed by flying trials on 13th-17th June, completing all trials on the 19th June.

HMS HERMES' ROLE CHANGES

Having entered refit in May 1976, HMS *Hermes* was to re-emerge with the primary role of ASW aircraft carrier, and with commando support as a secondary role which was a complete reversal of its previous roles. The ship was to complete the refit on 10th December 1976 and complete initial sea trials before Christmas.

The new year was to see the aviation trials take place which included a comprehensive series of Harrier trials with the RAF squadrons and with BAe aircraft. These were successfully completed and the ship was cleared to operate the aircraft from her deck. This was also in preparation for the Sea Harrier (SHAR), the prototype aircraft operating from her deck during November the following year, with the first SHAR landing accomplished on 13th November 1977.

This was not to be the ship's last role change. Operating as the RN's ASW carrier for 40 months, the ship would enter a final refit for the RN from 24th March 1980 to 5th June 1981 when she would be returned to fixed-wing carrier operations.

SILVER JUBILEE FLEET REVIEW

The Fleet Review in honour of HM Queen Elizabeth II's Silver Jubilee was held between 24th and 29th June 1977 in the Solent off Spithead, the venue for assembled fleets and reviews for over 200 years. The FAA was present in numbers with a flypast of 150 aircraft led by a single Wessex flown by Radm. J Roberts, Flag Officer Naval Air Command.

The flypast was formed into three waves, the first wave from some of the helicopter training squadrons; No. 700L Sqdn. Lynx, No. 703 Sqdn. Wasp, No. 705 Sqdn. Gazelle and Hiller HT2, No. 737 Sqdn. Wessex HAS3 and No. 771 Sqdn. Wessex HAS1, and the small ships' flight from Nos. 737 and 829 Sqdn. Wasps plus the Gazelles of the RM 3CBAS.

In the second wave was the Wessex Mk5s of Nos. 707, 845 and 846 Sqdns. and the Sea Kings of Nos. 706, 814, 819, 820, 824 and 826 Sqdns. as well as the Sea Kings from No. 817 Sqdn. RAN. This was followed by the heavy brigade of fixed-wing aircraft; No. 809 Sqdn. Buccaneers, No. 849 Sqdn. Gannets, No. 809 Sqdn. Phantoms and the Canberras and Hunters from the FRADU.

The assembled ships were led by HMS *Ark Royal* with HMS *Hermes* and HMAS *Melbourne* in attendance. The hovercraft from the Naval Hovercraft Trials Unit, the assault ship HMS *Intrepid* and both helicopter cruisers, HMSs *Blake* and *Tiger*, were also present amongst the 100 RN ships. There were twenty ships from sixteen NATO, Commonwealth and Foreign

Ex-RAF Scottish Aviation Jetstream TMk2

New BAe Jetstream T Mk3

HMS Ark Royal flying her last paying off penant

navies including two from Iran and one from Brunei, as well as 27 ships from other organisations (RFA, RMAS, RNAuxS, Trinity House and others). The RFA *Engadine* was used during the rehearsal as the replacement for the Royal Yacht HMY *Britannia*, whilst the NHTU used their hovercraft as mail and personnel delivery vessels operating alongside the supporting RMAS ships during the period the Fleet was assembled.

The RN ships were assembled first on Friday 24th June, followed by the visiting ships the following day and, at 11.00am on the 25th, there was a full flypast rehearsal in beautiful clear skies. The helicopters were operating from HMS Daedalus at Lee-on-Solent (over 100 helicopters) whilst the fixed-wing were at HMS Heron at Yeovilton. The Queen embarked aboard the Royal Yacht on the Monday evening but unfortunately the weather was overcast when the review took place the following day. During the flypast late afternoon it had not lifted and some of the helicopter formations disappeared into the low flying cloud, but even so it was a magnificent sight for those who witnessed the event.

A ROYAL FIRST

The first (and only) time any member of a royal family was to have an arrested carrier landing and catapult take-off in a jet aircraft was completed by HRH Prince Charles flying in the rear seat of a Buccaneer Mk2 of No. 809 Sqdn. on 21st September 1977.

The Prince took off from Yeovilton in the back seat of the aircraft heading for HMS *Ark Royal* in the Moray Firth. After completing two roller landings, the aircraft took the wire at 11.45 hours then, after a four hour visit to the ship, he was catapulted off at 15.45 hours for the short flight to RNAS Lossiemouth.

FAA IN NORTHERN IRELAND

The problems in Northern Ireland can be traced back to the eve of W.W.I, when members of the Curragh military barracks refused to accept 'Home Rule' (under the control of Southern Ireland) in Ulster, resigning on 20th March 1914. The result

Fairey Gannet AEW3 landing onboard HMS Ark Royal

was that Ulster remained part of the UK and was not governed by the South. After this, much unrest spread in the country with a rebellion in 1916 which was quickly crushed and the perpetrators tried and executed.

The Irish patriotic society (Sinn Fein) declared Irish Independence on 21st January 1919 and further disturbances occurred until peace was established in December, with the south of the island becoming the Irish Free State during 1922, eventually to become Eire. During the next 40 years an illegal army, the Irish Republican Army, carried out a campaign of disturbances against Protestant dominated Ulster in an attempt to reunite the island.

British troops were deployed to Northern Ireland in April 1969 to assist the security forces against the actions of the terrorists. Since then, troops have been in the province, including RMC's, and helicopters have been deployed to assist them in their security tasks.

The first deployment of FAA helicopters was the Wessex Vs of No. 845 Sqdn. which arrived at RAF Aldergrove on 10th October 1977 and were to remain in support of the security forces until needed for the Falklands war in 1982, leaving on 10th May.

THE SHAR FLIES

The first SHAR took to the air on 20th August 1978 when Mr. John Farley carried out a 35 minute handling flight. The following month it appeared at the Farnborough airshow and had its first deck operating trials aboard HMS *Hermes*, landing for the first time on 13th December. No prototype aircraft were to be built, as the three development aircraft would act as the prototypes although they were all completed as full production examples. The first SHAR to be delivered to the FAA was accepted by Admiral Sir Terence Lewin, the 1st Sea Lord on 18th June 1979.

Westland Wessex HAS Mk1 SAR Flt. The last operators of the venerable Mk1

NEW FIXED-WING AIRCRAFT

The Jetstream had entered service with the RAF in 1974 for multi-engine training but this was to be short lived as they were put into store the following year. One of these aircraft, known as the Jetstream T Mk1, was loaned to No. 750 Sqdn., the FAA observer's training squadron, for evaluation and trials as a replacement for the ageing Sea Prince. The trials proved successful so it was decided the FAA would replace the Sea Prince with these 'off the shelf' aircraft.

Fourteen of the stored RAF aircraft were acquired as were two ex-civil aircraft and these were converted into 'classrooms' with consoles for two students in the rear. They entered service on 26th October 1978 as Jetstream T Mk2s equipped with weather and ground mapping radar, with its radar scanner protruding from the nose. Four Jetstream T Mk3s supplemented the Mk2, entering service in 1986, and these differed by having a ventral ASR360 multi mode search radar beneath the fuselage. Some of the aircraft are based at Yeovilton for use as VIP and communications aircraft, replacing the Devons and Herons.

THE RFA's FIRST 'ASW' SUPPLY SHIPS

The Royal Fleet Auxiliary supply ships had been carrying helicopters for many years for use as an aid to replenishment vertreps and for helicopter delivery flights (HDS). They had also been home to detachments of ASW helicopters but were not equipped with support facilities for these roles, the

McDonnell Douglas F4K Phantom II about to launch from HMS Ark Royal

HMS *Bulwark*

helicopters having to rely on 'Mother' carriers.

Two ships were to join the Fleet, the 'Forts'- RFA *Fort Austin* and *Fort Grange*, later to become *Fort Rosalie*. These ships had two flight decks, a hangar and workshops to enable a flight of Sea Kings to operate independently from them. Fort Grange commissioned on 6th April 1978 followed by her sister on 11th May 1979, with the former conducting first of type operating trials using a detachment of Sea Kings from No. 824 Sqdn. off HMS *Ark Royal*, embarking four aircraft on 17th June 1978.

This squadron was redesignated the RFA Sea King Unit after leaving the carrier when it decommissioned. Its first operational embarkation in Fort Grange was in January 1979 for a tour of the Far East, the helicopters supplying the task force with its main ASW contingent. Its sister ship was to begin operating Sea Kings upon commissioning in February 1980. The RN now had two large deep water RFAs capable of immediate supply ASW patrols to ships devoid of larger aircraft carriers.

FAREWELL ARK ROYAL

After completing its final deployment (a Mediterranean cruise with its last port of call being Palma Majorca), HMS *Ark Royal* launched her air group for the last time on 27th November 1978. The last aircraft, Phantom '012', flown by Flt. Lt. Murdo Macleod RAF and Lt. Denis McCullam was launched at 15.11 hours. All the Buccaneers and Phantoms flew directly to the RAF base at St. Athan near Barry in South Wales for de-navalising and storage for later use by the RAF. The squadrons disbanded on 15th December 1978, ending the FAA's conventional carrier aircraft operations.

The ship sailed through the mist into Devonport in the early morning of 4th December amid much publicity. Having disembarked all but one of her Sea Kings to Culdrose the day before, the ship still had the last elements of her air group on board, the Wessex HAS1s of the SAR Flight, the last operators of the type in service. The ship's engines were rung off at 08.50 hours and the Royal Navy strike carrier force was no more. Since first commissioning 23 years earlier, Ark Royal had sailed 900,000 miles.

The ship was de-stored and finally paid off on 13th February 1979, thus ending the era of fixed-wing carrier aviation with catapults and arrestor wires. The horizon was not as bleak as it had appeared when the end of this era had been announced twelve years earlier, with Sea Harriers and new carriers to operate from them soon entering service, bringing a new era to the FAA.

CARRIER BORNE GROUND LIAISON GROUP

With her demise a special army unit also passed into history, the Carrier Borne Ground Liaison Group (CBGLO), a small unit of Army personnel carried aboard the strike carrier since W.W.II. This was a team of four Army and one Royal Marine personnel who liaised with the air group in supporting Army units on the ground. These units remained after the war, nominally consisting of a Major, Captain, Sergeant, Clerk and Driver.

The CBGLOs were detached from the HQ located at Lee-on-Solent, tasked with briefing aircrews in close air support of army units ashore, photographic interpretation, intelligence matters and the tasking of strike missions. All the members of the unit were experienced forward air controllers, and operated a specially equipped land rover and trailer equipped with communications equipment.

There were five elements of the group; HQ and training units at Lee-on-Solent and three teams for carrier detachment. Training was given by the Army at Old Sarum prior to the men joining the training unit and eventually an operational team. The operational unit attached to the ship was No. 55 CBGLO, the last of the little known department important to the operations of a British Carrier strike force.

CARRIERS OLD AND NEW

After being laid up in a state of P by O in Portsmouth and a possible sale to Peru, the venerable carrier HMS *Bulwark* rejoined the Fleet, re-commissioning on 23rd February 1979 as an ASW Commando carrier to bridge the gap until the arrival of the new Invincible class. It embarked its air group, Nos. 826 and 846 Sqdns. four days later for operational trials. After many role changes and periods of uncertainty, HMS *Bulwark* was to fly the flag as the FAA's major asset.

Her Majesty Queen Elizabeth launched HMS *Invincible* on 3rd May 1977, the first of three ships which would eventually be identified as aircraft carriers. The ship was required to be fitted with a 7 degree ski ramp for the operation of her small group of Sea Harriers, and this was built onto the front end of the flight deck by the builders after initially building the deck as a flush deck.

She conducted her contractor's sea trials during March and April, sailing from Barrow on 26th March 1979, the first British carrier to be designed since W.W.II. During the trials, the First Sea Lord and the USN Chief of Staff flew on board (24th April) to view the ship then, after the trials, the ship returned to Barrow for final preparations for sailing to Portsmouth and the handing over to the RN on 19th March 1980.

The second of these ships, HMS *Illustrious*, was launched by HRH Princess Margaret on Tyneside on 1st December 1978, and entered service during the Falklands War of 1982 after being completed early. HMS *Indomitable*, now renamed HMS *Ark Royal*, was launched by HRH the Queen Mother on 2nd June 1981, commissioning on 1st November 1985. The latter was fitted with a 12.5 degree ski ramp which would be fitted to its two sister ships during their major refits.

HMS *Invincible*

LAST HOVERCRAFT JOINS THE NHU

On 3rd April 1979, after over 40 months on hire from the manufacturer, the NHU purchased the VT2 which was to complete the first circumnavigation of the British Isles by a hovercraft. Primarily purchased for logistic support operations and the movement of troops, she was the largest and last hovercraft to join the NHU before it disbanded in 1982.

The illegal entry of mainly Vietnamese refugees into the colony of Hong Kong resulted in an SRN6 operating in the shark infested waters around the colony. Naval party 1009 was sent out in 1979 to assist the authorities in stemming the flood of these illegal immigrants, and SAR operations for those unfortunate to be swept overboard from their vessels. The hovercraft also assisted in anti-drug enforcement operations mostly in the darkness, as the speed of the craft could outrun the motorised junks and speed boats, holding up the drugs runner until customs and police launches arrived to take the boat and its crew into custody. The flight was disbanded during 1982 after the hovercraft was damaged during a patrol.

THE SHAR ENTERS SERVICE

The SHAR IFTU, No. 700A Sqdn., formed at Yeovilton on 26th June 1979, commissioning on 19th September. The following day, the SHAR was introduced to

BAe Sea Harrier FRS1 (BAe Systems)

Westland Agusta EH101 Merlin

the British public when one of its aircraft was flown to the BBC studios of Pebble Mill to take part in the lunchtime programme.

The type's operational sea trials were held aboard HMS *Hermes* during the period 24th October to 8th November whilst the ship was operating in Carmarthen Bay in the Irish Sea. Five aircraft were embarked; two from the squadron, two from 'A' Flt. A&AEE and one from BAe.

The aircraft was the first multi-role aircraft to enter service designed for fighter and strike roles with an auxiliary role of reconnaissance. Its primary role was in defence of the task force, providing 'local' fighting capability, armed with Aden cannons and anti-aircraft missiles - the carrier was equipped with Sea Dart anti-aircraft missiles as were the defensive destroyers. In the strike mode it could be fitted with bombs and Sea Eagle anti-ship missiles.

The first FLS to commission was No. 800 Sqdn. on 23rd April 1980 for service aboard HMS *Hermes*. It was intended to have three FLS operating the type; Nos. 800, 801 and 809 Sqdns. with No. 899 Sqdn. as the training squadron equipped with Sea Harriers, T-4 training aircraft and the specially modified Hunter T Mk8M. The RN ordered three T Mk4N trainers which were similar to the RAF's T-4s but without the laser nose, instead a Sea Harrier type nose would be fitted. It seemed strange that the three FLSs would wear the numbers previously held by bomber units and not those of fighter units in the 89* series, when the aircraft was primarily a fleet fighter aircraft.

SEA KING REPLACEMENT

The Sea King ASW helicopter had been the backbone of ASW operations in the FAA for nearly a decade when Westlands began designing a replacement for both the ASW and troop carrying roles. The first studies, the WG34, were conducted in 1978 but were cancelled before any full designs were completed.

During 1979, both the British and Italian navies were looking for a replacement and the two major helicopter companies for the respective countries began joint studies. The results were a large three-engined, fully autonomous, all-weather helicopter which would satisfy the requirements for the RN, RAF and Italian Forces jointly by Westlands and Agusta. The two companies formed the European Helicopter Industries Ltd. to build and market this new helicopter which was designated the EH101 (it is reported that it should have been the EHI-01 but a typing error resulted in the EHI becoming EH1). It was available in ASW and troop carrying versions for the military and as a fully certificated civil heli-liner.

Meanwhile the Sea King would continue to be upgraded until this new helicopter became available. Since initial introduction to the service in 1969, the Sea King had been modified to the HAS2/2A standard, entering service during 1976. All of the FAA's Sea Kings were to this standard, and these were now to be upgraded once again, this time to the Mk5 ASW model.

This mark was to look different having a larger radome above the cabin to house the Sea Searcher radar and the starboard undercarriage sponson was to be modified to carry a magnetic anamoly detector (MAD). This equipment measures the earth's magnetic field to detect its deviations which would be caused by submarines. Internally it was to receive the Jezebel system proved by No. 814 Sqdn., a new information processing and display system, and a tactical navigation system, making it the most up-to-date ASW helicopter in the world.

The first flight of a Mk5, a converted Mk2, was on 14th August 1980 with the first deliveries to No. 820 Sqdn. in November. The FAA ordered 30 new build machines and was to modify the majority of the current Mk2 helicopters to serve until the EH101 became available, estimated to be in 1993.

Westland Sea King HASMk5

Westland Sea King HASMk5

SEA KING HC4 COMMANDO

The first Sea King HC Mk4 utility/troop helicopters were received by No. 846 Sqdn. during November 1979 to operate alongside the Wessex MkV which it would eventually replace. Its first flight had been only two months earlier on 26th September 1979 but, as the systems were proven, it only needed a short flight test programme to establish the type's operating parameters.

The Mk4 began as a Commando Mk1, a stripped out model of the ASW Mk1 without sponsons and was a non-amphibious version designed to carry 28 fully equipped troops and under-slung loads including heavy guns and vehicles. First built for the Egyptian Air Force in 1974, it was later improved by being fitted with the standard ASW Mk2 equipment. They were offered to the FAA as a replacement for the ageing Wessex Vs and fifteen were ordered in 1978, enough to equip one commando squadron - No. 846 Sqdn.

The Mk4 was soon to operate with the Royal Marines, operating from HMS *Bulwark* in Norway, supporting 45 RMC during the 1980 exercise 'Clockwork', the annual amphibious winter exercises. This was the first time the type was to operate from the deck of a ship, embarking on the ship on 24th February for the deployment.

RNR AIR RESERVE

The RNR is the reserve division of the navy, used to augment the Force in times of conflict. On 9th November 1979, the Air Reserve was introduced for ex-FAA personnel under 38 who had left the service for less than five years, with the first fifteen aircrew forming up in 1980. Its role was to augment training units and FLSs with a limited pool of professional engineers and aircrew for both fixed and rotary wing aircraft.

It was conceived that 40 officers would be members within twelve months with a maximum of 60 by 1983, and it was planned to eventually reform two RNR squadrons, Nos. 1831 and 1832, but this was later shelved. All members of the reserve air branch are committed to completing at least two weeks continuous training with the FAA per year. The branch size had reached 400 members by 1999, consisting of officers and ratings covering all departments of the FAA, joining ships and squadrons for their annual training.

THE THROUGH DECK CRUISER ARRIVES

HMS *Invincible* was commissioned on 11th July 1980 by HRH the Queen, and was the first British aircraft carrier designed and built since W.W.II to enter service. It was the first purpose built ship capable of operating V/STOL Harrier type aircraft fitted with the ski ramp and was also the "West's" largest gas turbine powered ship, capable of operating at speeds in excess of 30 knots.

Westland Lynx HASMk3 embarked aboard HMS Boxer

Two days before the commissioning ceremony, a SHAR from No. 800 Sqdn. was to make history when it landed onboard the ship whilst she was alongside the wall in Portsmouth. She became the first fixed-wing aircraft to land aboard a British ship at berth and was to be the centrepiece for the ceremony.

The next eighteen months were spent proving the ship's design, not only as an ASW/strike carrier but also in its role as a command and communications ship. This proved the ship to be capable of her primary roles, as well as being capable of supporting amphibious operations. There was however a niggling problem that would be present with the ship for its lifetime, that of propellor shaft vibration troubles. This problem had been in evidence since its very first sea trials and after many attempts to cure it, it still remains.

The RAN were showing an interest in the Sea Harrier and the Invincible class carrier, as their last operational carrier, HMAS *Melbourne,* needed a replacement after nearly 30 years service. The British Government announced in February 1982 that Invincible was to become a RAN ship the following year, sold to the Australians for £175 million. She was to be taken out of service and prepared for transfer, leaving the RN with her two sister ships as the RN carrier assets once HMS *Hermes* was retired.

LYNX FLS COMMISSIONS

The front line squadron for the Lynx helicopter, No. 815 Sqdn., commissioned on the first day of 1981 (the ceremony took place on the 27th), taking over the role of parenting the ship's flights from the training squadron. It was to operate the Lynx HAS Mk2 but would eventually have the more powerful Mk3 which was undergoing trials since its first flight on 26th August 1980.

Westland HAS3ICE from HMS Endurance

Westland Wessex VIP Mk5 'Green Parrot'

Due to additional equipment fits to this later mark of helicopter, it was delayed service entry, not arriving until March 1982.

It had a more powerful Gem engine which necessitated a modified transmission system which was strengthened to cope with the forces imparted to it. The helicopter was also to be equipped for the surface search and strike role having the Orange Crop electronic surveillance system fitted. Once the Mk3 had been developed, all the new build helicopters would be to this standard and the Mk2s would be upgraded when next due for major survey and repair and rectification period.

Further versions of the basic HAS Mk3 have been produced, three especially for operations aboard HMS *Endurance*, the HAS Mk3ICE, as the ship operates two at any one time whilst the other is under deep maintenance. This version has special camera fit modifications and downgraded systems as its major function is that of utility helicopter supporting the scientists in the Antarctic. Some seven helicopters were initially modified with secure speech

HMS Hermes embarks No. 800 Sqdn. BAe Sea Harriers

DH Sea Heron C20

systems for operations with the special forces, and these are designated HAS Mk3S.

HMS BULWARK REALLY PAYS OFF

After recommissioning as an ASW/commando carrier in February 1979, HMS *Bulwark* had been operating in Norway as the RN's only operational aircraft carrier for the 1981 Clockwork exercises, when the defence secretary Mr. John Nott announced in February that the ship would pay off immediately upon return to Portsmouth the following month.

This announcement came as a shock to the crew and the RN in general. The ship had been repaired after a hangar fire only three months before and was expected to pay off at the end of the year once HMS *Hermes* was recommissioned. She returned to Portsmouth on 27th March for the final procedure alpha entering the harbour whilst aircraft and helicopters flew over in salute.

Her 'final final' commission (as it was known by those who were to be part of it), was a memorable one. The ship had had a major fire whilst in Philadelphia when a hydrogen fire in 'A' boiler room broke out. The ship's crew and the local fire brigade eventually put the fire out, somehow without sinking the ship (15th March 1980), and she continued operations on three boilers for the remainder of her life.

The ship was affectionately known as 'the Rusty B' and had remained a happy ship. She had successfully bridged the gap when, without her, the RN would have had no operational aircraft carriers - the first time since 1913. She remained alongside the wall at Portsmouth for de-storing after which she was laid up in Fareham Creek before going to the breakers yard at Cairnryan, the graveyard of many fine ships.

There was a glimmer of hope during 1982 when she was considered for a return to service for action in the South Atlantic but this was not to be. She left Portsmouth on her final voyage on 10th April 1984, rendezvousing with HMS *Hermes* on her passage to the breakers yard.

HMS DAEDALUS's SQUADRON RETIRES

The FAA's longest serving squadron (at that time), No. 781 Sqdn., retired after nearly 42 years operating as the FAA's communication squadron. With the exception of an eleven month spell when it was designated No. 799 Sqdn., the squadron had been providing the Fleet with communications aircraft based at Lee-on-Solent.

During its span it had been a training unit for bad weather flying training, a conversion unit, an instrument flying examining squadron, a Junior Officers' Air Course unit, a SAR flight and a VIP transport flight. By the time she decommissioned on 31st March 1981, she had operated over 80 different aircraft types both fixed-wing, rotary wing, piston and jet powered aircraft.

HMS HERMES - STRIKE CARRIER ONCE AGAIN

Now wearing a 12.5 degree ski ramp welded to the forward end of the flight deck on the port side, HMS *Hermes* recommissioned on 5th June 1981. The ship was now the Fleet's largest carrier capable of SHAR operations, and was also a multi-role ship with ASW as her primary role, strike as her secondary and still retaining some commando carrier facilities.

The refit was completed in early May and the first sea trials began on the 12th May. After the ship recommissioned, she began work up trials in June followed by the embarkation of five SHAR aircraft of No. 800 Sqdn. for the fixed-wing trials on 13th July. This was the first time a 12.5 degree ramp had been used operationally, as the ramps at Yeovilton and Bedford were for training. Whilst alongside the wall in Mayport Naval Yard on 26th September, she launched her Harriers for the first ever launching of aircraft by a ship alongside.

HMS ILLUSTRIOUS' SEA TRIALS

The second of the Invincible class carriers, HMS *Illustrious,* sailed from its berth at the Swan Hunters fitting out yard on the Tyne for sea trials in the North Sea on 4th November 1981. The trials were cut short due to a few minor problems which it was thought would be better sorted out before the trials were to continue.

Recommencing the trials on the 11th January 1982, it was envisaged the ship would be handed over to the RN in the Autumn but because of developments in the South Atlantic, the ship was needed sooner than expected. The first helicopter landed onboard on 12th January, a Sea King Mk4 of No. 845 Sqdn. used as an HDS aircraft during the trials.

***Left:* HMS Endurance 'down the ice' when operating Westland Whirlwind HAR Mk9s**

***Below:* HMS Invincible leaves Portsmouth Harbour**

***Bottom:* HMS Hermes leaves Portsmouth Harbour**

The Falklands War

TROUBLE BREWING

The Islands of the Falklands and South Georgia in the South Atlantic Ocean have been administered by Britain since 1833. The Argentineans first arrived on the island four years before but it was already occupied by British settlers. During those four years, the two groups of settlers often opposed each other and thus the Administration was established. The Administration expelled the Argentineans, who have claimed these 'Malvina' islands as part of their territory since then.

Argentina and Chile reached agreement over their rights in the Antarctic and Malvinas against British occupation on 4th March 1948, but this was to be a constant area of debate and argument at political level. Britain attempted negotiations with Argentina in 1971 but refused to relinquish sovereignty. For five years, talks continued to result in stalemate and eventually the Argentinean Ambassador in London was placed on indefinite leave (14th January 1976). Five days later the British Ambassador in Buenos Aires was also placed 'on leave'.

The following month, an Argentinean destroyer fired on the British Royal Research Ship *Shackleton* as she was making for Port Stanley. The Ambassadors were reinstated during November 1979 after three years of protracted talks, but the position of sovereignty remained unchanged.

THE FALKLAND MILITARY UNITS

During the 1970s, the Argentinean Navy established an 'illegal' research station on South Thule in the South Sandwich Islands, arriving aboard their icebreaker, the ARA *General San Martin*. The station, known as Corbeta Uruguay, was a series of huts, a hangar and landing strip and was discussed during the sovereignty negotiations but remained manned by the Argentinean Navy.

The Falkland Islands had a garrison of 84 Royal Marines and were infrequently visited by RN ships as they passed the islands. The ice patrol ship, HMS *Endurance*, carried out annual tours to the South Atlantic area during the summer periods (September-March) in support of British Antarctic research teams. The ship carried a flight of two helicopters, originally unarmed Whirlwind HAR9s, but hurriedly replaced these with missile capable Wasp HAS1s for the 1976 deployment.

ARGENTINIANS INVADE SOUTH GEORGIA

Lt. Gen. Leopoldo Galtieri took over as the leader of the Argentine military Junta, thus becoming President on 21st December 1981. Within a month he promised the people that the Malvinas would return to Argentinean control by 1st January 1983, a statement that was to be the start of another period of unease within the islands. This was further increased with the knowledge that the annual tour by the ice patrol ship Endurance was to finish after her 1982 tour, to be sold to Brazil as part of Mr. John Nott's defence cuts.

On 19th March, a group of Argentine scrap merchants arrived at Leith in South Georgia uninvited, raising protests from Britain. The Argentinean Navy sent five ships to the area in support of these workers and meanwhile, at Port Stanley, an Argentine Learjet was circuiting the airfield reportedly on a spying mission. The political situation deteriorated resulting in the British Parliament being informed on 30th March that there was the potential for a 'situation' in the Falklands. Three days later, Galtieri sent an invasion force to oppose the Royal Marines and take the islands for Argentina.

Intelligence reports showed the Argentinean Navy was at sea supposedly heading for the islands and it was decided, on 31st March, that a Task Force should be despatched to the area. There were seven ships in Gibraltar which had been involved in a NATO exercise and, instead of returning home, they were redirected south, leaving on Thursday 1st April - but this was to be no April Fool. This was no real surprise as the support ship RFA *Fort Austin* had left the group three days earlier on the premise of resupplying Endurance.

ARGENTINA RECLAIMS THE 'MALVINAS'

The invasion on 2nd April resulted in a three hour skirmish between the two opposing forces until the RMs surrendered. The following day, a detachment of RMs at South Georgia, which had been landed from HMS *Endurance*, fought off the invaders for seven hours before they too were captured. During this fight the 22 Marines damaged an Argentinean Navy corvette ARA

Westland Sea Kings embarking HMS Invincible, note the SHAR already embarked

SS Atlantic Conveyor carries out SHAR trials, the helicopters are already embarked (Crown copyright MoD via the FAA publication 'Flight Deck')

Guerrico (which was never to return to service after reaching Argentina), and a Puma and Gazelle helicopter were damaged by rifle fire and put out of action.

The British protest to the UN resulted in the resolution demanding the Argentineans withdraw immediately. This was refused by the Junta although they did offer to negotiate, but this in turn was rejected by the British Government until all invading forces were withdrawn.

BAe Sea Harrier FRS1 of No. 809 Sqdn. commissioned for duties in the South Atlantic

THE TASK FORCE SAILS

At this time the British Forces were mostly on leave for the Easter period and both of the British carriers were in Portsmouth - HMS *Invincible* with her crew on leave and HMS *Hermes* who was in for maintenance. The FAA's squadrons were at their home bases and their men were also on leave. All military leave was cancelled on Friday 2nd April with a total recall back to bases and ships, squadrons and airfields, barracks and logistic establishments.

It was announced that Britain was going to send a Task Force led by the two carriers, with Hermes as the flagship, to liberate the Islands. The weekend was spent putting Hermes back together and loading up stores, weapons and provisions to all available ships of the Fleet and RFAs. The Harriers and Sea Kings were prepared for a rapid return to their ships, embarking over the weekend whilst the ships were in Portsmouth.

With aircraft ranged on the decks and the men in procedure alpha, the Task Force left for the South Atlantic on Monday 5th April from Portsmouth and Plymouth, to the cheers of many thousands of people who had come to witness the largest British Task Force to sail since W.W.II.

Over the next few days, both dockyards were to despatch ships which were all to sail to the assembly point at Ascension Islands. On 8th April, the British Government declared an 'Exclusion Zone (EZ)' of 200 miles around the islands to protect the Fleet once it arrived, and this was implemented by a fleet of hunter killer submarines patrolling the zone.

EXTRA SHIPS FOR THE FLEET

Once the Task Force had sailed, it left the workforce to prepare those ships that could be made available to join the Force. British merchant ships were to be requisitioned and hastily modified for military service. The first of these was the SS *Uganda* which was converted to a hospital ship. She was in the Mediterranean with a group of school children who were dropped off in Naples before going south via Gibraltar where she was prepared for her new role. This was the first British civilian ship to be used for military operations since the end of W.W.II in 1945.

SS *Canberra* was the next ship to be called up, and she was fitted out at Southampton as a troop ship for the men of the British 3rd Brigade, Nos. 40, 42 and 45 RMC and No. 3 Parachute Regiment. She was fitted with two flight decks, one between the bridge and funnels, with the other on the ship's for-castle. All the work was completed in three days and the ship sailed to join the Force on the evening of 9th April.

The pride of the British Merchant fleet, SS *Queen Elizabeth 2nd (QE2)*, was to join the Task Force sailing from Southampton on 12th May, converted in eleven days from luxurious liner to troopship. Trawlers were taken up and modified as minesweepers, merchant supply ships were used to resupply the RFAs and as additional troopships and military equipment resupply ships. These consisted of tugs, a cable ship, tankers, ferries and even a banana boat.

Soon ships laid up in the naval dockyards awaiting disposal after the recent defence cuts were to be given a new lease of life. The dockyard workers performed miracles; RFA *Stromness* was fitted out as a troop transporter in days, the assault ship HMS *Fearless* was to sail south to join the Task Force after being put up for disposal, and RFA *Tidepool* on her way to join the Chilean Navy was to join the Force. Six frigates were also to be reprieved; HMSs *Berwick, Falmouth, Gurka, Londonderry, Tartar* and *Zulu*, specifically to operate in UK waters in place of the ships in the South Atlantic.

THE FAA GETS MORE SHIPS, AIRCRAFT AND SQUADRONS

The FAA was to get some 'new carriers' during the conflict when two of Cunard's laid-up container ships, SS *Atlantic Conveyor* and SS *Atlantic Causeway*, were fitted out as aircraft carriers, taking replacement aircraft south then acting as a deck for operations. Unfortunately the former was lost during the war. The MV *Astronomer* and SS *Contender Bezant* were both converted as carrier type ships which could operate helicopters or Harriers if needed.

Any ships that could take on helicopters or could be adapted for helicopter operations were to sail south with a helicopter flight. The Sea King squadrons, both ASW and Commando units, were to operate individual flights from all varieties of ships. Aircraft in storage for disposal were returned to operational use, even some training fuselages were to fly again.

Four new squadrons were formed; two commando squadrons with Wessex Vs, No. 847 Sqdn. from the two training and SAR units Nos. 771 and 772 Sqdns., and No. 848 Sqdn. was formed from the Wessex V training squadron No. 707 Sqdn., with both squadrons receiving additional aircraft out of storage. The Sea King training unit No. 706 Sqdn. became No. 825 Sqdn. and the SHAR training squadron recommmissioned as No. 809 Sqdn. No. 824 D Flight would equip itself with the two trials Sea King AEW aircraft.

HMS Endurance's Westland Wasp HAS1

OPERATION PARAQUAT - SOUTH GEORGIA

A small naval force led by HMS *Antrim* with 60 men from the SAS and SBS, accompanied by HMS *Plymouth* with 100 men from 42 RMC, HMS *Endurance* and RFA *Tidespring* set off for South Georgia. The ships had six helicopters for the operation; three Wasps from Endurance and Plymouth, Humphrey the Wessex HAS3 from Antrim, and two Wessex Vs from No. 845 C Flight.

Unfortunately the two Wessex Vs were both to crash during white-out conditions on the island whilst attempting to drop off an advanced party of SAS and SBS personnel. All the crew and troops were safely recovered by 'Humphrey' the Wessex HAS Mk3, thankfully with only a few minor injuries. The helicopter, not designed to carry many passengers, flew all the men and the two crews back to Antrim and, in one flight, carried seventeen men and their equipment. The two lost aircraft were supplemented by the two Lynx helicopters aboard HMS *Brilliant* which had joined the group, but the weather was causing problems for the landing of the men. Whilst waiting for a break in the weather, 'Humphrey' picked up a radar signal on 25th April. This proved to be the ARA *Santa Fe*, an Argentinean submarine leaving Grytviken harbour which 'Humphrey' attacked with her depth charges. The attack was continued by the Wasps and Lynx helicopters, with AS 12 missiles fired by the Wasps and the Lynx dropping a homing torpedo at the submarine. The Lynx and Wessex continued the attack with their cabin mounted GPMG guns, and the Santa

ARA Submarine Sante Fe beached with HMS Endurance's Wasp overhead

Hastily painted SHAR onboard HMS Hermes. Note the aircraft behind still wears the type's 'old' scheme.

Fe was disabled and beached herself alongside a jetty.

Although all the group were not available, No. 42 RMC were aboard the RFA which was 200 miles away outside the 'EZ'. It was decided to attack the Argentine positions whilst they were in a state of demoralisation and, in a three hour operation, the British flag replaced that of Argentina and the main battle was over. All that remained was a small group of sixteen enemy troops who surrendered the following day. Only two casualties were sustained, both from the submarine, one injured and one lost. The surrender document was signed on 26th April, 23 days after the island was taken by the enemy.

THE TASK FORCE ASSEMBLES

It was assumed, in the early stages of the Task Force sailing south, that Galtieri would back down, especially after the successful retaking of South Georgia, but this was not to be. The ships were to assemble at Ascension and, during their passage, the ships, aircrew and troops were to hone their skills in preparation for the conflict to come. The British Government increased the restriction in the 'EZ' to all non-British aircraft or shipping (the Total Exclusion Zone {TEZ}) on 28th April.

The Island of Ascension was the scene of intense activity as the ships and troops assembled, with much work carried out moving stores, equipment and troops around the Fleet, with over 300 sorties being flown. Many troops were to go ashore to check and 'zero' their weapons, practice amphibious landings and complete training prior to re-embarking for the transit to the Falklands. This island airfield in the South Atlantic was the base for the RAF tanker fleet and the operating base for the Vulcan bombers to be used for the 'Black Buck' bombing sorties, a return journey of nearly 4,000 miles.

OPERATION CORPORATE - FREEDOM FOR THE FALKLANDS

The fight for the Falklands began in earnest on 1st May. The RAF bombed the airport at Port Stanley with a Vulcan bomber, and the first naval casualty was received when HMS *Arrow* suffered damage after being hit by shells from a Mirage whilst bombarding the airport.

The first aircraft destroyed by SHAR aircraft were two Mirages, a Dagger and a Canberra bomber, shot down when they came within the Task Force operating areas by No. 801 Sqdn. which was supplying CAP aircraft. The SHAR of No. 800 Sqdn. carried out bombing missions to the airfield to inflict more damage, and they also attacked the airfields at Goose Green destroying a Pucara aircraft and Darwin.

A busy time on HMS Hermes: SHAR of Nos. 800, 899 and the new 809 Sqdns., a visiting Lynx and the only surviving RAF Chinook.

The submarine HMS *Conqueror* sank the battleship ARA *General Belgrano* on the second day after she became a threat to the Task Force. The first firings of Sea Skua missiles by Lynx helicopters resulted in destroying the ARA *Comodoro Somellera* and the damaging of its sister ship the ARA *Alferez*, two gun boats, on 3rd May. By the end of the war, the Argentineans would have lost six more vessels, but they were to revenge the sinking of their battleship when the destroyer HMS *Sheffield* was hit by an Exocet missile on 4th May. This was the first of seven British ships lost in the battle. The same day saw the loss of the first SHAR shot down with the loss of its pilot whilst attacking Goose Green, and two more SHAR were to disappear two days later. It is thought they had a mid-air collision whilst flying CAP in atrocious weather.

The RAF Vulcans continued their night missions with four more attacks, whilst the SHAR carried out daytime missions softening up Forces on the land and fighting off the enemy Skyhawks, Mirage and Dagger aircraft. Holding their own, they shot down many aircraft, destroying many on the ground whilst losing no aircraft in air-to-air combat.

RAF Harrier GR3 fitted with cluster bombs onboard HMS Hermes after arriving in the theatre aboard the SS Atlantic Conveyor

THE FIRST CONTAINERSHIP AIRCRAFT CARRIER

The requirement to supply additional aircraft for the Task Force with the additional facility of having an operating deck to fly them from, resulted in the MOD acquiring the two container ships from Cunard to be converted to aircraft carriers. The first was Atlantic Conveyor, a 15,000 ton containership with two vehicle decks, ideal for the role of support carrier able to transfer vehicles and stores. Taken to Devonport on 13th April for conversion so she could take aircraft as deck cargo and retain an aircraft operating area, she was completed on the scheduled date of 25th. Below decks were loaded with aircraft stores, ammunition, provisions and vehicles, then the ship moved out to Plymouth Sound to receive the aircraft.

The deck had been redesigned to give a storage area for aircraft in front of the bridge with the for'castle as an operating area. Embarking the Wessex of No. 848 Sqdn., Chinooks of No. 18 Sqdn. RAF and the helicopters of No. 656 Sqdn. AAC which were mostly put into the parking area, she then received a No. 809 Sqdn. SHAR to prove her deck could operate the aircraft.

The ship sailed for the Task Force arriving at Ascension on 5th May to join the amphibious group. The eight SHAR of the new No. 809 Sqdn., and eight Harrier GR3s of No. 1(F) Sqdn., flew from the UK direct to Ascension completing the longest transit flight flown by both types. The eight SHAR and six of the GR3s embarked on the ship on the 6th. This amphibious Force (HMSs *Fearless* and *Intrepid*, SSs *Canberra, Norland* and *Atlantic Conveyor*) headed south on the 7th to join up firstly with the remaining amphibious units and then the main Force on 18th May.

During the voyage, one of the SHARs was kept on alert to intercept any Argentine aircraft encountered. Upon joining the carriers, the SHARs disembarked in two flights of four, one to each carrier, whilst the GR3s joined Hermes which left the deck free to prepare and deliver the helicopters. Tragedy was to strike only one week later when Hermes was struck by two Exocet missiles on the 25th causing major fires. Eventually sinking, she took with her ten helicopters and the stores and equipment below decks. Only one of the four Chinooks was to make it ashore, the other three would be badly missed.

THE LAND BATTLE

The land battle began with the attack on Pebble Beach by the SAS using Sea King Mk4 helicopters. The men were flown ashore on the night of 14th May to attack the Argentine air field established at the site where they destroyed eleven aircraft, Pucaras, MB339s, Shorts Skyvan and Puma helicopters. The radio station, ammunition dump and large fuel dump were also destroyed, effectively removing the threat from the airfield.

Westland Sea King HCMk4

Westland Wessex HUMk5

The Sea Kings and Wessex began moving men and equipment to the amphibious ships, and it was during one such transfer that a Sea King was hit by an Albatross as it was operating from Hermes with SAS men aboard. The helicopter crashed into the sea with the loss of eighteen SAS members. The helicopters landed many raiding parties ashore to various locations with the aim of confusing the enemy as to where and when the landings were to commence.

The landings were to begin with an assault on San Carlos beach on East Falklands during the night of 20th/21st May, with the Paras and RMCs getting ashore to establish defensive positions around the beachhead. The night before, Sea Kings and Gazelle helicopters were flying over the area supporting an advance party of 3 Para, but unfortunately two Gazelles were shot down with the loss of three crew.

Once ashore the other amphibious forces were landed, and a total of 3000 British troops were ashore on East Falklands by the end of the day. The FAA helicopters were busy bringing ashore all the support equipment whilst the Sea Harriers provided air cover and the GR3s ground support.

During the assault, intensive strikes by the Argentine aircraft produced hits on three ships, with HMS *Ardent* being lost on the first day. One Harrier was also lost to ground fire whilst the enemy lost fifteen aircraft. This phase was to last four days resulting in the landing of all the first phase troops ashore, some 5000, along with their equipment. It had been costly for both sides. The RN had suffered the loss of two ships with strikes on a further eight, although these survived due to the bombs failing to explode. The cost to the Argentineans was at least 36 aircraft.

ADVANCING TO PORT STANLEY

After the landings, assaults were made on Darwin and Goose Green and the SHAR took on the unfamiliar role of ground support alongside the GR3s. The helicopters were in support transferring troops and equipment and spotting for the enemy. Whilst these assaults were in progress, two brigades began the long march to Port Stanley. It was originally planned they would be airlifted but the loss of the helicopters on the Atlantic Conveyor meant there were no helicopters available.

The two groups were to head in different directions fighting against enemy positions en-route, rejoining at Teal Inlet about half way, with the helicopters resupplying the troops throughout the 'Yomp'. Eventually the troops were to arrive and capture Mount Kent, an area of high ground overlooking Port Stanley, the final objective.

REINFORCEMENTS ARRIVE

Back home in the UK, the British 5th Brigade (Welsh and Scots Guards and the Gurka Regiments) were embarking aboard the SS *QE2* for the long haul south. The ship sailed on 12th May from Southampton arriving at Grytviken, South Georgia on the 27th. Here she offloaded her troops to the ships of the amphibious force for transit to San Carlos.

The Brigade assisted in the 'clearing up operations' before re-embarking on the assault ships for transit around the island to join the assault on Port Stanley. The ships moved around to Bluff Cove south of Port Stanley but whilst offloading on 8th June, they were attacked by Skyhawks and Mirages which bombed two of the LSLs, RFAs *Sir Galahad* and *Sir Tristram*. RFA *Sir Tristram* was carrying equipment and stores and was struck by the Skyhawks, whilst the former had the Welsh Guards aboard awaiting transfer to Fitzroy when she was struck by bombs during the attack by the Mirages and exploded in a ball of fire.

The Sea Kings of No. 825 Sqdn. went immediately into action in the rescuing of the Welsh Guards. Repeatedly flying into the smoke and fire, the crews ignored their own safety as they winched men out of the freezing water. The life boats began to drift back in the tide to the burning ship, and the Sea King pilots positioned their helicopters between the life rafts and the boat and, using the downwash of the rotors, drove the life boats away to the shore. Without the bravery of these helicopter crews, the attack would have cost many more than the 150 men lost or injured.

THE FINAL PUSH

The British Forces were closing in on Port Stanley and over the nights of 11th-13th, they were to take strategic high grounds allowing them to fire on the Argentineans. The troops were supported by the force of helicopters moving troops, heavy equipment and replacement ammunition to these advanced positions, returning with the casualties. They were also to be used in the attack mode, firing machine guns from their cabins and firing wire guided missiles at targets.

One such target was the Argentine headquarters set up in the police station which was attacked by an AS12 wire guided missile fired by Petty Officer Arthur Balls. It had been observed that there was a daily meeting of Argentine Officers held in the Town Hall and it was an ideal target which, if successful, could bring the conflict to an early end. No. 845 Sqdn. was tasked with the mission.

A single Wessex V armed with two AS12s attacked on the morning of 12th June, arriving at the target after a low level flight and taking the Argentineans by surprise. Having no time to ensure correct positioning of the helicopter due to the enemy troops concentrated in the area, PO Balls quickly took aim and fired. One missile hit the police station but the other unfortunately struck a telegraph pole en-route and veered into the harbour. The helicopter made its escape through a hail of gunfire from the defending troops. Although the daring attack failed in its objective of wiping out the Argentine senior command, it did have the desired effect of scaring them and the troops in the city.

NAVAL BOMBARDMENT HAS A COST

The ships of the Task Force were using their heavy guns to bombard the enemy's positions during this final push. HMS *Glamorgan* had been relieved from this role and was sent to protect the smaller ships, minesweepers, tugs, repair ships and stores ships which were not needed in the combat zone. She was recalled to supply gunfire for the final push, and so moved to a position about eighteen miles offshore out of the range of the Argentine Howitzers.

Unknown to the British Forces, however, was the fact that the enemy had some land launched Exocet missiles and one of these was to strike the aft end of the ship, entering the helicopter hangar and going down into the galley below. Fires were started but fortunately the missile failed to explode. Nevertheless, the fires cost the lives of thirteen men, mostly from the flight, but the crew saved the ship which was to return to Portsmouth during July.

THE ARGENTINE SURRENDER

The Gurka Regiment took the last vantage point overlooking Port Stanley on the night of the 13th, and the city was now surrounded. A Gazelle helicopter was despatched from Fearless with a negotiating party to meet with General Menendez, the Argentine garrison commander. Later General Moore, the British Commander, was flown to Port Stanley and the surrender document was signed at 23.59 on the 14th.

The only remaining Argentine group were on the island of South Thule, and the detachment of RMs defending South Georgia were given the task of removing the Argentinean naval unit from the island. The small force which had been patrolling South Georgia (Endurance and Yarmouth, RFA *Olmeda* and the tug Salvageman) took the men of 42 RMC to take the research station. Upon arriving, the Marines were landed and advanced on the station, but the Argentineans surrendered on 19th June without fighting. Thus ended the conflict, 79 days after the Argentinean Forces took Port Stanley.

TRIUMPHANT RETURN POST FALKLANDS TO THE PRESENT DAY

Although the RN had been reduced in size both in men, ships and aircraft, the professionalism was still to remain. This had been the first British war since the Boer War, which was fought a considerable distance away from home. Without the aircraft of the FAA it would have been impossible to win, and the Argentine Air Force would have sunk the Fleet before it could reach the islands.

The role played by the helicopters, initially in the movement of troops, materials and weapons amongst the ships, landing the special forces for clandestine and disruptive operations, was of great importance, including the movement of troops once ashore and supporting them in the battle, casualty evacuation and SAR missions by all units. All these operations reiterated the necessity for this machine for amphibious assaults and land warfare. The ASW helicopters maintained a round-the-clock operation to ensure the Fleet was not attacked by enemy submarines, as well as assisting in the supporting roles.

Without the SHARs, the Fleet would have been vulnerable to air attacks, and such was their success that the Argentine Skyhawks, Mirage and Daggers were no match, none being lost in air combat. After the surrender, the carriers remained on station with the SHAR continuing CAP missions 'just in case' the Argentineans returned.

The ships were to return home victorious receiving tumultuous welcomes at all the dockyards, the civilian ships were handed back to their respective operators and leave was granted to allow recuperation. It was a costly operation, over £750 million without the cost of replacing equipment. One good point was that the defence review would be reassessed - ships would be reprieved and more aircraft would be ordered. Mr. John Nott had been fortunate in that the ships he had written off were still available for service.

If the Argentineans had delayed their operations for another year, it may have been a different story. For a start, HMS *Invincible* would have been an Australian

HMS Hermes returns to Portsmouth Harbour (Crown copyright MoD via the FAA Publication 'Flight Deck')

Westland Sea King AEW Mk2 of No. 824 D Flt.

warship - but this was now not to be and she would remain in the RN.

PROJECT LAST

Since the withdrawal of the Gannet AEW3 with the decommissioning of HMS *Ark Royal*, the Fleet had to rely mainly on the RAF to supply AEW information during operations backed up by information from destroyers acting as a 'picket'. With the sinking of HMS *Sheffield* whilst operating as a picket, the urgency for a carrier borne AEW equipped aircraft was deemed paramount and efforts were concentrated on producing a solution.

The RN, Thorn EMI and Westlands proposed that the Searchwater radar, as fitted to the Nimrod, could be accommodated within a Sea King fuselage. This was titled Project Last (Low Altitude Surveillance Task), the detection of low level aircraft in any sea state at distances of up to 125 miles from the Fleet. This would be achieved using the Searchwater with the helicopter flying above 10,000ft.

Two aircraft were converted by removing the ASW equipment and installing the Searchwater operating equipment inside the Sea King's cabin. The radar scanner was attached to the outside starboard side of the fuselage housed in a protective bag which inflates when the radar is operated. The scanner was mounted such that when in operation it scanned below the helicopter's hull and, to allow this to work, it was designed to swivel through 90 degrees to a stowage position when the helicopter was on the deck.

The first trials of the Sea King AEW Mk2A began in June 1982 as D Flight of No. 824 Sqdn. which was formed on the 14th, eleven weeks after conception. It continued with its trials until embarking in HMS *Illustrious* on 2nd August for service in the South Atlantic where it continued its operational trials whilst the aircraft were attached to No. 814 Sqdn. These aircraft gave the Fleet AEW cover wherever the ships were operating without having to rely on land based aircraft.

THE NEW HMS ILLUSTRIOUS

Completed three months early, the second Invincible class carrier HMS *Illustrious* left the Tyne on 18th June. The need for her early completion was so she could relieve her sister ship on station in the South Atlantic. One modification to the ship as a direct result of the actions in the Falklands was the fitting of a pair of Phalanx close quarters weapons, the first RN ship so fitted.

The ship set sail for the Falklands on 2nd August, 45 days after leaving the builders yard, and she completed her trials in record time. Embarked were the ten SHAR from No. 809 Sqdn., nine ASW Sea Kings from No. 814 Sqdn. and No. 824 D Flight Sea King AEW aircraft. She relieved Invincible on 28th August remaining on station protecting the Falkland Island Protection Zone until relieved by RAF F4 Phantoms from No. 29 Sqdn. during November.

GIBRALTAR STATION

For the first time since W.W.II, the FAA was to establish a permanent aircraft presence in Gibraltar when Gibraltar Flight was ensconced at RAF North Front from July 1982. Initially tasked with patrolling the Straights during the Falklands conflict, it was now tasked with monitoring the movement of Soviet ships passing through to and from the Black sea.

The Russian Navy mostly operated in their territorial waters but had now become a large deep water navy, especially with their growing fleet of submarines. The Lynx flight was responsible for the monitoring of these movements, and submarines passing through the Straits on the surface were photographed. The tasking was to last nearly nine years, with the final surveillance flight taking place during April 1991.

Gibraltar Flt Lynx HAS Mk3

CHANGING FACES CHANGING ROLES

THE ROLE OF THE WRNS

One WRNS Officer, 1st Officer Karen Shepherd, a meteorological specialist, was to serve in RFA *Fort Grange* in the South Atlantic. The WRNS had been an integral part of the FAA since reforming in 1939 as a temporary department of the RN. The first FAA attached ladies were employed as aircraft engineers releasing the men for employment on FLSs, and worked as mechanical, electrical and radio mechanics supporting shore-based squadrons. The WRNS became a permanent department of the Navy in 1949 and has continued to provide ladies for service within the FAA.

Karen was not the first FAA Wren to see sea service as many Wrens had been aboard the helicopter training ship RFA *Engadine*. FAA Wrens are employed in all engineering and servicing roles, both as artificers and mechanics, photography, handlers, met, ATC, AEOs and air hostesses. They have been employed in the same employment as their male counterparts and when WRNS were given the opportunity to go to sea from 1990, FAA Wrens were amongst the first to embark on British warships.

The first WRNS Officer as an AEO was 1st Officer Debbie Iles who qualified after graduation at RN Engineering College Manadon in June 1989. She was initially appointed as an AEO on No. 845 Sqdn. Joining the navy as a weapons analyst, she successfully passed for officer training, eventually joining Manadon as the first female engineering officer to take a degree course.

Females are also employed as helicopter pilots, and the first to qualify was Lt. Claire Donegan who earned her wings on 11th December 1998 and then joined No. 820 Sqdn. with the Sea King for continuation training. The term 'Wrens' is no longer used, females in the RN are now known as Ratings and Officers.

FAREWELL TO THE FAA HOVERCRAFT

The final flight of a NHTU was to be flown on 29th November 1982 with the delivery of their last and largest hovercraft, the 100 ton Vosper Thorneycroft VT2, to a ferry company in Kent. After forming on 1st January 1975 with the demise of the IHU, the Unit continued evaluation of the role of the craft as an MCM vehicle, troop and logistics transport, drugs and illegal immigrant patrol vehicle and bomb disposal operations.

The operations and trials carried out, not only by the NHU but also the IHTU, all proved the worth of the craft as a useful tool for maritime operations. However this was not considered when the axe fell on the Unit in the 1981 Defence Review.

RFA RELIANT SPECIALISED HELICOPTER SHIP

Although the Falklands are protected now with a permanent detachment of RAF fighters and RN ships on patrol, it was deemed that an ASW presence was also needed. During the conflict one ship, the MV *Astronomer*, had been used successfully for helicopter operations, and this ship was purchased for the ASW operations in the South Atlantic. It was to serve in the area supporting No. 826 Sqdn. which had been reorganised into three flights for continuous ASW operations in the South Atlantic from February 1983. It would continue until the requirement ceased in August 1986 when the ship would be sold off.

The ship was fitted out with a hangar capable of taking four Sea Kings, briefing rooms and support facilities. The deck could also operate two Chinooks and was the largest helicopter deck in the Fleet after the three Invincible class ships. Accepted in November as the RFA *Reliant*, she began trials in December but these were rushed through and her sea training took place over the Christmas period using helicopters from No. 772 Sqdn. at Portland as she was needed to relieve HMS *Fearless* supporting actions of the Lebanon detachment.

The situation in Lebanon was deteriorating

RFA Reliant which saw service off Beirut

Westland Wessex HAS Mk3

with Syrian-backed terrorist organisations attacking the Peace Keeping Forces. The FAA was tasked with supplying helicopter support for the British contingent in the country, and a detachment of three Sea King Mk4s from No. 846 Sqdn. in HMS *Hermes* was despatched aboard HMS *Fearless* on 20th November 1983.

The helicopters, wearing large Union Jacks on the fuselage, operated low level sorties in Beirut in support of the British troops in the city. The new helicopter support ship, RFA *Reliant*, arrived on 2nd January whilst Fearless left the theatre on 11th January, leaving the RFA to remain as support and operations ship.

The multi-national Peace Keeping Force was ordered to withdraw on 7th February 1984 after the Lebanese army had been defeated by the terrorist forces. The first withdrawal consisted of 100 personnel, stores and equipment by the Sea Kings and RAF Chinooks, flown from the town of Juneih ten miles north of Beirut, on the 8th and taken to Cyprus.

The next phase involved 191 British civilians and embassy staff and 330 international personnel from 31 nations who were lifted from Juneih to the RFA and to a Greek ferry, the SS *Sol Georgeios*, chartered for the operation which ended on 31st March. These people were also taken to Cyprus.

Westland Sea King HCMk4 prior to embarking onboard HMS Fearless for duties in Lebanon. Note the large Union Jack on the aircraft fuselage.

With the operations completed, the ship and helicopters returned home, but not until they had been retained in the Mediterranean for SAR cover for the Queen who was to fly to Jordan. The ship returned to the UK on 5th April after four months during which she displayed her capability in supporting operations with a detachment of helicopters.

HMS HERMES AND HUMPHREY BOW OUT

Leaving Gibraltar, her last foreign port of call, HMS *Hermes* headed for a short refit in Plymouth. Whilst on passage, she was to conduct Sea Harrier trials yet again - this time with the Sea Harrier Mk51 of the Indian Navy. Little was it realised that in less than three years she would be their own ship. These trials were to be her last aircraft operations in RN service, and the ship arrived in Portsmouth on 22nd November 1983.

After de-storing and reducing the ship's company to less than 400 men, the ship returned to Devonport for a short refit in preparation for her last role, that of a dockside training ship with the ability to be readied for sea in 30 days. The ship left Devonport for its voyage to Portsmouth on 6th April, completing post refit trials en route.

She was to rendezvous with HMS *Bulwark* under tow to the breakers yard whilst passing the Edistone lighthouse, and arrived in Portsmouth for the final time on the 12th April. One member of the ship's company was Second Officer Liz Nuttall WRNS, the first female to serve on an active ship of the Fleet.

She was sold to the Indian Navy (to be renamed INS *Viraat*) to operate their Sea Harriers, transferring to them when the last of the three Invincible class ships HMS *Ark Royal (V)* became operational in 1986. After 27 years as an aircraft carrier in all roles designated for RN operations - strike, ASW, commando and Harrier carrier - with a memorable contribution to the British success over the Argentineans, the ship was to remain operational in the Indian Ocean.

The final Wessex HAS Mk3 was retired from service on 20th January 1984 when HMS *Antrim* Flight disbanded. This was the last Wessex small ships' flight, and the last county-class destroyer flight with the type (two other ships were equipped with the Lynx, HMS *Fife* being the last county-class to retire from RN service in November 1990). It was fitting that it should be the Humphrey from the ship that had been involved in the recapturing of South Georgia and the destroying of the ARA *Santa Fe* during the Falklands War. The ASW Mk3 helicopter had been in service a little over fifteen years, first operated by No. 814 Sqdn. from August 1967.

AEW SQUADRON REFORMS

Recommissioning on 1st November 1984, once again as the FAA's AEW squadron, No. 849 Sqdn. was equipped with the Sea King AEW Mk2A Searchwater equipped helicopters. As with the previous squadron, it would consist of an HQ flight and two flights for carrier deployments. It was reformed from the current operators of the type, No. 824 Sqdn. D Flight, which had been operating the two prototype helicopters since June 1982.

The two FL Flights would consist of three helicopters each, the first to commission being A Flight on 31st May 1985 for service aboard HMS *Illustrious*. The flights were equipped with the full standard AEW helicopter, and the first two prototypes which had effectively proved and developed the concept were to be upgraded. Embarking during August for exercise 'Ocean Safari', the three aircraft succeeded in detecting 'enemy' aircraft and directing defending SHAR aircraft to intercept the attacking aircraft.

COMMANDO HELICOPTER OPERATIONS & SUPPORT CELL

With the retirement of HMS *Ark Royal* in 1978 went the CBGLO Units, the services not seeing a need for this specialised team aboard carriers. Four years later came 'Operation Corporate' when it was seen to have been the wrong decision. During the war, the tasking of the support helicopters was not well co-ordinated and, although the operations were successfully completed, they may have benefited from an expert team co-ordinating the requirements in support of the land forces.

Thus, after careful planning, a specialist group was formed on 20th June 1984 (the Commando Helicopter Operations Support Cell located at Yeovilton), tasked with working with the commando squadrons, for co-ordinating operations ashore, tasking of helicopters and training details. Incorporated in the Unit are four mobile air operations teams (MOAT) who advise the amphibious forces of landing sites, logistic support and vehicle requirements.

Each commando squadron operation has an attached MOAT which advises the ground forces of the availability of the helicopters and liaises as to the tasking of them to ensure maximum use during the operation.

SEA HARRIER FRS2

British Aerospace was asked in 1983 to produce a study for the upgrading of the Sea Harrier fleet, which resulted in the MoD issuing a contract to upgrade 30 aircraft to FRS Mk2 standard during January 1985. The modifications were centred round the installation of the Blue Vixen radar which needed a more bulbous radome in the nose and a fuselage 'plug' behind the wing to accommodate the additional equipment. The aircraft was to be better equipped as a fighting machine with additional under-wing pylons and the ability to use AMRAAM (advanced medium range air-air missiles) missiles. The radar had a 'look down, shoot down' capability and the aircraft radar warning receiving equipment was upgraded. The proposed wing tip missile rails were deleted from the upgrade but the cockpit was completely revised, designed to reduce the pilot's workload, and the engine was the more advanced version as fitted to the USMC's AV-8B.

Two aircraft were to be converted from FRS1 to FRS2 status for evaluation and trials. The first flight was on 19th September 1988 and, after initial trials proved successful, the MoD issued a contract for 31 FRS1s to be converted on 7th December. This was to be followed with an order for five more conversions and a total of 28 new build aircraft.

The development of the new radar commenced using an RAE BAC 111 during 1987. This was followed by using two modified HS125s, also with the RAE, with the second HS125 being modified with a complete FRS Mk2 cockpit on the right-hand side. This enabled much research flying to be completed prior to the type's first flight and RN pilots gained experience using these aircraft. One of the aircraft became the only HS125 operated by the FAA.

HMS ARK ROYAL(V) AT SEA

The last of the through-deck cruisers, HMS *Ark Royal*, sailed from Wallsend for its Contractor's Sea Trials on 19th October

Westland Sea King AEW Mk2 wearing DDAY commemorative invasion stripes

BAe Sea Harrier FRS2 fitted with AMRAAM Missiles (BAe)

1984. She differed from the other two ships having a 12.5 degree ramp and Phalanx close quarters gun sponsons forward and aft. A detachment from No. 845 Sqdn. was to operate from the shipbuilder's yard as an HDS for the duration of the trials, with the Wessex making the first landing on board once the ship was in the North Sea.

The ship's aviation crew during the trials was made up of the AED personnel, the ship's regulating PO and stokers, and the DAEO acting as 'F'. The crew were tasked with receiving visiting aircraft and refuelling them using a bowser on the deck (possibly the first time a bowser had been on a carrier deck). This was the first time that aircraft carrier flying operations were co-ordinated by the ship's AEO and a team of aircraft engineers and non-FAA personnel.

The ship was to meet up with both its sister ships during its sixteen days at sea. Over 50 landings were achieved, not only by the Wessex, but also from visiting Sea Kings and a Tiger helicopter from Bristow's Helicopters. These helicopters transferred 192 passengers, stores and equipment and the Wessex also winched six people onto the deck. Quite a busy aviation work up - it was after all a Contractor's Sea Trial.

MOD CHANGES AFFECT THE FAA's STRUCTURE

The MoD announced changes to the structure of naval aviation elements and their use with the Fleet, and created two new departments, both under the command of Captains. The first, the Directorate of Naval Warfare (DNW), was responsible for the effectiveness of the assets available whilst the second, the Director of Operational Requirements (DOR), was to define future requirements and introduce them into service.

Dassault Falcon 2

This did not infringe on the incumbent flags, but rather gave them more say in the future roles of the FAA. The Flag Officer Naval Air Command (FONAC) was still responsible for training and second line squadrons, Flag Officer Fleet 3 (FOF3) was responsible for sea-going assets, whilst the Director General Aircraft (Navy) DGA(N) was responsible for engineering support.

FRADU FALCONS

Arriving in 1985 as the replacement for the FRADU Canberras were second-hand Dassault Falcon 20s. These bizjets were acquired by Flight Refuelling for operations from their Bournemouth facilities, in the aggressor aircraft role; fitted with under-wing hard points which enabled them to carry the EW and simulation pods and towed targets in support of Fleet exercises.

The Canberra TT18s were phased out as more of the Falcon aircraft became available post modifications. These bizjets were designed as passenger aircraft initially and were used for freight by their previous owners. FRADU also use the aircraft for these roles, operating from various locations both in the UK and abroad in support of Fleet exercises. The Falcons are used to transport the support crews and associated equipment to these locations.

HMS ARK ROYAL (V) JOINS THE FLEET

After completing her fitting out, HMS *Ark Royal* sailed for Portsmouth on 25th June 1985. As well as members of the ship's company, she still had some of Swan Hunters' staff on board including twenty

HMS Ark Royal (V) third and last of the Invincible class of carriers

cleaning ladies carrying out final work before the acceptance after arriving in Portsmouth. Embarked for the departure was a Wessex from No. 845 Sdqn., a Fairey Swordfish from HMS *Daedalus* and the RM band. Accompanying the Swordfish were a team of engineers to look after the aircraft, this included two Wrens (the first Wrens to officially wear a sea-going ship's cap tally).

Sailing into her home port on 1st July, she had the first SHAR to land on her deck ranged on the ramp. This aircraft landed as the ship approached Portsmouth flown by Lt. Cdr. Slade, CO of No. 899 Sqdn. It was an historic accession as he had completed the final recovery of an aircraft in the previous Ark Royal. The Swordfish was ranged on the stern, and both aircraft were used as the backdrop for the handing over ceremony. The ship conducted sea acceptance trials prior to commissioning on 1st November 1985.

June 1987 was to see the first aircraft carrier to visit London since the Festival of Britain in 1951 when HMS *Campania* was moored on the River Thames. To celebrate the 400th Anniversary of the first HMS *Ark Royal*, the 50th anniversary of the Maritime Museum and the 30th anniversary of the White Ensign Association, Ark Royal (V) was moored off the Royal Naval College Greenwich on the 3rd June for a six day visit. It was the largest ship to pass through the Thames Barrier at that time.

ARMILLA PATROLS

The Gulf confrontation between Iran and Iraq was threatening non-aligned shipping in the area which needed protection. Armilla patrols were established in 1984, and RN ships were to escort oil tankers proceeding through the Gulf to ensure safe passage. During 1986, the embarked Lynx were modified with a missile jamming system to protect them against 'stray' missiles.

Further modifications were embodied as defence against attacking Iranian/Iraqi aircraft after the USS *Stark* was hit by an Iraqi Exocet missile. These modifications included a chaff dispenser, improved Infra-red jamming equipment and a heavy machine gun pod fitted with a 0.5' machine gun, and they would all prove effective at a later date

HMS Ark Royal in the Thames opposite the RN College at Greenwich

Lynx HAS Mk 8

against Iraqi Forces during the Gulf War.

The Armilla patrol ships were also called upon to evacuate British civilians caught up in the civil war in the Democratic Republic of Yemen during January 1986. The Lynx helicopters from HMSs *Newcastle* and *Jupiter* airlifted 208 people to the Royal Yacht *Britannia* and the P & O ship *Diamond Princess* from Aden and Mukala. The patrols continue to provide safe passage in an unstable area of the world.

LYNX MK8

The Lynx helicopter had been developed and purchased for many navies and Westlands developed the Super Lynx for South Korea and Portugal which incorporated the radar mounted below the nose having a 360 degree capability. Whilst this was being produced, a British Experimental Rotor Programme was being conducted using composite rotor blades which were swept and designed with an anhedral. This gave the rotors a higher tip speed producing greater speed and lift and increased helicopter performance.

The company designed the Lynx HAS Mk8 which incorporated these two designs and, to complete the identifiable modifications, the Sea Owl passive ID thermal imaging turret was also fitted in the nose. Other modifications were the reverse direction tail rotor, secure speech, an automated tactical system (CTS), satellite navigation systems, a MAD and a floatation bag.

Due to the amount of work required to upgrade the 65 Lynx to this new standard, it was completed in phases beginning with all the helicopters having secure speech, followed by six trials aircraft fitted with the CTS equipment, floatation gear, BERP blades and revised tail rotor, and finally the remainder of the upgrade equipment. In effect, these helicopters were going to be new models.

THE MERLIN EH101 FLIES

After initial conception in 1979 and four years in build, the first EH101 Merlin helicopter was presented to the public at a roll-out ceremony on 9th October 1987, to be followed by the type's first flight. The ASW version for the FAA replaced the Sea Kings and can carry homing torpedoes and anti-ship missiles, and is to be fitted with the latest avionics and ASW/ASV equipment available. Taking a further nine years to develop, this helicopter would be the main ASW helicopter in the new millennium.

SMALL SHIPS AND SEA KINGS

The later batch of Type 22 frigates and subsequent designed ships were built to allow larger helicopters to be operated - this was aimed around the arrival of the Merlin helicopter. The first trials with the Sea King were the clearance trials by the A & AEE followed by No. 826 Sqdn.'s trials aboard HMS *London*, followed by a spell in HMS *Brave* during October 1987.

The results were to establish that helicopters could detach to these smaller ships for short periods whilst relying on their mother ships for engineering and stores support. This was put to the test when another trial was conducted aboard HMS *Brave* during autumn 1988 for exercise Teamwork, showing that the reliance on the mother ship had limitations to the length of time the flight could remain detached.

HMS *London* was thus equipped with facilities for the independent operation of a Sea King for ASW operations and began operating with its own Sea King flight, A Flight of No. 826 Sqdn., during 1989. The concept proved to be compatible as an ASW system, thus two flights were formed specifically to operate from Type 22 frigates.

SEA KING HAS MK6

The last model of the Sea King ASW helicopter for the FAA was the HAS Mk6 with modified ASW, sonar and MAD

Sea King HAS Mk 6

Westland Agusta EH101 (Westlands)

equipment. The helicopter had some digital systems and the Super Searcher radar, as well as a new dipping sonar with a cable length of 700ft (compared to the standard 245ft).

The modifications were incorporated into 73 Mk5 helicopters plus five new build examples, with the first converted aircraft flying on 15th December 1987 followed by the first new aircraft two years later. The IFTU, No. 824 Sqdn., received its aircraft during April 1988 for twelve months of evaluation. On completion of the IFTU duties, further operational work was required and for this an OEU (Operational Evaluation Unit), No. 826 E Flight, was formed (June 1991, becoming No. 810 Sqdn. on 27th July 1993). This was the equivalent of an IFTU but was based on the evaluation system used by the RAF for their fixed-wing fighter aircraft, responsible for developing the service use of aircraft and equipment needed to improve their safety and reliability.

One of the favourite modifications to the aircraft is the introduction of an emergency breathing system for use if the aircraft were to ditch. This STASS (Short Term Air Supply System) gives the crew a two minute supply of nitrogen/oxygen mix, thus reducing the risk of the bends (decompression sickness) when surfacing from a sinking helicopter. This system would be introduced to other FAA helicopters.

WORKHORSES GO TO GRAZE

After 25 years since its first flight, the Wessex HU Mk5 was finally retired at Culdrose on 31st March 1988 when No. 771 Sqdn. converted to the Sea King HAR Mk5. The type was the stalwart of the Wessex breed of helicopters seeing service with all the commando squadrons and as a useful SAR helicopter at RNAS Culdrose, Lee-on-Solent and Portland. Two aircraft were also fitted out as VIP aircraft for use as 'Green Parrots' with No. 781 Sqdn.

The last operational sortie for the Wessex HU Mk5 took place on 28th October 1986, after twenty years in FLS. The type was operated in all areas of the world, if not with troops then as an HDS between ships or during RASs. It was an aircraft used successfully as a SAR vehicle rescuing many people on the south coast and west country. The final operational flight was flown by the Unit that introduced it to FLS, No. 845 Sqdn.

Another helicopter to disappear was the Wasp, retired after twenty-one years continuous service with No. 829 Sqdn., mostly at Portland. This small but effective helicopter was to give the Fleet an effective weapons system for attacking both submarines and surface vessels. It was a great improvement from the Hiller and Whirlwinds used by HMSs *Vidal* and *Protector* as it was an armed helicopter, and Vidal was to operate the Wasp from

Westland Wessex HUMk5

RFA Engadine

January 1968 until withdrawn from service in August 1971.

It was the world's first attack helicopter specifically for use on frigates and destroyers setting the standards for the world's navies. Proving itself in the Falklands, the helicopter has now been replaced by the Lynx and Merlin helicopter. It finally bowed out during May 1988 when the flight from HMS *Plymouth* was disbanded.

BILL RETURNS TO ARK

To celebrate the 25th anniversary of the first aircraft carrier V/STOL landing by Bill Bedford, (P1127 in *HMS Ark Royal {IV}*), he was flown aboard the present Ark Royal on 13th April 1988, exactly 25 years to the date, embarking in a T4N from No. 899 Sqdn. This was the first time that a Sea Harrier T4N aircraft had embarked onboard an Invincible class carrier. The later Mk T8N embarked for deck training for the first time during 2003, once again in Ark Royal.

Sea Harrier T4N aboard Ark Royal

Whilst the T4N was onboard, it gave the opportunity for another first to be achieved when the ship's captain, Capt. M Harris (a submariner), flew a sortie in the aircraft. This was the first time the commanding officer of an Invincible class carrier had launched and recovered to the ship in a Harrier.

RFA ARGUS - THE NEW TRAINING AIRCRAFT CARRIER

Following on from RFA *Reliant*, another ship to be used successfully as a helicopter deck during the Falklands War was the SS *Container Bezant*, a 28,000 ton roll-on roll-off container ship. This ship was also purchased and after converting to an aviation training carrier in Belfast as a replacement for RFA *Engadine*, she was commissioned on 1st June 1988. The ship began service as RFA *Argus* during 1988 when No. 810 Sqdn. joined for trials on 18th July, with the final training series in Engadine completed on 1st February 1989 by the Lynx of No. 702 Sqdn. The ship was paid off the following month and then sold for scrap in 1990.

Argus is capable of operating both helicopters and Sea Harriers from its five spot flight deck. The large hold below the deck was converted to four hangars, divided by hydraulic water tight bulkheads, and is capable of holding twelve SHAR and six Sea Kings. There are also two lifts serving the flight deck and, in effect, it was the RN's largest aircraft carrier at that time. Although capable of SHAR operations, she is primarily a helicopter training and support ship.

SUPER LYNX

The uprated Lynx was a different 'cat' to the original HAS Mk2 or HAS Mk3, and prior to the Mk8 aircraft joining, six aircraft were modified to HAS Mk3CTS incorporating the Central Tactical System. To operate these, the Lynx Operational Flying Training Unit was established on 1st September 1989 tasked with evaluation, flying trials, support and maintenance requirements for the new Mk8 helicopter before the IFTU formed.

To introduce the Mk8 to the FAA, No. 700L Sqdn. Lynx IFTU reformed on 6th July 1990 equipped with three HAS Mk3CTS helicopters, receiving the first fully modified models in mid 1992. The only change to the proposed design was the retaining of the original Sea Spray 180 degree radar.

Both the training squadron and the FL squadron operated a mix of HAS Mk3s and HAS Mk8s whilst the helicopters underwent the modification programme at the Fleetlands aircraft yard. The Unit eventually joined No. 815 Sqdn. as the Lynx

RFA Argus

OEU on 14th June 1994, and the first Mk8 sea trials were completed in HMS *Montrose* during January 1995.

THE FAA UNDER ONE FLAG

A major development in FAA control came into effect on 23rd March 1990 with the establishing of the Flag Officer Naval Aviation (FONA), responsible for all aspects of naval aviation. Since aircraft were first introduced into RN service, the control and operation of them has been divided under the control of different flag officers. Now it was to be under a single Flag Officer accountable for all naval aviation matters.

The first FONA was R. Adm. M Layard with his headquarters at Yeovilton, and it was fitting that this Officer was the first FONA as he was the first OIC for DNW with the MoD changes of 1985. This would remain extant until the new millennium when FONA would cease to exist as the British Forces combined their assets.

NAVY MERLIN GOES TO SEA

The naval prototype EH101 Merlin helicopter carried out its first sea trials aboard HMS *Norfolk*, a Type 23 Destroyer, with the first landing taking place on 15th November 1990. Designed to operate the helicopter when it comes into service, the ship has the support facilities embodied including a new auto deck handling equipment, the first class of RN ships to have this fitted. The system allows for the moving of the helicopter from the deck into the hangar and vice versa. It stands proud of the deck, so to produce a flush deck it is fitted with teak planks.

The first time the naval Merlin embarked on an Invincible class ship was for the Royal Navy Equipment Exhibition of September 1991, when the helicopter operated from HMS *Ark Royal's* flight deck.

THE GULF WAR

After the war with Iran, Iraq owed the small oil rich state of Kuwait many millions of dollars in loan repayments. The Iraqi President, Saddam Hussein, was pressurising the State (which had been declared part of Iraq) for concessions, with the threat that without them he would invade the State. No concessions were forthcoming so on 2nd August 1990 he invaded, taking control of Kuwait on the 4th. His actions were condemned by most of the world including the majority of Arab States and, from the first invasion, the UN demanded he withdraw. Instead, on the 8th August, he declared Kuwait as the nineteenth province of Iraq.

Westland Lynx HAS Mk8

The crisis worsened when Saddam declared all Western people in Iraq were now 'Guests' of his country and would remain in the country. If the indicated aggression by the US resulted in military action, he would use these guests as human shields around military installations.

The UN imposed economic sanctions in an attempt to force Saddam to back down on 6th August, followed on the 25th by authority for the Gulf Allies to use military force to ensure the sanctions were upheld. A blockade of Iraq ports was established by the Allies' warships, and this blockade was to progress to an air embargo on 25th September. The UN finally gave Saddam an ultimatum to comply to the UN resolutions by 15th January 1991 unconditionally and, if he failed to do so, permission was granted for the Allies to use whatever means necessary to remove him from Kuwait.

OPERATION GRANBY

President Bush ordered his Forces to neighbouring Saudi Arabia to prevent Saddam entering the country, known as operation Desert Shield. The world united in supporting the UN sanctions for Saddam to withdraw, and then joined forces with the might of the USA. Military forces from all over the world began to build up around Kuwait, with Forces assembling in Turkey, the eastern Mediterranean, the Red Sea and the Persian Gulf, and in the gulf states of Saudi Arabia, United Arab Emirates and Oman. British Forces were to join the Allied Force under the code Operation Granby, with the RAF and Army providing the bulk of the forces.

Ten Lynx helicopters were operated in the Gulf from both No. 815 and No. 829 Sqdns., embarked aboard the frigates and destroyers. Some of these were the first

Westland Lynx HAS Mk3CTS

Westland Sea King HCMk4s at Al Jubail in Saudi Arabia during the Gulf War

FAA aircraft on patrol having been in the Gulf on Armilla Patrol escorting friendly oil tankers through the Gulf. They were tasked with enforcing the embargo and regularly landed boarding parties aboard suspect ships. Another role was identifying and watching the Iraqi Navy patrol boats who were laying minefields around the coast of Iraq and Kuwait.

Once the UN action to liberate Kuwait began on 17th January 1991, the FAA Lynx helicopters were the main naval helicopter force searching out and attacking Exocet capable Iraqi patrol boats. The Lynx flights accounted for fifteen Iraqi warships using their Sea Skua missiles, most of which were fast patrol boats, and the aircraft were also used to assist in the capturing of Iraqi occupied oil platforms. The combined FAA Lynx Force flew the equivalent of seven months of operations in the six weeks of action.

COMMANDO SQUADRONS

The FAA was to supply three squadrons of Sea King Mk4 Commandos; Nos. 845, 846 and 848 Sqdns. The first unit to be sent to the theatre, No. 846, went to the Gulf during October 1990 aboard the RFAs *Argus*, *Fort Grange* and *Olna*. RFA *Argus* was in the theatre in the role of hospital ship and had beds and operating theatres erected in the hangar.

The Sea Kings operated as casualty evacuation helicopters fitted with cabin stretchers for the transferring of men from the front line back to Argus. All the Sea King Mk4 helicopters were wearing a pink desert camouflage scheme, and were fitted with secure speech, IR jammers and radar warning, satellite communications and IFF equipment and sand filters for operations in the theatre.

The twelve aircraft of the other two squadrons were being delivered to the Gulf aboard SS *Atlantic Conveyor*, flying to Southampton for onward shipment. Arriving in the theatre on 5th January, they were offloaded to Al Jubail in Saudi Arabia in support of the 1st Armoured Division and the 4/7 Armoured Division of the British Army. No. 848 Sqdn. had been formed specifically for the Gulf War, commissioned on 16th November 1990, and would be disbanded upon returning after the conflict.

The two assault squadrons carried out their usual tasks of transferring men and equipment alongside the RAF Chinooks and Pumas as part of the Support Helicopter Force Middle East, operating initially from King Abdul Aziz Naval Academy (named NAS 'Flip Flop' by the crews), where they carried out two weeks of desert operation familiarisation.

Westland Sea King HCMk4s over the desert

Moving to King Khalad Military City (Strawberry Fields), the two squadrons operated a 48-hour shift routine supporting the Forces build up. They were to accompany the Forces as they advanced into Iraq carrying out SAR and casualty evacuation operations, some deep inside enemy territory and, after the Iraqi surrender on 26th February, they would transport POWs to holding camps. The Sea Kings were mostly withdrawn in March, with the final detachment from No. 845 Sqdn. leaving on 12th May 1991.

SEA KING MINESWEEPERS

Two Sea King HAS Mk5s of D Flight, No. 826 Sqdn., arrived aboard RFA *Olna* before transferring to the Dutch Oiler HrMS *Zuiderkruis* for the enforcing of the embargo, intercepting shipping heading for Iraqi ports. This flight was relieved by C

Westland Sea King HCMk4 at King Abdul Aziz Naval Academy 'NAS Flip Flop'

Flight on 13th December who were used during the Desert Storm operations to look for Iraqi mines and to patrol the southern Persian Gulf for sanction busters.

Operating on Argus and Sir Galahad, the squadron maintained a rapid mine detection alert state as their aircraft had been fitted with mine spotting equipment. Once the war began, they were busy locating mines in the proposed amphibious assault and naval bombardment areas and, by the time a cease fire was called, the squadron had located 44 mines, 30% of those discovered by the MCM fleet. The honour of being the first British helicopter in Kuwait City on the morning of liberation was bestowed to the squadron who now had the role of controlling Lynx and Sea Cobra probing flights looking for Iraqi troops.

Sea Harriers were prepared for operations in the war including the trial of a special colour scheme, however they were not deployed.

OPERATION SAFE HAVEN

With the war in Kuwait over, Saddam concentrated his efforts on annihilating the Kurds in the north of Iraq. UN Forces were required to provide protection and emergency relief for these people and again the commando squadrons were to be used. No. 845 Sqdn. was to send four aircraft from the Gulf to the large Turkish base of Incirlik aboard the merchant ship SS *Baltic Eagle*. The detachment was on passage back to the UK when it was diverted to Turkey, arriving on 22nd April.

In support was No. 846 Sqdn. operating in southern Turkey at Silopi, a US tented city on the Iraqi/Syrian/Turkey border. The squadron arrived on 30th April after being transported by Argus, the ship they had been on during the Gulf War only two weeks previous. The squadron later divided, with one detachment going to Incirlik and returning to the UK on 5th July aboard SS *Arcadian Queen*, whilst the remainder returned to the UK on 30th May from Silopi aboard SS *Baltic Eagle*.

The squadrons joined the multi-national Force as part of Joint Task Force Bravo, establishing a safe haven for the Kurds away from the interference of the Iraqis. The helicopters supported the RMs, moving them and their equipment as required, and carrying out medical evacuations and humanitarian missions. For the latter, the squadron transported the Kurdish leaders to convince the Kurds that they were going to be safe in the refugee camps. During the operation, the Sea Kings transported 500,000 tons of stores and 7600 troops flying a total of nearly 1200 hours.

BAe SHAR FRSMk1 wearing special colour scheme to be adopted for the Gulf Theatre. This was not to be and no other aircraft received the scheme

NEW COLOURS FOR THE FAA

The FAA was presented with its new colours by HM Queen Elizabeth during a ceremony at Yeovilton on 27th June 1991. Each air station supplied a platoon for the parade, and the old colours were trooped by a platoon of artificer apprentices whilst the new colours were trooped by a platoon of mechanics, both from the air engineering school at HMS Daedalus.

The static and flying display involved all the types of aircraft in service and some older types including the only air-worthy Sea Vixen D3, a target drone from RAE Llanbedr. In all, 56 aircraft took part in the flying display.

NEW AMPHIBIOUS SHIPS ANNOUNCED

The Defence White Paper of February 1992 announced the intention to replace the two assault ships HMSs *Fearless* and *Intrepid* with two new amphibious ships to be named HMS *Albion* and HMS *Bulwark* in the early part of the next century. Project definition contracts were awarded for the design of the new ships to be submitted for these two Landing Platform Docking Ships to enter service in 2001/2002.

The paper also announced a new helicopter carrier was to be built as a commando support ship with combined command capabilities. With the increasing number of tasks supporting UN operations, it was identified that since the scrapping of HMS *Bulwark* ten years earlier and the unreliability of the two old amphibious ships, the RMC have been relying on RFAs and merchant ships to provide transportation and operating facilities for the 3CB and the commando helicopter squadrons.

Exercises had frequently been carried out using the Invincible class carriers, but these were also involved supplying patrols over UN theatres, thus it was seen that this new ship was a priority. The ship, ordered in May 1993, was designed around the hull of the Invincible class with the same propulsion as the new RFAs. This use of similarity resulted in the 21,000 ton ship being launched on 11th October 1995, 32 months after it was first announced.

HMS Albion

Westland Sea King HC4 dropping chaff (Crown copyright MoD via the FAA publication 'Flight Deck')

FAREWELL TO THE SHARKS

After seventeen years as the premier FAA display team, the Sharks of No. 705 Sqdn. were to disband at the end of the 1992 display season. It was a volunteer team supported by civilian operators, with the helicopters flown by instructors from the squadron. Initially forming with six Gazelles, it was to reduce to four before finally retiring. No. 705 Sqdn. continued to provide aircraft for air displays using either a single Gazelle or two known as the Gazelle Pair until the type was withdrawn at the end of the 1996 season.

THE FORMER YUGOSLAVIA

With the breakdown of communism throughout Eastern Europe, the former country of Yugoslavia began to divide producing fighting amongst rival factions of Slovacs and Serbs. The first fighting broke out in the Serb province of Kosovo, the home to Ethnic Albanians on 24th January 1990. Eventually the Albanians declared independence from Serbia on 2nd July which was refuted by the Serbian Government. Slovenia declared itself a republic the following day and after an election in December, it declared independence from Yugoslavia.

The break-up of this once quiet country began to reveal hidden hatred between the different communities, producing much fighting and loss of life. In Bosnia Herzegovina, there were three communities of equal size - Croatians, Muslims and Serbs who all wanted to control their own lands. Intense fighting began in late 1992 resulting in the UN sending a Peace Keeping Force to protect the Bosnians and Muslims from the Serbs who had decided they wanted all the land for themselves, beginning a campaign of 'ethnic cleansing'.

OPERATION GRAPPLE

British assistance was given to the UN Forces providing aid to the Croatians in November. No. 845 Sqdn. sent four Sea King Mk4 Commandos to Split to assist in the humanitarian aid, arriving aboard RFA *Argus* on 14th December 1992, wearing the standard all-white UN colours.

Continuing where they left off during the Gulf War, the squadron was involved with supporting the British troops and CASEVAC missions. However their role was to change when they were called upon to evacuate 300 injured Muslims in Srebrenica who had been attacked by the Bosnian Serb army intending to eradicate them. This was to be a joint FAA/French Army operation involving the aircraft operating over hostile Serb held territory.

The three Sea Kings moved to the UN HQ at Kiseljak whilst the French Pumas operated from their base at Tuzla. The UN had gained Serb permission to overfly their territory provided they were inspected at Zvornik for weapons. The French began the operations but after arriving at Srebrenica, the Serbs began shelling the landing site, resulting in the cessation of the operation.

Two Sea Kings arrived at the town, one landing to rescue the Muslims whilst the other maintained an orbit over the site, then they reversed roles. Returning to Tuzla, they were shelled whilst disembarking their human cargo, but eventually the mission was completed although the aircraft were constantly fired at by the Serbs.

OPERATION DENY FLIGHT

The UN placed a 'no fly' zone over the area which was to be patrolled by the SHAR of the FAA. First to arrive were the FRS1s of No. 801 Sqdn. embarked in HMS *Ark Royal*, which arrived in the Adriatic on 26th January 1993. Sailing with the carrier was Argus returning with 350 troops, their vehicles and equipment supported by No. 846 Sqdn.

The SHARs enforced the 'no fly' zone operating alongside the aircraft of other NATO countries involved in the operation. They were tasked with preventing non-UN flights in Bosnian air space, CAP flights above the Fleet operating in the Adriatic, support for the UN F16s on offensive counter strikes, close air support for the ground troops and reconnaissance missions. For this latter role, RM Ground Liaison Officers were used as the direct link between the squadrons and ground forces.

Reconnaissance flights were to become the primary mission, the results from the flights were able to be interpreted in quick time, and counter strikes against

Sharks Display Team

No. 800 Sqdn. SHAR Mk1 in flight (BAe Systems)

Serb positions could be implemented before they were relocated. One such strike by two SHARs of No. 801 Sqdn. on 16th April ended when one of the aircraft was hit by an anti-aircraft missile, the pilot ejected and was successfully rescued. This was the first UN aircraft hit by ground fire and the first FAA aircraft lost since the Falklands War. The British carriers were to continue operations with the two operational ships rotating, ensuring the pressure was kept up.

Ark Royal finished her final tour on 4th September 1994 before going to refit. Taking her place in the rota would be HMS *Illustrious* returning to the Fleet after a five year lay off and refit. Invincible arrived off-station on 23rd August with No. 800 Sqdn. on the last deployment with the FRS1, as the SHARs aboard Illustrious would be the new FRS Mk2s of No. 801 Sqdn. During the operations, two SHARs were fired on by Serbs, their missiles missing the aircraft which returned back to the ship safely.

OPERATION SHARP GUARD

The UN Fleet operating in the Adriatic during June 1993 was to enforce the embargo on unauthorised ships entering Yugoslavia. Operating along the Montenegro coast, the helicopters of the FAA had a major role to play, with the AEW Sea Kings active in the locating of possible renegade ships. The AEW task for the fighter operations was from the NATO AWACS aircraft. Once a target was detected, the AEW would task one of the Lynx flights to intercept the ship and land a UN boarding party.

PROPOSED PEACE

With indications that an end to the hostilities could be found, a ceasefire was called on 23rd February 1994 between the Croatians and Muslims. The Sea Kings of No. 845 Sqdn. were active in flying the delegates for the talks held at the Winter Olympic Hotel in Sarajevo. Until the talks, the only route the helicopters could fly was at 2000ft in designated air corridors (even then they were fired upon). Now the talks were in progress, unrestricted operations over the Croatian and Muslim areas could be flown.

Until now, the helicopters had remained at Split but a detachment was moved forward to Gorni Vakuf (7th June), tasked with reconnaissance flights over Mostar and Sarajevo combined with VIP and UN observer transport flights in the area. These were to ensure the Serbs observed the Sarajevo exclusion zone, and the squadron still continued its CASEVAC and humanitarian missions throughout the theatre.

Westland Sea King AEWMk2

Above: BAe SHAR FRS Mk2 OEU

Below: BAe SHAR FRS2 trials onboard HMS Ark Royal

Bottom: HMS Illustrious post refit - after five years in reserve and a refit

Toward The Millenium

THE SHAR FRS MK2 JOINS THE FAA

With the arrival into service of the new aircraft, the SHAR OEU was formed at the A & AEE at Boscombe Down on 1st June 1993. The OEU was part of the SHAR training squadron, No. 899 Sqdn. based at Yeovilton, the aircraft wearing their mail fist emblem with the letter OEU on the top of the fin.

The first FRS Mk2 was delivered to the Unit soon after commissioning and a comprehensive series of trials and evaluation programmes were held over a six month period. The OEU is responsible for validating the aircraft's operational roles and for developing the service operating tactics. The initial type trials were held using the first two completed aircraft attached to the A & AEE and BAe. These included carrier qualification trials aboard HMS *Ark Royal* during November 1990 when both aircraft embarked. Further sea trials with OEU aircraft were conducted during October 1993 to evaluate night flying operations aboard Ark Royal.

ALL ONE REPLENISHMENT SHIPS

The RFA Fleet was increased with the commissioning of the two Fort Victoria class All One Replenishment (AOR) ships designed to operate independently from a fleet capable of supplying fuel, stores and ammunition to the ships it was supporting. These two 'one stop' ships, RFAs *Fort George* and *Fort Victoria*, were the first armed ships of the navy's merchant fleet, armed with vertical launched Sea Wolf missiles. They were designed to embark up to three EH101s, the ships being fitted out to support the embarked flight during long deployments. Until the arrival of the Merlin, they would operate Sea Kings.

Both ships were laid down in 1988, capable of operating and supporting large ASW helicopters as well as being available as an emergency deck for SHARs if necessary. Fort George was the first to be commissioned during October 1993 after which she conducted helicopter operating trials, embarking her first squadron, No. 819 Sqdn., in June 1994.

Fort Victoria entered service in 1994. Until now, RFAs had detachments of FAA personnel attached to them to operate the ship's aviation element. With these new ships, the crew also included operations and weapons electrical personnel to look after, maintain and operate the Sea Wolf missiles. These Unit (RFANSU) personnel would become part of the RFA naval support organisation at Culdrose.

HMS ILLUSTRIOUS REFITTED

HMS *Illustrious* sailed from Devonport for its first set of sea trials during February 1994. It received its first aircraft on the deck for five years when a Sea King of No. 810 Sqdn., the Mk6 OEU, paid a visit. It sailed for its final sea trials on 25th April, and embarked Sea Kings from No. 706 Sqdn. and SHAR FRS Mk2s during May for aviation trials. It was the flag ship for the international D-Day 50th anniversary commemorations in the Solent during June, and embarked another FRS Mk2 and the civil EH101 Merlin whilst at anchor on the review day, 6th June.

The Royal Yacht, with Her Majesty the Queen on board, passed through the assembled ships after the massed flypast which consisted of over 160 aircraft and helicopters from sixteen nations. It then commenced two weeks of aircraft operational trials at the end of the month which included embarking three Harrier GR Mk7s from the RAF's Harrier OEU at Boscombe Down, onboard to gain operational status on the class. It was the first time that a GR7 had operated from the decks of the Invincible class and, after gaining clearance, the type was to see many operations in the Adriatic alongside the SHARs.

SEA HARRIER REPLACEMENT

By 1994, plans were proposed to replace the SHAR with a combined USMC/FAA Future Carrier Borne Aircraft, a single engined, multi-role short take-off and vertical landing (STOVL) strike fighter.

By December 1995 the requirements had changed and an aircraft was required for all the US Forces as well as the RN. This new project was the joint advanced strike technology programme, to be altered again six months later when it became a Joint Service Fighter capable of a short take-off but arrested landing (STOBAR).

Boeing Aircraft (X32/32B) and Lockheed Martin (X35/35B) aircraft companies were awarded development contracts for 2 aircraft each; one conventional, the other a STOVL design. The aircraft were to take part in trials by 2000 when the most suitable design would be selected as the replacement aircraft.

RAF TYPES JOIN INVENTORY

The Hawker Hunters of Flight Refuelling were replaced with ex-RAF Hawk jet trainers, joining the FRADU fleet in May

Lockheed Martin X35 (Lockheed Martin)

Boeing X32 (Boeing)

Ex-RAF BAe Hawk on initial receipt still wearing its training colours

1994 at Yeovilton. The aircraft began replacing the Hunter which was retired at the end of the year. The compliment of Hawks was to increase from eight at the end of 1994 to fifteen by the time the contract to operate the Hawks was awarded to Huntings with effect from 1st December 1995. The aircraft are operated from Culdrose.

Fully fledged RN Hawks at RNAS Culdrose.

After 28 years providing electronic counter-measure training for all the services' ECM units, No. 360 Sqdn. RAF disbanded on 31st October 1994. The Unit had formed with the amalgamation of No. 831 Sqdn. FAA and No. 97 Sqdn. RAF on 1st April 1966 and was originally titled the Joint Trials & Training Squadron, receiving full squadron status on 1st September 1966.

It was manned with 25% FAA engineers, and every fourth squadron CO was to be from the FAA. It was to receive a squadron standard from HRH the Duke of Kent on 8th July 1992, a standard which is awarded after 25 years continuous service. The last squadron commanding officer fell to an FAA pilot, Lt. Cdr. P Shaw, who was also the last pilot to receive conversion training to the Canberra, the type's operational conversion unit (OCU) disbanding in March 1993 after over 40 years.

The last operational flight of the squadron's Canberra T17A was flown on 21st October, a week before the disbanding parade when the last flight of the type in service was flown over the parade, thus ending the FAA's long association with the Canberra. The role has now been civilianised and Flight Refuelling has a contract using their Falcon 20s in the role.

BAe SHAR F/A2

SHAR MK2 JOINS FLS

The sun sets on the BAe SHAR FRSMk1 after a distinguished career, The first of the two FLSs to equip with the FRS Mk2 was No. 801 Sqdn. which received four aircraft in 1994. Its first operations whilst deployed in HMS *Invincible* was during the ship's Deny Flight operations over Bosnia in the Adriatic during the 1994/95 winter operations in the theatre. It operated the aircraft alongside the FRS Mk1s of its sister squadron, No. 800 Sqdn., which re-equipped with the new aircraft upon its return from the deployment during March 1995. The designation for the new Harrier was to change from FRS to F/A (Fighter/Attack) to follow the designations used by the NATO Forces. Pilot training for the FRS2 was carried out using four T-8Ns which are similar to the older trainers but fitted with the FRS2's cockpit layout and avionics equipment plus it has a revised nose profile. These four aircraft entered service during 1996.

CIVILIAN HELICOPTERS RELIEVE THE LOAD

Whilst operational sea training was carried out at Portland, the HDS service to transport the staff of FOST around the ships was supplied by No. 772 Sqdn. When the training commitment moved to Plymouth on 11th September 1995, the squadron disbanded and Bond Helicopters were contracted to supply helicopters from Plymouth airport for the HDS task. These helicopters were of the size capable of recovering on small decks, and were to eventually wear the RN titles and military aircraft serials. Two bright red Dauphine helicopters were chartered under the HTUFT (Helicopters Taken Up From Trade) scheme, a scheme which came into being during the Falklands War and which has been increasingly used since.

From October 1996, all the basic helicopter

English Electric Canberra TT17

training for British military helicopter pilots would be using helicopters in the scheme. The Gazelles of No. 705 Sqdn. were retired on 31st October 1996, replaced with Squirrels and Griffons operated by the Defence Helicopter Flying School (DHFS) at RAF Shawbury.

A NEW CARRIER IS LAUNCHED

HMS *Ocean* was to sail to Barrow-in-Furness for final fitting out by Vickers Shipbuilding during November 1996 completing machinery trials en-route. Designed primarily as an amphibious ship, she is also capable of embarking Sea Harriers and ASW helicopters and, at 21,500 tons, she is the largest RN ship for 40 years.

Her normal compliment will be a mix of the commando helicopter force of Sea King Mk4s, Gazelles and Lynx helicopters. She can also operate the Puma, Chinook and Merlin helicopters. The hangar is large enough to accommodate twelve of the larger Merlin helicopters or fifteen Sea Harriers, and there are two lifts both situated alongside the large island superstructure.

Designed to carry 800 fully equipped marines from the joint UK/Neth commando force, the assault routes - passageways used by the troops to get from their messes to the hangar quickly - are purposely designed for convenience and the ladders to the hangar are wide and shallow. The embarking and disembarking routine for the marines is via the hangar deck. The four landing craft bays have direct access from the hangar, whilst the vehicle deck has a ramp giving direct access to the flight deck. A stern ramp gives the ability to embark vehicles directly from ashore similar to a car ferry into the vehicle deck which has the ability to accommodate up to 40 vehicles.

This is the first true commando carrier for the RN as the five previous carriers were built as fixed-wing carriers, three of which were converted for the role. The requirement for this ship came from the lack of a major commando carrying ship during the Falklands War, and it is the first carrier which does not have a permanent Air Engineering Department manning workshops. The facilities are available but are manned by squadron personnel when embarked, reducing the size of the permanent ship's company.

COMMANDO SQUADRONS REORGANISED

No. 848 Sqdn. commissioned on 9th February 1995 with the aircraft and staff of No. 707 Sqdn. continuing the role of training, RM support and UK security

Eurocopter Dauphine of Bond Helicopters

HMS Ocean, the amphibious LPH (Landing Platform Helicopter) ship

contingency operations, the latter role previously operated by No. 772 Sqdn. at Portland. The rebirth of the squadron was due to the need for FL use of the squadron's aircraft, as the two other squadrons, Nos. 845 and 846, have commitments that are reducing the availability of Sea King Mk4s for supporting roles.

The 3rd CBAS Lynx and Gazelles were to form the new No. 847 Sqdn. Although now an integral part of the FAA, the squadron is still manned by REME engineers and Royal Marine pilots and the aircraft are operated as previously when with the AAC. This gave the FAA four front line commando units.

OPERATION DENY FLIGHT/ DELIBERATE FORCE

HMS *Illustrious* arrived in the Adriatic to commence her first operations during February 1995, with the new SHAR FRS2s providing 24 hour cover for the relief flights into Sarajevo and Tuzla, continuing the Deny Flight operations. With the rebel Serbs not bowing to the UN demands and continuing with their brutal fighting against the ethnic minorities, the UN stepped up its campaign. Operation Deliberate Force gave the UN Forces the permission to commence strikes against Serb positions commencing in September. This gave the Mk2 SHAR its first strike missions. No. 800 Sqdn. in HMS *Invincible* (which had relieved Illustrious) attacked ammunition dumps and Serb storage facilities.

The strikes were by four SHARs loaded with two 1000lb bombs each, and they would carry out a steep dive at the target releasing their bombs at medium altitude which reduced their chances of being hit by ground fire. During the period 5th-14th September, twenty-one missions were completed. The aircraft were also tasked with completing PR missions for damage assessment after strikes by all the UN/NATO aircraft. The aircraft would then return to the ship where the film would be immediately studied and the results sent to HQ.

After two months of operations, the Dayton Peace Accord was signed and the role of the UN Forces was now one of implementation of the accord. Illustrious returned to the theatre in December 1995 and became part of the NATO Implementation Force (IFOR) for the operation coded Decisive Edge. The SHARs were to continue their PR operations and provide escort cover against some Serb rebels for the IFOR helicopters in the region.

HMS DAEDALUS CLOSES DOWN

The oldest FAA base at Lee-on-Solent

RM Lynx AH1 and Gazelle AH1 (Crown copyright MoD via the FAA publication 'Flight Deck')

Sea King HCMk4 No. 848 Sqdn.

BAe SHAR F/A2

closed its gates for the last time after 79 years operating aircraft involved with naval aviation. The closing down ceremony was held on 29th March 1996 when the White Ensign was ceremoniously lowered. At the top of the flag staff was a 75ft paying-off pennant, normally flown on ships as they sail into port for the last time. This is the first known occasion that a shore establishment has flown a pennant, and it was conceived and paid for by the Fleet Air Arm Association. This ceremony was followed by a parade marching through the local streets with the final salute being taken by Captain David Newberry.

The base began life as a seaplane base for the RNAS in 1917 and remained as an operational base with Coastal Command of the RAF. It became the headquarters of the FAA when it was re-established in 1939, and eventually became the FAA's training establishment whilst remaining an operational base with a variety of lodger units and home to the SAR and Communications Squadron, No. 781 Sqdn., until it disbanded on 31st March 1981.

Post war it was the operating base for aircraft and helicopters for two Fleet Reviews; the Coronation Review of 1953 and the Silver Jubilee Review in 1977. It hosted the international Helicopter Search and Rescue meeting during the 1970s and its final heyday was for the 50th anniversary commemorations of the D Day landings - 'Operation Overlord'- on 6th June 1994 when it was the support airfield for the event in Portsmouth and also hosted the US Presidential Flight helicopters. The weekend activities resulted in the busiest

Westland Sea King HC4 wearing IFOR markings

HMS Daedalus' ship's pennant

FAA Field Gun Crew

period in the base's post war period with over 500 aircraft movements. After the war, it became the FAA's drafting and discharge centre, but retained its status as the 'Front Line' disembarked flights' base until 1959 when the last front line aircraft departed.

The RN Aircraft Electrical School, previously based at Worthy Down near Winchester, began moving in to the establishment in 1957, paving the way for the eventual re-siting of all FAA Trade Training at the base. On 1st November, it was renamed HMS Ariel although the name Daedalus was still evident on the base. Wykeham Hall remained as the HQ for FONAC (Flag Officer Naval Air Command) retaining the name. Various Units (some with aircraft, some not) have been based at Lee since becoming Non-Operational, those with aircraft being: HMS Endurance Flight with its two Whirlwind aircraft, No. 781 Squadron with its mix of VIP aircraft, an RAF SAR Flight 1982-84 before being replaced by a Wessex V detachment from No. 772 Squadron Portland, and now the Coast Guard SAR Flight operated by Bristow's Helicopters.

The Southampton University Air Squadron operated from the establishment with their four SA Bulldogs, as well as the Hampshire Police Flight, the RN Portsmouth Gliding Club and the RN Hovercraft Unit. Non-aircraft units consisted of the Naval Aircraft Technical Evaluation Centre (NATEC) - this unit evaluated and procured equipment for use ashore and onboard ships operating aircraft; the Mobile Aircraft Recovery Transport & Salvage Unit which relocated to Fleetlands with the new title Mobile Aircraft Support Unit (MASU) responsible for repairing, transporting and recovering crashed helicopters of all three armed services, and the transporting of RN historic aircraft; the Naval Aircraft Trials & Installation Unit which was responsible for designing, procuring and carrying out equipment and aircraft modifications for RN aircraft, carrying out the initial proving fit of any equipment before fleet modification by user units.

Sea King AEW Mk5

This unit, although now absorbed by the MASU and the RN Aircraft Accident Investigation Unit - an autonomous unit which investigates all RN aircraft accidents on the same lines as the civilian aircraft accident investigation at Farnborough, hopefully solves the reason for any crashes and recommends actions to be taken to prevent them reoccurring. This Unit is now part of the RN Flight Safety Centre at Yeovilton still carrying out the task as it has done since 1946.

One of the most important public relations organisations within the RN was the Field Gun Crews who always delighted the crowds at the Royal Tournament, the FAA 'Men of Green'. The crew moved to Culdrose after the base closed down and remained there until after the last Royal Tournament in July 1999.

JOINT FORCE OPERATIONS

With the run down of requirements for the UN in the Adriatic, training programmes especially in ASW could be recommenced. Limited exercises had been carried out using the RFAs as the support ships, but now the carriers were released (including RFA *Argus*), the 'pingers' could practice their art with gusto and the ships could also carry out visits to exotic ports. It was not all fun though, and some units were still active in peace operations. No. 845 Sqdn. was still active in Bosnia and No. 846 Sdqn. was deployed to Northern Ireland supporting the Armagh Roulement Battalion in the province.

HMS *Invincible* was to exercise in the Persian Gulf during October and November, the first time the SHAR F/A2 had been in the theatre. Although not flying over the Iraqi 'No Fly Zone', the Iraqi Forces were aware the British carrier was in the Gulf.

On the development side, the Sea King

AEW Mk2 aircraft were being considered for upgrade for the first time since their introduction fourteen years earlier. Three ASW Mk5 aircraft were to be modified into AEW Mk5 aircraft by Westlands, thus relieving the older aircraft which would go into storage.

The Merlin helicopter was approaching introduction to the FAA, and was being assessed at A & AEE Boscombe Down for release into service, joining the IFTU in December 1998.

During the operations in the Adriatic, SHARs had been joined by RAF GR7s for joint operations. These operations with the two aircraft types proved complimentary, the SHAR providing radar cover whilst the GR7s completed the bulk of the strike missions. The requirements of the British Forces had changed dramatically over the last few years, and they were now an accepted part of the UN worldwide peace keeping force which could be called upon at short notice for joint nation operations.

The MOD introduced a Permanent Joint Force at Northwood Headquarters and the organisation was responsible for co-ordinating a Force for rapid deployment to trouble spots worldwide, based on the use of the Invincible class carrier as the main force. Upon deploying, the operation would be co-ordinated by the Joint Force HQ Afloat, a self-supported mobile HQ.

OPERATION DURAL/BOLTON

Whilst in the Gulf, the SHARs of No. 801 Sqdn. took part in operations over the Iraqi No-fly Zone during March. They were the first British fighter aircraft to operate in the 'Southern Watch' patrol areas of the Gulf, tasked with providing fighter cover for the RAF Tornado bombers. In all, eighteen operations were flown including six missions into Iraqi air space. More operations were to be flown early in 1998 when the SHARs of No. 800 Sqdn. would operate in the Gulf.

The Iraqis were denying admission to the weapon sites by UN monitors and HMS *Invincible*, on an autumn cruise to the Caribbean and USA, was redeployed to the Eastern Mediterranean with RFA *Fort Victoria* in company. As the ship entered the Mediterranean, she embarked the GR7s of No. 1 (F) Sqdn. RAF on 21st November for the first combined air operations as a joint force - Operation Bolton. HMS *Invincible* and RFA *Fort Victoria* moved into the Gulf on 25th January 1998 to operate alongside the two US carriers, the George Washington and Independence, for the combined operations against strategic and military targets in Iraq.

No 800 Sqdn SHAR

The Harriers would operate together, four SHAR providing fighter cover for four GR7s in the strike role. The intention was for the British aircraft to fly two eight-aircraft missions per day, one in the morning and one in the afternoon, and these were doubled as the pressure on Saddam Hussein was intensified. A second force of HMS *Illustrious* and RFA *Fort George* left the UK in late January to relieve Invincible. Embarked were the SHARs of No. 801 Sqdn. and the GR7s of No. 3 Sqdn. RAF. They relieved Invincible and Fort Victoria during March and continued the operations until the Force stood down in April 1998. Between the four squadrons, over 800 hours of operational missions were flown and the joint force concept was a proven success.

COMMANDO BRIGADE AIR SQUADRONS JOIN THE FAA

Having been conceived as an airborne RM Unit, No. 3 CBAS was a regiment of the Army Air Corps attached to the Royal Marines based at Middle Wallop. Post-war flying in the RMC began when Lt. R Learoyd RM gained his wings in 1961 and began flying AAC helicopters. By 1965 there were enough RM officers qualified as pilots for a detachment of three Sioux helicopters to be attached to No. 42 RMC. As more pilots qualified, a separate brigade was established on 12th August 1968 - 3 Commando Brigade Air Squadron (3CBAS). The Brigade annually moved its operations for the No. 45 RMC exercises in northern Norway, working as independent

RAF Harrier GR7

No 847 Sqdn. Westland Lynx AH1

units alongside the Wessex Vs and Sea King Mk4s of the Junglie squadrons and embarking on the amphibious ships. The Sioux were replaced with the Gazelle AH1s from the mid 1970s and were operated in flights from Coypool in Plymouth and Arbroath for liaison and observation duties. The last Sioux was passed to the FAA museum in 1984.

The Brigade received the Lynx AH1 helicopter with the armour piercing anti-tank missile system during the 1980s, and this has now been upgraded to the AH7. Moving to Yeovilton after the Falklands War, the Brigade took its eight Army Gazelles and six Lynx helicopters and REME engineers to operate more closely with the Sea King HC Mk4s of the 'Junglie' squadrons. The squadron was renumbered No. 847 Sqdn. during 1997 at Yeovilton with the same tasking and roles in support of the RM Corps. The aircraft are maintained to Army schedules and routines and flown by RM pilots, including the only NCO aircrew in the FAA. After initial and naval helicopter training at RAF Shawbury, the RM pilots receive their specialist 'Army style' training with the AAC No. 670 Sqdn. at Middle Wallop before receiving the Navy Wings (in recognition that they are naval pilots not army pilots). The first RM pilot to complete the course and receive these gilt wings (rather than previously receiving the AAC blue wings) was Lt. J Roylance RM when receiving his navy wings on 18th September 1998.

A DRAMATIC RESCUE

A dramatic rescue operation was carried out by No. 810 Sqdn. whilst embarked in RFA *Argus*, the training carrier, in the Atlantic Ocean during February 1998. The gales were so severe that flying was cancelled onboard the ship but a message was received that the SS *Delfin del Mediterreneo*, a Spanish container ship, had sunk 200 miles west of Lisbon. The ship launched two helicopters to attempt a rescue of the fourteen crew who were floating in lifeboats, at the extreme range of the Sea Kings' endurance. Both helicopters reached the scene and although not SAR crew, members of the crew were lowered into the sea to rescue the sailors, one CPO receiving injuries which rendered him unconscious. All the crew were saved and the helicopters safely returned to the ship. All ten members of the helicopter crews received bravery awards for volunteering their service for the rescue, the most awards given during a single peacetime operation. Three received the Air Force Cross, six the Queen's Commendation for Bravery in the Air, and one CinC Fleets Commendation.

JF2000

Following the successful joint missions during Operation Bolton in the Gulf, the Government announced in the 1998 Strategic Defence Review that the British Harrier Force of SHAR F/A Mk2 and GR7 aircraft were to combine as Joint Force 2000 (JF2000). The German-based Harriers and Yeovilton-based SHAR aircraft would all locate to RAF Cottesmore in 2003, whilst the Wittering-based Harriers would remain at their base.

The two bases would become joint operating facilities for this JF2000, and it was intended that this Force would equip with the proposed FCBA, the SHAR replacement. Since the proving trials for the GR7 aboard HMS *Illustrious* in 1994, the RAF aircraft had operated from both Illustrious and Invincible. The first move towards JF2000 was the modifications to the carriers to allow a squadron of GR7s to operate from the ships having full support facilities, and Illustrious was the first to be modified in 1998.

The review announced that the RN was to have two new attack aircraft carriers for offensive air support operations. These ships would be conventional ships in the range of 30-50,000 tons dependent on the final design requirements, based around the aircraft chosen as the replacement for the SHARs. They will be designed to operate between 40 and 50 aircraft and helicopters and should be in service around 2012/2015.

Since the first RAF Harrier deployment onboard HMS *Ark Royal (IV)*, it has been an accepted scenario for detachments of Harriers to embark on the fixed-wing carriers, especially after the operations during the Falklands War. The Invincible class of small carriers' limited space has meant control of the deck during these

No 847 Sqdn. Gazelle AH1

HMS Illustrious. Note the forward starboard flight deck extension

periods has been crucial due to the limited space available. More space has now been created by the removal of the ship's Sea Dart missile system from the forward end of the deck and the re-plating of the deck plus the covering of the open cable deck, producing a fully flush flight deck up to the forecastle. This will be the main parking and weapons loading area for the RAF GR7s when embarked.

The first ship to be refitted with this deck was HMS *Illustrious* which was refitted at Portsmouth over an eight month period from July to February 1998/9. The new deck has a special bomb lift which allows the RAF Harrier weapons to be supplied direct to the flight deck from the areas which were previously used as operating areas for the removed Sea Dart. The deck provides a large area for the storage of flight deck equipment and aircraft with an added helicopter operating spot.

Another feature fitted during the refit is a closed circuit TV system to monitor deck operations, with the cameras controlled by Flyco. The refit was completed after sea trials during February 1999 and the ship completed her operational trials during March/April before sailing to relieve HMS *Invincible* who was supporting the UN operations in the Eastern Mediterranean. Upon return to the UK, the latter ship was also refitted with the flush deck. The third ship of the class, HMS *Ark Royal* which had been placed into P by O in Portsmouth dockyard after decommissioning in 1993, was towed to Rosyth dockyard in 1999 for its first major refit when the flush deck was fitted.

THE AMPHIBIOUS FORCE

HMS *Ocean*, the RN's largest warship at 21,500 tons, commissioned at Plymouth on 30th September, seven months after the naming ceremony by HM the Queen (20th February 1998) in Barrow. She sailed for Plymouth in April carrying out sea trials en route. Whilst alongside in Plymouth she embarked aircraft for the first time when a Lynx from No. 847 Sqdn. and a Sea King Mk4 from No. 845 Sqdn. arrived on 19th August. The ship sailed on 7th September for the 'first of class' flying trials, when the various aircraft types joined the ship for trials using the deck and hangar. They were successfully completed before returning to Plymouth for the commissioning.

Operational flying trials began on 22nd October when four Sea Kings from No. 845 Sdqn. and two Gazelles and two Lynx of No. 847 Sqdn. embarked for an intensive series of exercises preparing for the first amphibious operations. The ship's amphibious trials would be unique in that they were carried out in the Caribbean embarking No. 45 RMC who were completing jungle training in Belize. The amphibious embarkation was delayed after the ship was diverted to lead an international rescue task force to Honduras and Nicaragua which had been struck by Hurricane Mitch. During eight days off the Central American coast, the ship distributed over 100 tons of food and the Royal Marines and Dutch Marines assisted ashore in clearing the damage and rescuing people. One of the Lynx helicopters rescued two Puerto Rican fishermen and another rescue mission resulted in finding and recovering the 34 crew members of a fishing boat.

ENTER THE MERLIN

The Merlin MH Mk1 IFTU, No. 700M Sqdn., commissioned at Culdrose on 1st December 1998. This new ASW helicopter has taken eleven years to reach squadron service since its first flight, but in that time the most potent ASW helicopter has been developed. The four aircraft of the IFTU will prove the operational capability of the type before it enters FL squadrons, and 44 have been ordered to replace the Sea Kings.

It is fitted with a 360 degree Blue Kestrel radar which can detect surface targets whilst using dunking sonar for submarine detection. It is the world's first helicopter capable of autonomous ASW missions, able to search, locate and attack

HMS Ocean

targets without the need of outside information sources. It is also the first ASW helicopter to require only one pilot throughout its missions, thus the crew component will be pilot, observer and crewman.

FURTHER UN SUPPORT OPERATIONS

After much warning from UN countries to Saddam Hussein that further strikes would be carried out if he continued his delaying tactics over the checking of his arms manufacturing, he continued unrelenting. It was agreed that in support of the US Forces, a British Force headed by HMS *Invincible* would be on station in the Arabian Gulf with the Joint Task Force by the end of January 1999 for operations Southern Watch and Bolton.

The ship sailed from Portsmouth after Christmas leave in company with HMS *Newcastle* and RFA *Fort Austin* arriving in theatre on the 31st of the month (as promised), after a journey of over 3000 miles. During the transit much training was carried out on the role the ship was going to play as this time it was not just a demonstration of power available, weapons were going to be used and the Iraqis would be firing back! The squadrons, No. 800 Sqdn. SHAR, No. 1(F) Sqdn. RAF GR7s, No. 814 Sqdn. ASW Sea Kings and No. 849A Flight AEW Sea Kings were trained and ready by the time they reached the Gulf. The Harriers were tasked with carrying out offensive strikes with the USN F14 Tomcat and RAF Tornado bombers in Southern attack against known weapon facilities and intercepting Iraqi aircraft that entered the 'no-fly' zone. Many missions were cancelled due to bad weather conditions but the squadrons did however achieve eighteen operational sorties without losing any aircraft.

EH101 Merlin of No. 824 Sqdn., the first commissioned unit

The helicopter squadrons played their part in the patrolling of the Gulf. The AEW Sea Kings were mainly used for searching for surface targets, looking for Iraqi fast patrol boats, and most AEW missions were by USN Hawkeye aircraft or Boeing 707 AWACS aircraft. The ASW aircraft, whilst not having an ASW role (except for training), was to carry out surveillance operations monitoring the shipping in the area. It was also busy in the HDS role between the Fleet and shore with many delivery flights taking place. The operation was completed on 1st April after successfully demonstrating the seriousness of the UN in achieving its goal of removing the huge weapons stock pile held by Hussein.

The ships headed for home but were unfortunately not to make it as they were to be diverted to assist the NATO operations in the Ionian Sea.

HMS *Invincible* was diverted to operate

with the NATO Forces assisting the Kosovon people against the Serbs, arriving in the Ionian Sea on 15th April. The helicopters of No. 814 Sqdn. were busy flying in stores and equipment for the refugees, whilst the AEW squadron was assisting in the CAP patrols being flown by the Sea Harriers. Eventually replaced by HMS *Illustrious* on its first operation since having the flight deck increased, Invincible was to return to Portsmouth to have the flight deck refit. The operations were continued until the Serbs were driven out of the area by the NATO and UN Forces during the summer when Illustrious returned to Portsmouth.

PORTLAND CLOSES

After 39 years and 341 days, the only British military helicopter base at RNAS Portland closed on 31st March 1999. A closing down open day was held on Saturday 17th October 1998, when an example of every type of helicopter that had operated from this, the busiest heliport in Europe (possibly the world), was on display. The base was the home to helicopters from small ships' flights, the ASW operational flying school and the helicopter trials squadron, No. 771 Sqdn., establishing themselves at the base. The first squadron to arrive was No. 815 Sqdn. on 14th April 1959 with its Whirlwind helicopters, and the honour of being the final squadron to depart was also given to No. 815 Sqdn., now the Lynx small ships' flight squadron departing for Yeovilton during February.

PILOT TRAINING

The training of all British military pilots is now carried out under Joint Service systems prior to their specialised courses. All the potential pilots begin with selection at the Officer and Aircrew Selection Centre at RAF Cranwell (originally HMS Daedalus when first commissioned as a RNAS base), then FAA pilots begin their path to flying with thirteen hours with the Grading Flight at Yeovilton, flying the Grob 115 D2 Heron. On successful grading, they join the Joint Elementary Flying Training School flying the Slingsby Firefly at RAF Barkston Heath. Upon completion, the standard achieved by the candidate and service requirements will determine whether he or she will be a fast jet pilot or a helicopter pilot.

The helicopter pilot moves to the Defence Helicopter Flying School at RAF Shawbury to complete a common basic flying course with Squirrel helicopters. All basic and advanced helicopter training is now done at this school using Squirrel and Griffon helicopters. The school has been formed as a combined school taking away the individual services' training squadrons.

Grob Heron of the RN Grading Flight

Slingsby Firefly primary training aircraft

Eurocopter Squirrel HT1

Bell Griffon HT1

Shorts Tucano

Westland Sea King AEW Mk7

Airship 500 at Lee on Solent during the early 1980s

The school is however split into two where both squadrons have retained an identification of previous training squadrons. The basic training is with No. 660 Sqdn. (AAC) and the advanced with No. 705 Sqdn. (FAA) (the previous No. 705 Sqdn. disbanded in October 1997). The aircraft are operated under a civil contract although they wear a military identification. After completing the advanced phase, the pilots are sent to their respective type training squadron - No. 702 Sqdn. for Lynx, No. 824 Sqdn. for Merlin, No. 848 Sqdn. for Commando Sea Kings and No. 847 for Lynx (RM pilots after training at Middle Wallop).

If selected for fast jet training and ultimately Harriers, the pilot goes to RAF Linton-on-Ouse for basic fast jet training in Tucanos. Final training is at RAF Valley for training on the Hawk jet aircraft for the advanced flying and tactical training. After completing the courses, the pilot joins RAF Cottesmore for Harrier conversion.

THE MILLENIUM ENDS

The fleet of Sea King AEW 2A aircraft have been upgraded to Mk7s. It is the most up-to-date system yet developed, producing 40% better signal definition and, through microchip technology, the 'black boxes' are more reliable and lighter, reducing the loading on the airframe of these old helicopters. These new systems have the ability to track multiple targets at all altitudes and include a pulse Doppler with integrated IFF facility able to track and identify targets both over land and sea, picking up any moving targets. The observers in the back of the aircraft are able to determine the threat of the target and relay the information to ships and aircraft using a high speed data link.

Trials have been held with airships since the development of the British Airships Industry series of airships at the end of the 1970s. Major trials were conducted in 1985 at HMS Daedalus which proved the airship could be useful as an AEW or ASW platform but these were not pursued. In June 1997, more trials were held at Culdrose using an Airship 600 which involved using the decks of RFAs as a landing platform. These trials also proved a success, especially in coastal survey and fishery protection roles.

The 1999 Strategic Defence Review confirmed the 1998 announcement that the RN was to have two large strike aircraft carriers to be ordered for service entry in 2012 and 2015 respectively. Unfortunately no further development had been pursued at this time.

Thales Aircraft Carrier

BA Systems original STOVL only design
(BA Systems)

BA Systems original STOVL combined deck design
(BAe Systems)

Top : Lockheed Martin X35 (Lockheed Martin)

Above: X35B (Lockheed Martin)

Combined Forces - The Future Of Britain's Services

UNITED NATIONS OPERATIONS STILL KEEP THE FAA BUSY

The new millennium continued with FAA squadrons operating in UN operations and humanitarian work. Mozambique suffered major floods in March and No. 820 Sqdn. embarked on RFA *Fort George* to assist in relief operations, arriving with four aircraft at the Port of Beira on the 11th March. During the two weeks of Operation Barwood, the squadron flew 343 hours delivering 532 tonnes of stores and transporting 350 people, mainly operating with the ship anchored off the mouth of the Save River. Utilising the deck of the ship saved hours of transit time and enabled the operation to be completed more efficiently in the hot and humid conditions.

Departing Portsmouth in January bound for the Gulf, HMS *Illustrious* and its supporting flotilla took part in further Southern Watch operations against Iraqi Forces protecting the 'No Fly' zones established after the Gulf War of 1991. The SHAR of No. 801 Sqdn. carried out both Air Defence and strike sorties against Iraqi missile sites during March and April.

This was immediately followed by Operation Palliser supporting the Parachute Regiment and 45 RMC in Sierra Leone. The war torn country was in the grip of civil war and British assistance was requested to help the government forces quell the actions of the rebel forces. The ship arrived off the coast on 11th May and immediately began operations supporting the Parachute Regiment, with the SHAR providing air defence and photo-reconnaissance sorties, the AEW Sea Kings controlling the airspace and the ASW Sea Kings providing transport and CASEVAC aircraft. HMS *Illustrious* withdrew from the area on 7th June to return home.

Arriving off Sierra Leone three days after HMS *Illustrious*, HMS *Ocean* took part in the operations for five weeks, with the Sea Kings of No. 846 Sqdn. supporting the Paras and Marines in the theatre. The

Top:* No. 845 Sqdn. Sea Kings on board HMS *Ocean
***Bottom:* HMS *Ocean* (both Crown copyright)**

No. 845 Sqdn. Sea King Mk4 (crown copyright)

operation was completed on the 14th June and control of the country was returned to the Government and UN Forces.

HMS *Ocean* was to return again in company with RFAs *Argus* and *Fort Austin* in November when once again the rebel Revolutionary United Front began threatening the stability of the country. The ships arrived after the rebels called a cease-fire, which changed the mode of Operation Silkman to one of a firepower demonstration. The eight-day operation began with No 846 Sqdn. Sea Kings dropping the RM's on the beach during a very public helicopter assault. The presence of the Marines and their supporting helicopters was sufficient to demonstrate to the rebels the UN's intent to keep the peace.

COMMAND RESTRUCTURING

Although the operations and training continued 'as normal', the restructuring of the FAA and maritime aviation as defined by the SDR was to see major changes in the command and control of FAA assets.

After many titles for the FAA's own 'brass hat' since control of naval aviation was regained from the RAF, the last Flag Officer for the service (FONA) was to disappear. In 2000 FONA was to take up the position of Flag Officer Maritime Aviation (FOMA), Air Officer Commanding 3 Group RAF Strike Command, although he was still the FAA's 'Brass Hat' and is the Commander of JF2000.

FOMA has responsibility for the RN and RAF maritime aircraft and the Joint Force Harriers (JFH). Assisting him are two Commodores; COMNA (Commodore Naval Aviation) - the head of Naval Air Command, responsible for manpower, training, disembarked FL squadrons and the air stations), and COM (Flt Av) responsible for the delivery of the Fleet's aviation capability.

Joint Force 2000 became operational as part of RAF Strike Command with effect from April Fool's Day 2000! The Sea Harrier squadrons were still at Yeovilton but progress was being made for their move to the RAF stations and combined training and deployments. On the 28th February 2002 this plan took a huge turn when it was announced in the House of Commons that the Sea Harriers F/A2 squadrons would disband by the end of 2006 as part of the 'Migration Strategy for Joint Force Harrier'. This will leave the FAA with no fighter aircraft until the arrival of the Joint Strike Fighter. The SHAR squadrons were now to remain at Yeovilton until their retirement.

MEMORIALS AND MERLINS

As a tribute to all members of the FAA in its 90 year history, a memorial has been erected in the Victoria Embankment Gardens in Westminster. The monument consists of a Portland stone pillar made from two curved sections with a bronze strip through the middle. On top of this pillar is the statue of Daedalus and at the bottom is a distinctive curved dedication stone with the FAA wings badge with the words FLEET AIR ARM, whilst the pillar has FAA battle honours engraved onto it. Dedicated to all the men and women of the FAA who have lost their lives whilst in the service, it was unveiled by HRH Prince Charles on 1st June 2000. A flypast of Sea King helicopters saluted it and the 2000 invited guests included three surviving aircrew from the ill-fated Channel Dash of February 1942. It is a fitting tribute to the oldest flying military institution in the world.

Commissioning in June 2000, the first squadron to operate the Merlin HMP Mk1 helicopter, No. 824 Sqdn. became the training squadron for the type, working with and alongside the IFTU, with aircraft being shared between the two squadrons. This second unit will not have FL status, the first FLS was No. 814 Sqdn. followed by No. 820 Sqdn. The IFTU No. 700M Sqdn. became the Merlin OEU, with two helicopters, on 1st September 2001 tasked with development and system operational evaluations for the helicopter. The MOEU is also the parenting unit for the Merlin ships' flights; the first of these for HMS *Lancaster* formed two days later on 3rd September and eventually the Merlin ships' flights became No. 829 Sqdn. when it reformed in 2004.

WITHDRAWAL FROM BOSNIA

After eight years of continuous operations, No. 845 Sqdn. finally pulled out of its base at 'NAS Banana' in Bosnia. War in Yugoslavia began in April 1992 when the different ethnic factions began fighting over control of the country and the British Army units were sent to the country to assist in the UN operations. The squadron was to

Merlin HM1

join them as a means of supplying CASEVAC availability, arriving in Split in November 1992 and setting up a base at the Divuljie Barracks, a former seaplane station.

Operating with four of its Sea Kings, a permanent detachment was to remain in support of the UN Forces until finally withdrawing on 1st January 2001. During its eight years of continuous 24-hour 365-day support (a record period of continuous front line operations by any aviation unit of the British military), the helicopters had flown over 13500 hours and had been hit by hostile fire 25 times.

The Mk4 Sea King proved to be a valuable asset to the UN Forces and was required to assist the SFOR elements in Bosnia. Less than eighteen months after No. 845 Sqdn. withdrew, No. 846 Sqdn. was tasked to send a detachment to assist the UN Forces during the summer of 2002, but their stay was short lived and they were replaced by RAF Merlin helicopters the following spring.

PILOTS NEEDED

With a shortfall in SHAR pilots, qualified helicopter pilots (RN and RM pilots) are offered the opportunity to qualify as Sea Harrier pilots. The first RM fixed-wing pilot to qualify as a SHAR pilot was Capt. Phillip Kelly RM on 29th March 2001, the Corps first fixed-wing pilot for over 40 years.

The RN Grading Flight was given squadron status on 6th December 2001 when it became No. 727 Sqdn., the RN Flight Training Squadron, manned and operated by civilian contractors from Vosper Thornycroft Aerospace. Although it is the smallest commissioned squadron within the British Forces, operating five Grob Heron aircraft at Roborough, it has a variety of tasks; the grading of prospective pilots, navigation courses for RM Aircrew, AEO's airborne classrooms, Air Traffic Controllers' flying training, fixed-wing refresher courses and hosting the university camps twice a year. The other civilian operated squadron No. 750 Sqdn. celebrated its 50th anniversary in continuous commission on 27th April 2002.

In 2007 the combined UK Military Flying Training System will come into force - a five year £12.5 billion project to replace all the UK Forces' training aircraft and helicopters for commonality aircrew training that will see an even more combined UK Forces' structure in full operation by 2012.

ARK ROYAL RETURNS

After seven years either in reserve at Portsmouth or undergoing the most expensive refit ever on a British Warship at £147m, HMS *Ark Royal* returned to Portsmouth as the most potent warship in the Fleet, having completed its refit which included completely replacing the catwalks and ringbolts, removal of the Sea Dart system and a new Flyco - a few of the modifications carried out so that the ship can operate the Harrier GR7 and Merlin helicopters more efficiently.

Sea King Mk4 with SFOR markings

Sailing from Rosyth for the first sea trials on 13th July 2001 - a date set prior to entering the refit two years previously, she embarked her first helicopters with the arrival of a No. 819 Sqdn. Sea King and a No. 824 Sqdn. Merlin the following day. After returning to the dockyard for the final work to be completed, she sailed for Portsmouth on 29th August arriving two days later.

The ship was re-dedicated on 22nd November when Her Majesty the Queen Mother arrived on board for the ceremony, twenty years after first launching the ship in Newcastle. This was to be the Queen Mother's last public engagement. Carrying out trials post re-dedication, Ark was to complete the initial Merlin/CVS operational trials during December when the helicopter flew 100 hours and completed 775 deck landings clearing the type to operate from the ship.

A MOST OUTRAGEOUS ACT OF TERRORISM

The largest exercise ever conducted by the British Military Forces (Exercise Saif Sarrea II) was planned for autumn 2001 in the Gulf region involving some 40% of the British Forces. All the available amphibious ships, carriers and embarked squadrons, the CHF and JF Harrier Squadrons, were to take part. The planned exercise was eventually altered after the dramatic attacks on the World Trade Centre and the Pentagon in America as elements were used in Operation Oracle - anti-terrorist operations.

No. 727 Sqdn. Heron

HMS Ocean with No. 845 Sqdn Sea King (Crown copyright)

No. 847 Sqdn. Lynx and Gazelle onboard HMS Ocean (Crown copyright)

The world is aware of the atrocities by Al Qaeda terrorists on 11th September 2001, and the resulting operations in Afghanistan involved elements of the FAA and RN. Many elements of the RN in the Gulf region became involved in operations against the Taliban and Al Qaeda terrorist forces in Afghanistan. HMSs *Illustrious, Ocean* and *Fearless* were directed to areas off the Pakistan coast operating alongside the US Forces during Operation Oracle (US operation Enduring Freedom) for three weeks.

On completion of the initial operations, HMS *Ocean* returned to Plymouth, whilst other elements of the Force remained either in the Gulf region, off Pakistan or in East Africa supporting Operation Resinate /Oracle. HMS *Fearless,* with Sea Kings, Lynx and Gazelles on board, carried out interdiction operations checking on shipping in the Gulf enforcing the UN sanctions against Iraq. The operations were to be the last for HMS *Fearless* as she was to finally retire later in the year after 36 years service, the last steam driven ship in the RN.

HMS *Illustrious* was eventually relieved by HMS *Ocean* returning during March 2002. During Illustrious' 5 month deployment carrying out operations against terrorism, she had been operating as a CVS (strike carrier), as an LPH (amphibious carrier) and as a Forward Operating Base embarking 11 different squadrons - a record for a RN aircraft carrier.

Operation Veritas was the code name for the continuous operations in the region. HMS *Ocean* remained on station in the Gulf region with No.s 845 and 847 Sqdns. embarked as part of the joint Task Force including the USS *John C Stennis* and *JF Kennedy* and the French carrier FNS *Charles De Gaulle*. The ship and squadrons were stood down in June 2002 after off-loading 45RMC to Bagram Air Base near Baghdad with the Chinooks of No. 27 Sqdn. RAF from HMS *Ocean*. On return to the UK, Ocean went into a four-month refit in Portsmouth dockyard, completed on 19th November 2002.

SEA KING MK7

The Mk7 AS&C (Airborne Surveillance and Control) Sea King is probably the last variant of this formidable helicopter to be developed anywhere in the world. Entering service with the FAA's AEW squadron No. 849 during March 2002, it replaces the original AEW Sea Kings designed in 1982 after twenty years of operations. This aircraft is the most advanced AEW type aircraft in service today after five years of development.

The HQ flight and 'A' Flt began using the aircraft upon receipt of the first two aircraft; 'A' flight would go to sea as an operational unit aboard HMS *Ark Royal* in September, and 'B' Flt would be the last operators of the retiring Mk2/5 AEW, embarked in Ark Royal until replaced by 'A' Flt.

FLEET FIRST CONCEPT

The 'Fleet First' concept, the new Fleet Command structure of the Royal Navy, is to have a significant effect on the future of aviation as perceived by the Commander In Chief (CinC). COMNA moved to the Fleet Headquarters at Whale Island as Commodore Fleet Aviation (Carrier Strike and Aviation) as a single aviation authority with a direct input to the CinC. For the first time in the history of the Royal Navy, the FAA has an Assistant Chief of Staff - ACOS(Flt Av), a member of the CinC Fleet staff tasked with integrating the aviation assets of the service. This makes the FAA a fully-fledged part of the senior service and ensures that naval aviation is given the priority it warrants after 90 years of service.

NEW CARRIERS AND AIRCRAFT CONFIRMED

The Lockheed Martin X35 was announced as the winner of the JSF contest to be the future combat aircraft for the FAA, RAF, USAF, USN and USMC. On 30th September 2002, Britain announced that the STOVL version of the F35 would be acquired for use with the RAF and FAA for operating off the proposed new carriers. The main reason that this version has been chosen for the FAA (in particular) is the availability date for service. This version should reach the squadrons by 2015 - now the in-service date for the first of the two carriers. A conventional version for use at sea would be some years later.

After the initial announcement of the Strategic Defence Review of 1998 and the awarding of design contracts in 2000, the two companies (BAe Systems and Thales) awarded the design phase of the new aircraft carriers submitted their completed designs at the end of November 2002 for selection. It was announced on 30th January 2003 that two 50-60,000 ton aircraft carriers, the largest warships to serve in the RN, were to be built at a cost of £1.5 billion each to replace the three Invincible class carriers. This decision was later revoked following a MOD requirement for even further discussions on the actual allotment of work and who was to lead the project - negotiations that were to last a further $4^{1/2}$ years.

INVINCIBLE AND ARGUS

After completing what is to be the ship's last major refit, HMS *Invincible* returned to Portsmouth in January 2003. Departing Portsmouth for Rosyth in July 2001, the sixteen month refit began in September with the aim of extending the 23 year-old ship's operational life to retirement in 2006. She carried out post refit trials until rejoining the Fleet at the end of May, eventually to replace HMS *Ark Royal* as the RN Flagship.

The FAA's training ship, RFA *Argus*, had served as a hospital ship during the first Gulf War in 1992 when her hangar was hastily fitted out with bunks and theatres. With the possibility of military action against Iraq looming, the need for a hospital ship for the RN was seen as a necessary requirement, resulting in the refit of Argus in the role of Primary Casualty Receiving Ship. Emerging from the refit, her exterior design had not changed but internally she could be converted from training carrier to hospital ship in a short time with 100 beds and three operating theatres.

HMS Invincible now devoid of the Sea Dart weapons system

HMS Ocean at anchor (Crown copyright

No. 847 Sqdn. over Iraq (Crown copyright)

OPERATION TELIC

The last action against Saddam Hussein and his Regime began on 20th March 2003 after many weeks of preparation. Since the Gulf War of 1991, there have been many actions against the regime in Iraq, mainly over Saddam's non-compliance with UN mandates. In 2002 the UN agreed a new resolution for arms inspectors to seek out 'weapons of mass destruction' in the Iraqi arsenal and to check on the destruction of weapons as laid down by previous resolutions.

As usual, the Regime was not giving the inspectors its full assistance in the inspections, resulting in President George W Bush proposing military action backed by Prime Minister Blair. The British Forces were to be an Amphibious Ready Group (ARG) led by HMS *Ark Royal* operating as a commando carrier leaving behind its SHAR squadron and embarking No. 814 Sqdn. with Merlin MPH Mk1s, No. 849 Sqdn 'A' Flt. with AEW Mk7s, Chinooks of No. 18 Sqdn. RAF and 40 RMC.

The main flotilla departed Portsmouth on 11th January 2003 whilst HMS *Ocean* departed Plymouth a few days later with the Commando Helicopter Force (CHF) embarked - Sea King Mk4s of No. 845 Sqdn, the Lynx and Gazelles of No. 847 Sqdn., and 42 RMC. She was accompanied by RFA *Argus* as a hospital ship, affectionately known as BUPA Baghdad, with No. 820 Sqdn. Sea King Mk6 helicopters on board for SAR and casualty evacuation aircraft. The 22 ships and 45 helicopters of the ARG - the largest British Amphibious Force since the Falklands War of 1982, assembled off Cyprus and set course for the Gulf arriving on 10th February to join up with the Coalition Fleet to begin exercising and planning the operations to come.

The operations to rid Iraq of the Regime began during the evening of 20th/21st March with the ships taking station seventeen miles off the Iraqi coast. Prior to the main assault, helicopters on board HMS *Ocean* carried out operations inserting and supporting Special Forces. The RM Commandos of 3CDO Brigade were put ashore using the Sea Kings and Chinooks assisted by USAF MH53 Sea Stallions airlifting marines and Special Forces' personnel into Iraq during the largest airborne amphibious assault since the Suez campaign nearly 50 years earlier. Their task was to secure the oil terminal at Al Faw to prevent Saddam's Forces from destroying it. The helicopters were given air support from the TOW equipped Lynx of No. 847 Sqdn., US Navy fighter aircraft and USMC Cobra gunships.

After securing the oil terminal the Royal Marines were to advance on the city of Basra, Iraq's second largest city. This phase was to be assisted by using USMC CH46 Sea Knight helicopters, but unfortunately one of the helicopters crashed in Kuwait with eight Royal Marines and four US Marines onboard, killing all twelve. The aircraft were withdrawn and the Sea King Mk4s and Chinooks carried the troops whilst the Lynx and Gazelles of No. 847 Sqdn. flew ahead of the Marines on a continuous airborne patrol, close air support, artillery fire spotting and attacking any hostile targets using their TOW missiles.

Flotilla (Crown copyright)

On the 24th, whilst the squadron was operating from HMS *Ocean,* with two aircraft airborne continuously before dawn until after dusk, one of the Lynx helicopters attacked and destroyed two Iraqi Armoured Division tanks at Abu Al Khesib using their TOW anti-tank missiles.

GROUP MARITIME HELICOPTERS

The Merlin helicopters operated from RFA *Fort Victoria* in their first operational missions since entering service. They were tasked with supplying the command with the surface picture and searching for suspect patrol boats. The four aircraft completed 800 hours of operations; this new helicopter proved a valuable asset in assessing the threat of small, hard to detect craft approaching within 40 miles of the Fleet.

The new Sea King AEW Mk7s were used to patrol the Gulf area against fast patrol boats and aircraft attacking the Coalition Fleet, but tragically two aircraft collided near HMS *Ark Royal* on the 22nd March killing all seven aircrew. The Sea King Mk6s aboard RFA *Argus* were busy with CASEVAC and personnel transfer missions.

The embarked small ships' flight Lynx helicopters of No. 815 Sqdn. were tasked with continuous round-the-clock patrols for mines and any boats possibly laying mines or on suicide missions. Two aircraft were airborne throughout the operations and all were equipped with the M3M machine gun operated from the cabin. They provided Force protection for the Amphibious Forces' landing craft, the aircraft carriers USS *Abraham Lincoln* and *Constellation* and for the Force of mine sweepers clearing the Gulf of mines.

With little resistance from the Iraqis during the war, the Iraqi Air Force kept on the ground or destroyed by coalition aircraft and no attacks by Iraqi gunboats, the objectives were quickly achieved; in little over three weeks the Coalition Forces had completed the liberation of the country. HMS *Ark Royal* was no longer needed and was released to return home arriving back in Portsmouth on 17th May. HMS *Ocean* and the amphibious group remained for a few more days supporting the Royal Marines in the south of Iraq, then she arrived back in Plymouth on the 28th. A few of the Mk4 Sea Kings remained in Iraq in support of the Royal Marines operating in Basra as part of the Support Helicopter Forces.

FAREWELL THE ASW SEA KING

The last front line Sea King ASW squadron, No. 820 Sqdn. was due to retire the last of the Mk6 aircraft in December 2002.

No. 814 Sqdn. Merlin

Sea Kings embark HMS Ocean (Crown copyright)

HMS Ark Royal with Chinooks (Crown copyright)

Chinook embarks Royal Marines (Crown copyright)

USMC CH46 on board HMS Ocean (Crown copyright)

HMS Ark Royal busy deck (Crown copyright)

However, due to the Merlin not being fully operational to take over all the ASW requirements, the squadron was to continue to operate the aircraft until 31st August 2003. The squadron operated the aircraft from RFS *Argus* during Operation Telic completing nearly 1300 hours of operational tasking, not in the ASW role but in the equally important role of SAR, CASEVAC and personnel transfer.

No. 771 Sqdn. supported two flights (A & B) of single Mk6 helicopters for operations aboard HMS *Campbeltown* and HMS *Cornwall* during 2004, the last time the type was used in the ASW role. The two flights were then tasked with HDS/SAR role aboard HMS *Illustrious* and HMS *Invincible* until November 2005 as individual flights. They were to combine as one flight for the last Mk6 maritime aircraft deployment aboard HMS *Ocean* for the 2006 winter exercises in Norwegian waters. The flight joined the ship in February for six weeks as the HDS/SAR/Troop transport and support flight until April when they finally disbanded on return to Culdrose.

Sea King Mk6 helicopters will remain in service with Gannet SAR Flight at Prestwick and No. 771 Sqdn. as the Culdrose SAR flight and training Squadron without their ASW equipment. Five fuselages have been converted to Mk6CR (Commando Role) helicopters to supplement the overstretched Mk4 Commando aircraft. This has involved removing all internal gear, refitting with troop seats and having their undercarriage fixed in the 'down' position.

The Merlin helicopters are now the mainstay of ASW operations with the Fleet deploying on carriers, RFA's and destroyers. Since Operation Telic the aircraft has developed another role that it will be called upon in future conflicts, that of Amphibious Support - using its detection systems to search for small targets posing a threat to any planned or current amphibious operations. It is planned to establish more Merlin small ships' flights which will be part of the newly reformed No. 829 Sqdn. re-commissioned in 2004 to be the parenting squadron of small ships' flights once again.

NEW SQUADRONS AND SHIPS

Two training units were to receive squadron status. The first No. 792 Sqdn, was re-commissioned from the Fleet Target Group based at Culdrose. The unit moved to Culdrose from its original base at Portland when the base closed, continuing its role of supplying pilotless target aircraft for naval gunners to practice their skills. The Defence Elementary Flying Training School at RAF Barkston Heath is responsible for the training of up to 60 potential RN pilots per year. In July 2004 the Naval unit of the DEFTS was given its own squadron status when it re-commissioned No. 703 Sqdn.

The first of the two LPD amphibious warfare ships, HMS *Albion* (launched 9th March 2001) began contractor's sea trials in December 2002. On successful completion she sailed into Plymouth in April 2003. The first deck landing by a Sea King Mk4 took place 13th May 2003 and the ship was commissioned on June 19th 2003. After completing the First of Class trials, she was declared ready for service in May 2004 and entered service in July as part of the Amphibious Ready Group.

The ship (and HMS *Bulwark*) was originally conceived complete with a hangar deck, however due to cost constraints this was not included in the build. There are already plans to have a telescopic hangar incorporated when the ships enter their first refits! HMS *Albion* had the honour of being the deck for a rare event in FAA history, the presenting of new colours to the FAA by Her Majesty the Queen onboard a ship, during the summer of 2004.

HMS *Bulwark,* the sister ship to Albion, left Barrow-in-Furness in June 2004 for its first sea trials. It arrived in its homeport of Plymouth six weeks later in July (it was planned to be ready for delivery in September but was completed ahead of schedule). The two ships met at sea for the first time in October when they rendezvoused in the English Channel.

With the commissioning of these two ships, their predecessors HMS *Fearless* and HMS *Intrepid* were finally moved from the Fleet reserve list and moved from Portsmouth basin to Fareham creek awaiting disposal. There are proposals for one of them to become a museum depicting amphibious operations.

The replacement ships for the Knight Class logistic landing ships, the Bay Class, were all launched during 2003 (RFA *Largs Bay*) and 2004 (RFAs *Mounts Bay, Lyme Bay* and *Cardigan Bay*). Mounts Bay began trials in July 2006 followed by the ship's acceptance into the RFA Fleet on 19th September 2006 with dedication the following month.

These bigger ships have large flight decks capable of operating helicopters and vertical lift aircraft, a vehicle deck and a landing craft dock, allowing them to operate as assault ships within an ARG. Lyme Bay, the last of the class to join the RFA Fleet, was accepted in service on 31st August 2007.

No 771 Sqdn. Sea King

HARRIERS AND GAZELLES RETIRE

After the decision that the Sea Harrier squadrons were to be disbanded, it fell on the shoulders of No. 800 Sqdn. to be the first to go when the squadron disbanded on 31st March 2004. The week prior to disbanding the squadron took part in the JF Harrier bombing contest and, to prove the point that it was still in business, it won the overall competition - going out with a bang you could say. No. 801 Sqdn. was to continue as the only FAA fighter squadron until it too disbanded on 31st March 2006. The last SHAR flight was the squadron flypast over Yeovilton three days before standing down.

Following the 2002 announcement, training continued with No. 899 Sqdn. including deck landing training onboard HMS *Ark Royal* during 2003 with the T8N, the first time the type had been operated from a carrier deck. The ship had also been the deck for the first operations from a carrier deck of its predecessor, the T4N, some 15 years earlier.

No 820 Sqdn. Sea King

703 Sqdn. Firefly

899 Sqdn. Harrier

899 Sqdn. Harrier T8

It continued training SHAR pilots until the squadron disbanded on 1st April 2005. Training will be continued by a joint RAF/RN squadron based at RAF Wittering.

No. 847 Sqdn. gave up its Gazelle helicopters in April 2005 and their observation helicopter role was taken over by the Lynx Mk7. With the AAC Apache attack helicopter receiving its carrier operational qualification, there is no longer a need for No. 847 Sqdn. to use its Lynx as attack helicopters using anti-tank missiles. The Gazelles had given sterling service since replacing the Bell 47's in the observation role.

NEW LEASES OF LIFE

RFA *Argus* entered a five month refit in Plymouth, emerging for sea trials early February 2004 before rejoining the Fleet after Easter, now as a fully fitted training carrier/hospital ship. The ship is expected to remain in service until 2020.

With the planned life expectancy of the MK4 Commando Sea King due to continue until 2015, the Fleet entered a 4 year programme of avionics upgrading during 2004. This would mean a shortage of aircraft for use by the three commando squadrons. To overcome this deficiency, five of the retired MK6 ASW helicopters have been converted into Mk6CR (Commando Role) helicopters having their ASW equipment, ASW weapons carriers and associated systems and the ECM equipment removed. The first two aircraft were delivered to the 'Junglie' Force on 16th July 2004.

OPERATION TELIC II

Peace in Iraq is a long way off and until the Iraqi forces can police the country, elements of the FAA will remain there. The RN continuously protects the two offshore oil platforms in the Iraqi territorial waters exclusion zone, whilst Lynx helicopters from the ships carry out interdiction operations against suspect targets. The Mk8 helicopters used in the Gulf are now all fitted with full NVG capability, have a defensive suite and also the M3M gun mounted outside the cabin door.

The Commando Helicopter Force (CHF) units, comprising Sea King MK4s from No. 845 and No. 846 Sqdns. and the Lynx of No. 847 Sqdn., returned to Basra in April 2005 to provide 24 hour support carrying out troop transport and casualty evacuation, surveillance operations and to have Immediate Response Teams based in Basra and Al Amarah.

INVINCIBLE RETIRES

A busy final 6 months were in store for HMS *Invincible*. She began by taking part in

Operation Marstrike in the Gulf, operating RAF GR7s on strike missions supporting coalition forces. On return to Portsmouth at the end of May, she began destoring prior to her paying off. She did however have one last duty, Flagship at the largest international fleet review ever held - Trafalgar 200 in the Solent.

Sailing out of Portsmouth, she took up her position at the head of a fleet of 188 military and support ships from 38 Navies and 60 non-military ships and sail training boats. The fleet review, in celebration of Nelson's victory in 1805, was on the 28th June 2005 when the Queen sailed through the lines of ships along the Solent whilst a small flypast of aircraft and helicopters from the RN, RAF and Commonwealth countries flew overhead. A magnificent sight probably never to be repeated with such a large fleet in attendance.

The ship entered Portsmouth Harbour for the last time on 1st August flying her paying off pennant following 25 years with the Fleet; the decommissioning ceremony was held two days later. The next eight months were spent being stripped of all remaining stores and reusable items before the last of her fifty crew departed the ship in March 2006. The ship will remain as a source of spares (in reserve) until her planned scrapping in 2010.

HMS *Illustrious* assumed the role of the RN's flagship following her return from her final refit in 2005 when she was redesigned to operate the JF Harrier and CHF as TAGs. The refit involved removing the ski ramp completely and fitting a new one, the third ramp the ship has had built onto her deck. Also refitted were the old briefing rooms that were previously designed to the requirements of specific aircraft types - these are now four planning rooms that can be used for any unit embarked.

VAAC HARRIER

The new F35 strike fighter being developed as the Harrier replacement will be the world's most up-to-date aircraft. The UK STOVL version will be a combined fighter strike aircraft with air-to-air and air-to-ground capability. The pilots will fly the aircraft using touch screen computer technology and information will be displayed on their helmet's visor. The aircraft will be built with sensors on the fuselage giving the pilot a 360-degree field of view and for landing he will have a view below the cockpit floor when the undercarriage is lowered.

A British development that may be incorporated into the design is an automatic landing facility for use in severe weather

801 Sqdn. Harrier

RFA Argus

HMS Invincible

VAAC Harrier

conditions. Trials of the system using the specially adapted Active Control Harrier from Boscombe Down were carried out on board HMS *Invincible* during May 2005, the last aircraft operations on the ship's deck before retiring. The VAAC Harrier landed on the ship on the 16th May "hands free" to complete the world's first automated carrier landing. The aircraft successfully completed 101 landings during the eight days of trials. The Harrier departed from the ship on 23rd May, the last launch of a Harrier from the ship's deck.

CONTINUED OPERATIONS

The RN/FAA is continuing its roles in international joint operations. The Lynx flights were busy in joint British/US operations against drugs trafficking in the Caribbean and in Operation Calash - the continued operation against terrorist organisations. The main role in these operations is armed search and reconnaissance flights when the helicopter is equipped with the M3M machine gun.

Following the dramatic Tsunami of December 2004 when the giant wave created devastation and destruction in the Indian Ocean, HMS *Chatham* and RFA *Diligence* were despatched to assist in the relief operations in Sri Lanka - Operation Garron.

Super Lynx (Agusta Westland)

During 14 days of continuous flying the two Lynx aircraft delivered stores, relief support teams and carried out photographic missions along the Island's coastline.

Support for the Forces in Northern Ireland was continuing however, to relieve the commitments on the Commando Sea Kings, Lynx flights from No. 815 Sqdn. took over the support task in Northern Ireland during 2005 and these support flights were to continue until final withdrawal of troops from the Province on 31st July 2007.

UN Forces in Bosnia continued to need the mighty Sea King MK4 for troop transport, thus No. 846 Sqdn. returned to Banja Luka in August 2004 with two of the (new) Mk6CR Sea Kings as part of the EUFOR Emergency Response Force, mainly tasked with transporting medical and mine clearance teams within their region of operations. The detachment returned during April 2005 when they were replaced by units of the AAC.

SQUADRON CHANGES

With the disbanding of No. 801 Sqdn. SHARs on the 31st March 2006, a new era in Naval Aviation was to begin the next day when the front line fixed-wing elements of the FAA were to become strike units as part of Joint Force Harrier (JFH). No. 800 Sqdn. recommissioned on 1st April with the Harrier GR7 as its mount, based at RAF Cottesmore alongside No. 801 Sqdn. who recommissioned on 1st October also with the GR7. The two squadrons form half of the JFH alongside two RAF squadrons, and all will be equipped with the Harrier GR9 as they become available.

December 2006 saw the relocation of No. 727 Sqdn. and the establishment of two new squadrons. On completion of the final Grading Flight at Roborough course No. 127, No. 727 Sqdn. took leave of Plymouth airport after a stay of 57 years and relocated to Yeovilton. After 24 years operating as detached flights from No. 849 Sqdn., the two ASaC Mk7 flights were given autonomous squadron status when A Flight became No. 854 Sqdn. and B Flight No. 857 Sqdn.

OPERATION TELIC II CONTINUES

Operations in Iraq continued under the guise of Operation Telic II. No. 846 Sqdn. relieved No. 845 Sqdn. at Basra during May 2003, supporting the British and UN Forces as part of the JHF(Iraq) with troop movement, reconnaissance and road convoy protection. By the time the five aircraft were returned to Yeovilton on 17th December, the squadron had completed over 1200 missions. No. 845 Sqdn.

returned in May 2005 as part of JFH(I), two years after leaving Iraq from its operations during Operation Telic.

No. 847 Sqdn. had mixed fortunes in Iraq. In May 2006, one of the Lynx helicopters was brought down by a missile strike on the tail pylon with the loss of five lives. The aircraft crashed into the roof of a building and valiant efforts by troops on the ground to rescue the crew were unsuccessful.

The following month a British Warrior armoured vehicle was under attack in Al Amarah. Major Will Chesarc USMC, an exchange pilot, flew his Lynx helicopter low over the hostile ground dispersing them, whilst avoiding small arms fire and grenades, before flying top cover over the scene. During this time he took command and control of the situation and directed a USAF F15 supporting the rescue operation to the scene. Finally, he evacuated a severely injured soldier, saving his life, and for this he received the DFC (the first awarded to a US service man since WWII).

Joining the surface ships protecting the oil platforms was HMS *Bulwark*. She joined up with the Task Force in June for three months prior to her commencing a seven month refit in September. This was the first time either of the two assault ships had taken part in Gulf operations.

OPERATION HIGHBROW

The uneasy peace between Lebanon and Israel disintegrated when Hezbollah factions attacked Israel with rockets launched from inside Lebanon in the summer of 2006. Israel retaliated and a fullscale conflict ensued. HMSs *Illustrious*, *Bulwark* and *York* were sent to the area to help evacuate civilians from Lebanon.

At Yeovilton, No.s 845 and 846 Sqdns. were tasked with a non-combatant evacuation operation supplying helicopters to assist. Given four hours notice to go, these heavily stretched squadrons flew 6 aircraft the 1700 miles to Cyprus taking 20 hours flying all the way in formation. The first mission was on the 21st July when an aircraft flew from Akrotiri to Lebanon and back with refugees. The helicopters embarked on the ships and Bulwark transferred 1300 people from Lebanon to Cyprus.

OPERATION HERRICK

Following an extensive six months of training with the strike aircraft, No. 800 Sqdn. took part in Operation Herrick, protecting and supporting the Royal Marines in Afghanistan on a four month deployment in Khandahar from October to January. The Squadron was tasked with supporting the coalition forces with ground support operations, reconnaissance flights and vehicle convoy escort.

No 800 Sqdn. GR7

The Squadron was the third unit to be deployed to the region since operations against the Taliban began in 2000. A detachment of aircraft engineers from MASU have been repairing the UK helicopter fleet at Khandahar since 2005. No. 846 Sqdn. moved from Iraq to Khandahar during October 2007 with modified Sea King Mk4 Plus helicopters.

EUROPE'S LARGEST SQUADRON

With a mix of 35 Lynx Mk3 and MK8 aircraft, No. 815 Sqdn. is Europe's largest squadron of military aircraft/helicopters. It is the parenting squadron for the 26 Lynx small ships' flights as well as being the Lynx OCU. With the heightened worldwide security, it is also the UK Maritime Counter Terrorism Unit tasked with protecting the UK coastline from potential terror attacks. For this role the Squadron has to supply helicopters to areas where a potential threat alarm has been raised to seek out the threat and co-ordinate the defence mechanisms required.

THE CARRIERS

Following three years of inactivity and a refit, HMS *Ark Royal* began sea trials in October 2006, now converted as a temporary Commando Carrier with accommodation for 600 marines, so that HMS *Ocean* can go into refit. Ark Royal returned to Portsmouth in March 2007 and was rededicated the following month. The ship still retains her Strike role, now fitted with the digital precision approach radar on a third mast at the back of the Island similar to her sister ship HMS *Illustrious*.

HMS Bulwark

Sea King Mk 4

No 800 Sqdn. GR7

No.815 Sqdn Lynx

With HMS Invincible retiring, Illustrious became the Fleet's strike carrier. In May 2007, she embarked No. 800 Sqdn. of the JFH Naval Strike Wing (NSW); this was the first time a FAA GR7 squadron had operated at sea. She followed this by becoming the first RN carrier to operate as a strike carrier with no FAA units involved except for No. 771 Sqdn. as the SAR support flight. USMC units operated from the ship from 15th - 31st July for exercises off the US east coast with 16 AV8Bs of VMA223 and an MV22 Osprey from Cherry Point USMC Station embarking. This was the first time an Osprey tilt wing aircraft had operated from the deck of a British warship.

For over three years the RN has been involved in anti-drug running operations in the Caribbean Sea working with the USN and Coastguard. This has normally been carried out with frigates, destroyers and RFA support ships. With HMS *Ark Royal* now operating as a Commando Carrier, HMS *Ocean* was free to go to the Caribbean to take over the role of Guard Ship - RN Drugs Buster for 4 months from April to July 2007, escorted by RFA *Wave Ruler* with a No. 815 Sqdn. Lynx embarked.

Embarked were four helicopters tasked with assisting the USCG with tracking down and watching for unidentified aircraft and boats trafficking drugs from South America. The helicopters, two ASaC MK7 aircraft from No. 854 Sqdn. and two Merlins from No. 700M Sqdn., supplemented by USMC CH46s, successfully tracked a variety of suspicious targets; two of these operations captured £53m of cocaine and heroin. On returning to Plymouth in July, she began a much needed 13 month refit.

RECRUITMENT TOOLS

Keeping up the tradition of providing display teams as promotional recruitment tools, the FAA currently has three such teams. No. 702 Sqdn., the Lynx training squadron, has been flying a pair of helicopters as the Black Cats since 2001, now in their sixth year. They have a superbly painted aircraft wearing a black cat on the fuselage.

Not to be outdone, the Jetstreams of No. 750 Sqdn. has a formation display team. The squadron has responsibility for training FAA Observers, a task they have been carrying out since forming from the Observers School in May 1939. The dedicated RN Observer has been serving since WWI; in respect of this the Jetstreams wore special 90th anniversary markings applied in 2007.

FRADU have an excellent display team comprising two Falcon 10 and four Hawk aircraft demonstrating the attack profile used for training our fleet in anti-aircraft and anti-missile warfare. The Falcons have the role of the attacker and the Hawks have the role of missiles launched from the aircraft. Their routine follows an attack pattern before the Hawks form a four aircraft display.

REPLACEMENT HELICOPTERS

The FAAs Lynx replacement was planned to be due in service by 2007 closely followed by Army's (and RM's) Battlefield Light Helicopter. It was announced in July 2002 that these replacement helicopters would be funded, however no firm dates for delivery were given. On 24th March 2005, a further announcement was made by the Defence Minister that the (Land Find and Maritime Surface Attack) helicopter was to be the Agusta Westland Future Lynx.

The MOD ordered 30 New Super Lynx maritime aircraft at the end of 2006. These new helicopters have a redesigned fuselage with more composite materials used in their construction and diagnostic equipment making them more maintainable and reliable. The more powerful and efficient engine combined with the redesigned tail rotor will make it a faster helicopter with increased handling characteristics. The helicopter will also have a new 360-degree surveillance scanning radar. The first flight is scheduled for 2009 with an in-service date of 2016.

Replacing the Lynx AH 7, No. 847 Sqdn. was re-equipped with the Battlefield Lynx AH Mk9 unarmed observation helicopter during the summer of 2007. Once the crews have completed familiarisation with this version of the Lynx, the Squadron will operate detachments in support of the Forces in Afghanistan and Iraq. It will continue to use this variant until the arrival of the replacement Army Lynx due to enter service in 2016.

Lockheed Martin were awarded the Merlin Capability Upgrade contract to modernise 30 FAA Merlin helicopters. They will have improved radar and sonar equipment, full NVG capability and new display screens. The contract requires all the aircraft to be completed and returned to operational flying by 2015.

UNMANNED AIRBORNE VEHICLE (UAV)

It can be argued that pilotless target aircraft were the original UAV's, but these are target aircraft for gunners to aim at during firing training. The Mirach 100/5 UAV used by No. 792 Sqdn. is an unmanned "aircraft" used in this role. The term UAV used today relates to unmanned

Black Cats

Jetstream wearing 90th anniversary markings

FRADU display team

Lynx Mk. 9

surveillance aircraft used as "eyes in the sky" over hostile territory.

The squadron began trials with the Boeing Scan Eagle UAV on board HMS *Sutherland* during April 2006. The UAV is capable of operating 70 miles from the ship for 15 hours sending back information to the Operations Room. Further trials were held jointly with the USN aboard the USS *Carter Hill* in the Indian Ocean in June 2007. These maritime operation trials included using the ASaC MK7s of No. 857 Sqdn. to track the UAV and recover it if it were to ditch.

There are proposals for the Fleet to acquire surveillance UAVs in the future, and these could be in the form of fixed or rotary wing similar to the Northrop Grumman UAV proposed for the British Forces. No. 792 Sqdn. will have the responsibility of operating any such vehicle introduced to the service.

JSF LIGHTNING II

The F35 first development aircraft (AA-1), now known as the Lightning II, flew on 15th December 2006. Progress with the build and testing of the strike fighter was continuing well following the January 2006 agreement with the US to share vital technical details of the aircraft and its equipment. However this came to an abrupt halt when the US retracted this agreement 12 months later - they wanted sole rights to these details "in the interest of homeland security". This was not acceptable to the British Government so the £140bn project stalled. Following protracted discussions, the US backed down and the UK signed to continue with the next phase on 23rd January 2007.

The aircraft is now due in service in 2018 when it will replace the Harrier GR9s. The first FAA personnel joined the development team during 2007 to assist in the 12,000 hours of flight testing and to learn how to operate and service the aircraft. The Lightning OEU will form at Edwards AFB in California in 2011 with a mix of US and UK pilots. Flying training will begin at Eglin AFB Florida in 2014 prior to the UK's own flying training commencing at RAF Lossiemouth.

SUPER CARRIERS

After nine years of indecision, on 25th July 2007 the Government announced the order for the two strike carriers, HMSs *Queen Elizabeth* and *The Prince of Wales* for service entry in 2014 and 2016 respectively. This follows an earlier announcement on 14th December 2005 for the go ahead of the demonstration phase; this was to evaluate the time to build, performance criteria and the cost for the construction of the ships. An alliance was formed with MOD, BAe Systems, Thales, Babcock, Kellogg Brown and Root, each with their independent responsibilities to the programme and build of the ships. The ships will be modular construction, a first for carrier design, with sections built by the various shipyards, then assembled in Rosyth.

The 65,000 ton gas turbine powered ships will be the largest to serve in the RN, have a full crew of 1500 and carry 40 aircraft and helicopters at a cruising speed of 25 knots. The ship will have all aircraft support facilities and workshops and a 155m x 33m hangar for 20 aircraft. The proposed service life of the ships will be 50 years and they will be home based in Portsmouth. The design is such that, if required later, catapults and arrestor wires can be installed for conventional carrier operations during their proposed life.

SEA KING REPLACEMENTS

Replacements for the remaining serving Sea King helicopters are planned to enter service at the time the two new carriers will be joining the Fleet. The replacement for the Mk4 Commando, the Future Amphibious Support Aircraft (FASA), was originally expected to enter service in 2008; this date has however slipped to 2012/15 with no decision as to which helicopter would be suitable. The indications are that a Merlin similar to RAF Mk3 will be chosen. The commando squadron crews

Helo UAV

have indicated that they would like a mix of helicopters and the 300mph V22 Osprey tilt rotor aircraft.

The future Maritime Amphibious Surveillance and Control (MASC) to replace the ASaC MK7 is expected in 2015/2018, although no final choice between the three contenders (Merlin, V22 Osprey or E3 Hawkeye) has been made. The Merlin helicopter is the probable platform for the role.

The current proposals for the SAR helicopter fleet are for all 12 SAR helicopter units (HMCG, RN and RAF) to amalgamate as the UK SAR Capability in 2012 using one type of helicopter. No choice of aircraft has yet been decided, however the main contender is a Merlin helicopter similar to the version operated by the Royal Canadian Air Force and the Japanese Self Defence Forces. This will be a civil organisation with its HQ at Lee-on-Solent, with no input from the military thus the two FAA units (Gannet SAR and No. 771 Sqdn.) will be disbanded.

AIRCREW TRAINING

From 1st April 2012, all British Military aircrew will be trained by a combined UKMFT (UK Military Flying Training) organisation, under civilian contract, from initial selection through to completion of basic and advanced training before joining second line units for type conversion. The future of the FAA's current training squadrons - No. 727 Sqdn. at Yeovilton, No. 703 Sqdn. at Barkston Heath, No. 705 Sqdn. at DHFS Shawbury and No. 750 Sqdn. at Culdrose, is unknown. It is planned that the latter squadron will replace its Jetstream aircraft by 2009, possibly with King Air aircraft, to fill the gap before the UKMFT becomes operational.

OPERATION BANNER

After 38 years, the FAA and RM units finally ceased operations in Northern Ireland (Operation Banner). The first operations in support of the army units in the country began in 1970 with Sioux helicopters flown by RM pilots, later replaced with Scouts and finally Lynx until they were withdrawn in 1980. Wessex MkVs from Nos 707, 845 and 846 Squadrons were operated from 1977 over many periods before eventually handing over to RAF Pumas and FAA Lynx flights, mostly operating from Bessbrook Barracks.

The final Lynx flight was on 31st July 2007 when their last support mission was flown by an aircraft from No. 815 Squadron operating from Aldergrove airport. This saw the end of the longest British military operation.

F35 Lightning

TELIC II AND HERRICK

After four years of supporting operations in Iraq, the Sea Kings from No.s 845 and 846 Squadrons were withdrawn from operations in Basra in October 2007. No. 846 Sqdn. were to redeploy supporting the efforts in Khandahar with modified aircraft fitted with special main and tail rotor blades to enable them to operate at the higher altitudes in Afghanistan. The aircraft also had uprated NVG capability and an extra defensive system for protection against the region's insurgents. These helicopters have been labelled Sea King MkIV Plus.

The Naval Strike Wing returned to Khandahar for a second tour supporting the UN Forces, returning nine months after completing their first operations in the theatre. The GR7 and GR9 aircraft again provided ground strikes and reconnaissance missions in the Helmand Province against the Taliban and rebel forces.

NEW ROLES NEW ACRONISMS

Since the end of 2003, the FAA has been governed by four commands all wanting to use the assets of the service, both ships and aircraft. The whole concept of the British military is one of a multi combined-service peacekeeping force. There is a Permanent Joint HQ at Northwood; the operational aircraft are either part of the Maritime Aviation (MA) or Joint Helicopter

Harrier GR 9

proposed CVS July 2007

Command (JHC) assets and all are under the umbrella of CinC Fleet.

Since the FAA began its humble beginnings in the early years of the 20th Century, the roles of the British Forces and the RN/FAA has changed from protecting British global interests to the main role of supporting international peacekeeping coalitions whilst still retaining the need to protect the British Isles and other British dependencies. With these changes have come the rethinking that the British Forces will operate more efficiently at a significantly reduced cost as a combined force and all changes within the MoD and different forces reflect this thinking. Note: combined forces have not faired well in countries such as New Zealand and Canada. With this comes new definitions of the RN/FAA roles with phrases that are now in constant use:

UK Security - Integrity of UK Territorial Waters.

V22 Osprey

Littoral Manoeuvres - the positioning of ships and aircraft in coastal areas and on land to apply force or influence where necessary.

Maritime Strike - an attack by maritime forces to inflict damage on or destroy an object or force.

Theatre Entry - Operations to allow main forces to enter a battle zone.

Flexible Global Reach - positioning of the maritime forces ready to intervene in UN operations where and when required.

Tailored Air Group (TAG) - the embarked aviation package of FAA/RAF/AAC units embarked on the carriers. No longer are squadrons designated to specific carriers, the embarked aircraft and helicopters are now determined by whatever the ship is being tasked with by C in C Fleet.

Amphibious Ready Group (ARG) - the embarked amphibious group deployed in the various amphibious ships - HMSs *Ocean*, *Albion* and *Bulwark* plus supporting assets and carriers when configured in the role.

Maritime Aviation (MA) - maritime assets of the RN (Lynx, Sea King and Merlin) and the RAF (Nimrod and Sea Kings) and Joint Force Harriers (JFH).

Joint Helicopter Command/Force (JHC/F) - British Forces helicopter commander controlling all assets of the FAA Commando Helicopter Force (CHF) - Sea King MK4 and Lynx, AAC Lynx, Gazelle, Apache and RAF Puma, Chinooks and Merlin helicopters.

Is British Naval Aviation going back 80 years to the period that was detrimental to the progress of British naval aviation assets? The country is assured this will not be the case, more so it will give the RN a much better aviation facility. Only time will tell. The Fleet Air Arm may reach its 100th anniversary as a fully accepted arm of the Royal Navy and as a major force in the British Forces with new equipment and ships to operate them from. It will probably by then be part of a combined British Defence Force but this will not detract from the fact that the British naval aviators and engineers can be credited with the development of all the major inventions and developments used to operate aircraft at sea and that many of the operational tactics used today are developments of those designed by the RNAS 90 years ago.

Bibliography

Allen Patrick – Wessex, Airlife 1988

Andrews CF & Morgan EB – Supermarine Aircraft since 1914, Putnam 1989

Birtles Philip - Vampire, Venon & Sea Vixen, Ian Allen 1986

Braybrook Roy - Harrier & Sea Harrier, Osprey 1984

Burns Michael - Phantom II, Osprey 1984

Chartres John - Sea King, Ian Allen 1984

Chesneau Roger - Aircraft Carriers of the World, Arms & Armour 1984

Dupuy R Ernest & Trevor N - Collins Encyclopedia of Military History, BCA 1993

Dyson Tony Lt. Cdr. - HMS Hermes 1959-84, Maritime Press 1984

Friedman Norman - British Carrier Aviation, Naval Institute Press 1988

Harrison W - Fairey Firefly, Airlife 1992

Jackson A J - De Havilland Aircraft since 1909, Putnam 1987

Jackson Robert - Sea Harrier & AV-8B, Blandford Press 1988

Jackson Robert - Air War Korea 1950-53, Airlife 1998

Jefford C G - RAF Squadrons, Airlife 1994

Lansdown John RP - With the Carriers in Korea, Crecy 1997

Layman R D - Before the Aircraft Carrier, Conway Press 1989

London Peter - Saunders & Saro Aircraft since 1917, Putnam 1988

Longstaff Reginald - FAA-A Pictorial History, Robert Hale 1981

Marriott Leo - RN Aircraft Carriers 1945-1990, Ian Allen 1985

Mason Francis K - Hawker Aircraft since 1920, Putnam 1991

Sturtivant Ray & Ballance Theo - The Squadrons of the FAA, Air Britain 1994

Russell Brian J - The Interservice Hovercraft (Trials) Unit, Hover Publications

Sturtivant Ray - British Naval Aviation, The FAA 1917-1990, Arms & Armour 1990

Taylor H A - Fairey Aircraft since 1915, Putnam 1988

Thetford Owen - British Naval Aircraft since 1912, Putnam 1971

Williams Ray - Fly Navy Aircraft of the FAA since 1945, Airlife 1989

Falklands Task Force - Portfolio Books 1 and 2, Maritime Press 1982

Glossary & Abbreviations

AAC: .... Army Air Corps
A&AE: Aircraft & Armament Experimental Establishment
ACOS: .... Assistant Chief of Staff
A/C: .... Aircraft
AD: .... Air Department of the Navy
AED: .... Air Engineering Department
AEO: .... Air Engineering Officer
AEW: .... Airborne Early Warning
AMRAAM: Advanced Medium Range Air-to-Air Missile
AOR: .... All One Replenishment
ARA: .... Argentine Armada Ship
ARG: .... Amphibious Ready Group
AS: .... Anti-submarine
ASaC: .... Airborne Surveillance and Control
ASP: .... Anti-submarine Patrols
ASV: .... Air to Surface Vessel Radar
ASW: .... Anti-submarine Warfare
ATC: .... Air Traffic Control
ATDU: .... A/c Torpedo Development Unit
AWACS: ... Airborne Warfare and Command System
AWTU: .... Amphibious Warfare Trials Unit
BAe: .... British Aerospace
BEF: .... British Expeditionary Force
BPF: .... British Pacific Fleet
BRNC: .... Britannia Royal Naval College
CAM: .... Catapult Armed Merchant Ship
CAP: .... Combat Air Patrols
Capt: .... Captain
CAS: .... Close Air Support
CASEVAC: .... Casualty Evacuation
CBGLO: ..... Carrier Borne Ground Liaison Group
Cdr: .... Commander
3CB: .... 3rd Commando Brigade
CHF: .... Commando Helicopter Force
CinC: .... Commander in Chief
CO: .... Commanding Officer
COD: .... Carrier Onboard Dispatch/Delivery
COMNA: ..... Commodore Maritime Naval Aviation
CPO: .... Chief Petty Officer
CTS: .... Central Tactical System
CVA: .... Attack Carrier
DAEO: .... Deputy Air Engineering Officer
DFC: .... Distinguished Flying Cross
DGA(N): .... Director General Aircraft (Navy)
DHSF: .... Defence Helicopter Flying School
DNW: .... Directorate of Naval Warfare
DOR: .... Direct Operational Requirement
DSC: .... Distinguished Service Cross
DSO: .... Distinguished Service Order
EHI: .... European Helicopter Industries
EUFOR: .... European Force
EW: .... Electronic Warfare
EZ: .... Exclusion Zone
F: .... Commander Flying
F/A: .... Fighter Attack
FAA: .... Fleet Air Arm
FAW: .... Fighter All Weather
FB: .... Fighter Bomber
FCBA: .... Future Carrier Borne Aircraft
FG/FGA: .... Fighter Ground Attack
FLS: .... Front Line Squadron
Flyco: .... Flying Control
FNS: .... French Navy Ship
FO2FEF: .... Flag Officer Two Far East Fleet
FOF3: .... Flag Officer Fleet Three
FOB: .... Forward Operating Base
FOMA: .... Flag Officer Maritime Aviation
FONA: .... Flag Officer Naval Aviation
FONAC: .... Flag Officer Naval Air Command
FOST: .... Flag Officer Sea Training
FR: .... Fighter Reconnaissance
FRADU: ... Fleet Requirements & Air Direction Unit
FRS: .... Fighter Reconnaissance Strike
FRU: .... Fleet Requirements Unit
GPMG: .... General Purpose Machine Gun
GPO: .... General Post Officer
HAR: .... Helicopter Air Rescue
HAS: .... Helicopter Anti-Submarine
HDS: .... Helicopter Delivery Service
HMAS: .... His/Her Majesty's Australian Ship
HMCG: .... His/Her Majesty's Coast Guard
HMS: .... His/Her Majesty's Ship
HQ: .... Headquarters
HT: .... Helicopter Training
HTUFT: .... Helicopters Taken Up From Trade
HU: .... Helicopter Utility
IFOR: .... Implementation Force
IFTU: .... Intensive Flying Trials Unit
IHTU: .... Interservice Hovercraft Trials Unit
IJS: .... Imperial Japanese Ship
INS: .... Indian Navy Ship
JFH: .... Joint Force Harrier
JHC: .... Joint Helicopter Command
JOAC: .... Junior Officers Air Course
JSF: .... Joint Strike Fighter
LPH: .... Landing Platform Helicopter
LSL: .... Landing Ship Logistics
LSO: .... Landing Sight Officer
Lt: .... Lieutenant

Lt Cdr: . . . . .Lieutenant Commander
Lt Gen: . . . . .Lieutenant General
MAC: . . . . .Merchant Aircraft Carrier
MAD: . . . . .Magnetic Anomoly Detector
MASC: . . .Maritime Amphibious Support and Control
MASU: . . . . .Mobile Aircraft Support Unit
MCM: . . . . .Mine Counter Measures
MDAP: . . . . . .Mutual Defence Assistance Programme
Mk: . . . . .Mark
MLS: . . . . .Mirror Landing Sight
MOAT: . . . . .Mobile Air Operations Team
MOD: . . . . .Ministry of Defence
MONAB: . . . . .Mobile Operational Naval Air Base
MPH: . . . . .Maritime Patrol Helicopter
NAD: . . . . .Naval Air Department
NAFDU: . . . . . . .Naval Air Fighter Development Unit
NAS: . . . . .Naval Air Station
NATEC: . . . . . .Naval Air Technical Evaluation Centre
NATO: . . . . .North Atlantic Treaty Organisation
NCO: . . . . .Non-Commissioned Officer
NES: .Naval Evaluation Trials
NF: . . . . .Night Fighter
NFSF: . . . . .Naval Flying Standards Flight
NFW: . . . . .Naval Fighter Wing
NHU: .Naval Hovercraft Unit
NHTU: . . . . .Naval Hovercraft Trials Unit
No: . . . . .Number
OCU: . . . . .Operational Conversion Unit
OEU: . . . . .Operational Evaluation Unit
OIC: . . . . .Officer in Charge
Op: . . . . .Operation
P by O: . . . . .Preservation by Operation
PO: . . . . Petty Officer
POW: . . . . .Prisoner of War
PR: . . . . .Photo Reconnaissance
RAC: . . . . .Royal Aero Club
Radm: . . . . .Rear Admiral
RAE: . . . . .Royal Aircraft Establishment
RAF: . . . . .Royal Air Force
RAN: .Royal Australian Navy
RAS: . . . . .Replenishment at Sea
RATOG: . . . . .Rocket Assisted Take Off Gear
RCN: . . . . .Royal Canadian Navy
RFA: . . . . .Royal Fleet Auxiliary
RFANSU: . . .Royal Fleet Auxiliary Naval Support Unit
RFC: . . . . .Royal Flying Corps
RMAS: . . . . .Royal Maritime Auxiliary Service
RMC: . . . . .Royal Marine Commando
RN: . . . . .Royal Navy
RNAS: . . . . .Royal Naval Air Station
RNR: . . . . .Royal Naval Reserve
RNVR: . . . . .Royal Naval Volunteer Reserve
ROK: . . . . .Republic of Korea
Rtd: . . . . .Retired
RSwN: . . . . .Royal Swedish Navy
SAS: . . . . .Special Air Service
SAR: . . . . .Search and Rescue
SBAC: . . . . .Society of British Aircraft Companies
SBS: .Special Boats Squadron
SDR: . . . . .Strategic Defence Review
SHAR: . . . . .Sea Harrier
SMR: . . . . .Senior Maintenance Rating
SP: . . . . .Senior Pilot
Sqdn: . . . . .Squadron
SRN: . . . . .Saunders Roe Number
SS: . . . . .Steam Ship
SS: . . . . .Submarine Scout
STOBAR: . . . . . .Short Take-Off But Arrested Landing
STOVL: . . . . .Short Take-Off Vertical Landing
Sub Lt: . . . . .Sub-Lieutenant
TAG: . . . . .Tailored Air Group
TAG: .Telegraphist Air Gunner
TAMY: . . . . .Transportable Aircraft Maintenance Yard
TARC: Tactical Air Reconnaissance and Combat Air . . . . .Patrols
TARCAP: . . . . .Target Combat Air Patrol
TEZ: . . . . .Total Exclusion Zone
TF: . . . . .Torpedo Fighter
TSR: . . . . .Torpedo Strike Reconnaissance
UAR: . . . . .United Arab Republic
UAV: . . . . .Unmanned Airborne Vehicle
UDI: . . . . .Unilateral Declaration of Independence
UKMFT: . . .United Kingdom Military Flying Training
UN: . . . . .United Nations
USAF: . . . . .United States Air Force
USN: . . . . .United States Navy
USMC: . . . . .United States Marine Corps
USS: . . . . .United States Ship
VC: . . . . .Victoria Cross
VIP: . . . . .Very Important Person
VJ: . . . . .Victory over Japan
VSTOL: . . . . .Vertical Standing Take-Off and Landing
WWI: . . . . .World War One
WWII: . . . . .World War Two

The FAA Firsts in Naval Aviation

Military flying machine: . . . . Mayfly, 7th May 1909

British military pilot training: . . . . 2nd March 1911

Pilot “ground school”: . . . . 2nd March 1911

Take-off and landing from water: Oliver Schwann, November 1911

Received first military aircraft: 1912

Take-off from a ship underway: . Charles Samson, 2nd May 1912

Military air force: . . . . 13th May 1912

Message between aircraft and ship: 1912

Aerial photography: 1912

Bomb dropped from an aircraft: . . . . Charles Samson, 1912

Strategic bombing operations conceived: . . Samson and Winston . . . . .Churchill, 1912

Spin recovery: . . . . Wilfred Parke, 25th August 1912

Mobile air station used: 1912

Bomb sight developed: . . . . Samson and R Hall, 1912

Ships converted as seaplane carriers: . . . . Abercrombie class . . . . .monitors, 1913

Aircraft with folding wings: . . . . Shorts Type 807, 1912

Aircraft flotation gear: . . . . Shorts S27, 1912

Aircraft carrier in service: . . . . HMS Hermes, 7th May 1913

Navy and aircraft exercises: . . . . July 1913

Torpedo/aircraft flights: . . . . Shorts Canton-Unne, 1913

Air launch of a torpedo: . . . . Gordon Bell, 27th July 1914

Aircraft 1.5lb gun firings: . . . . . . C Hall/Sopwith Gun Bus, 1914

Formation flying display: . . . . Fleet Review, July 1914

Night flying: . . . . Travers/Sopwith Bat Boat, July 1914

Armoured cars: . . . . Charles Samson, September 1914

Aerial bombing mission: . . . . . . C Collet, 22nd September 1914

Successful bombing mission: . . . . . . R Marix/ Zepplin Sheds, 7th . . . . .October 1914

Aircraft carrier sunk: . . . . HMS Hermes, 30th October 1914

Long-range bombing mission: . . Friedrichshaven, 21st November 1914

Purpose built aircraft (seaplane) carrier: . . HMS Ark Royal, 10th . . . . .December 1914

Night bombing mission: . . Charles Samson, 21st December 1914

Aircraft (seaplane) carrier operations: . . . . Cuxhaven Raid, 25th . . . . .December 1914

Bomber designed: . Murray Sueter/Handley Page, December 1914

Naval balloon operations: . . . . Dardenelles, 17th February 1915

Aerial reconnaissance operations: . C Butler, 17th February 1915

500lb bomb dropped: . . . . Charles Samson, March 1915

Incendiary bomb dropped: . . . . . . Charles Samson, March 1915

Wheeled take-off from a ship: . . Modified Sopwith Schneider, 6th . . . . .August 1915

Torpedo attack on a ship: . . . . . . C Edmonds, 12th August 1915

Aircraft carrier with island designed: Hugh Williamson, August 1915

Clandestine operations: . . . . 18th Jan 1915

Naval aircraft in naval engagements: . . . . 6th July 1915

Wheeled aircraft take-off from a ship at sea: . . . . Towler, 3rd . . . . .November 1915

SAR rescue on land: . . Richard Bell Davies, 15th November 1915

Aircraft carrier force operations: . . . . January 1916

Aircraft launched from an airship: . . . Be2C, 21st February 1916

Arrester equipment designed: . . . . . H Williamson/ Wright, 1916

Aircraft piggy back flight: . . Porte Baby/ Bristol Scout, March 1916

Aircraft operations from a submarine: . . E22/ Sopwith Schneider, ...April 1916

Mercy stores air drop: . . . . April 1916

British aircraft with a syncronised gun: . . . Sopwith 1½ Strutter, ...April 1916

Two seat fighter bomber: . . . . . Sopwith 1½ Strutter, April 1916

Battle aerial reconnaissance - .F Rutland/ Trewin, 30th May 1916

Inflight refuelling from a ship: . . C1 Airship/ HMS Carysfort, May 1916

“Pathfinder” operations: . Sopwith 1½ Strutter, 2nd August 1916

Strategic bombing unit: . . . Sopwith 1½ Strutter, 27th July 1916

Last air operations of WWI: 214 Sqdn. RAF, 10th November 1918

Transatlantic crossing: . . . . R34, 2nd-6th July 1919

Two-way transatlantic crossing: . . . . . . R34, 2nd-13th July 1919

True designed aircraft carrier commissioned: . . . HMS Hermes, ...23rd July 1923

Catapult launch of an aircraft from a ship: . . . Burlington/IIID, ...30th October 1925

Carrier night landing: . . . . Boyce/Dart, 1st July 1926

Spring loaded deck hook fitted: . . . . Fairey IIIF, 1931

British military a/c with retractable undercarriage: . Walrus, 21st . . . . .June 1933

Full military loaded aircraft catapult launch: . . . . . Walrus, 1935

Vertical take-off from a ship: . . . . Cierva C30, 1935

Use of landing control officer on carrier deck: . . . . "Bats", 1936

British monoplane dive bomber: . . . . . Skua, 9th February 1937

Steam catapult patented: . . . . C Mitchell, 1938

Aircraft shot down in WWII: . . . . . . Skua/DO18, 26th September

Flares used in aerial attack of WWII (Pathfinders): . . . . .Swordfish/Taranto, 11th November 1940

Military helicopters ordered: . . . . Sikorsky R4 Gadfly, 1943

Helicopter trials at sea: . . . . R4/SS Dagheston, 1944

Airborne air operations co-ordinator missions: . . Major Hay, 4th . . . . .January 1945

Helicopter squadron: . . . . No. 771 Sqdn., February 1945

Jet aircraft carrier landing and trials: . . . . . Vampire/Brown, 5th . . . . .December 1945

Landing of helicopter aboard a warship: . . A Bristow, September 1946

Landing of a helicopter on a battleship: . . . K Reed, 1st February 1947

Aircraft with retractable radar scanner: . . . . Gannet, 19th . . . . .September 1949

Carrier turbo prop aircraft deck landing: . . . . Gannet, 19th June 1950

British aircrew ejection: . . Attacker/McDermott, 21st March 1951

Night flying operations: 1916

Inflight crew change: . . . C1 Airship/HMS Canterbury, September 1916

Flotation equipment fitted to aircraft: Pup, 1½ Strutter & WBIII, ...1916

Aircraft designed specifically for British aircraft carriers first flight: . . . . Fairey Campania, 16th February 1917

Anti-submarine patrol system developed: . . Spiders Web System, ...13th April 1917

Submarine sunk by aircraft: . . . . 20th May 1917

Use of microphone for detecting submarines: . . . . . .Seaplanes/ . . . . .Airships, 1917

Deck landing of a ship underway: . Dunning/Pup, 2nd August 1917

Aircraft simulator: . . . . Schwann, August 1917

Sea SAR mission: . Leckie/H12 Flying Boat, 5th September 1917

Take-off from rotateable gun turret: .. F Rutland/ HMS Repulse, ...1st October 1917

Purpose designed carrier (conversion) launched: . . HMS Argus, ...2nd December 1917

Two seat take-off from a ship: Sopwith 1½ Strutter, 4th April 1918

Aircraft for carrier operations designed: . Beardmore WBIII, 1918

Two seat aircraft from a carrier: 1918

Take-off from a towed lighter: . . . . S Culley, Summer 1918

Multi-role aircraft first flight: . . . . . . Fairey IIIA, 6th June 1918

Aircraft carrier (with island) launched: . . . HMS Eagle, 8th June 1918

Purpose designed aircraft carrier laid down: . . . HMS Hermes, 15th . . . . .June 1918

Air combat operations from carrier-borne aircraft: . . . .Camels/HMS . . . . .Furious, 18th June 1918

Aircraft carrier aircraft strike operation: . . . Camels/ HMS Furious, ...19th July 1918

Purpose built aircraft carrier commissioned: . . . . . . HMS Argus, ...September 1918

Ship with safety barrier: . . . . HMS Argus, September 1918

Naval twin-engined aircraft in service: . . . . Shorts Sturgeon, August 1951

Mirror landing sight developed: . . . . N Goodhart, 1951

Angle deck designed: . . . . Cambell/Boddington, 7th August 1951

Sproule rescue net developed: . . . . J Sproule/A Lock, 1951

SAR rescue strop developed: . . . . A Lock, 1952

Jet shot down by piston aircraft: . . P Carmichael, 9th August 1952

Pilot rescued by SAR strop: . . . . W Davis, 4th August 1953

Helicopter amphibious assault: . . . . . . Suez, 5th November 1953

Helicopter small ships flight: . . . HMS Vidal/Hiller, August 1954

Helicopter deck harpoon developed: . . . . J Sproule, 1955

Maritime low level strike bomber designed: . . Buccaneer, July 1955

Jet powered helicopter: . . . . Wessex 'P', 17th May 1957

ASW helicopter: . . . . Wessex HAS1, 20th June 1958

Pure helicopter base commissioned: RNAS Portland, 14th April 1959

Amphibious (commando) carrier in service: . . . HMS Bulwark, 19th January 1960

Military hovercraft unit: . . . . IH(T)U/SRN1, 28th February 1962

Vertical take-off from a ship: . . . . . . Kestrel, 8th February 1963

Helicopter designed for small ships flights: . . . Wasp, 4th June 1963

Ship designed to operate a helicopter flight: . . HMS Devonshire, 14th March 1964

Last British military aircraft to leave Aden: . . . Sea Vixen/Wasp, 29th November 1967

FAA Phantom won Transatlantic Air Race: . . . B Davies/P Goddard, 11th May 1969

Ski ramp designed: . . . . D Taylor, 1972

Submarine sunk by helicopter: . . Wessex HAS3/ Wasp, 25th April 1982

AEW helicopter: . . . . Sea King, June 1982

British Aircraft and Carrier Designs

Depth charge invented . . . . .Hugh Williamson

Strategic Bombing Concept . . . . .Charles Samson

1st bomber aircraft . . . . .HP 0/100

Folding wings . . . . .Winston Churchill

Aircraft carrier trials . . . . .HMS Hermes

Seaplane carriers (conversions) . . . . .HMS Ark Royal

Purpose built aircraft carrier (conversion) . . . . .HMS Argus

Designed aircraft carrier from conception . . . . .HMS Hermes

Island design developed . . . . .Hugh Williamson

Aircraft simulator . . . . .Schwann

Flight deck arrestor wire . . . . .Hugh Williamson

Carrier aircraft safety barrier . . . . .HMS Argus/Furious

Aircraft flotation equipment . . . . .Sopwith Pup, 1½ Strutter & WBIII

Hydrophones for submarine detection . . . . .Airships and Seaplanes

Aircraft catapults . . . . .Carey

The angled deck . . . . .Dennis Cambell & Lewis Boddinton

Steam catapults . . . . .Mitchell

Mirror landing sight . . . . .Nick Goodhart

Ski Ramp . . . . .David Taylor

Amphibious carrier operations . . . . .Suez

Gas turbine powered helicopters . . . . .Wessex HAS 1

True ASW helicopters . . . . .HMS Vidal with Hiller HTE-2's

Small ships helicopter operations . . . . .Wessex Mk5

Commando helicopters . . . . .Sea King

AEW helicopter . . . . .Sea King AEW2

Multi-role fixed-wing aircraft . . . . .Sea Harrier

Index

Ships

BASES

OPERATIONS

MEN

SCOVAL
PUBLISHING LTD